East Timor at the Crossroads

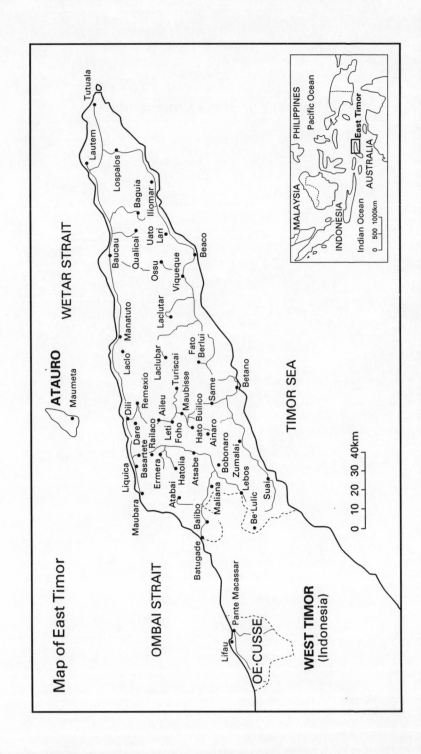

Map of East Timor

East Timor at the Crossroads:
The Forging of a Nation

Edited by Peter Carey and G. Carter Bentley

With a Foreword by General António
dos Santos Ramalho Eanes
(President of Portugal 1982–6)

DS
646.57
E255
1995

University of Hawai'i Press
2840 Kolowalu Street
Honolulu, Hawai'i 96822

Sponsored by the Joint Committee on Southeast Asia of the Social Science
Research Council, New York, and the American Council of Learned
Societies.

First published 1995

ISBN 0–8248–1787–7 (hardback)
        0–8248–1788–5 (paperback)

Front cover photograph by Penny Tweedie: Timor Highlands, November
1975, just prior to the Indonesian invasion.

Typesetting and design by Ben Cracknell
Printed and bound in Great Britain by Biddles Ltd,
Guildford and King's Lynn

**To the memory of the late Paramita Abdurachman
Historian of the Portuguese in Southeast Asia**

Bukan ku menangis di sepi kubur
Ibu yang hilang hanya tubuhnya
Walaupun tubuh hancur dan lebur
Jasanya kekal berbilang masa

adapted from Abu Zaky,
'Aku tidak meratap lagi',
Pedoman Rakyat [1941]

Contents

Contributors

Benedict R.O'G. Anderson is Professor of Government at Cornell University, Associate Director of Southeast Asian Studies, and Director of the Cornell Modern Indonesia Project. In addition to having written extensively on Indonesian culture, history and politics, Professor Anderson is the author of *Imagined Communities: Reflections on the Origin and Spread of Nationalism* (1983).

Robert Archer is Policy Coordinator at Christian Aid (London) and has worked for the Catholic Institute for International Relations (London), where he was the founder of the quarterly journal *Timor Link* (1985 to present), which focuses on the role of the Catholic Church in East Timor.

G. Carter Bentley has taught Southeast Asian Studies and cultural anthropology in several American universities. Currently a consultant specializing in organizational culture change, Dr Bentley has written on nationality formation among Philippine Muslims. He is the author of *Ethnicity and Nationality: A Bibliographic Guide* (1981).

Peter Carey is a Fellow and Tutor in Modern History at Trinity College, Oxford, and a specialist in modern Indonesian history. In addition to having written extensively on early nineteenth-century Java, he is a patron of the British Coalition for East Timor. He is the author of *The British in Java, 1811–1816. A Javanese Account* (1992).

Roger S. Clark is Distinguished Professor of Law at Rutgers University. Since the 1970s, he has represented the International League for Human Rights in presenting material on East Timor to the Fourth Committee of the United Nations General Assembly, and to the Assembly's Special Committee on Decolonization.

James Dunn served as Australian Consul-General in Portuguese Timor during the 1960s. He has since served as senior foreign affairs advisor to the Australian Parliament, and as a foreign affairs correspondent. He is the author of *Timor: A People Betrayed* (1983).

António dos Santos Ramalho Eanes was President of Portugal (1982–6) and served as a senior officer (lieutenant-general) in the Portuguese Army and was a leading figure in the Armed Forces Movement (*Movimento das Forças Armadas*) which toppled the Caetano regime in April 1974. His close personal interest in East Timor helped to revive national interest in the issue in the early 1980s.

Paulino Gama (Mauk Muruk) was born in East Timor in 1955 and served as a Fretilin operational commander for ten years (1975–85) during the most intense period of fighting against the Indonesians. Since October 1990, he has been a refugee, first in Portugal, and then in the Netherlands where he is the founder President of the International Timorese Secretariat for Human Rights in Europe.

Donaciano Gomes was born in East Timor in 1969 and lived through the first fifteen years of Indonesian military occupation (1975–90). Active in the high-school and student resistance in the late 1980s, he played a key role in the independence demonstration during the Pope's visit to East Timor on 12 October 1989. After a period of imprisonment and torture, he arrived in Portugal as a political refugee in September 1990.

Sue Rabbitt Roff is currently at the Centre for Medical Education at Dundee University in Scotland. She was associated with the New York office of the Petitioning Delegation of the Democratic Republic of East Timor in 1975 and 1976, and was Non-Governmental Representative of the Minority Rights Group to the UN in New York (1980–90). She is the author of *Timor's Anschluss: Indonesian and Australian Policies in East Timor 1974–1976* (1992).

Shirley Shackleton is the wife of Greg Shackleton, the most well-known of the five Western journalists who died at Balibo on 16 October 1975. Since her husband's death, she has developed a deep concern for East Timor and its people, and has travelled extensively to give public talks both in Australia and abroad. A trained nursing sister, she lives in Melbourne.

John G. Taylor is Principal Lecturer in Social Sciences at the University of the South Bank, London, where he is also Director of the Centre for Chinese Studies. He edits *Timor Link* for the Catholic Institute for International Relations, and is the author of *Indonesia's Forgotten War. The Hidden History of East Timor* (1991).

Elizabeth G. Traube, Professor of Anthropology at Wesleyan University, conducted ethnographic field research in East Timor (1972–4) and is the author of a monograph on the Mambai of East Timor, *Cosmology and Social Life* (1986).

Pat Walsh is Director of the Human Rights Office at the Australian Council for Overseas Aid and Coordinator of the East Timor Talks Campaign. He has taught Indonesian language and studies and is general editor of the quarterly magazine *Inside Indonesia* (1983 to present). He is also co-author of *East Timor: Towards a Just Peace in the 1990s* (1991).

Foreword

East Timor: Twenty Years of Miraculous Resistance Struggle

by António dos Santos Ramalho Eanes
(President of Portugal, 1982–6)

The response of the East Timorese population to the Javanese invasion defies imagination. Over 200,000 people, a third of the pre-invasion population, have been put to the sword, yet the guerrilla resistance has survived, maintaining to this day an effective presence in East Timor's rugged mountains. It is a case unparalleled in the history of guerrilla warfare, especially when one considers that the theatre of war is a small island territory without the benefit of sanctuaries over contiguous borders.

The determination of the resistance is rooted in the fact that the Timorese are a distinct ethnic group, whose culture and history are quite different from those of the invading Javanese. These differences have been enhanced by 450 years of Portuguese contact and colonization. The Portuguese language has affected most of the local dialects and is the basis of the modern script. Catholicism is also now practised by 80 per cent of the population. At the same time, Timorese art has been deeply influenced by the European Renaissance and the Baroque, Christian images infusing animist myths and rituals.

The resistance continues to this day because the people will not sacrifice their principles. They continue to fight for liberty and human rights, for the freedom to determine, in the land of their forebears, the present and future course of their lives. The East Timorese want to follow the path of their ancestors, rather than serve an Indonesian empire which strangely does not have a federal structure but a unitary one, and this despite the fact that its 190 million people are scattered over 13,000 islands and speak around three hundred different languages.

The Timor problem is, unquestionably, an international issue. It is not, and never was, a mere quarrel between the Indonesian invaders and Portugal. Portugal, still recognized by the UN as the administering power, only acts for the international community, represented by the

United Nations. It is, in fact, the United Nations which has the greatest responsibility, and it should not be allowed to forget its ten Security Council and General Assembly resolutions regarding East Timor's right to decolonization.

As the genocide and violation of human rights in East Timor continue, the problem becomes ever more an international one, and the responsibility of the United Nations becomes ever greater. More than at any other time since 1975, East Timor represents an inescapable political obligation for the United Nations and a major piece of unfinished business for the international community.

Since the Second World War, the United States has enjoyed a significant maritime advantage, which the former Soviet Union tried to counter by establishing a strong continental presence. Before the end of the Cold War in the late 1980s, the US responded to Soviet strategies by pursuing its traditional policy of political expansion through the key archipelagos and their principal sea lanes. The Soviet position in the Pacific was further affected by the age-old Sino-Russian enmity. At a certain point in the postwar period the Soviet Union ceased to challenge American strategic domination of the region, concentrating instead on weakening the Chinese empire and trying to obstruct its southwards expansion through its support for Hanoi during the Second Indochina War (1964–73), the Vietnamese invasion of Cambodia (December 1978), and the sale of arms to Sukarno's Indonesia in 1963–5, as well as obliging it to deploy considerable military resources on its southern frontier.

It is in this broader geopolitical context that the Indonesian invasion of East Timor must be considered. It was the logic of the Cold War which caused the US to stimulate the 'national security states', thereby supporting the late President Marcos in the Philippines (1965–86), the late Marshal Lon Nol in Cambodia (1970–75), and President Suharto in Indonesia (1967 to present). These are states which have the army in power, communism identified as the principal enemy, and the assumed need for security against outside aggression. The same geopolitical logic encouraged the US to 'authorize' the Indonesian invasion of East Timor (7 December 1975), and to recognize the *de facto* validity of its integration into the Javanese empire as its twenty-seventh province.

Similar Cold War logic caused the former Soviet Union to consider the invasion of East Timor a 'minor act', and an indirect setback for its traditional enemy, China. China itself, given its tacit alliance with the US after President Nixon's 1972 visit, and its internal and external vulnerability, reacted with caution, limiting itself, in practice, to supporting the Portuguese position. The regional powers – in particular Indonesia's

ASEAN partners – had no economic interest in alienating Indonesia, nor any political or strategic reason for opposing US policy in the region.

Today, nearly twenty years after the invasion, the situation is very different. The US has allowed Marcos to fall in the Philippines (25 February 1986), and the Cold War has come to an end with the collapse of the Soviet Union, leaving a new balance of power in the Pacific with an increasingly assertive China confronting the established power of the US and its allies. As the international situation has made it more difficult for the US to support the national security states, Indonesia is trying to appease both domestic and international opinion.

The end of the Cold War, the 1990–91 Gulf Crisis, and the threat of future conflicts demands a new international order. Indeed, the Gulf Crisis has paradoxically demonstrated that no one nation has the right or the means to bring about this 'New Order' on its own. Rather, it is the UN which should energetically strive to create this by a radical change in the way it responds to breaches of international law. It cannot continue to use two weights and two measures.

Lasting peace can only exist when fortified by certain legal principles, such as the inviolability of frontiers, and the protection of people's rights and property. UN principles and objectives, which were kept in abeyance during the Cold War, such as that of 'preserving future generations from the scourge of war', and 'opposing all acts of aggression' as stated in the preamble to Article One of the UN Charter, can be achieved today. Saddam Hussein flew in the face of international opinion in August 1990 when he invaded Kuwait. Others did it before him such as Indonesia in East Timor (1975 to present), an example referred to by Saddam after his Kuwait invasion when he asked why, if Indonesia could make East Timor its twenty-seventh province, he could not make Kuwait his nineteenth province. Others will do it in the future. But no one superpower can be judge and policeman of the whole world. Only the UN should fulfil this role.

The United Nations can turn to its Security Council to guarantee the maintenance of peace and to restore the damaged fabric of international law. If the UN does not enforce international law, the world will continue to suffer endless conflicts, both economic and military, and will experience ever graver breaches of human rights. To resolve the problem in the Gulf, but to ignore East Timor, is to embark on a new world order based on the wilful negligence of human rights, and a lack of respect for the sacred UN principles of the right of all peoples to self-determination and independence. It would be tantamount to continuing the old double standards of international policy. The responsibilities of all nations are great, especially those of the states represented on the Security Council.

And this includes the government and people of Great Britain, currently Indonesia's principal foreign arms supplier.

The Timorese fight and die because they have faith in their ideals and have hope in the people who have fought and still fight for liberty everywhere in the world.

António dos Santos Ramalho Eanes
(President of Portugal, 1982-6)
Lisbon, July 1994

Preface

by Peter Carey

It was mid–October 1975 and I was on a research visit to Leiden. Sitting in a café after a long day in the library, I opened the newspaper and my eye fell on a map of the border between East and West Timor, and an article describing how five Western newsmen had gone missing at the small border village of Balibo. I can remember thinking: 'How strange! One could understand the death of a single journalist, but for *five* to disappear all at once...?' My question was to remain unanswered for the next eight years. It was my first contact with the unfolding tragedy of East Timor as the long shadow of Suharto's Indonesia fell over it.

During the intervening period, I scarcely gave a thought to East Timor. Why should I? There was too much going on in my life as an academic historian specializing in modern Indonesia to risk enquiring too closely. Although I did not articulate this very clearly to myself at the time, I can now see that I was prey to a subtle form of self-censorship, with an all too plausible inner voice prompting me to question whether I really wanted to jeopardize my access to the Indonesian archives, my contacts with my Indonesian family and friends, and my relations with the Indonesian Embassy in London for the sake of some God-forsaken ex-Portuguese colony? Surely, if one studied the map of Indonesia closely enough, anyone could see that, given its proximity, East Timor was destined to become part of the Republic?

Eight years later, in November 1983, the telephone rang. It was the editor of the *Times Literary Supplement* in London asking me if I would review a book on a place he had never heard about by an Australian author by the name of James Dunn. I agreed. The book was *Timor. A People Betrayed*. As I read it, I went into a state of shock. In great detail, Dunn told of the barbarities which had attended the Indonesian invasion of 7 December 1975, of the murder, rape and pillage of a whole society, a third of the pre-invasion population of 680,000 succumbing to the effects of war, famine and disease. The gruesome murder of the five Western newsmen at Balibo (16 October 1975) was now set in context: not an aberration, but part of a ruthless Indonesian campaign to take over the former Portuguese territory, and secure its annexation. In this, according to Dunn, it had been massively assisted by the connivance and duplicity of the major Western powers.

What could I do? I could not pretend that I had not read the book. But, if I published a long review article, surely that would mean the end of my career as an Indonesianist, certainly the end of my access to the Indonesian archives? I hesitated, and eventually sought a shabby compromise. I would write the review, but would publish it under a pseudonym, my mother's maiden name. With dread in my heart, I delivered my copy to the editor and the piece eventually appeared as the lead article in the *TLS* of 16 December 1983: 'From Decolonisation to Destruction: The Tragedy of East Timor'. The Indonesian reaction was apparently strong: when I visited the *TLS* offices later that month, an armed policeman was on duty in the lobby. This was still at a time when public knowledge of East Timor, at least in Britain, was almost non-existent. Jakarta wanted to keep it that way.

I was later to experience at first hand just how far it was prepared to go to ensure silence. It was 3 August 1990, and I was attending a conference at the School of Oriental and African Studies. In the intervening period I had cast caution to the winds and begun to write on East Timor under my own name, most recently contributing a preface to John Taylor's *The Indonesian Occupation of East Timor, 1974–1989. A Chronology,* where the destruction wrought in the former Portuguese territory had been compared to Pol Pot's Cambodia. Across the aisle from my seat, I noticed the Indonesian information attaché gesticulating vigorously. 'I need to talk to you urgently, but not here, it is too public. Can you come over to the Embassy?' I agreed. 'Now this is off the record, elder sister to younger brother. A friendly piece of advice if you don't mind?' The attaché's mellifluous words hung in the air. 'I have to say…hmm…how *very* disappointed I was to go into Dillons the other day and read your preface to Taylor's book. How can you, a friend of Indonesia, say these terrible things about our army? You know they are not true!' Brushing aside my mumbled demurrers, she went straight to the point. 'Now I hope you remember that you are married to an Indonesian. What *would* your Indonesian relatives – your father-in-law in particular – think if you fell into disrepute?' So that was it: under the guise of friendship, an unspecified threat to my family connections with Indonesia.

Half a decade later, despite the crude pressures from Jakarta, the transformation wrought in public perceptions has been remarkable. What had been an issue known only to a tiny group of human rights activists and Indonesia specialists (most of whom were conspicuous by their silence), has begun to enter the public domain. Credit for this largely goes to a handful of courageous photographers, documentary film makers, and journalists, who have risked their lives to bear witness to the ongoing massacres and atrocities perpetrated by the Indonesians in East Timor. One thinks here especially of the dramatic footage shot by Max Stahl in the Santa Cruz cemetery at the time of the 12 November 1991 massacre, the still photographs taken by Steve Cox, and the two documentaries made by Peter Gordon ('In Cold Blood: The Massacre of East Timor', Yorkshire TV, 7 January 1992), and John Pilger and David Munro ('Death of a Nation: The Timor Conspiracy', Central TV, 22 February 1994). At the same time, the remarkable changes in the international order since the late 1980s – the end of the Cold War, and the triumph of long suppressed nationalist movements in eastern Europe, Africa and the Middle East – as well as the new pressures which are bearing down on the Suharto regime, both domestically and internationally, have opened new possibilities for a resolution of the Timor conflict. The silence which had condemned the East Timorese to obscene obscurity for so long has been broken.

This book is the child of these transformations. Born out of two conferences, held at St Antony's College, Oxford on 8 December 1990 ('East Timor: Fifteen Years On') and the American University in Washington DC on 25–6 April 1991 (SSRC 'Workshop on East Timor'), this volume takes a new look at East Timor's history, both pre- and post-1975, the generational changes in East Timorese society, the role of the Catholic Church, the socio-economic impact of Indonesian military occupation, and the prospects for a future political settlement. Particular attention has also been paid to producing as comprehensive as possible a bibliography of East Timor titles published during the nearly quarter century since 1970, a bibliography which is aimed at complementing that of Kevin Sherlock, which deals mainly with pre-1970 publications. It is hoped that this will constitute both a useful research tool, and the basis for any future national library collection which may one day be established in East Timor to safeguard the heritage of the *maubere*.

A wide variety of different viewpoints are expressed in this volume, all of which are the authors' own and in no way reflect the official policy of either the University of Oxford or the Social Science Research Council in New York. While we are pleased to have been able to include two contributions from East Timorese, representing the pre- and post-1975 generations, it is a matter of regret to us that there are no Indonesians represented here, apart from the brief contributions made at the SSRC Colloquy ('Dimensions of Domination') by Professor Mubyarto of the Gadjah Mada Centre for Rural and Regional Development Studies, and Colonel Luhud Panjaitan of the Indonesian Army's Special Forces, a

Timor veteran. Now that Dr George Aditjondro of the Universitas Kristen Satyawacana (Salatiga), a young Indonesian academic with special interests in East Timor and Irian Jaya, has begun to speak out publicly on the East Timor problem, it is to be hoped that more Indonesian academics and area specialists will be prepared to come forward to make their voices heard. I should add here that I was particularly struck by the remark made by one of Indonesia's leading historians of the Portuguese period, namely the late Paramita Abdurachman, who told me just before her death how much she deplored the way in which Jakarta had sought to incorporate the former Portuguese territory. Coming from someone whose judgement I respected and whose nationalist credentials were so impeccable (in her heart she had clearly hoped for East Timor's peaceful incorporation), her remark had a deep and lasting effect. It is thus fitting that this book should be dedicated to her memory.

Many are the friends, colleagues and institutions to whom thanks are due for their help in the organization of the original conferences, and the preparation of the present volume. For help with the Oxford Conference, I would like to express my particular gratitude to Dr Nicholas van Hear of the Refugee Studies Programme (Oxford), Robert Archer of Christian Aid (then working for the Catholic Institute for International Relations [CIIR]), and Dr John Taylor of the University of the South Bank (London); and to CIIR, Christian Aid, and the Foreign and Commonwealth Office (through a grant to St Antony's Asian Studies Centre) for their much appreciated financial support. Arnold Kohen, of the Timor Project of Washington DC, organized the American University conference. Sponsored by the Joint Committee on Southeast Asia of the Social Science Research Council and the American Council of Learned Societies, under the direction of Dr. Toby Alice Volkman, the conference and preparation of this volume were made possible by the generous support of the Ford Foundation. The bibliography, originally compiled by Sue Roff, received important inputs from Kevin Sherlock and Wendy Lambourne of the Peace Research Institute of the Australian National University.

Our fervent hope is that this book will contribute in some practical way to the resolution of the East Timor conflict, a conflict which has spelt disaster both for the people of East Timor, and for the people of Indonesia, whose leaders have betrayed every principle on which the Republic of Indonesia was founded just half a century ago. In 1975, the East Timorese were abandoned to their fate. Those who should have known better remained silent; those who had the power to act did not. Today, none can plead ignorance.

Peter Carey, Trinity College, Oxford, 17 August 1994

Preface

by G. Carter Bentley

This book originated in the 1991 Workshop on East Timor held at the American University (Washington DC). Dr Toby Volkman, Staff Associate at the Social Science Research Council (New York), felt the information presented at that workshop deserved wider circulation and, at her urging, I began developing the papers and a transcript of workshop discussions into a book. When an opportunity arose to combine the materials from the SSRC workshop with those from the Oxford Conference organized by Peter Carey, we gladly joined forces.

For several years, I have studied minority nationalist movements, most particularly that among the Bangsa Moro, the Islamic minority in the southern Philippines. In the light of that experience, I find the situation in East Timor distressingly familiar, from the political centre's often brutal drive to dominate peoples on its geographic periphery, to religion as a key element in emerging national identities and as a medium for organizing resistance, to a shift in movement leadership from an organization waging guerrilla war in the countryside to an *intifada* led by 'integrated' young people in the cities. East Timor reminds us again of the tragic consequences of military occupation and displacement, the immense loss of life, deculturation, alienation, anger, and despair. On a more theoretical level, the experience of East Timor demonstrates, once more, the distortions and poverty of the conventional paradigms of 'nation building' and 'national integration'. As refugee accounts attest and events clearly demonstrate, East Timorese national feeling shows few signs of abating. If the lines of difference between Indonesian and East Timorese identities are changing form, they remain potent signifiers.

We have consciously chosen to include a wide range of perspectives in this volume. The contributors are drawn from many countries and settings, among them academia, human rights and other non-governmental organizations, and the refugee community. The discussions in the 'Colloquy' represent an even participation, including representatives from the US government, the Indonesian Special Forces, American business interests, the clergy, and others. As Peter Carey notes, we would like to have included greater representation of Indonesian points of view. Those we invited to contribute demurred, perhaps illustrating the difficulty of creating a constructive dialogue at this time. Even so, as Anderson and Walsh have indicated, new openings and opportunities will certainly arise as configurations of interest and power continue to shift in our rapidly changing world. We hope that those in power will recognize and seize any openings toward a just and lasting peace in East Timor.

G. Carter Bentley
Seattle, Washington
21 September 1994

Abbreviations

ABRI Angkatan Bersenjata Republik Indonesia (Armed Forces of the Republic of Indonesia)

ACFOA Australian Council for Overseas Aid (Canberra)

Apodeti Associação Popular Democrática Timorense (Timorese Popular Democratic Association)

ASDT Associação Social Democrata Timorense (Association of Timorese Social Democrats)

ASEAN Association of South-East Asian Nations

BAKIN Badan Koordinasi Intelijens Nasional (Coordinating Body for [Indonesian] National Intelligence)

CNRM Conselho Nacional da Resistência Maubere (National Council of Maubere Resistance)

CNT Convergência Nacional Timorense (Timorese National Convergence)

Falintil Forças Armadas de Libertação Nacional de Timor-Leste (Armed Forces for the National Liberation of East Timor)

Fretilin Frente Revolucionária de Timor-Leste Independente (Revolutionary Front for an Independent East Timor)

ICRC International Committee of the Red Cross

Intel Indonesian Military Intelligence; secret police

Kolakops Komando Pelaksana Operasi (Operations Execution Command [East Timor Operations Command]), disbanded 1992

Koopskam Komando Operasi Keamanan (Security Operations Command [for East Timor]), disbanded 1992

Kopassandha Komando Pasukan Sandi Yudha (Para Commando Forces [of the Indonesian Army/ABRI]), becomes *Kopassus* April 1985

Kopassus Komando Pasukan Khusus (Special Forces Command). Pre-1985 *Kopassandha*

liurai clan chief/ruler

maubere 'son of Timor' (from Mambai '*mau bere*' 'my brother/friend')

nurep *núcleos de resistência popular* (popular resistance centres)

Opsus Operasi Khusus (Special Operations [Executive]), disbanded 1974

UDT União Democrática Timorense (Timorese Democratic Union)

Introduction

The Forging of a Nation: East Timor
Peter Carey

Because it is our blood, it is not lost, and I think the whole world can [now] understand the phenomenon of Maubere nationalism. It is not our propaganda, it is not an ephemeral, temporary phenomenon, but it is in the soul of the people, transmitted from parents to children

**(East Timorese Resistance leader, Xanana Gusmão,
to Robert Domm, September 1990)**

We are dying as a People and as a Nation

**(Bishop Belo in a letter to the United Nations Secretary-General,
Perez de Cuellar, 6 February 1989)**

Introduction

East Timor – the very name has now become synonymous with ethnocide, Third World colonialism and the crushing of a people in the interests of *realpolitik*. In the nineteen years which have elapsed since the Indonesian invasion of 7 December 1975, so much blood has flowed, so much destruction wrought, that it is easy to become mesmerized by the sheer scale of the suffering and forget the inner dynamics which have sustained resistance to Indonesian rule for so long. What is for the regime in Jakarta a lingering international embarrassment – 'grit in one's shoe' as the present Indonesian Foreign Minister, Ali Alatas, has put it – is, for the East Timorese themselves, a matter of life and death. At stake is their very survival as a nation.

From the vantage point of the mid-1970s, as both President Eanes and Ben Anderson have pointed out in their contributions to this volume, hopes that the East Timorese might ultimately win their freedom and constitute themselves as an independent nation-state, seemed frankly far-fetched. This was the height of the Cold War with the United States and its allies unflinching in their backing for the anti-Communist Suharto regime in the wake of the April 1975 Communist victories in Indochina. The collapse of Communism in eastern Europe, the dismantling of the Berlin Wall, and the triumph of long suppressed nationalist movements in the Horn of Africa (Eritrea), the Middle East (Palestine), South Africa and the former Soviet Union, were still more than a decade and a half away. Nineteen years on, the prospects for a new political future for the long-suffering East Timorese no longer seem so remote. Indeed, it is increasingly recognized in Indonesia itself that the East Timor problem is at heart a nationalist one, and not just a 'regional' problem (*unsur kedaerahan*) as Jakarta has long tried to portray it. In this introduction, I will draw on the more detailed discussions presented in this volume to look at the changes wrought in the East Timorese (*maubere*) nationalist movement during the past nineteen years and to assess the forces which are likely to shape its future.

The Colonial Heritage

The remote colony with which the Portuguese had traded since the six-teenth century and fitfully administered from the late eighteenth century, is a land of striking contrasts. As both Taylor[1] and Traube[2] have indicat-ed, despite its small size it has at least three clearly distinct ecological zones – a mountainous central upland flanked to the north and south by two very different coastal plains, the first semi-arid and the latter – with its relatively high rainfall – much more lush and tropical. Its linguistic sit-uation reflects a similar division, the island being occupied by two differ-ent language 'families' – Austronesian and non-Austronesian (or 'Papuan'), the former being distantly related to languages spoken in the Indonesian Republic, and the latter with those of New Guinea. In West Timor, Dutch controlled since the mid-eighteenth century and formally demarcated from Portuguese East Timor by the *Sentença Arbitral* bound-ary agreement of 1913, two principal languages (both Austronesian) – Tetum and Atoni (also known as Timorese) – hold sway. But, in the east, as Traube has pointed out in her contribution to the Colloquy, where there are at least eleven distinct languages spoken by ethnic groups which range in size from a few thousand to over 100,000 members (the total population of East Timor now being some 700,000, of whom at least 150,000 are newcomers from Indonesia [particularly Bali and Sulawesi]), Tetum is used as a kind of *lingua franca* and has, since the Indonesian inva-sion (7 December 1975), but particularly since the Vatican's decision of

October 1981 to allow its use in the Mass (Portuguese having been banned by the Indonesians), assumed an increasingly pivotal role as the 'national' language of the East Timorese.

Prior to 1975, Portuguese was the official government language in East Timor, and, as such, was the principal language of both Church and state. Interestingly, when the Fretilin (*Frente Revolucionária de Timor-Leste Independente*) leadership formally declared East Timorese independence on 28 November 1975, Portuguese was declared the official language of the new state 'at least for the time being'.[3] This reflected the background of the Fretilin leadership, who had all been educated in Portuguese-language high schools and/or Catholic seminaries in the colonial capital Dili. Knowledge of Portuguese was a prerequisite for Portuguese citizenship, Lisbon's *assimilados* policy encouraging cultural and linguistic assimilation, with only a tiny percentage (about 0.25 per cent) of East Timorese being recognized as '*assimilados*' or '*civilizados*' before 1975.[4] Today, the situation has been further complicated by the effects of nearly a decade and a half of Indonesian-language schooling in East Timor, which has produced a younger generation of educated East Timorese whose principal foreign language is *Bahasa Indonesia* not Portuguese. This linguistic gap between the older and the younger generations in East Timor could well have political implications – perhaps even splits along generational lines – if the territory achieves its independence before the older Portuguese-educated group (which includes Xanana Gusmão) has passed from the scene. As Anderson has shown, there are interesting parallels to be drawn out here with the generational gap which opened out along linguistic lines in post-1945 Indonesia between the prewar Dutch-educated elite and the younger group of military officers and civilian leaders who had been educated in the Indonesian-language schools of the independent Republic.[5]

The cultural and ethno-linguistic diversity of East Timorese society is clearly reflected in its oral traditions. In her chapter, Traube, who did pioneering fieldwork amongst the Mambai people of central East Timor prior to the Indonesian invasion, has stressed the dualistic or diarchic political ideologies prevailing which distinguished the 'original, autochtonous' inhabitants from the 'ancestral invaders' from overseas, a distinction which separated 'insiders' and 'outsiders', and the 'people of the land (mountains)' from the 'people of the sea (coast)', the former being endowed with special ritual powers and the latter more conversant with worldly affairs. This distinction between 'inner' and 'outer' can be seen in many other Indonesian cultures. Despite the importance of kinship and locality, she also stresses the significance of inter-ethnic contacts which were later to be central to the growth of a wider Timorese national identity. Formal exchange obligations helped to link the small indigenous domains of eastern Timor into complex political alliances, many of which transcended ethnic boundaries – the colony-wide revolt of Dom Boaventura (1910-12) being one famous example. Indeed, in Traube's view, it was Portuguese colonialism which engendered a wider sense of unity with the common experience of subordination to a European power heightening awareness of inter-ethnic ties and providing an enabling condition for the later development of Timorese nationalism.

The East Timorese experience during the Pacific War (1941–5) was certainly crucial here in developing this wider sense of 'national' community, a community forged in the shared suffering of foreign occupation. It is estimated that upwards of 60,000 East Timorese, or roughly 14 per cent of the pre-1941 population (490,000) died during the thirty-six month Japanese occupation, many of them killed in reprisal for the support given to the two companies of Australian commandos (2/2nd and 2/4th Independent Companies) between December 1941 and February 1943 when Australia was fighting to prevent a Japanese landing in the Northern Territory.[6] In the aftermath of the Indonesian invasion of December 1975, the two periods of foreign occupation began to be talked of in the same breath as that of the '*Japoneses*' (Japanese) and the '*Javaneses*' (Javanese), of which the latter was by far the more severe. 'When speaking to me', the Australian researcher Michele Turner recently reported, 'Timorese continually called the 1975 invasion and occupation "Javanese". Although troops from all over Indonesia serve there, it is the Javanese who are seen in larger numbers, who are usually in command, and who are most offensive to Timorese, especially in their treatment of women.'[7]

This sense of nationhood, however, remained embryonic up to the mid-1970s when the sudden political events of the April 1974 'Carnation' Revolution in Lisbon, the formation of the first East Timorese political parties the following May, and the accelerating decolonization process, contributed to a growing awareness of the wider 'national' community.

The Rise of Fretilin (1974-5)

As Taylor has made clear, the leadership of all the main political parties formed at this time – the right of centre lusophone UDT (*União Democrática Timorense* or 'Timorese Democratic Union'), the socialist inspired Fretilin (from May to September 1974 known as the *Associação Social Democrata Timorense* or ASDT, 'Association of Timorese Social Democrats'), and the tiny pro-integrationist Apodeti (*Associação Popular Democrática Timorense* or 'Timorese Popular Democratic Association') – were sprung from the very restricted *assimilado/civilizado* Portuguese-speaking Timorese elite, which numbered barely 1200 people in the mid-1970s, nearly all domiciled in Dili.[8] But, it was not long before the Fretilin leadership, at least, began to look beyond their privileged position and see that the future lay in the hands of the East Timorese peasantry who made up over 90 per cent of the population.[9]

Influenced by the example of successful liberation movements in the other Portuguese colonies, especially the martyred Amilcar Cabral's PAIGC (*Partido Africano da Independência da Guiné e Cabo Verde*) in Guinea-Bissau and Frelimo (*Frente de Libertação de Moçambique*) in Mozambique, Fretilin's social and political programme, as Taylor has shown, called for fundamental economic re-construction with production, distribution and consumption cooperatives becoming the basic economic units, thus ending excessive dependence on imports. They also called for the expropriation of large landholdings, the inclusion of unused fertile land in the cooperative system, the implementation of agrarian reform and the diversification of monoculture, especially reliance on cash crops such as coffee. Stressing the overwhelming need for self-reliance, the dismantlement of colonial structures and the rapid development of Timorese participation in local decision-making, they likewise drew up policies relating to education and culture (the former heavily influenced by Fr Paulo Freire's rural literacy/adult-education programmes in Brazil), social justice, health, internal administration and national defence.[10]

It is clear from their showing in the local elections of July 1975 – when their candidates won 55 per cent of the vote in rural areas – that their popularity was growing rapidly in the period leading up to the UDT-inspired coup and civil war of August, which eventually left Fretilin in sole charge of the colony until the Indonesian invasion on 7 December. Taylor, for example, stresses that support for Fretilin after the departure of the Portuguese in August 1975 extended to all the territory's ethnic groups, even the normally rather self-sufficient Fataluku people in the Ponta Leste region of the extreme east. However, despite the success of their programmes – especially their adult literacy campaign, a sense of Timorese 'nationhood' was almost certainly still in its infancy at this time, something which Traube makes clear at the end of her discussion of the Mambai when she speaks of the grievance felt by their ritual leaders at what they perceived to be Fretilin's cavalier disregard for traditional authorities. But against this must be set the fact that most Mambai (who numbered at this time about 80,000 or nearly 12 per cent of the population of East Timor) harboured a deep sense of moral superiority to their colonial rulers and a pervasive discontent that things were not 'as they ought to be', feelings which would have made many receptive to the nationalist promise of a new future.

The Indonesian Invasion and its Aftermath (1975 to present)

Without detailed research, it is difficult to speak with confidence about the impact of the Indonesian invasion (7 December 1975) and the subsequent military occupation on groups such as the Mambai. Indeed, we do not really know whether such groups continue to exist. Dunn, for example, speaks of 'a systematic campaign of terror' against the local population with, in some villages, whole communities (apart from very young children) being slaughtered. Furthermore, as Paulino Gama (Mauk Muruk) has written in his moving personal memoir of the guerrilla war, the first five years (1975–80) of Indonesian rule were so devastating for East Timorese society, involving the deaths of perhaps as much as 40 per cent of the pre-invasion population[11], the destruction of swidden agricultural systems in the highlands, and the forcible removal of populations from the hills to 'strategic villages' situated for the most part in insalubrious locations on the coastal plains, where many died of famine and disease, that the surviving population are living today in a very different world from that of 1974–5.

However, in terms of the development of a sense of nationhood, it is clear that this whole period of Indonesian occupation, will be looked back to as a defining moment in the birth of a new East Timorese identity, much in the same way as the short-lived Japanese occupation (1942-5) of the former Netherlands East Indies was a defining moment for the future Indonesian Republic. The key developments here are: first, the complete reorganization of the Fretilin leadership structures and resistance tactics in the aftermath of the Indonesian conquest of Mt Matebian in November 1978; second, the changes in the attitude of the East Timorese Catholic Church; third, the coming of age of a new generation of Indonesian-educated East Timorese student leaders and the emergence of an urban-based *intifada*; and, finally, the clear failure of Indonesian 'development' policies – especially since the 'opening' of East Timor to outside investment in January 1989 – in terms of winning East Timorese support for their rule.

The Reorganization of Fretilin Leadership and Resistance (1981-6)

At its conference at Mabai, Lacluta in March 1981, the first after the fall of Matebian, as Gama explains, the Fretilin leadership had to come to terms with the crippling losses it had sustained in the 1977–9 period: 79 per cent of the members of the Supreme Command killed (only three of the Fretilin Central Committee who remained in East Timor after 1975 had survived and today these are either dead [Sera Key] or in Indonesian custody [Ma'Huno, Xanana]); 80 per cent of the 4,000 Falintil (*Forças Armadas de Libertação Nacional de Timor-Leste*) troops lost together with 90

6

per cent of their weapons; all Fretilin support bases destroyed and Indonesian troops in control of the surviving population; all lines of communication between the remaining resistance fighters severed, and communications with the outside world cut off (there had been no contact with the Fretilin mission abroad since 1978), making it impossible to channel information to supporters overseas.

As Gama has described so graphically, the first task of the Fretilin leadership was to restore links between the scattered Fretilin units still capable of mounting attacks on Indonesian positions. Once those had been established, pre-1979 military and political strategies were completely revised: the policy of maintaining permanent bases was abandoned, Falintil units were now to function as highly mobile columns, continually moving from place to place. At the same time, a network of clandestine organizations was created behind enemy lines and in the concentration camps (a.k.a. 'strategic villages') and population centres under Indonesian control. The vital link between the resistance movement in the bush and the clandestine organizations was henceforth maintained through the *núrep* (*núcleos de resistência popular* or 'popular resistance centres') which had a presence in most of the main population centres.[12]

In the words of Budiardjo and Liem 'reliance on weaponry strength was replaced by reliance on the strength of the people'[13] with guerrilla units henceforth being made responsible for securing their own food supplies, weapons and ammunition. The new strategy adopted in 1981 was clearly remarkably successful for by March 1983, on the initiative of the local Indonesian military commanders, a whole series of ceasefires had come into place, which later resulted in a general ceasefire (March–August 1983) and negotiations between Xanana and Colonel Purwanto, the Javanese commander of the East Timor Security Command (*Koopskam*). In terms of popular solidarity with Fretilin, as Taylor explains, Indonesian attempts to use local inhabitants to 'flush out' the guerrilla remnants in the countryside through the infamous 'fence of legs' (*pagar betis*) tactics of the 1981 'Operation Security' ('*Operasi Keamanan*') were sabotaged by the Timorese who either led the Indonesian troops in the opposite direction to the Fretilin encampments or enabled guerrillas and their families to pass unhindered through their ranks.

In 1986, according to Gama's account, in order to reflect the new relationship between the resistance leaders and the people, Xanana Gusmão declared the formation of a new nationalist organization, the 'National Council of Maubere Resistance' (CNRM or *Conselho Nacional da Resistência Maubere*) with himself as head and Ma'Huno as his deputy. At the same time, he announced that, although he would remain

Commander-in-Chief of Falintil, the armed wing of the CNRM, he no longer wished to be seen solely as the President of Fretilin, thus enabling him to stand above party politics. Henceforth the struggle against the Indonesian military would be fought on a truly national front, one which embraced all East Timorese political parties and groups dedicated to securing national independence (e.g. Fretilin, Falintil, Renetil [*Resistência Nacional Estudantil de Timor-Leste*, the East Timorese Students' National Resistance movement], and UDT). The decision taken in Lisbon in late March 1986 by Fretilin's external delegation and exiled representatives of UDT to form a coalition certainly facilitated the establishment of this broad national grouping.[14]

The Role of the East Timorese Catholic Church

It was during this period, faced with the deepening suffering of the Timorese people, as Archer has shown, that the Timorese Church began to speak out publicly for the first time. Their first important statement was contained in a *Reflection* written in July 1981 (Feast of Our Lady) by East Timorese religious and approved by the Apostolic Administrator, Mgr Martinho da Costa Lopes (in office, 1977–83), which referred to their feelings of 'solidarity' with the people and the bitterness they felt at the seeming indifference of the wider Catholic Church, in particular their fellow co-religionists in Indonesia. Isolation was not a new experience for East Timor. Indeed, it was the norm under Portuguese rule: throughout the colonial period, and especially after Rome signed a concordat in 1941 with the Portuguese dictator, Dr Salazar, the Catholic Church in East Timor was fully integrated into the colonial system. It was at heart a *foreign* Church, outwardly symbolized by the use of Latin and Portuguese in the liturgy, and the majority of East Timorese did not identify with it. In 1970, Church statistics quoted by Archer show that most Timorese were animists, with fewer than a third (180,000) registered as practising Catholics. Far from showing solidarity with the people, it is significant that when serious crises did occur, such as the Japanese landings in February 1942 or the Fretilin-UDT civil war of August 1975, the vast majority of foreign priests and religious (in total about forty priests and over a hundred sisters from eight different orders) left Timor for Australia and Portugal.

All this changed with the Indonesian invasion of 7 December 1975. The priests and religious who remained were not able to leave and many (including six foreign priests) went with the population to the mountains to escape the Indonesian army. With their Portuguese links severed, and deeply influenced by the development of East Timorese nationalism, they were constrained to build a new – more indigenous – Church out of the wreckage of war. Gama's recollection that the first account of events in East Timor came from the mouth of a recently exiled Timorese priest in Australia in June 1979 is an interesting reflection of this development. The outward signs of this were the enhanced role of the East Timorese priests (there are today [1994] some 22 in a priesthood of over 68, the others being divided equally between Indonesians and foreigners), the official use (from October 1981) of Tetum as the language of the liturgy, and the appointment of an East Timorese Apostolic Administrator on the retirement of the Portuguese Bishop of Dili, Dom José Joaquim Ribeiro, in 1977, a post first filled by Mgr Martinho da Costa Lopes (in office, 1977–83), and then by Mgr (post-1988, Dom) Carlos Filipe Ximenes Belo (in office, May 1983 to present) who was elevated as Bishop in 1988.

The 'new' East Timorese Church began to emphasize national identity and culture, human rights and justice. In sharp contrast to the situation which prevailed in the colonial era, as Archer argues, the Church began to define itself in terms of its service to the people, not to the state. This new outspokenness, especially the willingness of the Church to condemn Indonesian atrocities, such as the September 1981 Lacluta massacre in the central highlands in which at least 500 East Timorese perished (Gama gives a number as high as 3,000), cost Mgr da Costa Lopes his job (16 May 1983) when intense Indonesian pressure forced him to resign.

Undeterred, on 1 January 1985, the East Timorese Council of Priests, in another *Reflection*, which Bishop Belo was later forced by the Indonesian authorities to disown, came out in explicit support of the right of East Timor's population to an act of self-determination, a goal which Belo subsequently adhered to – witness his 6 February 1989 letter to the UN Secretary-General, Perez de Cuellar, calling on the UN to use its good offices.[15] At the same time, as Archer has shown, the priests, while continuing to protest the numerous Indonesian human rights abuses, affirmed the importance of Timor's specific cultural heritage in the face of 'Indonesianization'.

Throughout the period from December 1975 to January 1989, when East Timor (with the exception of seven eastern districts between Baucau, Viqueque and Lospalos where fighting was still raging) was officially 'opened' to Indonesians and foreigners by Jakarta, the Catholic Church was the *only* local institution capable of communicating independently with the outside world and of articulating the deep trauma of the East Timorese people. Centrally important here was the special relationship with Rome which the East Timorese Church enjoyed following the invasion. Since East Timor remained the subject of an international dispute (between 1975 and 1982 there were no less than ten UN

Security Council and General Assembly resolutions on the issue demanding – *inter alia* – an immediate Indonesian withdrawal and a genuine act of self-determination), the Vatican decided to administer the diocese directly rather than attach it to the Bishops' Conference of Indonesia or Portugal. As Archer comments, the Church represented both continuity for the Timorese, and also a 'public space' not occupied by the Indonesian authorities.

It is indeed striking that some of the most important public protests of the late 1980s and early 1990s, for example the East Timorese youths' pro-independence demonstration during the Papal Mass of 12 October 1989, the pro-independence protest on the occasion of the 50th anniversary celebration of the diocese of Dili on 4 September 1990, an event which Donaciano Gomes refers to in his brief memoir of the student *intifada*, and, most recently, the march to the Santa Cruz cemetery on 12 November 1991 which turned into a bloodbath (271 dead, 382 wounded and 250 'disappeared'[16]) when Indonesian troops fired indiscriminately on the packed mourners, have been associated with Church events.[17] At the same time, it is hardly surprising that in the circumstances of war and foreign occupation in which the East Timorese find themselves, the great majority opted for Catholicism when they were required to adopt a religion recognized by Indonesia's state ideology, the *pancasila*. In just two decades, the proportion of nominal Catholics shot up from less than 30 per cent to over 80 per cent of the population – from 180,000 in 1970 to over half a million in 1990. As Ben Anderson has pointed out, with regard to the Catholic Church in East Timor, Jakarta finds itself in a strange bind for it has found itself both wanting and distrusting Catholicism's spread, recognizing, on the one hand, that as official members of the Catholic Church the population will enjoy protection according to the logic of the religious provisions of the *pancasila* state ideology, and, on the other hand, fearing the emergence of a popular Catholicism, which, as in nineteenth-century Ireland or Communist-ruled Poland, has become a powerful expression of common suffering.[18]

A recent interview with Bishop Belo (8 September 1993)[19] gives a useful insight into the current situation of the East Timorese Church.

Q: 'How [can] the Timorese people express their faith ?'

Bishop Belo: *'There are many ways: their presence in the Church, in the Eucharist, in the chapels. They also pray in their own homes, [use] the rosary [and] organize processions with a statue of the Virgin, which they carry from house to house...[But] other kinds of group meeting, to sit down together to read the Bible and to pray is not allowed because the [Indonesian] military don't trust them. They think they will discuss politics — this is not allowed. But really, the Catholic faith for the people is a kind of symbol to unite them, it is a way to express the fact that they are Timorese, they don't like any other religion [and] they [certainly] don't like Indonesia.'*

Q: 'Have you tried complaining about this lack of freedom for Church activities?'

Bishop Belo: *'They say they don't beat anyone, they respect the people, that they work for the prosperity of the people. But for me it is a pure lie. From [May] 1983 [i.e. the time of Belo's appointment as Apostolic Administrator] until now, I hear only lies from them.'*

Q: 'I would have thought from the doctrine of 'pancasila' that people [would be] free to worship?'

Bishop Belo: *'This is the theory, but in practice it is very difficult because they are intent on Islamisation. I hear[d] yesterday [that] there are about 400 [East Timorese] boys [who have been] taken to Java to attend Islamic centres of studies [i.e. pesantrèn].... The theory is all very well, but in practice [it's] different.'*

In this oppressive situation, where the very life of the Church is threatened by the ubiquitous presence of what seems, to most Timorese, a Muslim military occupation, parishes, especially those run by East Timorese priests, cannot function in the normal sense of Christian Community. Instead, the priests have to operate under great pressure, running vast parishes (especially to the south and west of Dili) whose numbers are constantly swollen by refugees from other parishes run by Indonesian priests or foreign missionaries. Even though this often means travelling much further for church services, East Timorese parishioners are prepared to do this in order to hear Mass and receive the Eucharist from the hands of their fellow countrymen.

The critical question now is clearly one of the Church's support for the popular desire for an act of self-determination, the question over which Bishop Belo aroused so much passion by his 6 February 1989 letter to the UN Secretary-General. On the one side, amongst the East Timorese priests and some of their foreign colleagues, there is virtual unanimity that self-determination is a realizable goal. For most of the 32 Indonesian priests now serving in East Timor, however, this aspiration is regarded as unrealistic, if not illegitimate. As Archer has stressed, on this vital matter the East Timorese Church is deeply divided, and unless these divisions are somehow resolved, it could again, in the eyes of the Timorese, become a Church which is partly foreign.

As already noted, one area where the Church has made a crucial contribution to the growth of East Timorese nationalism has been that of language. Pivotal here was the decision taken by the Catholic hierarchy in East Timor in 1981, when Portuguese was banned by the Indonesian authorities, to use Tetum, and not Indonesian, as the language of the Church. This decision, which was endorsed by the Vatican in October of that year, has raised Tetum from being a mere local language or *lingua franca* in parts of East Timor to becoming, in Anderson's words 'for the first time, the language of "East Timorese" religion and identity'.[20] Indeed, recent observers have confirmed the way language is used on Church occasions to underscore the intense rejection of the Indonesian presence by the East Timorese. Thus, in a Mass celebrated in September 1993 in the southern parish of Suai, the congregation refused to join in singing hymns in Indonesian (*Bahasa*) led by visiting Indonesian seminarians from Atambua in West Timor when these were introduced into the service.[21]

The Failure of Indonesian Development Policies and the Rise of a New Generation of East Timorese Nationalists

Besides the East Timorese Church, there are also two other developments which have been determinant in the rise of East Timorese nationalism during the past decade: first, the coming of age of a new generation of East Timorese student leaders – young men and women of Donaciano Gomes's ilk – who have been educated in the Indonesian school and university system, and have been radicalized by the gap between this system and the reality of contemporary East Timor; and, second, the failure of Indonesian development policies and the Indonesian-staffed local administration in East Timor to address the key concerns of the East Timorese themselves. This failure, a failure all the more striking given the large sums of money poured into East Timor by the central government, has been most poignantly illustrated by the recent (1990) study undertaken by a Gadjah Mada University (UGM) team led by Professor Mubyarto of the Gadjah Mada Centre for Village and Regional Development.[22]

The study's principal findings are that the sources of alienation in East Timor, which are currently fuelling both the student-led resistance movement/*intifada* and widespread popular support for the remaining Fretilin guerrillas, are traceable to two main sources – military conflict and the exclusion of East Timorese from meaningful political and economic participation in the development of their territory. The Indonesian takeover in all its dimensions – military, educational, economic and political – was so rapid and violent that the East Timorese were subjected to deep trauma and 'culture shock' from which the Mubyarto report, penned fifteen years after the initial invasion, found they had in no way recovered. This profoundly negative experience –

most tragically illustrated in the huge death toll especially in the early years of the occupation – has been compounded by what the study calls an 'overdose' of the military which has maintained (despite the January 1989 'opening') a strong and active presence in East Timor. There are still upwards of ten battalions with several special force (*Kopassus*/*Kopassandha*) units in the territory (perhaps as many as 8,000 men in all), and their continued perpetration of the most gross human rights abuses against the local population has kept alive deep feelings of mistrust between the East Timorese and the Indonesian authorities.

The second set of 'blockages' identified by the report derives from the denial to key groups in traditional East Timorese society – for example, the *'umapukun'* (traditional leaders) and *'katuas'* (elders) of Traube's Mambai – of any meaningful role in the social, political and economic life of their localities. None of the leaders and elders are, for example, invited to sit on the village deliberative councils (*Lembaga Ketahanan Masyarakyat Desa*) controlled by the Indonesian Interior Ministry, nor on any other Indonesian-sponsored representative institution at the local level. Besides these traditional community leaders, these groups also include the educated youth and, most important, the Catholic Church, which may lack coercive power and wealth (currently the prerogative of the Indonesians) but which, unlike the local government, in the view of the Mubyarto report, 'controls the people'. The strong antipathies which have developed between these sectors have been compounded by the insensitivity of the many thousands of 'newcomers' (currently 150,000 or over 20 per cent of the population living in East Timor are non-East Timorese), who have taken over key administrative and commercial positions, but show no understanding of local culture and practices.

Furthermore, outside interests, especially the military through its commercial operations run by the PT Batara Indra Group of companies, which grew out of a holding company (PT Denok Hernandes) set up by three senior officers (Benny Murdani, Dading Kalbuadi and Adolf Sahala Rajagukguk) in command of the Timor invasion operation ('*Operasi Seroja*'/'Operation [Blossoming] Lotus'), have monopolized East Timor's small modern economy, in particular coffee, sandalwood and marble, and have been exploiting it like a 'milking cow' (*sapi perahan*).[23] The infamous 'Timor Gap Treaty' (11 December 1989), which has attempted to divide East Timor's offshore oil resources between Indonesia and Australia, a matter now subject to Portuguese litigation at the International Court of Justice in The Hague (a judgment is due in late 1995), is perhaps the most blatant manifestation of this exploitation, as Roger Clark explains, because nowhere in the treaty is there any mention of the rights and interests of the East Timorese people themselves.

Even the much vaunted '*Pembangunan*' ('Development') supposedly brought by the Indonesians has been shown to be vitiated by corruption and by a blatant concern for military security rather than local welfare – it is striking here that most of the serviceable roads, bridges and harbours are in the eastern sectors (Baucau and Lautem), where fighting is still taking place, whereas in the relatively more 'peaceful' regions such as Ermera, Maliana and Suai in the south and west, local infrastructure is deplorable.[24] At the same time, new environmental problems, particularly land disputes, are being generated by the official Indonesian transmigration programme, which has brought Balinese farmers to sites near the Indonesian border (Bobonaro and Kovalima) and spurred a rush of 'spontaneous' transmigrants from Atambua (Belu district) in West Timor.[25] The overall result has been the fostering of deep divisions within East Timorese society and what the Mubyarto study presciently calls (it was written over a year before the 12 November 1991 Santa Cruz massacre) 'various [adverse] social dynamics which are developing quickly'.[26]

As Donaciano Gomes's memoir makes clear, the deepest of these cleavages undoubtedly affects East Timorese youth, particularly high school students and those 1,000 or more who have been sent to universities in inner Indonesia since the mid-1980s. Their resentment of the non-Timorese newcomers – the so-called 'Battalion 702' (the numbers referring to their leaving for work early in the morning [7], not bringing any benefit to the local economy [0], and then going home early in the afternoon [2]) – is particularly keen. The Makassarese and Bugis, who have engrossed nearly all the retail trade of Dili and other important towns, are seen here as especially extortionate. As an East Timorese secondary school student from Gleno put it:

> What's the good of school if there's no way we are going to get a decent job? These days all office jobs are closed to us. If the Regional Office Head [Kakanwil] in a department is a newcomer, he will only be interested in having his relatives, or at least people from the same region as him, working in his office. [27]

Large numbers of educated East Timorese job seekers are unable to be absorbed into a work force now dominated by inner island 'newcomers'. Of 4,707 job seekers in 1987, only 166, or 3.4 per cent found jobs, a much lower percentage than in previous years (15 per cent in 1979 and 21 per cent in 1983). Neither private companies nor government are able to provide jobs for school leavers, and the fact that the monopolistic practices of military-dominated companies have effectively 'closed off' the modern economic sector to East Timorese high school and university graduates has led them to question the relevance of educational institutions for their future.[28] At the same time, as Anderson has pointed out, their mastery of Indonesian has given them access to a world beyond Indonesia, much in the same fashion that Dutch gave Indonesian intellectuals, at the turn of the century, access to a world beyond the Netherlands-Indies.[29]

It is this unemployment and resentment of non-Timorese 'newcomers' that has been the main breeding ground of the new leaders – young men like Donaciano Gomes – of the East Timorese underground resistance network, the group whom Xanana has described as 'of great significance' for the future of East Timor. They are strongly committed to independence for their country and are prepared to face considerable risks without any of the protection of high political connections and press sympathy (now admittedly somewhat muted in the aftermath of the June 1994 government press crackdown) which their fellow Indonesian student activists enjoy – one has only to compare here the relatively relaxed atmosphere of the 1993 'Golput' student trial in Semarang with the savage sentencing meted out to those deemed the 'ringleaders' of the Santa Cruz demonstration (12 November 1991).[30] Besides keeping the flame of resistance alive in East Timor itself, as Pat Walsh describes, some of the more educated East Timorese are making contact with key Indonesian academics and non-governmental organization workers, who are now questioning the limits of Indonesian nationalism and believe that, after years of neglect, East Timor should be placed much higher on the domestic agenda. It is possible that these connections will become increasingly important as a new generation comes to power in Indonesia in the late 1990s.

Conclusions

Surveying the growth of East Timorese nationalism in the nearly two decades since the first political parties were formed in Dili in May 1974, it is possible to discern some salient themes. First, the crucial role played by Fretilin in the military and political struggle against Indonesia between 1975 and the early 1990s. Without the Fretilin leadership there would have been no unified basis of popular resistance against the overwhelming might of the Indonesian army. It is true that to this day not all East Timorese are pro-Fretilin, but nearly all would acknowledge its critical contribution to keeping the ideal of an independent East Timor alive. If there were free elections in the territory in the near future, it would certainly win a landslide victory at the polls. Having said that, one can sense that the leadership is now passing into the hands of a younger generation of educated East Timorese, who are at the heart of the urban *intifada* and the underground resistance network, which is now as important amongst East Timorese in Indonesia, as it is in East Timor itself. As Xanana has pointed out in his interview with Robert Domm in September 1990:

> We know we cannot hope for a military victory, but the underground resistance is more active today than it has been at any time during the past fifteen years of war. There are organized groups in each village and the youth [now] feel involved in the struggle for independence...actually, for us, just to resist is already to have won, and if the Indonesians imagine that by exterminating Falintil, they will put an end to the war, they are very much mistaken.[31]

Later, in his trial statement, which the Indonesian judge refused to allow him to read, he acknowledged that as Commander of Falintil he was not ashamed to acknowledge military defeat on the ground,[32] but he also indicated that the struggle against the Indonesians would be ultimately won in the political arena, precisely the area where the new student leadership can make the greatest contribution. However, the possibility of generational conflict – somewhat akin to that of the Indonesian *pemuda* (youth activists) and the older nationalist elite in Indonesia in 1944–6[33] or to the current inter-generational debate over the role of the army and its 'dual function' (*dwifungsi*) powers in the dying days of Suharto's 'New Order' – is something which might develop in the future in East Timor, especially if the territory achieves its independence. Indeed, one could imagine a situation in which the older generation of Timorese nationalist leaders, who had grown up in the Portuguese colonial period (and thus speak Portuguese rather than Indonesian) and who had risen to high positions in the Falintil, might find themselves at loggerheads with a younger group of Indonesian-schooled student activists, who might be critical of any attempt to carve out a special role for the Timorese armed forces and Falintil veterans. In this sense, young East Timorese might find a measure of common ground with their fellow students in Indonesia as Walsh has surmised. At the moment, however, there is no evidence for this.

Second, in this political sphere, the role of the East Timorese Church will continue to be central, especially in terms of deepening a specifically East Timorese sense of cultural and religious identity. However, as Archer has warned, there are problems on the horizon, not least the diminishing numbers of East Timorese priests when compared with those from Indonesia (it will be nearly a decade before the next generation of local-born priests are ordained, the lack of a local training seminary being keenly felt), and pressures from Jakarta to split the Dili diocese and incorporate it in the Indonesian Bishops' Conference, moves being presented by Jakarta as a way of serving the needs of East Timor's bur-geoning Catholic population, but whose inner design seems to be to reduce Bishop Belo's growing influence.[34] Finally, the very nature of the Indonesian presence in East Timor, especially its economic exploitation, will ensure that the struggles of the new generation of East Timorese nationalists will continue to enjoy widespread popular support amongst all sections of East Timorese society, and in the exile communities abroad. This is something which Indonesian Foreign Minister Alatas seems at last to be aware of now that there is talk of bringing anti-integrationist East Timorese leaders, perhaps even Xanana Gusmão, into the current UN-sponsored talks. The tragedy of East Timor is still a long way from resolution, but, in the late twentieth-century, Indonesia may at last be realising that Third World colonialism tends to create its own gravediggers.

Notes

1 See below, chapter 1.

2. See below, chapter 2.

3 Jolliffe, Jill, *East Timor. Nationalism and Colonialism*. St Lucia: University of Queensland Press, 1978, p. 76.

4 Weatherbee, Donald, 'Portuguese Timor: An Indonesian Dilemma', *Asian Survey*, 6(12), pp. 684; and Mubyarto, *East Timor. The Impact of Integration. An Indonesian Socio-Anthropological Study*, ed. Pat Walsh. Northcote (Australia): Indonesia Resources and Information Program [IRIP], 1991,pp. 45–60.

5 Anderson, B.R.O'G., 'The Languages of Indonesian Politics', *Indonesia*, No.1 (April 1966), pp. 101–9.

6 Dunn, James, *Timor. A People Betrayed*, Milton [Queensland]: Jacaranda Press, 1983, p.26; and Turner, Michele, *Telling. East Timor: Personal Testimonies 1942–1992*. Kensington: New South Wales University Press, 1992, pp. 51–2.

7 Turner, Michele, *Telling. East Timor: Personal Testimonies, 1942–1992*. Kensington: New South Wales University Press, 1992, p. 84.

8 Hill, Helen, 'Fretilin: The Origins, Ideologies and Strategies of a Nationalist Movement in East Timor', MA thesis, Monash University, Melbourne, 1978, p. 98; Weatherbee, Donald, 'Portuguese Timor: An Indonesian Dilemma', *Asian Survey* (1966) 6(12), p. 684; and Budiarjo, Carmel and Liem Soei Liong, *The War Against East Timor*, London: Zed Books, 1984, p. 54.

9 *Op cit.*, Hill, Helen, note 8.

10 Jolliffe, Jill, *East Timor. Nationalism and Colonialism*. St Lucia: University of Queensland Press, 1978, pp.75–6; and Budiarjo, Carmel and Liem Soei Liong, *The War Against East Timor*. London: Zed Books, 1984, p. 53

11 Defert, Gabriel, *Timor Est. Le Génocide Oublié. Droit d'un Peuple et Raisons d'États*. Paris: Éditions L'Harmattan, 1992, pp. 147–51. Defert quotes a figure, based on Church sources, of 308,000 out of an original 700,000.

12 Budiardjo, Carmel and Liem Soei Liong, *The War Against East Timor.* London: Zed Books, 1984, pp. 68–9.

13 *Ibid.*, p. 69.

14 Taylor, John, *The Indonesian Occupation of East Timor, 1974–1989. A Chronology.* London: Catholic Institute for International Relations, 1990, p. 60.

15 *Ibid.*,p. 93.

16 A Paz é Possível em Timor-Leste, *East Timor: The Santa Cruz Massacre* (Lisbon: A Paz é Possível em Timor-Leste, February 1992), p. 3.

17 Boavida, João Frederico, 'The Fusion of Religion and Nationalism in East Timor: A Culture in the Making', MPhil. thesis (Anthropology), Oxford University, Oxford, 1993, p. 97.

18 Anderson, B.R.O'G., 'Imagining "East Timor" ', *Arena Magazine* (April-May 1993), p. 27.

19 Catholic Institute for International Relations (CIIR), *Timor Link*, No. 27 (October 1993), p. 7.

20 *Op cit.*, note 18.

21 Catherine Scott, personal communication, October 1993.

22 Mubyarto, *East Timor: The Impact of Integration. An Indonesian Socio-Anthropological Study.* ed. Pat Walsh. Northcote (Australia): Indonesia Resources and Information Program [IRIP], 1991.

23 Aditjondro, George, 'From Memo to Tutuala. A Kaleidoscope of Environmental Problems in East Timor', in Aditjondro, *East Timor. An Indonesian Intellectual Speaks Out,* ed. Herb Feith, Emma Baulch and Pat Walsh, Australian Council for Overseas Aid (ACFOA) Development Dossier No. 33. Canberra: ACFOA, 1994, p. 17.

24 *Ibid.*, p. 14.

25 *Ibid.*, pp. 17–18.

26 See Walsh foreword to Mubyarto, *East Timor: The Impact of Integration. An Indonesian Socio-Anthropological Study*, ed. Pat Walsh. Northcote (Australia): Indonesia Resources and Infromation Program [IRIP], 1991, p. ix.

27 Mubyarto, *East Timor: The Impact of Integration. An Indonesian Socio-Anthropological Study*, ed. Pat Walsh. Northcote (Australia): Indonesia Resources and Infromation Program [IRIP], 1991, p. 55.

28 *Ibid.*, p. 58

29 Anderson, B.R.O'G., 'Imagining "East Timor" ', *Arena Magazine* (April-May 1993), p. 27.

30 Cohen, Margot, 'A Telling Trial: Students Test Limits of Government's Tolerance', *Far Eastern Economic Review*, 23 September 1993, p. 15; and *Indonesian Observer*, 27 August 1993.

31 Defert, Gabriel, *Timor Est. Le Génocide Oublié. Droit d'un Peuple et Raisons d'États.* Paris: Éditions L'Harmattan, 1992, p. 204, quoting Robert Domm, 'Timor Rebels Fight on with "Unshakeable Morale" ', *The Age* (Melbourne), 25 October 1990.

32 Tapol Bulletin, No.117 (June 1993), p. 3.

33 Anderson, B.R.O'G., *Java in a Time of Revolution, Occupation and Resistance, 1944–1946.* Ithaca: Cornell University Press, 1972.

34 Wagstaff, Jeremy, 'East Timor Catholic Church. A Refuge Under Siege', *Reuter* (4 March 1994).

PART I

Historical
Background

CHAPTER 1

The Emergence of a Nationalist Movement in East Timor

John G. Taylor

Introduction

Following the Indonesian invasion of East Timor in December 1975, and the subsequent annexation of the former Portuguese colony, many commentators were surprised both by the extent of opposition and by the ability of the population to resist Indonesian incorporation. Whilst the course of events in East Timor in recent years has been documented in a number of texts,[1] several important issues emerging from the conflict remain unanalysed.

One of the most important of these issues is to explain why, despite such overwhelming superiority, the Indonesian military experienced such difficulties in quelling resistance to its occupation. Various writers have tried to answer this by focusing on issues such as the suitability of East Timor's terrain to guerrilla warfare,[2] the brutal treatment of the population by Indonesian troops,[3] or the desire of the military to maintain East Timor as a counter-insurgency training ground for its troops. Whilst some of these, and notably the first two, are important in addressing this problem, it nevertheless seems to me that we also need to consider other areas. Most notable of these are the following: first, the structure of East Timor society as it emerged in the twentieth century after a prolonged period of colonial control; and second, the nature of the independence movement that developed in East Timor in the early 1970s. Analysing these will enable us to gain a deeper understanding of the strength of resistance to Indonesia's annexation.

Specifically, initial studies seem to suggest that the particular features of Timorese society which enabled it to contain the spread of European colonial control have continued to operate during the post-1975 period. Furthermore, that the nationalist movement which emerged in East Timor during the early 1970s, by relating itself to these features, was able to develop strategies and policies which resulted in widespread support for its campaign for independence.

What, then, are these aspects of Timorese society, and how are they related to the development of East Timorese nationalism? Answering this question involves us examining briefly a number of features of East Timor's recent history.

Settlement and Exchange

Prior to Portuguese and Dutch entry into Southeast Asia, Timor formed a part of the trading networks centred on East Java and the Celebes (Sulawesi). These networks were tied into commercial links with China and India. The commercial value of Timor is highlighted in documents published during the Ming Dynasty in 1436. The island is described as one in which, 'the mountains are covered with sandalwood trees, and the country produces nothing else'.[4] Duarte Barbosa, one of the first Portuguese to visit Timor, wrote in 1518, 'There is an abundance of white sandalwood, which the Moors in India and Persia value greatly, where much of it is used.'[5] Consequently, although other commodities – honey, wax, and slaves – were exported from Timor, its trade was focused primarily on its rich sandalwood reserves.

At first glance, it seems that Timor's role in the sandalwood trade influenced markedly the structure and development of its political system. Schulte Nordholt cites early sixteenth-century reports which seem to indicate that the predominance of coastal kingdoms in the north and south was a direct result of this trade. Each area appeared to be under the control of a chief who supervised all commercial dealings.[6] This illustrates the forms in which Timorese political organization appeared initially to Asian and European traders, with commerce founding a coastal political hierarchy. Colonial history took this form and adopted it as the basis for many of its subsequent analyses. Yet behind it there seems to have been a more complex political organization which needs to be analysed briefly if we are to understand the basic features of Timorese society.

A Timorese myth recounted by the ethnographer Jonker in Amabi (West Timor) in the early nineteenth century, cited by Middelkoop, begins: 'A long, long time ago there was one ruler of this island in Babiko-Babali' (the southern coastal plain).[7] The ritual ruler of this realm appears to have had three subordinate rulers (*liurai*) under him, each of whom exercised executive power in his own territory. The first *liurai* was located in South Belu (the coastal plain), the second in Sonbai (in the west of the island), and the third in Suai-Kamanasa (in the south-centre of the island). The triad of heads under one ruler had its origins in a substantial migration dating from the early fourteenth century. Myths describe how the original Melanesian inhabitants were displaced in this period by invaders coming from Malacca via Makassar in the Celebes and

Larantuka in Eastern Flores. These newcomers, of Malay origin, settled in the southern coastal plain, and moved north-west and north-east, displacing the original inhabitants, and forming the three kingdoms dominated by 'Babiko-Babali'.

These kingdoms were neither unified nor centrifugal in any sense which would be familiar to European historians. They combined loosely-knit localized territorial groups in a general hierarchy of clans, each related through exchange. These clans were ruled by chiefs who received tribute and organized marital alliances with neighbouring clans. Each clan paid tribute to the kingdom in which it existed. Consequently when these localised groups began to trade with the Dutch and Portuguese in the sixteenth century, their encounter with a more developed economic system, which itself operated through exchange, enabled this latter system to transform the clans' ties with their kingdoms by directing their exchange systems externally. Chiefs who could organize labour to produce and trade in commodities such as sandalwood received in return from the Portuguese trade items such as cloth, furs, and iron tools. This supply from the Portuguese enabled coastal groups to assert their identity over their erstwhile royal rulers. The resultant shifts in political control produced major changes in the distribution of power in the sixteenth and seventeenth centuries. These changes provided the backdrop for the turbulent events of this period, in particular the organization of resistance to European invasion.

Before examining the effects of European intrusions on the reproduction of Timorese society, we need to recount briefly the chronology of events.

Colonial Interplay

The first Portuguese settlement in the proximity of Timor was on the island of Solor, in 1566. Dominican friars built a fortress, which they filled with their recent converts from Solor and Flores. At this stage the Portuguese made annual trips to Timor to collect sandalwood and trade in finished goods. When their commercial rivals, the Dutch, managed to capture Solor in 1611, the population of the fortress moved to the neighbouring island of Larantuka. Whilst Solor experienced both Dutch and Portuguese rule in the seventeenth century, Larantuka remained firmly within the Portuguese orbit.

This relatively settled period of Dutch rule witnessed the consolidation of a group which was to dominate Timor's development in the seventeenth and eighteenth centuries. The Dutch termed them the 'Topasses',[8] and they first appear in colonial history as a 'mixed race...the offspring of Portuguese soldiers, sailors, and traders from Malacca and Macao, who intermarried with the local women of Solor,'⁹ and who moved with the Portuguese to Larantuka. After the move, the Topasses, initially with the help of groups of Dominican friars, began to control the trading networks between Solor, Larantuka, and Timor, particularly the lucrative sandalwood trade. During this process, they began to settle in Timor itself, although their presence was not really felt until after 1642.

This mid-seventeenth century date marked a watershed in Timorese history since it was during this year that the Portuguese invaded Timor in strength, attempting to extend their influence beyond the coast to control the island's internal trade. Justifying their attack by the need to defend recently Christianized coastal rulers, the Portuguese moved directly against the western kingdom of Sonbai, and its parent kingdom, Babali, or Wehale as they called it. Victory was swift and brutal. An observer described the campaign of the commander, Captain Major Francisco Fernandes of Solor, in the following words: 'Laying waste the regions through which he marched with his troops, the Captain Major held out in the face of pursuit by the enemy up to the place where Wehale had his residence; after reducing everything to ashes there he withdrew to Batimao.'¹⁰ Topasse migration to Timor increased markedly after this slaughter. The Topasse community was centred at Lifau (now Oecussi or Pontai Makassar) on the northern coast. From here the Topasses prepared to quell any internal threat to their position, either from local communities or from the Dutch, who, shortly after, in 1653, defeated the Portuguese garrison at Kupang in the west of the island, and landed a substantial military force in 1656. Unlike the earlier Portuguese invasion, the Dutch met with stiff resistance: Topasse families were provided with European weapons to contain the Dutch advance. They routed the Dutch in a short and brutal battle near Kupang which forced them to move to the neighbouring island of Roti, thereby giving effective control of Timor to the Topasses. Opposition to Topasse rule could now come only from three groups: the Portuguese merchants, the Dominican friars, and the Timorese themselves. The merchants tried to wrest control of the sandalwood trade from the Topasses, with the blessing of the Portuguese crown; the Dominicans attempted to build their own separate power base; and the Timorese kingdoms rose in periodic revolt against both the 'white' and 'black' (Topasse) Portuguese. Throughout the late seventeenth and early eighteenth centuries, conflicts between these groups were interspersed with periods in which their participants united in opposition to the spread of Dutch influence.

Thus, after the fall of Kupang, the Portuguese embarked on a campaign of enticing chiefs away from the Topasse sphere. This culminated in attempts to introduce a governor on to the island in Lifau in 1695 and

1702. On both occasions he was forced out by the combined efforts of the Timorese and Topasses. Subsequently, in 1720, the Dominicans were largely responsible for removing the governor. In 1729 another governor and his forces were besieged and defeated in Manatuto, after which the Portuguese withdrew until 1748.

Meanwhile, the Dutch had once again begun to reassert themselves in the western half of the island. Their spread of influence amongst local tribes in the 1730s culminated in their rebuilding Fort Kupang by 1746. Unlike earlier conflicts, the campaigns against the Dutch in 1735 and 1746 had only a limited impact, hence the Topasses turned to the Portuguese for assistance and invaded Dutch areas in 1749. The outcome of this invasion was a ferocious engagement which came to be known in Timor as the Battle of Penfui. The result was a Dutch victory, and a strengthening of Dutch presence in the west of the island. Indeed, with Dutch assistance, the kingdom of Servião was able to remove Topasse control. Penfui (1749) laid down a distinct territorial division of the island, with the Dutch in the west and the Portuguese in the east. The fact that the Topasses had requested help from the Portuguese ensured the latter a stronger political presence, and led to a reduction in Topasse power. The healthy respect engendered by the one for the other meant that neither attempted to extend their influence beyond the *liurai* (kingdom) level, thereby leaving Timorese society relatively free from incursion and disruption.

The Structure of Timorese Society

By the end of the eighteenth century Timorese society had thus managed to retain many of the features that had characterized its social, political, and cultural systems, prior to European contact. Although the island contains as many as eighteen distinct ethnolinguistic groups, these shared common features, whose reproduction rested on a number of mechanisms and were unified through elaborate systems of exchange. The basic structures of these systems can best be illustrated by focusing initially on the features of the Timorese economy.

The organization of production was profoundly influenced by the nature of the Timorese terrain. The main topographical feature of the island is its mountainous spine, interspersed with fertile valleys and permanent springs. To the north, mountains protrude into the sea, whilst in the south they give way to a broad coastal plain. Lowland areas are also found in the north and west. In this terrain the flow of water is seasonally based. The vegetation produced by the climate and terrain varies from savanna and grassland in the plain areas to bush land on the hill slopes, and to evergreen and tropical forests in the mountainous areas. Under these conditions only a limited amount of land use was possible. Irrigated cultivation could be undertaken only where water supplies were available from flood plains, in the vicinity of springs, or on swamp land. Most cultivation was of the swidden (slash and burn) type, with land use being rotated to preserve the soil. Several crops were grown: rice, maize, cassava, yams, sweet potatoes, and a variety of fruits. Livestock – pigs, goats, sheep, and buffalo – were grazed on the hill slopes. Production was mainly for local subsistence, but goods were regularly exchanged at local markets. The units in which production occurred were the household garden, the field, and the irrigated *padi*. Economic organization was based primarily on the extended family, which was responsible for the maintenance of each type of unit. Throughout the agricultural cycle, the low technical level necessitated extensive cooperation in the use of labour. Production took place in both extended kin and village contexts, each being characterized by distinct sexual divisions, and governed by ritual. In the cycle of rice cultivation, for example, planting was undertaken by women, and harvesting by men. Outside the agricultural cycle, weaving was a female task, whilst men produced iron implements, and so on. Economic relations were not solely influenced by divisions in the production process, however. They were also affected by a system of exchange which involved both goods and individuals. Goods were exacted from Timorese communities as tribute due to the chiefs of the various princedoms and kingdoms. In the Wehale kingdom, for example, through his officials the *nai boot* or 'lord of the land' granted land to families for their own use, in return for which they paid a token rent, of *rai teen* (literally, 'excrement of the land'). Goods were also exchanged for women and men in marriage. This exchange was only possible if the goods required could be produced in return for the provision of men and women in the village unit. Villagers had to work beyond the time required to produce their own subsistence crops, in order to produce the goods to be exchanged. In this fashion, the products of surplus labour time were exchanged for means of reproduction, and the elders, through their role in exchange, were responsible for distributing these products. Thus, in addition to the economic relations generated by production, there were also those generated by exchange and the consumption of goods exchanged.

These relations were expressed in systems of kinship and status distinction between various groups in each of Timor's kingdoms. Although these systems varied somewhat, their basic essentials were the same, having their base in a common structure of production and exchange. Kinship, for example, assumed varying forms. By the end of the seventeenth century, there were variations from a patrilineal system with patrilocal residence in the north and east, to a matrilineal system in the south, where matrilineal kinship combined with uxorilocal residence.[11]

Whatever the form taken by kinship, the exchange of men and women between groups was channelled through tribal elders, who arranged supplies of goods varying from buffaloes and horses to swords and gold ornaments. Consequently, just as the chiefs of the princedoms were able to gain status from their collection of surplus labour through tribute, so also were elders through their role in the system of kinship exchange. Although status accrued to individuals in other ways, such as size and fertility of land cultivated, knowledge of tradition, possession of sacred objects, accumulated wealth, and age, the most important hierarchy remained that generated by production and exchange. Thus, in Timor's political system, the predominant positions were occupied by the most elevated individuals in the tribute and exchange systems.

This political system had three main administrative levels: the village, princedom, and kingdom, each with its own head. Other sources of political power resided in clan leadership, and a royal and aristocratic status accorded to some kingdom and princedom leaders. The village comprised several hamlets, spread over a wide area. Each hamlet contained the members of a particular clan, generally tracing itself to six generations. Ruled by a headman in association with a council of elders, the village was part of a princedom (*suco*) headed by a family which was itself subject to the ruler (*liurai*) of the kingdom in which it existed. In kingdoms and princedoms where the *liurai* and princes possessed a royal or aristocratic status, the extended royal and aristocratic families distinguished themselves from the mass of the population, the latter being divided into commoners (*dato*) and, in certain cases, slaves (*ata*), mostly captured in wars between clans, princedoms, and kingdoms. In this system, those with the greatest political power were those in receipt of the most tribute and/or those in the most strategic positions in the kinship exchange system.

Each Timorese kingdom, princedom, and clan possessed value systems whose ideologies highlighted the importance of exchange, and justified the hierarchy influenced by this exchange. In the kingdoms of Belu and Servião, for example, tribute paid to the rulers controlling trade focused particularly on gifts at the end of the harvesting period. These gifts were called *poni pah* (literally, 'rice baskets of the land'). Similarly, gifts of 'homage' or *tuthais* were given to rulers whose political prominence had been established by their success in arranging marital exchanges. The exchange of gifts in return for access to means of production (land) and reproduction (the creation of new family units) was also expressed in the cultural rites accompanying birth, marriage, and death, all of which were

27

combined in a value system relating them to the place of the tribe in the cosmos. In death rites, for example, the dead person's descent group acted as an intermediary between its wife-givers and takers, coordinating exchanges between them, making 'death payments' to the deceased person's matrilineal kin. Just as marriage was characterized by an exchange of gifts for means of reproduction, so too were death rites part of a value system whose ethos centred on the notion of exchange. In marriage, food was exchanged for means of reproduction. In death, it was offered to spirits who, in exchange, ensured the fertility of the earth. The products of this fertility were then offered to different spirits who ensured the best climatic conditions for growth, and so on. Life was viewed as a system of inter-linked exchanges whose enactment was essential for the maintenance of economic and social stability.

Reproduction and Resistance

Bearing in mind these general characteriztics of Timor's social structure, and examining the events we have recounted earlier from the history of the sixteenth and seventeenth centuries, several trends emerge.

Whilst trade in the pre-sixteenth century period had led to a gradual increase in the cultivation of goods for export, the political and social effects of this had been minimal, largely confined to a limited increase in the political influence of the heads of coastal kingdoms. Inserting themselves into existing trading patterns, the Portuguese intensified this process, with the long-term aim of undermining the Timorese kingdoms, producing smaller, less powerful units, more amenable to European control. Throughout the sixteenth century, however, Portuguese attempts at divide and rule had only very limited success, and it was not until the mid-seventeenth century, with the defeat of the Wehale kingdom, that the control by kingdoms over their subordinate princedoms (*suco*) was lessened.

This decline in the kingdoms' powers enabled the invading group of Topasse families to take over the senior positions previously occupied by kingdom and princedom heads in the exchange of tribute, services, and men and women between clans and villages. Through their increasing assumption of this role in the course of the eighteenth century, the Topasses were able to exercise political influence within the Timorese princedoms.

The emphasis on the value of exchange in pre-Portuguese influenced Timor was thus reinforced by the Portuguese spreading the net of exchange economically downwards from the kingdom level, and by the Topasses reinforcing the system of kinship exchange for the purposes of their own political control. Consequently, although the Timorese economy was directed to external needs, and although control of its political system shifted to an external grouping, the effects of these changes were limited. What, in other societies, might have produced fundamental structural changes, resulted rather in the maintenance of basic aspects of Timorese society. This seems to indicate how Timorese society was able to reproduce its indigenous economic, cultural, and social systems despite foreign control. Once established, this co-existence of external control with indigenous structural reproduction continued throughout the eighteenth and nineteenth centuries. The history of this period is marked by the success of Timorese communities in restricting Topasse, European, and Chinese influence and control to the political sphere of princely kinship alliances.

This resistance took many forms. Throughout the eighteenth century, opposition focused largely on the Portuguese, with attacks on Portuguese troops launched from sheltered mountain areas. One of the most renowned battles took place in the mountains of Cailaco in 1726, when four thousand troops under Portuguese command were contained by a Timorese army less than a quarter its size.[12] As a result of such encounters, by the middle of the eighteenth century, the Portuguese had given up their attempts to administer the territory in any effective way. In 1769 they were routed in Lifau and moved their administrative centre eastwards to Dili. With the Portuguese threat reduced, the Timorese then found themselves defending their territory against the Topasses, who tried to extend their political control through kinship agreements. Topasse families tried to entice Timorese kingdom rulers by awarding them Portuguese titles such as '*Coronel*' (Colonel) or '*Brigadeiro*' (Brigadier), and providing them with military support for tribute exaction. Their success, however, was limited. Resistance continued into the nineteenth century as evidenced in eyewitness reports.

In 1825, a young Dutch lieutenant, Dirk Kolff, visited Dili. In a detailed account of his visit, he described how, 'the inhabitants of Dili expressed to me their strong desire to be freed from the hateful yoke of the Portuguese.'[13] At the end of the 1850s, the English traveller Alfred Russel Wallace spent several months in Timor during his travels in the 'Malay Archipelago'. Witnessing one of the regular attacks on Dili, he concluded that, 'Timor will for many years to come remain in its present state of chronic insurrection and misgovernment.'[14] When the naturalist H. O. Forbes travelled in Timor in 1882, he reported that the country was 'apportioned out under certain chiefs called Rajahs or Leoreis (*liurai*), each of whom is independent in his own kingdom.'[15] Their independence was attested by Forbes being conducted through the country without the presence of any Topasses or Portuguese, except in Dili. He noted that the Timorese had 'learnt' many of the customs of the Portuguese, in order to 'outwit' them more effectively. Forbes' observations on the 'independence' of the Timorese kingdoms, and on their ability to control Topasse or Portuguese encroachment, illustrate the constant complaints of Portuguese officials that they were unable to maintain with any degree of success their administrative posts in the interior.

Pacification: The Two Political Systems
At the end of the nineteenth century, however, this situation began to change, as the Portuguese tried once again, this time with much greater determination, to extend control over their colony. Colonial history initially recorded this as a 'reaction' to the assassination of a newly-appointed governor, Lacerda Maia, in 1887, but its causes ran rather deeper.

Faced with the rapid economic development of most of Europe, Portugal tried to improve its economic position by a more systematic exploitation of its colonies than had previously been the case. For Timor, this resulted in an expansion of cultivation for export, persuading villagers to increase their yield and diversify into new crops such as cocoa, copra, and rubber, and introducing plantations to grow coffee. Forced labour was used to develop the infrastructure, cultivate crops, and extend the trading system.

The success of these policies required a more widespread political control than previously. Yet the extension of Portuguese authority encountered a barrier. This was described by the Governor of Timor Affonso Castro in 1882 in the following terms:

> Marital exchange is our government's major enemy because it produces...an infinity of kin relations which comprise leagues of reaction against the orders of the governors and the dominion of our laws. There has not yet been a single rebellion against the Portuguese flag which is not based in the alliances which result from marital exchange.[16]

Exchange and the kinship system, which had been maintained throughout the years of Portuguese control, were now seen clearly by the Portuguese as the most important barriers to the extension of its administrative framework. Portuguese policies at the end of the century thus had two objectives: to undermine the indigenous kinship system, and to create a basis for the systematic exploitation of its colony.

Thus, between 1884 and 1890, a programme of road construction was organized with the use of forced labour (corvée). In 1897 a trading company (Sociedade Agrícola Pátria e Trabalho [SAPT]) was set up by the governor, José Celestino da Silva (in office, 1894–1908), which introduced coffee plantations into Ermera, in the north-west. From 1906, a head-tax was levied on all Timorese males between eighteen and sixty. The only way in which this could be paid, of course, was by peasant families cultivating and selling goods over and above their subsistence needs.

The introduction of these measures, and particularly the use of forced labour, produced widespread resentment amongst the Timorese. Kingdoms united under the leadership of a *liurai* from the southern district of Manufuhi (Same), named Dom Boaventura. The rebellion simmered for sixteen years (1894–1910), culminating in a major uprising which lasted throughout the colony for two years (1910–12), until Boaventura's forces were defeated in August 1912, an estimated 3,000 Timorese dying at the hands of the victorious Portuguese troops.[17] With resistance quelled, the Portuguese introduced their policies to undermine the system of political alliances produced by kinship exchanges. The position of the *liurais* was undercut by the abolition of their kingdoms. The colony was redivided into administrative units, based generally on *suco* boundaries. A measure of administrative power was thus given to the unit below the kingdom level in the indigenous hierarchy. This enhanced the position of the leaders of the *sucos*, although their election as administrators was now subject to Portuguese approval. The Portuguese created two new, additional administrative levels: the *posto*, comprising groups of *sucos*, and the *concelho*, which controlled *postos* via a Portuguese administrator. By these means, the Portuguese tried to replace the Timorese political system with one whose structure and hierarchy could be independent of kinship alliances. Thus, the essence of Portuguese 'pacification' was its attempted destruction of a crucial feature of Timor's social system, whose existence limited the influence of Portuguese control.

With pacification under way, the Portuguese turned to their Dutch colonial neighbours, and completed border discussions with them in 1913. This resulted in the 'Sentença Arbitral', a decision of the ICJ in The Hague 25 June 1914 which was signed in 1915. This divided the island equally, with the Dutch in the west and the Portuguese in the east. The Portuguese retained the enclave of Oecussi Ambeno on the north-west coast (the site of the former, pre-1769, Portuguese capital of Lifau), and the islands of Atauro and Jaco.

By these measures, the Portuguese hoped that, finally, they would be able to exercise a more effective control over their colony. In the coming years, however, it soon became apparent that the impact on the subsistence sector of the economic policies required for cash-crop cultivation was relatively minor, as were the social effects of these policies, with the sole exception being the regular demands for forced labour.

Furthermore, although the kingdoms had been formally abolished, the ideologies legitimizing the traditional political hierarchy and the rituals of exchange were perpetuated; *suco* heads, for example, had to ensure that they were supported by the *liurai* and his retinue. Consequently, two political systems, the colonial and indigenous, co-existed in a rather uneasy truce. Whilst the former was sanctioned through coercion and the use of force, the latter was underpinned by a powerful set of cultural traditions. Whereas in Portuguese East Timor, by such means, most of the population in the Dutch-controlled western part of island (present-day West Timor) were resettled by the end of the 1920s.

Invasion

The political changes accompanying the emergence of Dr Salazar's *Estado Novo* in 1926 had only a marginal effect on the co-existence of the two political systems. A handful of Timorese, a mere 0.25 per cent of the population, were brought into the Portuguese administrative system through their gaining *assimilado* status during the period leading up to the Second World War.

The Japanese invasion of East Timor in December 1941 encountered widespread resistance, organized within the framework of the indigenous political system. Whilst history has recorded the gallant campaign of 400 Dutch and Australian commandos in resisting 20,000 Japanese troops, little has been written about the participation of the Timorese.[18] As several of the commandos have subsequently stated,[19] their operations would have been impossible without the support of the Timorese, who suffered severely from harsh Japanese reprisals when the last group of commando units withdrew in February 1943. By the time the Japanese surrendered in August 1945, 60,000 Timorese, or nearly 14 per cent of the pre-war population had died, and many of the towns and villages had been destroyed.

Whilst West Timor became part of the Indonesian Republic when control was transferred from the Dutch in December 1949, East Timor remained under Portuguese rule. The rebuilding of East Timorese society was undertaken mostly within the indigenous system during the 1950s. The Portuguese recruited compulsory labour from the villages to reconstruct government buildings and port facilities, but their primary concern was to improve the conditions for the cultivation of export crops.

During the 1960s, Portuguese policies aimed to promote a further, but still very limited, recruitment of East Timorese into the colonial administration. Faced with the successes of independence movements in their African colonies, together with an increasingly heavy burden of military expenditure, the Portuguese attempted to create a political elite which could rule East Timor as an 'overseas territory' within a federal framework under Lisbon's benevolent tutelage, as an alternative to independence. Consequently, there occurred a limited extension of education at the secondary and tertiary level,[20] together with an increased recruitment of Timorese into the army, the health service and the lower echelons of government administration. Although the objective of socializing Timorese into the values of Portuguese culture as a precursor to federal rule was modified after the Armed Forces Movement (*Movimento das Forças Armadas*) coup of April 1974,[21] the overall aim of decolonization remained to ensure progress through the inculcation of Portuguese values.[22]

Party Formation

Consequently, several of the early political initiatives undertaken in East Timor after April 1974, most notably the creation of the first political party, the Timorese Democratic Union (*União Democrática Timorense, UDT*) on 11 May 1974, exhibited the Portuguese perspective of progress toward independence through the gradual acquisition of metropolitan culture by elites whose members would be recruited from the indigenous system. The co-existence of the colonial and indigenous systems would thus be superseded by the gradual assimilation of the latter into the former, principally through the recruitment of leading *liurai* and *suco* leaders.

It was in this context that, on 12 May 1974, the Association of Timorese Social Democrats (*Associação Social Democrata Timorense, ASDT*) was formed. This party, which subsequently became the *Frente Revolucionária de Timor-Leste Independente* (Fretilin) on 12 September 1974, differed from the other political groups emerging during this period in its policies, strategy, and attitudes towards East Timorese society.[23] Rather than attempting to incorporate aspects of East Timorese culture, politics and society within the framework of Portuguese metropolitan culture, it directed its policies toward what it regarded as important areas of indigenous society, taking them as the basis for its organization and strategies. In doing this, it began tentatively to create a qualitatively new political culture, by combining elements of the indigenous value system into a nationalist ideology. Furthermore, basing elements of its programme for political and economic development on the institutions of indigenous society, Fretilin attempted to build upon what its leaders saw as the strengths of this society in resisting colonial control, most notably its system of kinship alliances. This attempt to take traditional East Timorese culture and social organization as the basis for the development of a nationalist movement, seems to have formed the central part of Fretilin's project. In pursuing this, its support amongst the population increased steadily, particularly during 1975, the year leading up to the Indonesian invasion. Initially, Fretilin drew most of its support in the countryside from the central mountain peoples, in particular the Mambai and Makassae, the northern upland Ema, and the Tetum-speaking peoples of the south and west. The members of the majorities of East Timor's remaining twelve ethnolinguistic groups tended either to be aligned with none of the new political parties, to favour the UDT, or, in the case of some of the northern Tetum in the border villages, to support the minuscule integrationist Apodeti (*Associação Popular Democrática Timorense*) party. By the end of 1975, however, and particularly during the period August–December 1975, when Fretilin administered East Timor following the departure of the Portuguese, support for the movement increased dramatically, extending to all ethnic groups, even the Fatuluku people at the eastern extremity (*Ponta Leste*) of the island. This growing support, together with the organization it created, enabled Fretilin to sustain a campaign of resistance in the years following the massive Indonesian invasion in December 1975.

Fretilin's Programme

The nature of this support can best be illustrated by referring briefly to aspects of the development of Fretilin's programmes during the period from September 1974 to the Indonesian invasion in December 1975.

One of the most important areas of Fretilin's work was its programme to tackle widespread illiteracy which affected 93 per cent of the pre-1974 population. From October 1974, Fretilin members travelled widely, collecting material for a literacy handbook in Tetum, the most widely used of East Timor's many languages. Focusing on words in common use, the handbook, entitled *Tai Timor Rai Ita Niang* ('Timor Is Our Country'), broke these words into syllables, and then placed them in different contexts of village life, together with associated words. The essence of the handbook was its description of aspects of everyday life in the villages, as provided by the Timorese themselves.

The way in which this literacy campaign was undertaken illustrated the approach taken by Fretilin: ideas and notions in common use in East Timorese society were adopted as a means of improving the preconditions for development. A similar case was the health programme in which treatments to deal with East Timor's most common diseases, tuberculosis, malaria, elephantiasis, were introduced in a framework which combined modern treatments with the use of traditional cures.[24]

In the early stages of Fretilin's development, the idea was mooted of introducing rural cooperatives as a basis for economic development. As a result, several experimental cooperatives were set up, notably in Basartete, Aileu, and Bucoli. In these villages, Fretilin members, several of whom had given up their jobs in Dili and Baucau to work in their home areas, after consultation with *suco* leaders and villagers, selected areas to be worked collectively. Half the crop was delivered to the cooperative and half to the families involved in cultivation. The cooperative then marketed the crop, and, after distributing the income to the families, spent the remainder on expanding output. In Bucoli, cooperation was developed initially at the distributive level. A journalist visiting the cooperative in October 1974, reported that,

> Bucoli people were planning a cooperative for next year's harvest. Villagers will pool their surplus crops [after deducting family needs] for sale in Dili for higher prices than they would get through Chinese middlemen. The receipts will be used as the villagers decide, to buy a truck perhaps, or build a cooperative store to buy wholesale basic necessities, or to buy a small tractor.[25]

In developing this cooperative movement, Fretilin adopted methods similar to those in its other campaigns: beginning with rather vague, general notions, ideas for future development were concretized through the accumulated experiences of their members in working with villagers in areas where they had local links.

This stress on developing ideas for programmes through work in the villages was accompanied by the creation of an administrative system which emphasized political decentralization. As opposed to the UDT, in which power was held by Dili-based elites, Fretilin devolved a considerable degree of power over decision-making to regional committees, particularly in the areas of education and health. This decentralization enabled the regions of East Timor to be involved in the direction of the nationalist movement's development, yet to retain a considerable degree of autonomy in both organization and implementation of policies.

Fretilin's Popularity

During the initial phase of party formation and development, from April to June 1974, the ASDT remained much less popular than the UDT, although both attracted far greater support than the Indonesian sponsored party, Apodeti. This remained the case until the period from October to November, when the ASDT (now renamed Fretilin) began to be viewed by both East Timorese and foreign commentators as the party with the greater support, although it was not until the elections for village heads, held in July 1975, that this support was confirmed in a 55 per cent vote for Fretilin candidates. Throughout 1975, during the coalition with UDT from January to May, and after the coup attempt by the UDT in August followed by the departure of the Portuguese administration to Atauro island, Fretilin enjoyed a high degree of popularity within the population, as attested by a variety of visiting commentators, journalists and politicians.[26]

The reasons for this popularity owed much to the movement's attitude to indigenous society. As distinct from the UDT, whose leadership base was to be found in the lower echelons of the colonial administration, and amongst coffee plantation owners and *liurai* in the agriculturally richer areas of Ermera, Maliana and Maubara, Fretilin moved increasingly into the regions. Building up regional power by working with existing political alliances based on kinship, and taking concepts and ideas prevalent in traditional society as the bases for the development of its programmes, Fretilin emerged as a nationalist movement with extensive popular support and an effective decentralized political structure. Despite some support for more centralist notions of power put forward within Fretilin during the early months of 1975, when it was involved in its coalition with UDT, especially by a group of East Timorese sergeants from the former Portuguese army, Fretilin maintained this decentralized approach. Indeed, in recent years, it has been reemphasized by the movement's present leadership, stressing the importance of ethnic group identities and culture, despite the ethnic intermixing enforced by the Indonesian military through its resettlement programmes.

The Indonesian Invasion and Its Aftermath

In a series of campaigns carried out between 1975 and 1981 to 'pacify' the territory (1975–7), to 'encircle and annihilate' the population outside Indonesian-held areas (1977–8), and to hunt down Fretilin groups through 'fence of legs' (*pagar betis*) operations (1981 to present), the Indonesian government maintained a heavy military presence in East Timor.[27] In actions which have been thoroughly documented by refugees and visitors to the territory, the Indonesian army has exercised a brutal rule, trying to coerce the population through massacres of villages, saturation bombing, and widespread human rights abuses.[28] The administration set up by the military has attempted a 'resocialization' of East Timor through the enforced movement of the population into strategic hamlets, the reorganization of the economy, and a systematic outlawing or undermining of East Timorese culture and society.[29]

Throughout all this, opposition has been widespread, with a progressive alienation of almost all social groups from the Indonesian occupiers. The nationalist movement resisted the invasion, maintained substantial areas of the territory under its control until the end of 1978, and after devastating serial and ground attacks against it, managed to rebuild a framework for the organization of resistance in the early 1980s, which exists to this day.[30] Here, the support of the broad mass of East Timorese society has been crucial. There are many examples of this.

During late 1976 and the early months of 1977, the resistance movement's national framework began to be weakened as Indonesian forces maintained troop concentrations in strategically located villages. In this situation, as many refugee accounts have noted, the movement's successes in creating strong regional power centres, based on pre-existing political alliances, enabled it to maintain its areas despite the weakening of links between them.

Similarly, during the 'encirclement and annihilation' campaigns of 1977–8, the maintenance of Fretilin and its rebuilding in the eastern part of the territory were only possible because Fretilin members were protected and shielded by villagers.[31] Again, one of the most successful areas of the nationalist movement's strategy has been its development of systematic links with support groups, known as *núrep* (*núcleos de resistência popular*), inside the resettlement villages established by the Indonesian military. The groups have organized opposition and supplied the movement with information on Indonesian military intentions. In most cases, the cohesion and organization of these groups has depended to a considerable extent upon kinship ties which have been maintained despite attempts by the military to undermine them (principally through splitting up population from the same village, and settling groups on areas distant from their original villages).

Perhaps some of the most supportive actions, however, came during the 'fence of legs' (*pagar betis*) operations in 1981. In these, according to many refugee accounts, almost the entire male population between the ages of 16 and 60 was recruited to march across the territory in lines, with groups 500 metres apart, in front of Indonesian troops, in an attempt to round up Fretilin members. Despite the extent and duration of these campaigns, few Fretilin troops were captured. Refugees have documented a remarkable process in which Fretilin groups passed through the 'fence' unnoticed by the military, assisted by East Timorese 'human chain' conscripts, who either hid them or led the military away from their encampments. By such means, many Fretilin groups avoided capture.[32]

Such actions typify both the strength of support for the nationalist movement within the population, and the ability of the East Timorese to frustrate Indonesian objectives through a systematic social organization.

Conclusion

The pattern outlined above seems likely to continue and there seems to be little doubt that East Timor will continue to resist Indonesian incorporation for many years to come. Its capacity to resist owes much to the way in which its social structure developed during Portuguese colonialism.

This, in turn, resulted from the nature of the trading contacts with Portugal and from the Timorese ability to 'play off' one colonial faction against another, as well as their capacity to organize resistance through political alliances based upon kinship ties.

In the twentieth century, Portuguese attempts to undermine the reproduction of indigenous societal structures were unsuccessful, whilst the strength of East Timorese resistance to the Japanese invasion and occupation revealed again the ability of indigenous societal structures to contain attempts at incorporation.

With the demise of Portuguese colonialism, a nationalist movement emerged, drawing increasingly widespread support through policies aimed at developing aspects of the indigenous social structure and value systems in a largely successful attempt to create a national economy and community. The movement was able to mount its campaigns of resistance to the Indonesian occupation and reorganize itself under the most unfavourable conditions in the early 1980s, both because of the popularity of its policies and because of the strength of its organization within indigenous society.

The Indonesian military seems to have had only a very limited understanding of the nature of East Timorese society when its troops invaded, and was clearly taken aback by the strength of popular opposition to its annexation. Faced with such strong resistance, the military gradually realized that its main hope of success lay in the destruction of existing social structures and their replacement by ones more amenable to Indonesian control. Consequently, from the end of the 1970s, the military began its intensive resocialization and restructuring campaigns of economic reorganization, control of family life, resettlement, the undermining of East Timorese culture and a systematic inculcation of 'Indonesian' (i.e. 'Javanese') values. These campaigns were carried out brutally, and were accompanied by widespread military intimidation. They have been disastrous for the East Timorese, as many well-documented accounts of the results of the invasion and occupation have shown.[33]

Despite their determination, the Indonesian military have neither succeeded in fully controlling the territory, nor in establishing any meaningful support for its annexation amongst the wider East Timorese population. In spite of its policies, the social relations and values of the pre-invasion period persist, providing a framework for continuing opposition. Indeed, recently, opposition to the occupation has been led by a younger generation raised during Indonesian rule and largely Indonesian educated.[34] This has particularly angered military leaders, many of whom had pinned their hopes on a successful socialization of the second generation.

The success of the nationalist movement in maintaining opposition to the occupation under extremely adverse conditions and despite overwhelming Indonesian military superiority, is a truly remarkable achievement. The preceding analysis has indicated ways in which the strength and depth of opposition to Indonesian rule can be understood.

Notes

1 See, for example, J. S. Dunn, *Timor: A People Betrayed*, Milton (Queensland): Jacaranda Press, 1983. *See also* C. Budiardjo and Liem Soei Liong, *The War Against East Timor*. London: Zed Books, 1984; J. Jolliffe, *East Timor: Nationalism and Colonialism*. St Lucia: University of Queensland Press, 1978, and *Timor, Terra Sangrenta*. Lisbon: Editora O Jornal, 1989; J. Ramos-Horta, *Funu: The Unfinished Saga of East Timor*. Trenton (New Jersey): Red Sea Press, 1987.

2 See, for example, Budiardjo and Liem Soei Liong, *War Against East Timor*, Ch. 3.

3 See Dunn, *Timor: A People Betrayed*, Ch. 10. Also J. G. Taylor, *Indonesia's Forgotten War: The Hidden History of East Timor*. London: Zed Books, 1991.

4 Groeneveldt, W. P., *Historical Notes on Indonesia and Malaya, compiled from Chinese Sources*. Jakarta: Bhatara, 1960, p. 116.

5 Groeneveldt, *Historical Notes*, p. 117.

6 In similar vein, Groeneveldt (*op. cit.*, note 4) cites a Chinese report of 1618, which claims that trading could not begin until a figure he calls 'the king' appeared: 'When they see their king, they [the Timorese] sit down on the ground with folded hands,' and only then could negotiations over trading transactions commence.

7 Middelkoop P., 'Trektochten van Timorese Groepen', *Tijdschrift voor Indische Taal, Land en Volkenkunde* (Batavia/ Jakarta), **85**(2) (1952), p.52.

8 The term 'Topasse' originates either from the group's role as interpreters (from the Dravidian word *Tupasse*, 'interpreter'), or from their mode of dress (from the Indian *Topee Walas*, 'hat-men'). *See* C.R. Boxer, 'The Topasses of Timor', *Koninklijke Vereeniging Indisch Instituut (Medeling)*, **73**(24) (1947).

9 Boxer, C. R., 'Portuguese Timor: A Rough Island Story, 1515-1960', *History Today*, **10**(5) (May 1960), p. 351.

10 Cited in H. G. Schulte Nordholt, *The Political System of the Atoni of Timor*. (The Hague: Martinus Nijhoff, 1971), p.166.

11 See G. Francillon, 'Some Matrilineal Aspects of the Social System of the Southern Tetum', PhD thesis, Australian National University, 1967.

12 See M.A.R. Rodrigues, 'Da Campanha de 1726 às Pedras de Cailaco' [From the 1726 Campaign to the Stones of Cailaco], *Independência*, **5** (1987).

13 Kolff, D. H., *Voyages through the Southern and Little Known Parts of the Moluccan Archipelago, and along the previously unknown Southern Coast of New Guinea, 1825–26*, ed. G. W. Earl. London: Madden, 1840, p. 35.

14 Wallace, A. R., *The Malay Archipelago: The Land of the Orang-Utan and the Bird of Paradise, a Narrative of Travel, with Studies of Man and Nature*. New York: Dover, 1962 [originally published by Macmillan (London), 1869], p.153.

15 Forbes, H. O., 'On Some Tribes of the Island of Timor', *Journal of the Royal Anthropological Institute*, No. 13 (1883), p. 404.

16 Cited in S. Forman, 'East Timor: Exchange and Political Hierarchy at the Time of the European Discoveries', paper presented at a conference on 'Trade in Ancient Southeast Asia' (University of Michigan, 1976). Later published in K. Hutterer (ed.), *Economic Exchange and Social Interaction in Southeast Asia*, Ann Arbor (Michigan): Center for South and Southeast Asian Studies, 1978.

17 This figure is taken from a report published in the *Melbourne Argus,* August 1912.

18 Notable exceptions are Dunn, *Timor: A People Betrayed*, pp. 22–7, and Michele Turner, *Telling. East Timor: Personal Testimonies, 1942-1992.* Kensington: New South Wales Press, 1992, pp.1-30.

19 See, for example, B. J. Callinan, *Independent Company: The 2/2 and 2/4 Australian Independent Companies in Portuguese Timor.* Melbourne: Heinemann, 1953, and Turner, *op. cit.*, note 18, pp. 1–50. Also, Interview with C. Morris, former commando, on Australian Broadcasting Corporation (ABC) Radio, Melbourne, 6 April 1977, reprinted in *Retrieval*, No.36 (April–May 1977), p.14.

20 For analyses and data on this process, see Helen Hill, 'Fretilin: The Origins, Ideologies and Strategies of a Nationalist Movement in East Timor', MA thesis, Monash University, 1978, pp. 43–51.

21 Although, of course, this 'socialization' remained as a general aim for some months after the coup. Furthermore, elements of it were retained in General António de Spinola's notion of a 'Lusitanian Federation', to which the governor of East Timor, Colonel Mário Lemos Pires (in office, Nov. 1974 – Dec. 1975), subscribed.

22 Colonel Lemos Pires, on his appointment as governor of East Timor in November 1974, was given instructions that, no matter what the political outcome, he should try to preserve the legacy of Portuguese culture and traditions in East Timor.

23 In addition to the ASDT and the UDT, there were four other parties: the Indonesian-sponsored *Associação Popular Democrática Timorense (APODETI)*, the *Klibur Oan Timor Aswain (KOTA)* (literally, 'The Sons of the Mountain Warrior Dogs'), the *Partido Trabalhista* (Labour Party), and the *Associação Democrática Integração Timor-Leste Austrália (ADITLA)*. Apart from APODETI, whose support came from the border district (*suco*) of the pro-integrationist *liurai* of Atsabe, Guilherme Gonçalves, and from a small number of Dili-based administrators and members of the capital's tiny Moslem community, the other parties could never boast more than the most minuscule following.

24 Knowledge obtained in developing these cures was later used widely in Fretilin-held areas after the invasion, particularly from 1975–8, as refugees subsequently testified, see Taylor, *Indonesia's Forgotten War*, pp. 81–2.

25 Evans, Grant, 'Portuguese Timor', *New Left Review*, (London), No. 91 (May–June 1975), pp. 67–75.

26 Apart from visiting journalists, detailed reports were published after visits by delegations from the Australian Trades Union Movement and the Australian Parliament, in May and September 1975, respectively. The International Committee of the Red Cross (ICRC) also visited before and after the UDT coup attempt in August 1975, and produced a report.

27 Indonesian troop numbers during this period varied from 30,000 to 40,000.

28 See, for example, Amnesty International, *East Timor: Violations of Human Rights.* London, 1985.

29 For detailed discussions and refugee testimonies on this issue, see Taylor, *Indonesia's Forgotten War*, pp. 80–92.

30 For the most insightful reports on the condition of Fretilin, see the articles written by the Australian Trades Union lawyer, Robert Domm, following his meeting with Fretilin leader Kay Rala Xanana Gusmão, in September 1990. In particular see the *Sydney Morning Herald*, 25 October 1990, and *Indonesian News Service*, No. 267, Maryland (USA), 1 November 1990.

31 See Amnesty International, *East Timor: Violations of Human Rights*, London, 1985, pp. 29-34.

32 This, of course, did not prevent these *pagar betis* campaigns from being accompanied by the most brutal actions committed by Indonesian troops. See, for example, Cristiano Costa, 'Timorese Refugee on Indonesian Operations since 1975: The Aitana Massacre', *Tapol Bulletin*, (London), No. 87, June 1988.

33 See, in particular, Budiardjo and Liem Soei Liong, *War Against East Timor*, Ch. 5; and Taylor, *Indonesia's Forgotten War*, Ch. 9.

34 During the visits of the Pope, in October 1989, and the United States Ambassador to Indonesia, Mr. John Monjo, in January 1990, demonstrations against integration were led by young people in Dili (see below Donaciano Gomes' account). A similar pattern also occurred during a demonstration held at the end of a Mass to commemorate the fiftieth anniversary of the Dili diocese. The Mass, attended by Mgr Canalini, the Apostolic Nuncio in Jakarta, and the Governor of East Timor, Mário Carrascalão (in office, 1982-92), took place on 4 September 1990.

CHAPTER 2

Mambai Perspectives on Colonialism and Decolonization

Elizabeth G. Traube

Contemporary anthropologists who attribute an active role in history to culture also reject the view of cultural influence as inherently conservative in its effects. Culture, it is argued, is involved in the transformation as well as the reproduction of social systems over time. Recent historical studies by anthropologists have investigated specific cultural forms – categories, symbols, narrative patterns, and so on – that mediate local interpretations of new circumstances in complex ways, shaping a variety of possible responses. Both internal features of cultural forms themselves and the dynamics of their social use contribute to the openness and indeterminacy of culturally mediated historical processes.

Thus, the content of cultural forms may justify critiques of or departures from established practices. For example, Valerio Valeri argues, many societies represent their past as a complex process that provides arguments for change as well as for changelessness.[1] And from a somewhat different perspective, James Scott[2] points out that inasmuch as any legitimizing ideology idealizes the dominant order, it inevitably provides its members with the symbolic means for an internal critique.

If a cultural repertoire has a certain inbuilt dynamism, the possibilities for meaningful social action multiply from a sociological perspective. Within a society, actors' interpretations of shared cultural forms may vary according to social position, producing divergent but mutually intelligible versions of reality. Sherry Ortner[3] suggests that the very distance between actors' selves and particular cultural forms is shifting and variable. Certain people, at certain times, may internalize a given cultural 'schema' (Ortner's term for relatively generalized and transferable symbolic patterns) and use it in constructing their current situations, whereas for others, or at other times, that schema remains external to the self, perhaps apprehended as an abstract model of ancestral deeds but not as a structural dimension of ongoing, lived reality. With these ideas as a background, I will explore the responses of one East Timorese people to the prospects for their political future as these appeared to them in 1974, one and a half years before the Indonesian invasion of their island (7 December 1975).

At that time I was in the second year of ethnographic research among a group known as the Mambai. They are Austronesian-speakers who then numbered over 80,000 and inhabited the mountainous interior of central Timor.[4] One of approximately twelve distinct ethnolinguistic groups on the eastern half of the island, the Mambai are no more representative than any of their neighbours of what various parties in the contemporary controversy described as 'the East Timorese' or 'the people of East Timor'. Although there was a certain sense of unity among East Timorese peoples, it needs emphasis that diversity was a characteristic feature of social life on the island.[5] Before I turn to Mambai constructions of colonial domination, I want to give some idea of the wider socio-cultural matrix of which they are part.

The Peoples of East Timor: An Ethnographic Sketch

Despite its small size, Timor displays a number of striking ecological contrasts. The rugged central mountains divide the island into three major zones, a central upland flanked by two contrastive coastal plains. With its low rainfall and semi-arid conditions, the northern coast is the driest part of the island, while the southern coast is an area of relatively high rainfall and presents a more lush, tropical appearance.

East Timorese economies were based on subsistence agriculture and animal husbandry, supplemented with petty commodity production during the later colonial period. Both the forms of cultivation and the types of crops varied. Although wet-rice agriculture was practised in some areas in the east and along the northern coast, the predominant form of agricultural activity was shifting or swidden cultivation, with either maize or dry rice as a staple. Introduced by the Portuguese in the seventeenth century, maize displaced many precolonial food crops and transformed the indigenous agricultural systems.[6] Certain areas ecologically unsuited for maize cultivation retain evidence of the precolonial agricultural situation which appears to have included systems based on cereal agriculture similar to Indonesian economies as well as others dependent on taro and yams, reminiscent of Melanesian root crop economies.

The linguistic situation reflects a similar division. The island is occupied by two different language families, Austronesian and non-Austronesian or 'Papuan'. The Austronesian languages are related in complex ways to languages spoken within the Republic of Indonesia, whereas the non-Austronesian languages have affinities with the languages of New Guinea. In West Timor the great majority of the population speak one of two Austronesian languages, Tetum or Atoni (the latter also known as Timorese), but the situation is more complicated in the east where somewhere between eleven and fourteen distinct languages were spoken by ethnic groups which range in size from a few thousand to 100,000 members.

Ethnolinguistic diversity was recognized in oral traditions. Most Timorese peoples did not attribute a single origin place to the island's peoples in their myths and legends. Instead, each ethnic group distinguished between original, autochthonous inhabitants and ancestral invaders from overseas and represented itself as descended from one or the other, insiders or outsiders, the people of the land (mountains) or the people of the sea (coast). This distinction operated at multiple social levels. Within a social system, it structured dualistic or diarchic political ideologies in which ritual authority and jural power were distributed between two complementary functions. At another level, the distinction was of considerable importance in the classification of neighbouring groups and the delineation of ethnic boundaries. In any given inter-ethnic relationship, the group associated with origins and with the inside was also attributed special ritual powers, while the group identified as newcomers from the outside was said to be oriented toward worldly affairs. But with whichever plane they identified themselves, the peoples of East Timor took pride in their differences from one another, evoking language, myth, and custom as badges of their distinctive cultural identities.

Social and political existence on East Timor was shaped by kinship and locality. Individuals were affiliated at birth to descent groups of varying segmentary order that were incorporated into higher level political units, and such affiliations largely determined an individual's social universe. For an East Timorese, daily life unfolded within the confines of the household and the hamlet, among close kin and affines, while ritual occasions periodically mobilized wider networks, bringing together scattered clan members or uniting all those who recognized a common chief.

But neither the relative autonomy and inwardness of local communities nor the ideological stress on cultural differences precluded inter-ethnic contacts. Most East Timorese spoke Tetum, one of the local languages which had become a *lingua franca* during the colonial period, and many were fluent in the languages spoken by neighbouring groups. Excursions outside one's own territory for purposes of trade or social intercourse were common. Prior to colonial intervention, formal exchange obligations linked the small indigenous domains of eastern Timor into complex political alliances, many of them across ethnic lines. Coastal rulers associated with the outside received harvest gifts from chiefs in the interior who were attributed special powers over nature.

The interior chiefs received counter-prestations from the coast in return for their ritual services. It was Portuguese colonialism, however, that engendered a wider sense of unity. Out of the common experience of subordination to a particular European power there arose among the subjugated peoples a heightened awareness of their mutual ties to one another, an awareness that was eventually to provide an enabling condition for East Timorese nationalism.

Portuguese contact with Timor began in the early sixteenth century. At the time the island was already renowned for its abundant sandalwood. Since the seventh century, Javanese and Chinese merchants had maintained trade relations with the coastal rulers of Timor who controlled the sandalwood felling in the interior. It was sandalwood that initially drew the Portuguese to Timor, and the island soon became the centre of Portuguese commercial and missionary interests in the outer arc of the Lesser Sundas. In the seventeenth century, however, the situation was complicated by the arrival of the Dutch who established a foothold in western Timor and successfully challenged Portuguese political hegemony. The next two centuries saw a protracted struggle in which the European powers vied for control over Timor. In 1850 a diplomatic accord was reached. The western half of the island was formally incorporated into the Dutch East Indies, eventually to become part of the Republic of Indonesia. The eastern half, together with the enclave of Oi Kussi (Oecusse), where the Portuguese had established their original base on the island, was recognized as an overseas province of Portugal.

But despite the diplomatic solution, Portuguese rule remained precarious. It was based on shifting alliances with native rulers, who received Portuguese military patents and insignia of office in return for military assistance during the chronic rebellions. The Portuguese pursued their political and economic interests by inserting themselves into the indigenous systems of exchange between the coast and the interior, effectively taking over the position of the coastal chiefs. Only after the pacification campaigns carried out between 1894 and 1900 was colonial rule extended, consolidated, and rationalized. Coffee was introduced and grown for export, while the traditional systems of tribute paid in agricultural produce were replaced by a cash head-tax, policies that worked together to draw the subsistence farmers of Timor into petty commodity production. Collection of the head-tax and daily control of the province was effected through a new system of administration, uniformly imposed across the province. In this system the province was divided into colonially created administrative districts or *concelhos,* each under a colonially appointed (almost invariably European or mestizo) administrator. These units were subdivided into *postos* headed by *chefes.* Beneath these administrative groupings were the *reino* or 'kingdom', the *suku* (a Tetum term which designated a traditional political unit in some Tetum systems), and the *povoação* or village, all headed by Timorese who in many cases were appointed by the colonial administration and who reported to the *chefe de posto*. As we shall see, the colonial administrative hierarchy was not always coincident with indigenous political systems based on diarchic rule.

Nevertheless, even over the twentieth century, Portuguese intervention in Timorese life was not extensive. Apart from the short-lived Portuguese involvement in the sandalwood trade, the province was run at an economic loss. Peripheral to a colonial empire centred in Africa, Timor was spared the massive intervention characteristic of colonial involvement in areas more central to European economic interests. Ideological responses to Portuguese colonial intervention reflect its *relatively* benign character. It was my impression that among most East Timorese peoples the Portuguese were at least officially represented as legitimate rulers, while I myself became personally entangled in Mambai constructions of the Portuguese as their younger kin.

Mambai Responses to Colonial Domination and Decolonization

On Timor the Mambai were regarded by other groups as one of the poorest, oldest, and most 'backward' (*atrasado*) peoples of the land. Their economy was based on shifting cultivation and animal husbandry. Maize was the staple crop, and Mambai also cultivated dry rice (an important ceremonial food), as well as taro, yams, sweet potatoes, cassava, millet, pigeon peas, and beans. Coffee, introduced by the Portuguese and raised by individual families, was the most important cash crop, sold in order to purchase such commodities as clothing, school supplies, kerosene, and to pay the annual colonial head-tax.

Mambai social life was shaped at multiple levels by ideas of unity and division.[7] Individuals belonged to male-ordered units known as 'houses', *fada,* a term that designated both a group and its dwelling. The socially significant dwelling was not an everyday residence but a named ancestral origin house where the group's sacred heirlooms were stored. House members or 'people of one house' were scattered for most of the year, living in what Mambai represented as the 'outer' realm of space, but they reconvened at their origin houses on ritual occasions to reenact their mythical unity.

A conceptual premise of the house system is that all houses are ultimately derived from a single primordial origin house on the top of the sacred mountain, at the centre of the cosmos, where Mother Earth and Father Heaven are said to have brought forth the first ancestors of humankind. In this mythology of common origins, human history entails a process of separation and division that begins with the dispersal of the ancestors from the cosmic mountain and continues down to the present. Narratives of house formation describe how houses are divided and sub-divided by restless, mobile men. In these narratives elder brothers invariably remain behind at the paternal origin house, while their younger brothers 'go off to the outside', after having 'cut a slip' from the paternal house pillar to 'plant' as the foundation for new houses of their own. Repeated over generations, the centrifugal movements of younger brothers create what Mambai represented as an ever ramifying array of junior 'tip houses', centred by the senior 'trunk houses' of common ancestors. In the ideology of the house system, 'tip houses' are ritually dependent on their acknowledged 'trunk' and are expected to participate in its rituals.

Mambai houses were also ranked and organized at a higher level into hierarchically structured communities. Leadership in these communities was diarchic, divided between active political executives, the actual holders of power, and passive ritual authorities, who legitimize the power held by others. Narratives that were preserved by ritual authorities but were widely acknowledged in broad outline recount the origins of the diarchic division. In these narratives, mythical ancestors of the ritual figures are the original founders of order. Once they have established their dominion over outlying house groups, they renounce the power of rule, which is embodied in the regalia of office, swords, spears, and Portuguese flags and military drums. Newcomers from outside the realm receive these tokens and are henceforth empowered to regulate human affairs, while the old lords retain ritual authority over the cosmos and sta-bilize the community from its symbolic centre. As Mambai say, 'they sit down to look after the rock and to watch over the tree', the ubiquitous icons of cult life on Timor.

Mambai referred to these house-based political communities by the Portuguese term *reino*, 'kingdom', which also designated a unit in the colonially created administrative hierarchy. To distinguish their ritually organized communities from the administrative units, Mambai described the former as the 'ancient kingdoms' (*reinu antiku*) or 'kingdoms of long ago' (*reinu akin*), and the emphasis on antiquarianism was well-placed. Under Portuguese rule, annual and periodic ceremonies staged in the rit-ual centers still mobilized the communities in their ideal, hierarchical form, but to the Portuguese colonial authorities, these were purely 'reli-gious' as opposed to 'political' activities, and the house organization on which they rested went largely unrecognized by the colonial administra-tion. Mambai preserved their system of hierarchically ranked, decentral-ized house groups for ritual purposes, but the colonially imposed admin-istrative hierarchy regulated secular political affairs.

What Mambai came to regard as their traditional political units were not primordial residues of precolonial political life but products of an earlier stage in colonial intervention. After moving their capital to Dili in 1769, the hard-pressed Portuguese colonizers contracted alliances with local chiefs by distributing military patents. In return for the patents, recipients pledged their loyalty and military support to the Portuguese Crown, and they agreed to deliver tribute in agricultural produce to the Portuguese in Dili, who had usurped the position of the coastal rulers in the precolonial system of exchange relations.

According to traditions preserved by Mambai ritual leaders, the 'ancient kingdoms' originally united for the accumulation and distribution of harvest gifts. In this version of the past, ritual leaders used to receive harvest tribute from their people and display it in their villages. It was then the task of the local executives to convey the tribute to the Portuguese in Dili and return with counter-prestations of salt, lime, rice and livestock from indigenous chiefs on the coast. These gifts were formally presented to the old lords of rock and tree, those whose ritual influence over agricultural growth had made the entire cycle of transactions possible. As recalled by Mambai members of ritual centres, these exchanges had enacted and confirmed the hierarchical status of their houses, and at the time of my research, members of local executive houses were still required to bring symbolic gifts to the old lords on ritual occasions. But the system as a whole no longer operated. In 1903, when the Portuguese abolished the tributary arrangements of which they had once availed themselves and substituted the cash head-tax, they eliminated what Mambai continued to represent as a legitimate and meaningful exchange system. Indeed, in withdrawing from the older system the Portuguese appeared to many Mambai to have relinquished the role that legitimized their presence on Timor.

No doubt the ideological legitimation of foreign rulers had been facilitated by the limited extent of colonial intervention prior to the twentieth century and by the relatively benign system that was established after pacification. Still, legitimation took a striking cultural form. In the diarchic ideologies characteristic of Timorese political systems, power is assigned to the symbolic outsiders, strangers who come from overseas or from somewhere outside the realm and supplant original autochthonous rulers. What varied from group to group was which of the two categories represented their collective identity, outsider or insider, stranger or autochthon, people of the sea or people of the land, but in either case, it was logically possible and plausible to identify the Portuguese with the figure of the 'stranger king'.[8] Mambai not only made such an identification, but they gave it a distinctive twist.

Their mythology of the origins of colonial rule combines two sets of closely related dual categories, the distinction between elder and younger brothers and the diarchic distinction between insiders and outsiders. In the model that results, those opposed as elder people of the land and younger people of the sea also share a common ancestry. The story, known to Mambai as 'the walk of the flag', begins on the cosmic mountain, at the very start of human history, when the first children of Heaven and Earth still dwelt together in one abode. After washing in white water, their youngest son wandered far away, across the water and sea, taking with him all the regalia of political office, the signs of sovereignty that 'cause women to tremble and lead men to fear'. Left behind on Timor, his black elder brother retained 'only the rock and the tree', and he was unable to elicit respect from his realm. Thus the elder brother set off on an epic journey over the seas to Portugal. There his younger brother restored to him sufficient power tokens to found a realm and promised that his descendants would one day return to their homeland and resume their rightful place as defenders of order. Generations passed, but at last Portuguese ships sailed proudly into the harbour of Dili, where they were welcomed by their older kin and incorporated into the exchanges that linked the coast to the interior. Hence, from the perspective of Mambai ritual leaders, when modern Portuguese rulers abolished the tribute system which revolved around the old lords of rock and tree, they were turning their backs on the very figures whose ancestors had summoned them to Timor.

In the ritual centres the abolition of tribute was remembered with great bitterness, but it was not the Portuguese themselves who were held responsible. I was told repeatedly and with considerable fervour that local Mambai chiefs from the executive plane of the diarchy had somehow tricked the Portuguese into instituting the head-tax. What motivated the chiefs, according to local rumour, was an abiding but unfounded suspicion that the old lords were plotting to 'seize the chieftaincy' and restore the original mythical situation, when power and authority had been concentrated in a single function.

Colonial domination, especially in its modern, rationalized forms, has rarely been congenial to sacral authorities. In case after case, traditional rulers who claimed to have mystical influence over nature either fell back on more mundane military and jural prerogatives, if they possessed them, or else retreated before those who did and who thus conformed more closely to European conceptions of sovereignty. Mambai ritual leaders had been in retreat for much of the twentieth century, as Portuguese colonial policies strengthened the jural plane of the diarchic system. Their pragmatic ability to affect Portuguese colonial policy was nil, and their traditional moral influence over native holders of power was slowly eroding, yet they continued to wage an ideological struggle with the latter over the symbolic definition of political reality. In April of 1974, when the fall of the Caetano regime abruptly altered the possibilities for Timor's political future, this local ideological struggle conditioned divergent responses to the new situation.

Some Mambai executive leaders initially gravitated toward UDT, the political party calling for eventual federation with Portugal. Most, however, were receptive to Fretilin's goal of national independence and many openly declared their support for the party. The Fretilin supporters did not necessarily reject the mythology of common origins with the Portuguese, nor did they deny that ritual authorities were the original holders and ultimate legitimizers of power. Nevertheless, to use Sherry Ortner's formulation,[9] they kept these schemas at a distance, treating them as models of ancient events, with limited bearing on present political realities. Accustomed by their social position to look forward and outward rather than backward and inward, to concern themselves with the changing, worldly 'affairs of women and men' rather than with the timeless concerns 'of rock and tree', they became actively involved in the new nationalist politics that emanated from the coastal capital of Dili.

I witnessed most of this early stage in the debate from the perspective of a ritual centre, where the community had been convoked for a house-building ceremony. Throughout the lengthy ceremonial event, people met to discuss 'this matter', as one old man put it, 'of our younger brothers going away'. Episodes from the mythology of rule were repeatedly incorporated into ritual performances and recited or alluded to in ordinary conversations, which grew increasingly heated as events outside unfolded. In short, the hosts as well as many of their guests had internalized the mythic schema and were using it to interpret their current situation.

The most conservative way of deploying narrative constructions of colonialism was to categorically reject the possibility of independence. In this strategy, Portuguese colonial rule was portrayed as natural and necessary, legitimized by ties of kinship and by the primordial division of diarchic functions. 'They cannot go,' people protested over and over, 'for they are our younger brothers. Our ancestors crossed the water and sea to call them back here to rule over us.' Many speakers used diarchic symbolism to construct a collective Timorese identity that was incompatible with self-governance. 'How can we rule ourselves,' they would exclaim rhetorically, 'when we are old and ignorant (of worldly things) and know only the rock and the tree!'

In the mythic past, however, Mambai could also find arguments for change. Although usurpation is not a legitimating criterion for succession in Mambai political thought, as it was in ancient Hawaii,[10] their narrative representations of succession underscore the transferability of political power. A recurrent pattern in the narratives is for executive rulers to 'grow old and weary', at which point they voluntarily 'surrender the lordship' to younger, more vigorous claimants. After the first outburst of indignation and alarm, people began more calmly to discuss how best to deal with the fatigue which had apparently overtaken their Portuguese kinsmen. The assumption in these discussions was that the Portuguese *would* depart, and attention focused on the process whereby a successor might be selected.

In fact, Mambai contemplated their 'younger brothers going away' with mixed emotions. By means of their ingenious legitimation of colonial rule, not in spite of it, Mambai had also developed a distinctive popular culture of resistance. Open defiance of colonial power was rarely attempted, either individually or collectively, and Portuguese officials often remarked on the extreme deference that Mambai showed in their presence. But colonial stereotypes of native submissiveness ignored what James Scott[11] calls the 'hidden transcript', the 'backstage' situations in which subordinate groups take off their public masks and criticize the powerful. Outside of colonial power situations, Mambai complained bitterly and forcefully about their Portuguese rulers, without, however, denying the legitimacy of the colonial power structure. On the contrary, they formulated their complaints in terms of the ideal model of colonial rule, an ideal which the Portuguese repeatedly violated, both individually and collectively.

Portuguese transgressions ranging from rude, arrogant behaviour to the abolition of the tribute system coalesced to persuade Mambai of one inescapable fact: their younger kin and rightful rulers had forgotten their own origins and no longer understood their obligations to their elder kin. A poetic speech that two close informants once recited for me makes the point compellingly, in the form of a reprimand delivered by a Timorese to his younger Portuguese brother. I quote a few lines:

Maybe it is the rifle that you carry on your shoulder
Maybe it is the gun belt that you gird around your waist
For it is you who is stupid
It is you who is ignorant.
We two might converse
We two might talk together.
But you come with the sharp thing
You come with the pointed thing
To chase me like a deer
To hunt me like a wild pig
As if I had no words
As if I had no speech.

In this poem transgressions take their meaning from the order that the poem as a whole reaffirms. By treating kin as if they were non-kin, speaking to human beings as if they were speechless animals, subjects as if they were objects, the Portuguese brother demonstrates his limited understanding of reality. And from the all too apparent ignorance that the Portuguese displayed in actual power situations, Mambai derived a sense of moral superiority which is explicitly articulated in hidden transcripts such as the poem. Unlike Scott, however, I would not characterize public deference as a purely pragmatic, calculated submission to power, although it is partly that. But retrospectively, at least, maintaining a respectful silence in the presence of disrespectful or abusive Portuguese conduct also reinforced the considerable pride that Mambai took in their superior understanding of the contract between rulers and ruled.

Two points need emphasis. The first, which I suspect is generalizable to other Timorese groups, has to do with the difficulty of interpreting indigenous attitudes toward colonial authorities on the basis of outward appearances. Thus, to reiterate, in publicly reaffirming the legitimacy of Portuguese rule, Mambai were also implicitly reminding one another of an ideal order that seemed to have been violated, but the sense of violation found more open expression outside of colonial power relations. Secondly, certain features of Mambai culture placed ritual leaders at a particular disadvantage when it came to public expression of discontent with the existing order.

Collectively represented as 'the old men' or 'those who know', ritual leaders were the acknowledged custodians of the past in Mambai society, and their status was inseparable from their claims to possess special knowledge of origins. In theory, such knowledge was to be hoarded as treasure, withdrawn from circulation and stored 'inside the stomach' in the form of what Mambai, in their pervasive botanic idiom, described as 'trunk words'. Internalized, unspoken trunk words were contrasted with externalized 'tip words' which 'go out from the mouth', the partial, oblique, branching expressions of knowledge which were regarded as appropriate for public communicative occasions. Communication in ritual contexts was generally understood to be highly coded, deliberately opaque, and differentially understood by participants, who brought different degrees of understanding to ritual events. To reproduce hierarchical social relations, however, ritual discourse had to convey to all participants an impression of meaningfulness if not a hidden message. For ritual leaders, in other words, the trick was to mask the full content of their knowledge while simultaneously securing public recognition of their claims to possess it.[12]

These ideas about knowledge and its transmission organized Mambai interactions with outsiders and shaped their reputation as a withdrawn and secretive people. In this ethnic stereotype, which was held by Portuguese, other Timorese, and Mambai themselves, the group as a whole was represented by its ritual leaders, the appointed custodians of the past. Hence any interest in their culture on the part of outsiders tended to be widely interpreted by Mambai as interest in the special knowledge of origins that their ritual leaders were believed to possess. Any outsiders who actually ventured into Mambai ritual centres – the Portuguese administrator or Catholic priest with a penchant for collecting *usos e costumes*; the occasional tourist who strayed into the mountains in pursuit of the exotic; the soldiers stationed in their interior posts who went looking for diversion; and of course, the anthropologist – were assumed to have come 'in search of rock and tree', to uncover the secrets of the past. Such visitors were met with ambivalence. On the one hand, their visits were rhetorically appropriated as confirmation of the hierarchical status of the ritual centres; on the other hand, perceived as attempts to acquire sacred knowledge, the incursions of foreigners posed a threat to its custodians, and my Mambai friends liked to tell my of the skill with which they had deflected the inquiries of previous visitors. 'We gave them only the tip,' they would say, 'but we kept back the trunk'.

I stress these attitudes not to celebrate my own ethnographic skill, but to convey the tense, ambivalent character of interactions between Mambai and outsiders, even in periods of relative stability. In the more volatile and uncertain times initiated by the fall of the Caetano government and the formation of East Timorese political parties, ambivalence toward outsiders increased dramatically, to the benefit, it now appears to me, of my ethnographic project.

As Mambai ritual leaders confronted the paradoxes of the status they had negotiated, the costs of withholding the knowledge on which it was founded became all too apparent. To them, the ongoing debates over decolonization were notable for what they ignored, the origins of proper rule, order, and hierarchy. While Mambai associated with external affairs looked to the future embodied in Fretilin, in the ritual centres people called with growing urgency for consideration of the past; in the anthropologist, at least, they found an attentive audience.

When I left Timor at the end of 1974, few Mambai whom I knew showed signs of a fully developed nationalist consciousness. In Mambai ritual centres, people rallied around a traditional, backward-looking ideology of domination, in defence of the hierarchical values and political arrangements that colonial practice had cumulatively eroded. What they envisioned in this period was more on the lines of a restoration of an idealized past than a radical transformation of the existing order. Among the demands most vociferously, not to say petulantly, articulated was that

Mambai ritual leaders be consulted to legitimize any new claimants to power. In this respect, many people nurtured a sense of grievance against Fretilin for what they perceived as the party's disregard for traditional authorities.

Nevertheless, as I have argued, there were also oppositional elements to the consciousness that prevailed in the ritual centres. The ideology of Portuguese legitimacy also provided the terms for a critique of colonial practices and it sustained among Mambai a deep sense of their moral superiority to their colonial rulers. As the situation around them changed, Mambai from both the ritual and the executive planes of the diarchic system may well have found common interests and been drawn into increasingly radical forms of political action. Under colonial rule, Mambai discontents had multiplied to create a pervasive discontent. Their quietly maintained sense that things were not as they ought to be would, I believe, have made many Mambai receptive to the nationalist promise of a new future. That promise, however, today remains unfulfilled.

Notes

1 Valeri, Valerio, 'Constitutive History: Genealogy and Narrative in the Legitimation of Hawaiian Kingship', in Emiko Ohnuki-Tierney (ed.), *Culture Through Time*, Stanford, CA: Stanford University Press, 1990, p. 155.

2 Scott, James C., *Weapons of the Weak: Everyday Forms of Peasant Resistance*. New Haven, CT: Yale University Press, 1985.

3 Ortner, Sherry, 'Patterns of History: Cultural Schemas in the Foundings of Sherpa Religious Institutions', in Emiko Ohnuki-Tierney (ed.), *Culture Through Time*, Stanford, CA: Stanford University Press, 1990, pp. 57–93.

4 Although my use of the past tense in this chapter is not without ambiguity, the drastic changes that have occurred in East Timor since the Indonesian invasion make the use of the 'ethnographic present' particularly inappropriate. For example, given the Indonesian policy of forced relocation of peoples from the interior to the coast, not even the present location of populations can be assumed, and it is more than likely that indigenous cultures and social structures have been severely dislocated. In what follows the past tense is not to be read as signifying that the predicate in question no longer exists, but rather as acknowledging that I do not know its current status. Conversely, my occasional shifts to the ethnographic present in describing certain Mambai myths are not meant to represent mythology as a timeless product, unaffected by recent history. But the myths in question are now preserved in the texts that I recorded, and it is to their separated existence as texts that the ethnographic present refers.

5 Fox, James J. (ed.), *The Flow of Life: Essays on Eastern Indonesia.* Cambridge, MA: Harvard University Press, 1980, includes essays on a number of East Timorese societies and gives a good idea of the range of variation.

6 Fox, James J., *The Harvest of the Palm: Ecological Change in Eastern Indonesia.* Cambridge, MA: Harvard University Press, 1977, pp.73–8.

7 For a fuller analysis of Mambai social life, see Traube, Elizabeth G., *Cosmology and Social Life: Ritual Exchange among the Mambai of East Timor.* Chicago: The University of Chicago Press, 1986.

8 Sahlins, Marshall, 'The Stranger King', *The Journal of Pacific History* **16**(3) (1981), pp.107-32.

9 Ortner, Sherry, 'Patterns of History: Cultural Schemas in the Foundings of Sherpa Religious Institutions', in Emiko Ohnuki-Tierney (ed.) *Culture Through Time.* Stanford, CA: Stanford University Press, 1990.

10 Valeri, Valerio, *op cit.*, note 1.

11 Scott, James C. *op cit.*, note 2, pp. 284–9.

12 I analyse the Mambai sociology of knowledge in some detail in Elizabeth G.Traube, 'Obligations to the Source: Complementarity and Hierarchy in an Eastern Indonesian Society', in David Maybury-Lewis and Uri Almagor (eds), *The Attraction of Opposites: Thought and Society in the Dualistic Mode.* Ann Arbor: The University of Michigan Press, 1989, pp. 321–44.

PART II

International Dimensions

CHAPTER 3

The Timor Affair in International Perspective

James Dunn

Introduction

East Timor is a small country[1] but it is not insignificant by the standards of the size of the smaller member states of today's United Nations. On the eve of the Indonesian invasion in 1975 the colony had an area of about 7,300 square miles, and a population of about 680,000 people, with an annual growth rate of about 2 per cent.[2] This means that today there should be at least 950,000 people in the territory but, based on recent Indonesian statistics, the population of what is now designated the 27th province of Indonesia was in 1993 only about 740,000 people, of whom about 150,000 are non-Timorese who have in recent years moved into the territory. What these demographic statistics reveal is that the population of East Timor, eighteen years after the invasion began, has actually fallen by about 12 per cent, one of the most dramatic declines in postwar history.

Portuguese navigators first reached Timor about twenty years after Columbus completed his epic trans-Atlantic crossing in 1492, and about fifty years later their colonial rule of the area began in earnest. Therefore, for some four centuries in East Timor, Portugal has been the dominant, virtually exclusive, external influence – except for a brief Japanese inter-regnum lasting from January 1942 until their surrender in August 1945.

Until 1974 East Timor was apparently a subject of little concern or interest to Indonesia. From 1958 to 1966, the last eight years of Sukarno's presidency, Indonesia was to become one of the most aggressive anti-colonial states, vigorously asserting its own claim for the 'return' of West Irian. After that objective was secured in the early 1960s, the Sukarno Government embarked on a costly and futile *Konfrontasi* (1963–6) with Malaysia, which the President perceived as a British neo-colonial creation. However, at no stage did Indonesia seek to bring any real pressure to bear on the Portuguese in East Timor, although the

Salazar regime was at that time the only colonial power in open defiance of the post-war decolonization process, a process which had been rapidly gathering momentum by the early 1960s. While Dutch colonialism in West New Guinea was denounced in vitriolic terms, the more traditional form of colonial rule then being conducted by the Portuguese in neighbouring East Timor was rarely mentioned.

True, in the early 1960s, at about the time of *Konfrontasi*, there were occasional remarks by leading Indonesian political figures, hinting that East Timor's future lay with its big neighbour, but these statements were not taken further by the government of the time, and they certainly never evolved into any formal territorial claim or political campaign.[3] Even in the two years preceding Indonesia's military intervention, most official statements from Jakarta emphasized East Timor's right to self-determination.[4] Certainly, at no stage, under either Sukarno's *Orde Lama* (1945–67) or Suharto's *Orde Baru* (1967 to the present), was a claim to East Timor ever formally made by the government in Jakarta.[5]

From Portuguese Rule to Indonesian Intervention

In the postwar years most governments of the former European imperial powers wilted before the march of decolonization, and parted with their colonies. However, the Portuguese government led by Dr António de Oliveira Salazar (in office, 1926–68) and Marcelo Caetano (in office, 1968–74) ignored these winds of change. In the early 1960s the component parts of Portugal's rambling empire were designated 'overseas provinces', a device designed to counter the international political implications of the formal UN pronouncements on decolonization.[6] It was not until after the April coup in Lisbon in 1974 that these overseas territories were granted the right to self-determination. Prior to the coup most of Portugal's African colonies were engaged in armed struggles in pursuit of independence, but in East Timor a relative calm prevailed. However, the Timorese quickly organized themselves into political parties. Two major movements emerged: Fretilin (*Frente Revolucionária de Timor-Leste Independente*), a left-wing nationalist movement, and UDT (*União Democrática Timorense*), a more conservative grouping, both of which had come out in favour of independence by September 1974.

Of course, there were a few Timorese who were not averse to the notion of joining with Indonesia, but it was an option with little appeal among the population at large. A very small party, called Apodeti (*Associação Popular Democrática Timorense*), was formed with integration as its objective. But Apodeti was little more than a political contrivance, reflecting not the aspirations of an identifiable minority, but rather the opportunistic concerns of an elite group of Timorese, among them the more conservative feudal chiefs (*liurai*), who had always been pillars of support for the Salazar regime. Independence would mean popular government and an end to the privileges they had enjoyed under the Portuguese.[7]

Even with this support, Apodeti would not have existed without strong Indonesian financial and political backing, and discrete support from the Portuguese administration. By June 1974, some officials, especially the military, apparently felt that they had a responsibility to urge the Timorese to think positively about integration. They were also inclined to the view that the Indonesians would be more likely to accept the popular will if the option of joining with them was openly and impartially presented to the Timorese community.[8] Nevertheless, based on my own observations during a fact-finding visit in mid-1974, from the very outset, integration with Indonesia was the last thing the great majority of East Timorese wanted. Most preferred to continue links with Portugal rather than become part of Indonesia. To integrate with Indonesia would constitute, as one East Timorese put it, 'not decolonization but recolonization'.

At this juncture it should be stressed that the independence movement in Timor, in the early stages of the post-coup political awakening, was not antagonistic to Indonesia. The Timorese may have been apprehensive as to how the Suharto regime would react to the emergence of an independent East Timor, but they were not hostile to Indonesians as a people. In fact, a generous response by Indonesian Foreign Minister Adam Malik in May 1974 deeply impressed the young Timorese leaders in the Fretilin movement.[9] At the time José Ramos-Horta told the writer that if Malik's magnanimous response were to prevail in Jakarta, he felt that his party would consider inviting Indonesia to be responsible for East Timor's foreign affairs and defence when the territory eventually became independent.[10] But real power in Indonesia was not at Adam Malik's disposal, and the military establishment soon began to discredit his views.

By the end of 1974 Indonesia had already begun waging a propaganda war against the Timorese independence movement. As a party of the left Fretilin was its principal target. The Fretilin leaders were accused of being both Communist and anti-Indonesian. At the same time, falsified accounts of links between the Fretilin leadership and Peking and Hanoi were circulated among the more conservative Timorese groups. In reaction to this campaign, the Timorese inevitably became increasingly hostile to the Indonesian authorities.

In the first two months after April 1974, the Portuguese administration in Dili was rather indifferent towards the idea of independence for East Timor, with some military officers contending that joining with Indonesia made good sense for such a poorly developed territory. Indeed, one senior official believed he had a responsibility to promote the idea of integration.[11] However, a widespread popular enthusiasm for independence quickly manifested itself, eventually convincing Lisbon and the colonial authorities that the Timorese were simply not disposed to merge with Indonesia. The Timorese saw themselves as being different, culturally, politically, linguistically and religiously from their neighbour.[12] The aggressive and clumsy attempts by the Indonesians, after August 1974, to intimidate the Timorese merely served to strengthen their growing national consciousness.

In the event, the Portuguese authorities commenced a decolonization programme in late 1974, presenting the Timorese political elite with three options: full independence, continuing with Portugal under some new and more democratic arrangement, or integration with Indonesia.

It soon became clear to the Timorese themselves that the magnanimity displayed by Adam Malik was not shared by influential Indonesian military figures like Ali Murtopo and Benny Murdani, who harboured very different plans for East Timor's future. These generals were not motivated by a desire to acquire additional territory – East Timor was, in the days before the off-shore oil developments in the Timor Gap area, hardly an economic prize. As the guardians of Indonesia's national integrity, the military was principally concerned that an independent East Timor might stimulate or rekindle separatist tendencies among discontented ethnic groups in neighbouring Eastern Indonesia, such as the West Timorese and the Ambonese. In the aftermath of the Communist victories in Indochina in April 1975, Indonesia's military leadership was also obsessed with the risk of Communist infiltration and insurgency. To the military, therefore, integration was the only acceptable solution for East Timor.

As early as the end of 1974 a covert intelligence operation was launched by the aforementioned military group, including the head of Bakin (*Badan Koordinasi Intelijens Nasional*/Coordinating Body for [Indonesian] National Intelligence), Lieutenant-General Yoga Sugama, as well as General Murtopo and Benny Murdani. As senior intelligence officers they all enjoyed ready access to President Suharto. The existence of this operation, code-named *'Operasi Komodo'*,[13] became known to US and Australian intelligence agencies before the year was out. Its aim was to bring about the integration of East Timor by whatever means necessary. Its initial efforts, which included a clumsy propaganda campaign vilifying the independence movement, the open backing of Apodeti, and some thinly disguised subversive ventures, had the effect not of dividing the two major parties, but of bringing them together into a coalition dedicated to the goal of independence.

However, if the year 1975 proved to be a turbulent one for East Timor, it was no less difficult for Portugal. Political turmoil in Lisbon demoralized the overseas administration, undermining its administrative grip on the colony, a situation subtly and subversively exploited by the Indonesian generals heading *Operasi Komodo*. Economic conditions in Timor were also affected by the crisis in Portugal, but it should be pointed out that life in the colony was not a dark and dismal contrast of the more 'developed' TimTim of today. For a brief period in 1974–5, there was free political expression and movement, and there was great enthusiasm and optimism as to the future prospects of the territory. There was no oppression, little violence, no torture and a general feeling that the lot of the indigenous Timorese vis-à-vis the rest of the community was on the verge of radical transformation (see further Traube in this volume).

Portuguese colonial practice was undeniably authoritarian under Salazar, but its character had changed even before the Salazarist regime fell in 1974. Since the April 1974 coup the change had been radical. But the revolution had led to economic stagnation in Portugal, stalling plans for the economic development of distant East Timor. However, this situation had not daunted the confidence of the Timorese that their country could soon become self-sufficient in food, and the prospects of rapid political change had already attracted the attention of foreign investors, especially in the field of tourism.

By May 1975, however, serious differences had surfaced between the two major parties. In an *Operasi Komodo* operation, led by General Ali Murtopo himself, the Indonesians moved to exploit these divisions. Their propaganda offensive against Fretilin was intensified, while the UDT leaders were invited to Jakarta and courted. They were lectured, sometimes by Murtopo himself, on the threat of Communist subversion, and were sent on subsidized tours to anti-Communist countries in Asia, notably South Korea, the Philippines and Taiwan. At the same time, fabricated evidence of links between the Fretilin leaders and leading Communist powers in Asia, like China and Vietnam, was passed on to them. At least three of these Timorese leaders, Francisco Lopes da Cruz, José Martins and César Augusto da Costa Mouzinho, were actually recruited by Bakin, the powerful Indonesian central intelligence agency.[14] By May 1975, relations between the two Timorese parties had become so brittle that the coalition collapsed and talks aimed at healing the rift broke down completely. At this time rumours were circulated by Bakin agents that Fretilin was planning a coup, encouraging UDT leaders to act hastily and rashly.[15]

Early in August 1975 Murtopo himself told UDT leaders in Jakarta that a Fretilin coup was imminent, and encouraged them to take urgent preemptive action.[16] A few days after their return to Dili the UDT leaders, with what military support they could muster – mostly from the local Portuguese police commander in Dili – launched an abortive coup in Dili. Within three weeks the party and its followers had been over-whelmed by Fretilin, not because of external military support, but because most Timorese troops in the colonial military were in fact supporters of the independence movement. In this short but intense conflict,[17] the Portuguese, whose administrative apparatus had been reduced to a small number of officials and less than a hundred combat troops, withdrew to the offshore island of Atauro, the aptly named 'Isle of Goats'.

Having found themselves in administrative control of the colony, the Fretilin leaders immediately sought to reassure the Indonesian authorities. But the latter were dismayed to find that Fretilin was now in *de facto* control of the province, and its overtures were ignored. *Operasi Komodo*'s military commanders moved to persuade Suharto to authorize direct military intervention, but the President remained unenthusiastic. He continued to hold back until the end of September when Generals Murtopo, Murdani and Yoga Sugama were able to assure him that countries like the United States, Australia and Japan, not to speak of Indonesia's ASEAN neighbours, would not make a fuss if Indonesian troops moved into Timor. Two weeks later, on 16 October, Indonesia's first major military action, a covert operation, was launched: it was an attack on the border village of Balibo. Among those killed were two television crews from Australia.[18]

After its victory Fretilin moved quickly to set up an interim administration, and sought to assuage Indonesian fears by inviting the Portuguese to return and resume decolonization. But there was no response from the Portuguese, whose government in Lisbon was now in turmoil in the aftermath of General Spinola's failed right-wing putsch, and the deepening tensions within the Portuguese military and political parties. The Indonesian response was swift in coming. They launched attacks over the border from West Timor, the official news agency Antara telling the world that the 'anti-Fretilin forces' were counter-attacking. With the Portuguese ignoring their request to return, the Indonesians attacking from the west, and the international community turning a blind eye to their plight, Fretilin's unilateral declaration of an independent East Timor on 28 November 1975 should have surprised no–one.

The Invasion and Its Aftermath

Despite the fact that they themselves had provoked Fretilin's hasty UDI, the Indonesian authorities lost no time in making use of the event to justify their invasion plans to Western diplomats in Jakarta. A full-scale invasion, an amphibious operation involving thousands of troops (one of the largest operations of its kind in the nation's history since the 1958 PRRI – Permesta revolt), was unleashed, concentrated mainly on Dili. The status of East Timor was therefore changed abruptly on 7 December 1975,[19] when these forces, under the overall command of General Benny Murdani, stormed ashore. From the evidence accumulated over the past 19 years it is clear that the invasion and subjugation of East Timor, especially in the early stages, was carried out at huge human cost. With their capital under attack, the Fretilin leadership made a desperate appeal for help to the international community, but their cries fell on deaf ears. This unwarranted act of aggression was a blatant violation of the UN Charter. Even more serious was the brutality which accompanied it. In the very first days of the invasion rampaging Indonesian troops engaged in an orgy of indiscriminate killing, rape and torture. There were a number of large-scale public executions – victims including women as well as men – which constituted a systematic campaign of terror. In some villages whole communities were slaughtered or burnt alive, with only children of the age of four and under being spared.

Outraged by these atrocities the small but determined Timorese army, the Falintil (*Forças Armadas de Libertação Nacional de Timor-Leste*), bitterly contested the advance of the invading forces, inflicting heavy losses on the attackers (estimates range as high as 20,000). For more than three years they denied them effective control outside the main towns and administrative centres. In retaliation the invading force imposed a harsh and oppressive occupation. In the areas under Indonesian control, summary killings, torture and rape were a daily occurrence, forcing tens of thousands of Timorese to flee before the invading troops and seek refuge behind Fretilin lines.

The rugged mountainous interior of East Timor provided excellent terrain for Fretilin's guerrilla campaign, but the resistance forces were heavily outnumbered and outgunned. For about two years the Timorese managed to meet most of their basic food needs from their own hastily developed agricultural resources, but their farms began to come under ever more devastating attack from the air, and, by 1978, the Fretilin leaders were encouraging the Timorese to return to Indonesian-occupied areas, their limited food and medical resources having been exhausted.[20]

Initially, the way these 'refugees' were received by the Indonesians was anything but humane: Fretilin suspects were often summarily executed, while many were beaten or tortured at the slightest provocation. They were forced into resettlement camps, where there was precious little food and medicines. In 1979, even in the areas under Jakarta's control, thousands of Timorese died needlessly in these camps from famine and disease.

The International Reaction

Reports on the grim situation in East Timor began to filter out of the territory as early as the end of 1976. In that year a confidential report from Catholic Church sources depicted a scene of oppression and wanton killing. Its authors suggested that in the year since the invasion as many as 60,000 Timorese might have lost their lives.[21]

Was the international community aware of this very heavy loss of life and, if so, how did it react? In fact, these early reports aroused very little international attention. East Timor was no Kuwait: it was remote, little known, and was without any strategic or economic importance to the superpowers, even to the Portuguese, who at that time were anxious to divest themselves of their troublesome empire as quickly as possible. These alarming reports were thus dismissed as unreliable or exaggerations by Indonesia's Western friends.

This leads us to a sinister dimension of the Timor tragedy. The gravity of the humanitarian situation in this territory could easily have been made into an issue of international concern and reaction by Western governments, especially the United States, Australia, Japan, and the Netherlands, if they had chosen to react responsibly and compassionately.[22] Most chose the path of shielding Indonesia from international criticism, even to the extent of dismissing reports of this genocidal loss of population as being ill-founded and exaggerated. If the Western missions in Jakarta were aware of just how serious the humanitarian situation actually was, they appear not to have deigned to report it to their respective governments. In the case of the Australian, Canadian, and United States missions, the assessments of most diplomats were inhibited by their governments' complicity, that is their decision not to oppose Jakarta's military intervention.

Some of the reports that were made public by these Western governments could not have been honestly arrived at. For example, early in 1977, one State Department official told Congressmen that only 2,000 Timorese had died as a result of the invasion. A few weeks later another official, Robert Oakley, came up with a 'revised' figure of 10,000, which yet another official source later qualified with the comment that many of these deaths had occurred in the fighting between Fretilin and UDT.[23] The thrust of such comments was to suggest that the Timorese losses were largely self-inflicted.

In the 1970s most Australian official responses were delivered in this vein, that is, in a manner seemingly designed to diminish the seriousness of the situation on the ground in East Timor and to discredit reports suggesting that Indonesian troops were responsible for serious human rights violations, thus deflecting international concern. Early in 1978, a year in which tens of thousands of Timorese died as a consequence of Indonesian operations, the Australian Government, then led by Prime Minister Fraser, took the extraordinary step of according *de facto* recognition to the annexation of the territory, which by that time had been designated Indonesia's 27th province.[24]

The genocidal dimensions of the loss of life in East Timor emerged starkly in 1979, almost four years after the invasion, when Indonesian authorities finally allowed a small number of international aid workers to conduct a survey of the humanitarian needs of the province. The human misery they encountered shocked them deeply. Their estimates suggested that in the preceding four years Timor had lost between a tenth and a third of its population and that 200,000 of the remainder were in appalling conditions in 'resettlement camps', which one official, who had previously served in Cambodia, described as among the worst he had ever seen.[25]

These revelations should have galvanized the world community into demanding that Indonesia withdraw from the former Portuguese colony, but that did not happen. Not one of the major powers, who were later so affronted by Argentina's seizure of the Falkland Islands (April 1982) and Iraq's invasion of Kuwait (August 1990), was prepared to bring any real pressure to bear on Indonesia regarding the key issue of East Timor's denial of the right to self-determination. The best that Washington and Canberra could come up with was to urge the Suharto government to admit international humanitarian relief organizations to the territory. These requests, which elicited some response from Indonesia, resulted in the readmission to the province of an International Committee of the Red Cross (ICRC) mission.[26]

It was to be more than a decade after the invasion before Jakarta could claim to exercise administrative control over most of the island. Even today armed resistance continues, despite annual large-scale operations by Indonesian forces, who invariably outnumber the guerrillas by more than ten to one.[27] Thanks to the intervention of these international agencies, and the work of some dedicated East Timorese and Indonesians, conditions in Timor improved markedly during the 1980s. However, there was no major improvement in the human rights situation; serious abuses, mostly by the Indonesian military, have continued. The annual reports by Amnesty International and Asia Watch still speak of summary executions, 'disappearances', torture and imprisonment on the grounds of conscience.[28] Despite the decline in Fretilin guerrilla activities, large numbers of Indonesian troops continue to remain in the territory.[29]

Some Contemporary Considerations

It is now beyond doubt that East Timor suffered a catastrophic loss of population in the process of the annexation of the territory. From the very outset, the Indonesian military bear overwhelming responsibility for that loss. In 1975, based on my own assessment of the situation on the ground at that time, the majority of the Timorese, while preferring independence, would have remained in the towns with their families, rather than flee to the interior of the island, had the invading forces shown respect for the lives, property and rights of the civilian population. It was the invading forces' brutality, their senseless killing, their seizing and raping of girls, some of them children in their early teens, which caused the mass exodus into the mountains. There, behind Fretilin lines, they were eventually surrounded by the invading forces who sought to starve them into submission, a strategy which had devastating consequences, as testified by the arithmetic of East Timor's contemporary demographic statistics.

The principal targets of the occupation authorities for elimination, according to the likes of General Benny Murdani,[30] remain the independence movement leaders and their supporters. But opposition to integration goes far beyond the reduced ranks of the Fretilin guerrillas. From the observations of the many visitors to Timor since the territory was opened to foreign visitors in 1989, the majority of Timorese remain unequivocal in their hostility to integration. Paradoxically, while there are fewer signs of armed resistance, the population at large is more outspoken than ever before about integration. Even if few are prepared to take up arms, the majority of the population are at risk while the Indonesian military persists in the idea of eliminating all support for independence.

That economic conditions in East Timor have improved markedly over the past ten years is an indisputable fact, but the question is, just who are the real beneficiaries of this much-vaunted development? Is it the indigenous Timorese themselves? In fact, it is evident that most of this development carries few benefits outside the select group of the elite and the affluent, these days mostly Indonesian. The better roads are, therefore, for Indonesian use, not for the Timorese, few of whom own vehicles. Much of the improved housing is for the new Indonesian ruling class and commercial elite, or the transmigrants, not to speak of the military and their families.

Jakarta's central objective remains essentially the same: to achieve the full integration of the territory into Indonesia. That means eradicating a desire which is held by the vast majority of the people. The armed resistance from Fretilin guerrillas may no longer pose a serious threat, but popular opposition to integration has not diminished and the aspiration to some form of independence remains uppermost in Timorese minds, as the reports of most visitors attest. This aspiration has been kept alive not only by the oppressive character of Indonesian occupation, especially from the military side, but also by the rather patronizing attitudes of Indonesian civilians. Development policies have also had the effect of marginalizing the indigenous population.

It would be an exaggeration to say that Timorese aspirations have been kept alive by international support, for there has been precious little of this, especially at the official level. Their case has attracted attention and sympathy in the European Parliament, in the US Congress, and among parliamentarians in Europe, Canada, Japan and Australia but, so far, neither legislative action nor appeals by parliamentarians have budged the governments concerned.

Some recent developments, notably the liberation of the Baltic States and Kuwait in the early 1990s, the emergence of previously captive small states elsewhere in Eastern Europe and Africa, have, however, given the Timorese encouragement, especially in the light of the accompanying rhetoric by the great powers about the unacceptability of aggression by larger states against smaller neighbours. The war, the massive intrusion of outsiders, and Jakarta's efforts to effect a radical change in their ways and attitudes, is undermining the cultural identity of the Timorese. Such an intrusive presence did not occur under the Portuguese. The latter may have ruled Timor as a colony, but their interference in Timorese culture and society was minimal (see further Taylor and Traube above).

Twenty years ago, Timor was a world of tiny hamlets, which formed the nucleus of community life. In the years following the Indonesian invasion hundreds of these hamlets were destroyed, or their inhabitants simply forced by the Indonesian military into resettlements, resembling the strategic hamlets of Vietnam notoriety. The Timorese used to study their own language and cultures, but this has been replaced by a curriculum designed to promote a sense of Indonesian-ness and acceptance of *pancasila* (Indonesian state) ideology. In the last years of rule from Lisbon many of the indigenous population spoke Portuguese, but the teaching of this language is now denied them.[31] The intricate cultural patterns of the past, so fascinating to anthropologists, are steadily being eroded. East Timor was the least 'Indonesian' of the communities of the archipelago, its people not having shared with Irian Jaya, for example, the linking experience of Dutch colonialism. Indonesia's annexation of East Timor has, therefore, had a much more devastating impact on the fortunes of the Timorese people than other Eastern Indonesian societies subject to Jakarta's political and cultural hegemony.

An inkling of its terrible consequences may be deduced from the dramatic demographic changes: had the invasion not occurred East Timor should today have had a population of about one million people, but with the Timorese component today standing at about 650,000, the population remains significantly less than it was on the eve of Jakarta's military intervention. The current position of the Timorese is certainly weaker than it was in the last years of Portuguese rule and, unless there is a radical change in the attitude of the Indonesian authorities, the special cultural character of this former Portuguese colony is at risk of being lost for ever, as Bishop Belo has repeatedly warned.[32]

The annexation of East Timor constitutes an outrageous violation of the fundamental standards of conduct the international community has set for itself through the forums of the United Nations. No less disturbing than the behaviour of the Indonesian military is the shameful record of the governments like the United States, Britain, Japan and Australia, who were in a position to dissuade the Suharto regime from its act of aggression but did nothing: indeed, by letting the Indonesians know that the incorporation of the Portuguese colony was an acceptable, if not desirable, end, they virtually encouraged the annexation. No less shameful than their complicity at the time of the invasion was their later hasty support in principle for integration, their deflecting of criticism of the humanitarian consequences of the invasion and their continuing accommodation, especially at diplomatic and, in Britain's case, military levels, in the present. It is thanks to their shielding of the Suharto regime from international criticism that international interest in East Timor has yet to be translated into the kind of resolute measures that would offer the Timorese people some hope that colonization by Indonesia is not for ever.

Notes

1 As well as the eastern half of the island the Portuguese territory included the enclave of Oecussi, on the northern coast of the western sector.

2 Based on the assessment of the administration of the Catholic Church, whose population records were generally regarded as more accurate than those of the colonial authorities.

3 Curiously, the strongest argument for such an outcome was advanced in 1966 by an American academic, Professor Donald Weatherbee, who concluded that, 'in a sense, Portuguese Timor is a trust territory, the Portuguese holding it in trust for Indonesia', see Weatherbee, 'Portuguese Timor: An Indonesian Dilemma', *Asian Survey*, 6(12) (December 1966), pp. 683–95.

4 In June 1974, in contrast to most of his colleagues, who studiously avoided uttering the word 'independence', Foreign Minister Adam Malik generously assured the Timorese of Indonesia's support for East Timor's independence. In a letter to José Ramos-Horta, then Fretilin's foreign affairs spokesman, Malik wrote, *inter alia*, 'The independence of every country is the right of every nation, with no exception for the people of Timor', see José Ramos-Horta, *Funu. The Unfinished Saga of East Timor*. Trenton, NJ: Red Sea Press, 1987, p. 43.

5 In 1957, for example, Indonesia told the UN First Committee, in a reference to Timor: 'Indonesia has no claim to any territories which had not been part of the former Netherlands East Indies. No one should suggest otherwise or advance dangerous theories in that respect', quoted in Dunn, *Timor: A People Betrayed*. Milton, Qld.: Jacaranda Press, 1983, p. 101.

6 For example, UNGA Resolution 1514(XV), adopted in December 1960, *Declaration on the Granting of Independence to Colonial Countries and Peoples* (New York: Resolution of the 958th Plenary Session of the United Nations General Assembly, 14 December 1960).

7 Information based on interviews with Apodeti leaders in 1974–5.

8 Australia, too, encouraged the Portuguese to include integration as an option in the political context of decolonization.

9 For details of this letter, see Dunn, *Timor*, pp. 108–9; and Ramos-Horta, *Funu*, pp. 42–4.

10 Conversation with the author shortly after Horta's return to Dili in June 1974.

11 Based on conversations in June 1974 with Major Arnão Metelo, a senior member of the Armed Forces Movement (*Movimento das Forças Armadas*) in East Timor.

12 East Timor is today (1994) predominantly Roman Catholic, see Archer, 'The Catholic Church in East Timor' in this volume. It is estimated that some 180,000 of the pre-1975 population of 700,000 were practising Catholics, the remainder being, for the most part, animists.

13 Named after the 'dragon', or giant lizard, which is found on the nearby island of Alor.

14 Based on talks with Lopes da Cruz in Canberra in mid-1975, with César Mouzinho in Dili in October 1975, and, with José Martins (an Apodeti leader who defected after the Dili invasion of December 1975) in February 1975. All confirmed that Murtopo had pressed them to sever links with Fretilin.

15 An example of the provocative disinformation role of Bakin at this point was the deliberate circulating of a story by *Operasi Komodo* agents that a number of Vietnamese officers had been smuggled in to Timor, and were training a Fretilin military force.

16 There is no evidence that a coup was being planned at that time. In fact, most of the top leadership were out of the country.

17 The humanitarian consequences of this civil war were assessed by the International Committee of the Red Cross and the ACFOA (Australian Council for Overseas Aid) mission which I led in October and November 1975, with the former concluding that the total loss of life was about 1,500.

18 For an account of their fate, see Shackleton, chapter 7 below.

19 US intelligence officials in Jakarta were told by their Indonesian opposite numbers that the attack would take place on 6 December. However, the Americans reminded the Indonesians that President Ford and Dr Kissinger would be in Jakarta on that day, and their hosts obligingly delayed the attack 24 hours, see Philip Liechty, 'How Indonesia Engulfed East Timor', *The Washington Post*, 6 January. 1992; and Dunn, *Timor*, p. 277.

20 See the account by Paulino Gama (Mauk Muruk), chapter 5 below.

21 A copy of this report, *Notes on East Timor* (1976), is held by the present author.

22 Of Indonesia's major trading and aid-donor partners, namely the US, Japan, West Germany, Australia, and the Netherlands, only the last-mentioned displayed any serious concern at the government level, and this was short-lived.

23 Testimony of Robert Oakley contained in United States, House of Representatives, *Human Rights in East Timor and the Question of the Use of US Equipment by the Indonesian Armed Forces* (Hearings before the Subcommittee on International Organization and on Asian and Pacific Affairs of the Committee on International Relations). Washington DC: House of Representatives, Ninety-fifth Congress, First Session: US Government Printing Office, 23 March 1977; and letter, Edward C Ingraham (*sic*), Department of State, 13 May 1977.

24 Canberra waited only one more year before according *de jure* status to its recognition in February 1979, a move designed to facilitate negotiations with Jakarta on seabed rights and oil exploration in the Timor Gap, see further Roger Clark, chapter 4 below.

25 The confidential report, to which the author was later given access, stated that, of the 200,000, about ten per cent were in such bad shape that they could not be saved.

26 An ICRC mission, fully staffed by foreigners, had operated in East Timor until the eve of the invasion in December 1975.

27 Despite the withdrawal of some combat battalions, more than 10,000 troops are still believed to be in East Timor, with territorial units playing key administrative roles, see below, note 29.

28 See, in particular, the annual reports published by Amnesty International and also the publications of Asia Watch cited in Sue Roff's bibliography in this volume.

29 It is noteworthy that while the Portuguese exercised control with a military force never exceeding about 1500 men, the Indonesian military presence rose as high as 40,000 shortly after the invasion (1975–8), and is now estimated to be not much less than 17,000, a figure which includes some twenty battalions and numerous special force units (*Kopassus, Kopassandha*), see the report of the British Military Attaché on his visit to East Timor in May 1994, and his interview with the Indonesian Commander, Colonel Johny (*sic*) Lumintang, cited in John Pilger, 'True Brits, True to Mass Murderers', *New Statesman and Society* (3 June 1994), p. 14; and the list of Indonesian military units given by Bishop Belo in, 'Bishop Belo's Diary of Oppression', *Timor Link*, **27** (October 1993), p. 8.

30 In a speech to Timorese officials in Dili, in February 1990, Murdani warned that those who still sought to form a separate state 'will be crushed by ABRI [*Angkatan Bersenjata Republik Indonesi*a; Armed Forces of the Republic of Indonesia]. ABRI may fail the first time, so it will try for a second time, and for a third time'. Referring to Fretilin and its sympathisers, he went on to say, 'We will crush them all…to safeguard the unity of Indonesian territory', see *Inside Indonesia*, 23 (June 1990), 'Murdani's Dili Speech: Don't Dream or else…'.

31 It is argued that Portuguese was the language of the colonial past, but in most former colonies study of the language of the imperial power has been permitted, if not openly encouraged, see Ben Anderson, 'The Language of Indonesian Politics', *Indonesia*, **1** (April 1966), pp. 89–116 (esp. p. 101ff.); and *ibid.*, *Imagined Communities: Reflections on the Origins and Spread of Nationalism*. London: Verso, 1983.

32 See Muchlis Dj. Tolomundu, 'Kami Ingin Lebih Bebas. Uskup Belo, Integrasi, Insiden 12 November dan ABRI', *Matr*a (August 1992); 'Interview with Bishop Belo', *Inside Indonesia*, **32** (December 1992); and John Pilger, 'Bishop Belo Accuses the West', *New Statesman and Society*, **15** (July 1994).

CHAPTER 4

Timor Gap

The Legality of the 'Treaty on the Zone of Cooperation in an Area between the Indonesian Province of East Timor and Northern Australia'

Roger S. Clark[1]

Day of Infamy in East Timor

On 7 December 1975, the thirty-fourth anniversary of the day of infamy at Pearl Harbor, Indonesian forces invaded the territory of East Timor, a Portuguese colony for some four and a half centuries. Following the 1974 Portuguese revolution, East Timor, like other Portuguese non-self-governing territories, had been moving through a process of self-determination. Portuguese authorities evacuated the territory in August 1975 during civil disorders, condoned, if not fomented by the Indonesians. Fretilin,[2] a popular group which aimed at independence for the territory after a short transitional period, gained the upper hand in the struggle and, on 28 November 1975, declared independence hoping this would strengthen their hand in dealing with Indonesian border incursions. A full-scale Indonesian invasion followed. One might have thought that this was a plain breach of the norms of the United Nations Charter concerning the illegal use of force and self-determination.[3] Indeed, at the United Nations, the General Assembly and the Security Council both adopted resolutions[4] deploring the Indonesian actions, reaffirming the right of the Timorese to self-determination and calling for the withdrawal of the Indonesian forces. The political will has never been there to put teeth into these resolutions,[5] but the United Nations continues to treat Portugal as the legal administering power of the territory and the General Assembly has specifically rejected the claim that East Timor has been legally integrated into Indonesia.[6]

The Timor Gap

The continental shelf area between northern Australia and East Timor is believed to contain oil. Exploiting the area has been complicated by the difficulty of delimiting boundaries, given conflicting claims and sharp disagreement about the applicable legal principles.[7] Prior to 1975, Australia had some inconclusive negotiations with the Portuguese on the subject. More recently, the discussions have taken place with the Indonesians. The essence of the problem is that while the width of the sea in the relevant area between the two coastlines varies from some 250 to 290 nautical miles, there are, geographically-speaking, two continental margins between the two land masses, a more than 200 nautical mile Australian margin to the south and a 40 to 70 nautical mile margin to the north, separated by a deeper area, known as the Timor Trough. The issue is what are the legal implications – if any – of the shape of the shelf or shelves? Australia has argued essentially that it is entitled to the full natural prolongation of its shelf to the edge of the margin, while Portugal and Indonesia have argued that, since it is not possible to accommodate a full 200 mile shelf for both Timor and Australia, the median line of the shelf (ignoring the trough) is where the boundary should be. The law on such delimitations has been evolving in the past two decades and is still far from clear. Both Australia and Portugal are parties to the 1958 Geneva Convention on the Continental Shelf,[8] so that as between them, that Convention should provide the framework for a delimitation. The result of such an exercise is far from predictable.[9] Indonesia, while it signed the 1958 Convention, has not ratified it. It presumably argues that the relevant rules are those of customary law developed under the aegis of the 1982 Convention on the Law of the Sea.[10] This approach, especially when account is taken of the development of the concept of Exclusive Economic Zones,[11] would suggest that some kind of median line should probably be drawn – the force of the Australian argument, based on there being 'two' shelves as a result of the geographic features, appears to have weakened in the more recent practice.[12]

In 1971 and 1972 Indonesia and Australia agreed to a shelf boundary between them to the west and the east of East Timor, since no-one at that point disputed that it was Portuguese territory.[13] The agreed line tracked the shelf edge along the Timor Trough essentially in accord with the Australian position – Australia did much better than Indonesia in terms of area in this deal. Indonesia has apparently since regretted its generosity. The hole in the line of delimitation is known popularly as 'The Timor Gap'. It is in this context that Australia and Indonesia entered into what is titled the 'Treaty on the Zone of Cooperation in an Area between the Indonesian Province of East Timor and Northern

Australia"[14] (henceforth 'the Treaty'). The Treaty was signed on 11 December 1989 and subsequently ratified by the two parties.[15] The Treaty describes itself as a 'provisional' solution to the problem.[16] The relevant part of the shelf between East Timor and Australia ('the Zone of Cooperation')[17] has been divided under Articles 3 and 4 of the Treaty into three 'Areas'. One, Area A, in the middle, is to be jointly developed. Area B, nearest to Australia, is an area of sole Australian jurisdiction, but Australia will allocate 10 per cent of gross Resource Rent Tax revenues, equivalent to 16 per cent of net Resource Rent Tax, collected from this area to Indonesia. Area C, nearest to Indonesia, is an area of sole Indonesian jurisdiction, but Indonesia will allocate 10 per cent of Contractors' Income Tax revenues from this area to Australia. The whole deal – A, B and C – obviously comes as a package and the resources of the total package are thus subject to sharing.

Illegality of the Treaty

My object here is to expand upon a view that has been espoused by the government of Portugal in various protests to the Australian authorities and to the United Nations,[18] and which I have previously addressed in outline,[19] namely that the Australian government has acted in breach of its international obligations in entering into the Timor Gap Treaty[20] with Indonesia. I believe, moreover, that this Treaty is null and void under international law and that, if properly seized of the issue,[21] the International Court of Justice would so decide. Needless to say, in making this case, I do not mean in any way to minimize the blatant illegality of Indonesia's aggression against, and denial of self-determination to, East Timor. I have, indeed, addressed that issue at length elsewhere.[22] The illegality of Indonesia's actions are, I believe, not disputed by the Australian authorities[23] and they have, of course, been duly noted in resolutions of the Security Council and the General Assembly. One of the many tragedies of the Timor situation is, however, that otherwise decent governments – of Australia, of the United States, and of my own country, New Zealand – have for political reasons not been prepared to make the stand on this issue which I believe their own assessment of the facts should have required them to make. There are times when even one's friends should be called to account for acting wrongly and this is one of them![24]

The Duty Not To Recognize the Acquisition of Territory Through Unlawful Force

In its simplest form, my argument is that, by entering into the Treaty, Australia breached an international obligation not to recognize the legitimacy of the Indonesian presence in East Timor. That obligation is reflected[25] in two unanimously adopted resolutions of the United Nations General Assembly, the 1970 Declaration on Principles of International Law Concerning Friendly Relations and Co-operation Among States,[26] and the 1974 Resolution entitled Definition of Aggression.[27] The 1970 Resolution was adopted by the General Assembly in celebration of the occasion of the twenty-fifth anniversary of the United Nations, after a careful seven-year drafting period. It provides that:

> The territory of a state shall not be the object of acquisition by another state resulting from the threat or use of force. No territorial acquisition resulting from the threat or use of force shall be recognized as legal.[28]

The 1974 Resolution is perhaps couched in narrower terms,[29] but its language is equally apposite to the Timor situation as characterized by the Security Council[30] and the General Assembly[31]:

> No territorial acquisition or special advantage resulting from aggression shall be recognized as lawful.[32]

This language is rather blunt and has an obligatory ring about it. One might have thought just from reading it that it carried some obligations with it, moral or even legal. Note the mandatory sounding 'shall' in a context where less imperative requirements of the Friendly Relations instrument use the softer 'should'. Indeed, bearing in mind that the Australian government was represented on, and participated actively in, the committee that drafted the 1970 Resolution, and was a co-sponsor when the draft reached the General Assembly itself, one might have expected some embarrassment in ignoring it. But no, Senator Gareth Evans, a former law lecturer and presently Minister for Foreign Affairs and Trade, has on several occasions denied the relevance of the Friendly Principles resolution. In response to a question from Senator McIntosh in the Australian Senate on 20 March 1986 he claimed that: 'I make it plain that the legal status of [the Friendly Relations] declaration, which is not a treaty in any sense, has long been very hotly contested.'[33] In the Senate on 1 November 1989, he said, repeating much of the language that he had used in 1986:

> ...[W]e have taken the view since 1979 that whatever the unhappy circumstances and indeed, possible illegality, surrounding Indonesia's acquisition of East Timor in the mid-1970s, Indonesian sovereignty over that territory should be accepted not only on a de factor [sic] but on a de jure basis. There is no binding legal obligation not to recognise the acquisition of a territory that was acquired by force. Such a recognition does not, of

*course, imply approval of the circumstances of the acquisition. In interna-
tional law the legality of the original acquisition of territory by a state has
to be distinguished in subsequent dealings between the state acquiring that
new territory and other states – in this instance, Australia.*[34]

More recently, on 3 November 1990,[35] he added that '[t]his recognition does not mean that Australia condones the method of incorporation
– on the contrary, the Government has been forthright in protesting the
circumstances of incorporation.'[36] I believe that the Senator is totally
wrong on three fronts: he is wrong about the status of the Declaration
being hotly contested; he is wrong about there being no legal obligation
to comply with its requirement of non-recognition; and he is wrong in
suggesting that his government has paid its international dues once it 'has
been forthright in protesting the circumstances of incorporation'. It has
an obligation to go beyond that. (No doubt there are those who dispute
the forthrightness of the Australian protests!)

First, some discussion of the nature of General Assembly resolutions
and their role in the creation of international law in general is necessary.
Then it will be possible to say something about the two 'non-recognition'
resolutions in particular. One starting point is clear. An effort during the
drafting of the Charter to give the General Assembly a broad legislative
power failed.[37] Moreover, Article 38 of the Statute of the International
Court of Justice, which describes 'international law' at least for the purposes of the jurisdiction of the Court and is widely regarded as useful
more generally,[38] makes no reference to resolutions of international organizations amongst its 'sources' of law. Article 13 of the United Nations
Charter does, however, empower the General Assembly to 'initiate studies and make recommendations for the purpose of…encouraging the
progressive development of international law and its codification'. And
Article 38 lists among its sources 'international custom, as evidence of a
general practice accepted by law.' Customary law is said to comprise two
elements, state practice and some indication that the practice is regarded
by states as being legally obligatory rather than just coincidentally con-
cordant.[39] Since this second element partakes of some of the alchemist's
art, it is usual to describe it in Latin as *opinio juris*, in the hope that this
will sound more convincing. Traditionally (say before the latter part of
the nineteenth century and the rise of international organizations), most
state practice and expression of *opinio* took place in a bilateral setting. But
all that has changed, particularly with the dramatic alteration in the
nature of diplomacy wrought by the birth of the United Nations (1945)
and the membership in it of many new nations. Now much more
activity is multilateral.

Against this backdrop, assume that all the states of the United Nations (or even most of them) were to behave in a particular way, in pursuance of Article 13 of the Charter, by adopting a resolution espousing a particular point of international law, and that they were to express their *opinio juris* in that resolution, expressly or impliedly.[40] It must be the case that in some such situations this will pass muster as a contributor to custom, perhaps even a definitive contributor.[41] Suppose further that all of the parties to an international treaty, say the Charter of the United Nations, sit down and adopt fairly detailed rules spelling out the details of some of the general principles contained in the Charter. Might not this be fairly assimilated to the treaty itself?[42] Here, then, are two ways in which *some* resolutions, at least widely accepted ones might become 'law' – either as custom or as an authentic interpretation of the Charter. With these thoughts in mind, let me return to the Friendly Relations Declaration, a document which asserts that it is concerned with the 'progressive development' and 'codification' of the principles addressed therein.[43]

To take first the matter of 'hot contest' of the status of the Declaration. I have searched the literature in vain for this hot debate. We do not have the benefit of Senator Evans's sources for his assertion.[44] I thought that the obvious place to look was to see whether the Australian representatives involved in drafting the Declaration had placed some specific reservations about the whole exercise – or some substantial part of it – on the record. This was, however, not the case. The Australian representative on the Special Committee of 31 states that did the drafting stated on 1 May 1970 that 'his delegation was pleased at the progress reflected in the draft declaration and paid a tribute to those who had contributed to its production. The task of the Committee had not been to amend the Charter but, in accordance with Article 13 [of the Charter], to elaborate some of its most important principles for the purpose of encouraging the progressive development and codification of international law.'[45] He also made some remarks that must, in part at least,[46] have been aimed at Indonesia for its 'Confrontation' (*Konfrontasi*) against Malaysia 1963–6 in which it used guerrilla tactics to further territorial claims, efforts that Australia helped to overcome:

> The inclusion in the principle on the non-use of force of a paragraph stating that States had a duty to refrain from organizing or encouraging the organization of any form of irregular forces or armed bands was essential. So too, were references to the prohibition on organizing or participating in actions of civil strife in another State. These activities were unfortunately present in the area of which Australia formed a part, namely in South East Asia, and were a breach of Article 2 (4) of the Charter.[47]

In this statement, the representative seems to be supporting the proposition (which does not seem to be disputed) that this part of the Declaration amounted to a spelling out of the broad generalities of Article 2, paragraph 4 of the Charter. He also, however, addressed himself in a vague way to the role of General Assembly resolutions more generally in creating international law. Singling out the sixteenth preambular paragraph of the Declaration,[48] he said:

> On preambular paragraph 16, the Australian view was that General Assembly resolutions were recommendatory and not binding upon Member States. Resolutions of the General Assembly could therefore play on [sic. only?] a limited role in relation to the interpretation of the declaration [author's emphasis]. There would be different ideas about which resolutions, or parts thereof, were relevant, and in any case they could not be understood as overriding or amending provisions of the Charter.[49]

This is hardly a vigorous attack on the legal status of the Declaration. It is addressed to the role of *other* instruments in interpreting the Declaration. Indeed, the statement seems to concede that the Declaration has some status but is aimed at preventing the Declaration from bootstrapping up some other (unnamed and perhaps unknown) resolutions that the representative feared might surface to cause trouble. The argument goes to weight and relevance in particular cases and refers to other resolutions, not to the Declaration. And of course it is right. Some resolutions simply do not command the respect that the Friendly Relations one does and give less support to a law-making argument.

As vigour goes, however, it seems to have been the most vigorous assertion in the debates. A leading commentator on the Declaration is Robert Rosenstock, Adviser on Legal Affairs to the United States Mission to the United Nations, not a bold proponent of the law-making power of General Assembly resolutions. He makes the following comment, worth quoting at some length:

> There is some difference of opinion among Members of the United Nations as to whether the Declaration represents a mere recommendation[50] or a statement of binding legal rules. The truth would appear to lie somewhere between these two extremes, but closer to the latter. Two considerations point to the more limited view as to the effect of the adoption of the text on the state of international law. The first is that there is no difference in United Nations practice between the term 'declaration' and 'recommendation'. Secondly, statements accepted by the San Francisco Conference limit to some extent the efficacy of efforts at interpretation other than

through the amendment route. The principles involved, however, are acknowledged by all to be principles of the Charter. By accepting the respective texts, states have acknowledged that the principles represent their interpretations of the obligations of the Charter. The use of 'should' rather than 'shall' in those instances in which the Committee believed it was speaking de lege ferenda *or stating mere* desiderata *further supports the view that the states involved intended to assert binding rules of law where they used language of firm obligation.*[51]

Perhaps I was clutching at straws in an attempt to make Senator Evans's case. In any event, the death knell to the Evans argument about a hot contest − to say nothing of the legal status of the Declaration − is surely sounded by the decision of the International Court of Justice in the 'Case Concerning Military and Paramilitary Activities In and Against Nicaragua'.[52] That case concerned the United States support of the *contras* who were fighting against the Nicaraguan government. Because of the jurisdictional stance of the case,[53] Nicaragua was not able to rely on arguments based on Article 2, paragraph 4 of the United Nations Charter and analogous provisions of the Organization of American States (OAS) Charter. Nicaragua was therefore constrained to make a customary law argument based in substantial part on the Declaration on Friendly Relations. After noting that both Nicaragua and the United States had accepted the treaty obligation to refrain from the use of force contained in Article 2, paragraph 4, the Court continued:

The Court has however to be satisfied that there exists in customary international law an opinio juris *as to the binding character of such abstention. This* opinio juris *may, though with all due caution, be deduced from,* inter alia, *the attitude of the Parties and the attitude of States towards certain General Assembly resolutions, and particularly resolution 2625 (XXV) entitled 'Declaration on Principles on International Law concerning Friendly Relations and Co-operation among States in accordance with the Charter of the United Nations'. The effect of consent to the text of such resolutions cannot be understood as merely that of a 'reiteration or elucidation' of the treaty commitment undertaken in the Charter. On the contrary,* it may be understood as an acceptance of the validity of the rule or set of rules declared by the resolution by themselves *[author's emphasis].*[54]

In short, Senator Evans's argument that the legal status of the Declaration on Friendly Relations is hotly contested is a shaky one. In fact, there is strong authority that it represents a legal obligation. In the Nicaragua case, the Court was, of course, addressing itself to the basic rule on the non-use of force, rather than the corollary about the non-recognition of the fruits of illegal force. But the 1970 formulation came as a package and I can find no statements anywhere to the effect that some parts of the package are less obligatory than others.

Needless to say – and the reasoning of the International Court of Justice seems to proceed on this basis[55] – the Friendly Relations Declaration's rule of non-recognition hardly made its first appearance in 1970 from nowhere. At most, the 1970 declaration put the seal on a development in international law that had been occurring over a half century.[56] Some have traced the doctrine back to Article 10 of the League of Nations Covenant;[57] some to the Kellogg–Briand Pact (1928) under which the parties renounced war as an instrument of national policy in their relations with one another.[58] Others emphasize Article 2, paragraph 4 of the United Nations Charter.[59] I would certainly rely upon the cumulative effect of much reiteration of the doctrine. Robert Langer asserted the existence of a legal obligation not to recognize territorial changes effected by force in his classic 1947 work on seizure of territory.[60] Ian Brownlie espoused a similar position in 1963.[61] Nor is the rule a dead letter in subsequent United Nations practice. In one of its resolutions on Iraq's 1990 invasion of Kuwait the Security Council insisted that 'annexation of Kuwait by Iraq under any form and whatever pretext has no legal validity, and is considered null and void'. It called upon all states and international organizations, moreover, 'not to recognize that annexation, and to refrain from any action or dealing that might be interpreted as an indirect recognition of the annexation'.[62]

Not wishing to belabour the point, I merely note that the repetition of the principle of non-recognition in the Resolution on Definition of Aggression in 1974[63] demonstrates no hot contest either. I have found no statements by Australia – or anyone else – disassociating themselves from it. Australia was a member of the Committee that laboured for seven years on the drafting and co-sponsored the resolution when it was adopted by a unanimous General Assembly.[64] The relevant language of the Definition of Aggression is written in equally mandatory terms to the 1970 formulation, even if its field of application is arguably narrower in ways not relevant in the present context.[65]

To summarize, the Australian government had an international obligation not to recognize Indonesia's forcible acquisition of the territory of East Timor.[66] Merely being 'forthright in protesting the circumstances of incorporation'[67] is not enough.

One might reasonably ask how I think Australia might have behaved differently. Plainly, from what I have said elsewhere about the utter illegality of the Indonesian position,[68] I think that the principled position for

Australia to have taken was to refuse to deal with the Indonesians, even if this meant that the boundaries would not be delimited and the area in question would remain, for the foreseeable future, unexploited. There is nothing obviously objectionable about leaving resources untapped for reasons of principle – consider the case of Antarctica, for instance, in respect of which Australia has played a leading protective role.

But let me, for the purposes of argument only, concede what I believe is the kernel of the Australian position: at some point it is necessary to 'get on with it' and accept that the Indonesians are in control and that they have to be dealt with to some degree. There is, indeed, some force to the argument thus stated. Assume, for instance, that it is necessary to deal with the Indonesians to make humanitarian arrangements for refugees; assume that a question arises in an Australian court or even in an international tribunal about the validity of a marriage (or divorce) or the registration of a birth performed by Indonesian authorities in East Timor after the takeover. It is probably the case that some exceptions to the general rule will be made. The hard question is where to draw the lines.[69] The Advisory Opinion of the International Court of Justice on Namibia, a comparable case of illegal occupation, indicates that such exceptions must be narrowly drawn.[70]

How might that line of reasoning apply to the Timor Gap? I suggest that at the very least it indicates that if some treaty arrangement has to be made, it must be one which itself asserts the basic non-recognition point and reserves a position on it. Apparently no attempt was made to do this. The Australian authorities conceded from early in the negotiations that dealing with the Indonesians on the issue required that they accept and recognize Indonesian sovereignty *de jure*.[71] Yet why should this be so? And where is the authority for this position in international law? Surely it is not beyond the wit of the diplomatic mind to say something like, 'I am dealing with you because necessity demands, but I do not thereby concede your legitimacy'. The case for asserting that the act of entering the deal amounts to recognition is stronger when the completed treaty is signed or ratified, and this one certainly concedes the Indonesian position. But did it need to? Indeed, the Indonesians apparently went out of their way to rub the Australian negotiators' noses in the Indonesian position. Note the title of the Treaty: it refers to 'An Area Between *the Indonesian Province of East Timor* and Northern Australia' (author's emphasis). If Australia objects to the mode of incorporation, why not insist all along on a formula such as 'the territory currently under the *de facto* control of Indonesia'[72] or something of that ilk. I am certainly not privy to any departmental material on the drafting history of the Timor Gap Treaty, but it does seem to me that the Australian negotiators fell

over themselves to accommodate the Indonesian position on incorporation right from the start. Even accepting their premise that some deal had
to be cut, I am not persuaded that it was lawful to cut one that gives away
so much on the recognition point.[73]

Moreover, when the Treaty shares out the proceeds of exploitation of
the area, why did Australia not insist on putting some of its share -
Indonesia's too – in a trust fund for the people of East Timor? In a 1990
speech, Senator Evans commented that the Australian recognition of the
Indonesian incorporation means that 'Australia has been able to work
together constructively and effectively with the Indonesian authorities in
improving the economic situation of the people of East Timor'.[74] I take it
that this is not a contention that the profits from the exploitation of the
area will flow – or even trickle – inexorably down to the people of
Timor as a matter of treaty obligation, although some may in practice. It
is true that the Treaty refers to the desire of the governments to 'cooper-
ate further for the mutual benefit of their peoples in the development of
the resources of the area'[75] and to 'taking appropriate measures to ensure
that preference is given in employment in Area A to nationals and permanent residents of Australia and the Republic of Indonesia.'[76] But
'Indonesia' here probably means 'Jakarta' – there is not a word in it about
anything for the people of Timor. Why should not one or both of the
parties to the Treaty be earmarking some of the proceeds for the people
of East Timor?

The Treaty is Null and Void

I come then to the point that the Timor Gap Treaty may be regarded as a
nullity under international law. Now there is a fairly fundamental assumption, but I think a correct one, in what follows. It is that if Australia and
the legitimate sovereign over East Timor were to embark on a judicial or
arbitral delimitation of the three areas,[77] it is unlikely that Australia would
be held to be entitled to the whole of areas A, B, and C. My guess is that
it would succeed in respect of Area B and some, but not all, of Area A and
probably none of Area C. If it were to win in respect of all three areas, my
argument about recognition, while it would be applicable to the actual
territory of East Timor, would be irrelevant in respect of territory that by
virtue of the delimitation would belong to Australia. Australia is presumably entitled to give away some of its own resources to its good neighbour. My contention of course is that, far from giving away its own
resources, it is engaged with an aggressor in sharing out somebody else's.
The Timor Gap Treaty, in some significant part at least, shares resources
obtained by aggression, even if, in the absence of a final delimitation, one
cannot be sure exactly which part this is.

There are at least two lines of argument why I believe this effort to be null and void. I shall call them the 'nemo dat' and 'jus cogens' arguments. They both lead inexorably to the same conclusion.

Nemo dat quod non habet

Ian Brownlie in his leading text on public international law notes that the maxim *nemo dat quod non habet*, the principle that you cannot give a better title than you have, is a 'familiar feature of English commercial law, and the principle which the maxim represents is undoubtedly a part of international law.'[78] A domestic law analogy helps to grasp the point. I buy your car from a thief. You find me in possession of it. You are entitled to it back and I am left with trying to get my purchase price back from the thief. This is true whether I know or do not know of the circumstances of the thief's acquisition. The thief gets no title and I cannot get a good title through the thief. Notice that in domestic law my legal problems get potentially worse, much worse, if it can be shown that I know of the thief's thievery. Then I may be a receiver of stolen property or an accessory after the fact. I would thus be liable to criminal sanctions as well as being liable to suit in tort or delict.[79] Australia seems to be in this worse position since it has known the circumstances all along. But it does not seem necessary to pursue the argument that far. On any theory, it cannot get a good title through the bad Indonesian one.

Jus cogens

The alternative argument[80] is the jus cogens one. Article 53 of the Vienna Convention on the Law of Treaties (a treaty to which Australia acceded without reservation in 1974) provides for what it calls Treaties Conflicting with a Peremptory Norm of General International Law (Jus Cogens):

> *A treaty is void if, at the time of its conclusion, it conflicts with a peremptory norm of general international law. For the purposes of the present Convention, a peremptory norm of general international law is a norm accepted and recognized by the international community of States as a whole as a norm from which no derogation is permitted and which can be modified only by a subsequent norm of general international law having the same character.*[81]

The exact scope of Article 53 is disputed, notably the categories of breaches of international law to which it applies. One thing though is striking: the basic Charter/Friendly Relations Declaration rule proscribing the use of force is on every significant commentator's agreed list of what are the jus cogens norms, starting with the Commentary by the International Law Commission which drafted the Convention.[82]

If Australia were to enter into an arrangement with Indonesia to jointly invade and take over the territory of East Timor, that agreement would clearly be void under the peremptory norm doctrine. I think the logic of the argument is that the same result follows if the territory is shared out after the invasion, even if Australia had completely clean hands at the point of conquest.

Conclusion

Now the way in which Australia has tried to avoid the application of one or other of the 'nemo dat' or 'jus cogens' arguments is by suggesting that its recognition of Indonesian title gets it off the hook. This will simply not work, for the reasons I suggested earlier in the paper. The sleight of hand in trying to avoid the problem by 'recognizing' Indonesia's title will not work under the modern international law which Australia itself helped to create. The recognition itself is void!

Notes

1 This is a revised version of a paper delivered by Professor Clark at the East Timor Conference, St. Antony's College, Oxford, 8 December 1990. It first appeared in [1992] *Pace Yearbook of International Law*, p. 69, and is reprinted here with permission. Many of the issues discussed herein are canvassed in the context of Australian law in a lawsuit filed in the High Court of Australia at Melbourne, No. M88 of 1993, *Horta* v. *The Commonwealth of Australia*. That case, which seeks to have the Timor Gap Treaty declared void by the High Court, was thrown out in late Aug. 1994. The present discussion considers international legal issues and does not deal with the particular problems presented by Australian domestic law.

2 *Frente Revolucionária de Timor-Leste Independente*.

3 See generally Roger Clark, 'The "Decolonization" of East Timor and the United Nations Norms on Self-Determination and Aggression', *Yale Journal of World Public Order* 7(1) (1980), p. 2.

4 GA Res. 3485 (XXX), 30 U.N. GAOR, Supp. (No. 34) 118, UN Doc. A/10034 (1976); SC Res. 384, 30 UN ESCOR, *Resolutions and Decisions* 10, UN Doc. S/Res/384 (1975).

5 Although the matter refuses to go away. Note the widespread coverage of the 12 November 1991 massacre by Indonesian troops in Dili, the capital of East Timor. See, for example, Alan Nairn, 'The Talk of the Town: Notes and Comment', *The New Yorker* (9 December 1991), p. 41.

6 In July 1976, Indonesia purported to annex the territory. The General Assembly rejected this claim, inasmuch as the people of the territory had been prevented from freely exercising their right to self-determination. GA Res. 31/53, 31 UN GAOR, Supp. (No. 39) 125, UN Doc. A/31/39 (1976).

7 On the area and its potential resources, see Mark Valencia, *Southeast Asian Seas: Oil Under Troubled Waters. Hydrocarbon Potential, Jurisdictional Issues, and International Relations*. Singapore and Oxford: Oxford University Press, 1985, Chapter 2. See also Note 15 below.

8 449 UN.TS 311. Art. 6 (1) provides:
'Where the same continental shelf is adjacent to the territories of two or more States whose coasts are opposite to each other, the boundary of the continental shelf appertaining to such States shall be determined by agreement between them. In the absence of such agreement, and unless another boundary line is justified by special circumstances, the boundary is the median line, every point of which is equidistant from the nearest points of the baselines from which the breadth of the territorial sea of each State is measured.'

9 Australia would argue that there are two shelves – not one that is the 'same'. Portugal would argue for the equidistance rule. Contemporaneously with an Application to the International Court of Justice concerning the Timor Gap Treaty, (see below, note 21), Portugal insisted that Australia continue efforts to negotiate a delimitation of the shelf with Portugal by application of the 1958 Convention. See Letter handed on 22 February 1991 to the Minister of Foreign Affairs of Australia by the Ambassador of Portugal at Canberra, in UN Doc. A/46/97 (1991).

10 UN Doc. A/CONF. 62/122 (1982). Art. 83's 'non-rule' on the subject provides that *'The delimitation of the continental shelf between States with opposite or adjacent coasts shall be effected by agreement on the basis of international law, as referred to in Article 38 of the Statute of the International Court of Justice, in order to achieve an equitable solution.'* And see the extended definition of the shelf in Art. 76 (1): *'…or to a distance of 200 nautical miles from the baselines from which the breadth of the territorial sea is measured where the outer edge of the continental margin does not extend up to that distance'*.

11 Indonesia lays general claim to a 200 mile EEZ. Arts 56 and 57 of the 1982 Convention appear to permit claims to be made over the sea-bed in an exclusive economic zone (EEZ) of up to 200 nautical miles regardless of the shape of the shelf. They may well supersede some of the earlier legal notions of the continental shelf, but it is all very uncertain.

12 See 'Case Concerning the Continental Shelf, Libyan Arab Jamahiriya/Malta', [1985] I.C.J.6,56: *'Each coastal State is enti-*

tled to exercise sovereign rights over the continental shelf off its coasts for the purpose of exploiting its natural resource…up to a distance of 200 miles from the baselines – subject, of course, to delimitation with neighbouring States – whatever the geophysical or geological features of the sea-bed within the area comprised between the coast and the 200-mile limit'. But see the separate opinions of Judges Sette-Camara at 61–2, and Valticos at 105. They perhaps see the Timor Trough as exceptional, although their argument is obviously influenced by viewing the 1971–2 Indonesian-Australian agreements as state practice, practice, as it turns out, Indonesia came to regret.

13 See *International Legal Materials* 10 (1971), p. 830; *International Legal Materials* 11 (1972), p. 1272; *International Legal Materials* 12 (1973), p. 357.

14 The Treaty is reproduced in *International Legal Materials*, **29** (1990), p. 469.

15 The exploitation is now continuing apace, notwithstanding the uncertainties caused by the Portuguese case (see below, note 21). On 12 December 1991 the Australian Federal Minister for Resources announced that eleven production sharing contracts with oil companies had been approved for exploration in Area A of the Zone of Cooperation, see *Media Release*, [Australian] Minister for Resources, DPIE91/320G. On 4 March 1994 Australian Resources Minister, David Beddall, announced the discovery of oil in the Australian zone (Area B) of the Timor Gap, see *Summary of World Broadcasts*, FE 1940/B1, 8 March 1994. Twenty-three more wells are due to be drilled by Australia in 1994 alone. According to another report, 'Timor Sea exploration has turned up a hefty oil flow in the Australian-Indonesian Zone of Cooperation Area A', see 'Timor Sea Exploration Yields 5,800 b/d Oil Flow', *Oil & Gas Journal*, (7 March 1994), p. 30.

16 See first preambular paragraph and Article 33 of the Treaty. 'Provisional' is defined therein to mean a minimum of forty years, subject to renewal for 20 year periods. According to a note issued by the Australian Department of Foreign Affairs

and Trade in January 1990, 'Australia continues to assert sovereign rights over the seabed extending to the geomorphological edge of the natural prolongation of Australia's continental shelf, marked by the Timor Trough, i.e. slightly to the north of the Zone of Cooperation'.

17 Onorato, W.T. and M.J. Valencia, 'International Cooperation for Petroleum Development: The Timor Gap Treaty', *Foreign Investment Law Journal* (International Centre for Settlement of Investment Disputes), **5**(1) (Spring 1990), p. 5, describe the zone thus:
The Zone is delineated on the northern side by a simplified bathymetric axis line; on the southern side by a 200 [nautical mile] line measured from the Indonesian archipelagic baselines; on the eastern and western sides by equidistant lines. Thus both States conceded the extreme boundary claims of the other and presumably the principles on which they were based. These equidistant lines are determined by the former relationships between the coasts of Indonesia and Portuguese Timor. The northern limit of the coffin-shaped Zone is a simplified line marking the axis of the Timor Trough. The southern limit lies 200 [nautical miles] from the coast of Timor. The two other intermediate lines that separate the three areas are a straight line in the general vicinity of the 1,500 meter isobath and median lines between Australian and Indonesian territories.'

18 See, for example, Letter dated 10 November 1988 from the Permanent Representative of Portugal to the Chairman of the Special Committee on Decolonization, UN Doc. A/AC.109/981 (1989).

19 See my 'Submissions to the Senate Standing Committee on Foreign Affairs and Defence (Reference: East Timor)', Commonwealth of Australia, *Official Hansard Report* (1982), pp. 1388, 1400; Letter to Gordon McIntosh, Senator for Western Australia, 27 February 1986. I was assisted in honing my views by exchanges with Sasha S. Stepan during the writing of her excellent monograph entitled, *Credibility Gap: Australia and the Timor Gap Treaty*, ACFOA Development Dossier No. 28, Canberra: Australian Council for Overseas Aid, 1990. See also John Pilger, *Distant Voices*, London: Vintage, rev. ed 1994,

p. 312; Mark Aarons, and Robert Domm, *East Timor. A Western Made Tragedy*, Sydney: The Left Book Club, 1992, p. 77.

20 It is not my purpose here to criticize the details of the arrangements. Were the Treaty validly entered into with a party which – unlike Indonesia – had legitimate status to strike the deal, it would certainly seem to be a creative solution to an awkward delimitation problem. See generally, Onorato and Valencia (note 17 above). Here, however, I am interested in the legitimacy of the whole enterprise. On principles of delimitation in such cases, see generally Catriona Cook, 'The Australia–Indonesia Maritime Boundary', Occasional Papers in Maritime Affairs No. 3, Canberra: Australian Centre for Maritime Studies, 1985, p. 40. On the Treaty, see also E. Willheim, 'Australia–Indonesia Sea-Bed Boundary Negotiations: Proposals for a Joint Development Zone in the "Timor Gap"', *Natural Resources Journal,* **29** (3), 1989, p. 821 (which contains some useful maps); A. Smart, 'Timor Gap Zone of Cooperation', *The APEA (Australian Petroleum Exploration Association) Journal* (1990), p. 368; K. Suter, 'Oil in Troubled Waters', *Inside Indonesia* (December 1988), p. 7; H. Burmester, 'The Timor Gap Treaty', *Australian Mining and Petroleum Association Yearbook* (1990), p. 233 (and several commentaries on the Burmester piece in that volume); K. Livesley, 'The Timor Gap Treaty – An Update', *Australian Mining and Petroleum Law Association Bulletin*, **10** (1991), p. 213; G. Moloney, 'Australian–Indonesian Timor Gap Zone of Cooperation Treaty: A New Offshore Petroleum Regime', *Journal of Energy and Natural Resources Law*, **8** (1990), p. 128; A. Bergin 'The Australian–Indonesian Timor Gap Maritime Boundary Agreement', *International Journal of Estuarine and Coastal Law*, **5** (199), p. 383.

21 As in a case brought by Portugal, or some time in the future by an independent East Timor. Litigating all the issues is complicated since, while Australia and Portugal have made declarations accepting the jurisdiction of the Court, Indonesia has not. Portugal, in fact, instituted proceedings against Australia in the International Court

on 22 February 1991, making a somewhat different case than mine. As of August 1994 Portugal's Application was public, but neither its initial Memorial nor that of Australia are. It did not appear that the case would be set down for oral argument in the Court before early 1995. In the way in which it has presented the issue in its Application, Portugal does not apparently need to assert the invalidity of the Timor Gap Treaty or to stress the duty not to recognize the acquisition of territory obtained by force. Instead, it emphasizes Australia's obligation not to act contrary to the duties of Portugal as administering power, and the interests of the people of the territory. Para. 1 of the Application reads:

'1. The dispute relates to the opposability to Australia:

(a) of the duties of, and delegation of authority to, Portugal as the administering Power of the Territory of East Timor; and

(b) of the right of the people of East Timor to self-determination, and the related rights (right to territorial integrity and unity and permanent sovereignty over natural wealth and resources).

Portugal maintains that, in its capacity of administering Power within the meaning of Article 73 of the Charter, it is performing an international public service and that, so long as the United Nations has not discharged it from its responsibility, it is invested with the corresponding duties and powers, which continue to be opposable, as do the rights of the people of East Timor, erga omnes, and in particular to all the member States of the United Nations and hence to Australia.

2. The dispute has arisen from the actions, recounted below, by which Australia has, in the view of Portugal, failed to observe, at least, the obligation to respect the duties and powers of the administering Power as mentioned in the preceding paragraph, the right of the people of East Timor to self-determination and the related rights, and Article 25 of the Charter; Australia by so doing has incurred international responsibility vis-à-vis both the people of East Timor and Portugal.

Those activities, shortly stated, have taken the form of the negotiation and conclusion by Australia with a third State of an agreement relating to the exploration and exploitation of the continental shelf in the area of the 'Timor Gap' and the negotiation, currently in progress,

of the delimitation of that same shelf with that same third State.'

Presumably, in spite of this effort to draft the pleadings in such a way as to emphasize Australia's breaches of international law rather than those of Indonesia, Australia will argue some variations on the theme that Indonesia is an indispensable party in the proceedings which should not, therefore, go forward to the merits. See generally I. Scobbie, 'The East Timor Case. The Implications of Procedure for Litigation Strategy', *Oil and Gas Law and Taxation Review,* **273** (1991). I have speculated about the Portugal/Australia case in 'Presentation by Professor Roger S. Clark concerning the substance of the East Timor case in the International Court of Justice, CIIR/IPJET Conference, London 5–6 December 1992' (manuscript available from the author).

22 See above, note 3. See also the excellent analysis in Paula Escarameia, *Formation of Concepts Under International Law: Subsumption Under Self-Determination in the Case of East Timor.* Lisbon: Fundação Oriente, 1993.

23 As the Department of Foreign Affairs and Trade put it (*op. cit.*, note 16), '[t]his recognition in no way implies approval of the circumstances of acquisition'. And see the comments of Minister of Foreign Affairs and Trade at note 34 below.

24 New Zealand diplomatic material on East Timor between 1975 and 1994, released in July 1994 to Member of Parliament, Phil Goff, pursuant to the Official Information Act, highlights the way in which New Zealand officials have emphasized the 'bilateral relationship' with Indonesia at the expense of principle. The only time a hint of outrage creeps into the cable traffic is when a New Zealand citizen was killed in the 12 November 1991 Dili massacre.

25 'Reflected' is chosen deliberately. See below, note 56.

26 GA Res. 2625 (XXV), 25 UN GAOR, Supp. (No. 28), UN Doc. A/8028 (1970).

27 GA Res. 3314, 29 UN GAOR, Supp. (No. 31) 142, UN Doc. A/9631 (1974).

28 'Declaration of Principles on Friendly Relations', *op. cit.*, note 26. The paragraphs are not numbered in this resolution.

29 The 1970 Resolution speaks of 'threat or use of force' while the 1974 one speaks of 'aggression'. In the context of the territories occupied by Israel, debate has been joined about whether territory can be properly acquired following a *lawful* use of force – as in self-defence. See, for example, M. Halberstam, 'Recognition, Use of Force and the Legal Effect of United Nations Resolutions Under the Revised Restatement of the Foreign Relations Law of the United States', *Israel Law Review,* **19** (1984), p. 495; John Dugard, *Recognition and the United Nations.* Cambridge: Grotius Publications, 1987, p.156. Dugard goes so far as to contend that even acquisition following lawful force is contrary to principles of *jus cogens* (see notes 80–2 below). It is not necessary to pursue this line of debate since the Indonesian actions come within the core meaning of *unlawful* force condemned by both resolutions.

30 In its resolutions calling for the withdrawal of Indonesian forces, SC Res. 384, 30 UN SCOR, Resolutions and Decisions 10, UN Doc. S/Res/384 (1975) and SC Res. 389, 31 SCOR, Resolutions and Decisions 18, UN Doc. S/Res/389 (1976).

31 In its resolution GA Res. 3485 (XXX), 30 UN GAOR, Supp. (No. 34) 118, UN Doc. A/10034 (1975).

32 'Definition of Aggression', *op. cit.*, note 27, Art. 5, para. 3.

33 *Hansard, Senate,* 20 March 1986, p. 1377.

34 *Hansard, Senate,* 1 November 1989, p. 2702. I am puzzled by the last sentence (which also appears almost verbatim in other statements by the Minister). The way 'distinguished' is used, it seems to suggest that the legality of the acquisition (why 'original acquisition'?) is to be distinguished from something else but the fragment of the sentence that explains the something else has not been included. I take it that the something else is the way other states treat the title in later dealings. If this is what it means, then this sentence is a restatement of the basic point that there is no obligation to deny recognition to title acquired by what the recognizer acknowledges to be illegal force. This is the point that I dissent from in the text. If it means something different and is a distinct argument, I have missed it.

35 'Statement by Senator Gareth Evans to Timor Gap Forum, Darwin, 3 November 1990', p. 3 (on file with the author).

36 In light of this statement, which is part of a consistent pattern of Australian statements, Australia is surely precluded from now arguing that, contrary to the assessment of others, what the Indonesians did was perfectly legitimate. Had Australia from the start argued that the incorporation was legal, it could now, at least as a rhetorical posture, tough out the contrary assessment of others (including a majority of the General Assembly) and argue that, on the facts as Australia sees it, the norm of non-recognition does not apply. My position is simply that a state like Australia, acting in good faith *on the basis of its own assessment of the facts*, must apply the rule of non-recognition. Because of the clarity of the facts, Senator Evans has found it necessary to try to take the high ground and deny the legal status of the obligation.

37 A proposal to this effect (subject to further approval by a majority vote in the Security Council) by the Philippines was rejected 26–1 in Commission II at the 1945 San Francisco Conference, see *UNCIO Docs.* **9** (1945), p. 316.

38 Note the reference to it in Art. 83 of the 1982 Convention on the Law of the Sea, see above, note 10.

39 See generally Clive Parry, *The Sources and Evidences of International Law.* Manchester: Manchester University Press, 1965.

40 Article 13 of the Charter speaks both of 'progressive development' and of 'codification'. Where a rule is in the fluid stage reasonable people might differ about whether its clarification amounts to mere codification or whether more is being done to develop it. My point about the Friendly Relations Declaration is that whether it codified or developed does not particularly matter. Whichever, development was complete by then.

ROGER S. CLARK

41 See R. Falk, 'On the Quasi-Legislative
Competence of the General Assembly',
American Journal of International Law, **60**
(1966), p. 782; and see generally American
Law Institute, *Restatement of the Law Third,
The Foreign Relations Law of the United
States*, (St Paul: American Law Institute,
1987), Section 102, Comments b and c
and Reporters' Note 2, and authorities
there cited espousing the basic view suggested in the text.

42 Unlike some constitutions that grant a
power to make definitive interpretations of
the constitution to a particular organ of
government – typically the US Supreme
Court – the Charter is silent on who has
the final power of interpretation. This
means that, in the first instance at least, the
General Assembly can make its own determination, see United Nations Conference
on International Organization, Report of
Rapporteur of Committee IV/2, San
Francisco 1945, excerpted in Frederic
Kirgis, *International Organizations in their
Legal Setting*. St Paul: West Publishing Co.,
2nd edn. 1993, p. 482. If an organ such as
the Assembly asks the Court for advice,
the Court at least gives considerable
weight to what the organ has done in the
past. See 'Advisory Opinion on Legal
Consequences for States of the Continued
Presence of South Africa in Namibia
(South West Africa) Notwithstanding
Security Council Resolution 276 (1970)',
[1971] ICJ 16.

43 See the Declaration, note 26 above,
preambular para. 17.

44 It is believed that Professor Don Greig
of the Australian National University gave
the Government some unpublished advice
on the matter. Efforts by a Member of the
Australian House of Representatives,
Laurie Ferguson, to obtain a copy of that
advice were rebuffed. After some discussion about the benefits of the treaty for
Australia 'in terms of strengthening our ties
with an important regional neighbour and
providing an interim solution to a maritime boundary dispute', the departmental
response continued: 'You will appreciate
therefore that it is Government policy not
to make public any confidential and privileged legal advice which may have been
prepared in relation to the treaty. The

release of such material would be contrary
to the national interests which the
Government is seeking to promote'. Letter
from Department of Foreign Affairs and
Trade to Laurie Ferguson, Member for
Reid, dated 6 September 1990.

45 Report of the Special Committee on
Principles of International Law concerning
Friendly Relations and Co-operation
among States, 25 UN GAOR, Supp. (No.
18) at 104, UN Doc. A/8018 (1970).

46 The remarks may also have been
prompted in part by Australia's position in
the Vietnam War (1963-73).

47 See above, note 45.

48 See above, note 26. '*Considering* the
provisions of the Charter as a whole and
taking into account the role of relevant
resolutions adopted by the competent
organs of the United Nations relating to
the content of the principles.'

49 *Op. cit.*, note 26 above (author's
emphasis). It appears from the Summary
records of the Sixth Committee of the
General Assembly that a Mr Brennan
repeated the same speech for Australia on
23 September 1970, see UN Doc.
A/C.6/SR. 1178 at 8–9 (1970).

50 Here Rosenstock cites the Brennan
statement on behalf of Australia in the
Sixth Committee, see above, note 49. In
my view it is not even as strong as
Rosenstock reads it, or even relevant since
it is addressed to *other* resolutions.

51 R. Rosenstock, 'The Declaration of
Principles of International Law
Concerning Friendly Relations: A Survey',
American Journal of International Law, **65**
(1971) p. 713, at 714–15 (footnotes omit-
ted). The Indonesian representative was at
the binding end of the spectrum. 'He
agreed with other delegations that the formulation of the seven principles *was of a
legal character* and hoped that it would
receive widespread support when it was
considered by the General Assembly.' UN
Doc. A/C.6/SR.1182 at 33 (1970) (author's
italics) (Mr Rachmad for Indonesia).

52 [1986] ICJ. 14.

53 The United States's 1946 acceptance of
the jurisdiction excepted 'disputes arising

under a multilateral treaty, unless (1) all parties to the treaty affected by the decision are also parties to the case before the Court, or (2) the United States of America specially agrees to the jurisdiction.' The Court found that El Salvador, at least, was a party 'affected', see [1986] ICJ at 38.

54 [1986] ICJ at 89–90. The Court seems to have taken for granted that there was plenty of supporting state practice and that all that remained was the *opinio* problem. The Court went on to note the expression of the same principle in the resolution of the Sixth Annual Conference of American States condemning aggression (18 February 1928), the Montevideo Convention on Rights and Duties of States (26 December 1933) and the Helsinki Accords of 1975. In context, in referring to these items, the Court was addressing the *opinio juris* of the United States which this represented. Even if the *opinio* of such acts cannot be attributed to Australia there is certainly plenty of state practice represented in such events. Australia's *opinio* is demonstrated by the Charter itself and by Resolution 2625 (XXV).

55 See above, note 54.

56 Which is why I chose the word 'reflected' earlier to describe what the 1970 resolution does with the principle – the resolution merely crystallizes what had long been developing, if not developed.

57 'The members of the League undertake to respect and preserve as against external aggression the territorial integrity and existing political independence of all the Members of the League. In case of any threat or danger of such aggression the Council should advise upon the means by which this obligation shall be fulfilled.'

58 'Treaty Providing for the Renunciation of War as an Instrument of National Policy', done at Paris, 27 August 1928.

59 'All Members shall refrain in their international relations from the threat or use of force against the territorial integrity or political independence of any state, or in any other manner inconsistent with the Purposes of the United Nations.'

60 Robert Langer, *Seizure of Territory: The Stimson Doctrine and Related Principles in*

Legal Theory and Diplomatic Practice. New York: Greenwood Press, 1947. Langer refers, as state practice, notably to the Stimson notes on Manchuria to Japan and China on 7 January 1932 and the subsequent reaffirmations of the principles therein; the Resolution of the League of Nations Assembly of 11 March 1932, also on Manchuria; the Chaco Declaration of 3 August 1932 by 19 American republics asserting non-recognition of territory obtained by conquest; the Saavedra Lamas Anti-War Treaty of 10 October 1933; and the Montevideo Convention on the Rights and Duties of States of 21 December 1933, see Langer, *Seizure*, p.95. And see his discussion of Article 10 of the Covenant of the League of Nations and attempts to either amend or interpret it (depending on your point of view) so as to assert a rule of non-recognition, Langer, *Seizure*, pp. 40–9.

61 I. Brownlie, *International Law and the Use of Force by States.* Oxford: Clarendon Press, 1963, p. 418. And see J. Crawford, *The Creation of States in International Law.* Oxford: Clarendon Press, 1979, pp. 106–7, 122–3, 418–9. Crawford speaks of a general principle that *ex injuria jus non oritur.* Much of the literature, and state practice, deals with non-recognition of the Soviet acquisition of the Baltic States. See, for example, A. Heino, 'Nonrecognition - Its Development in International Law and Application by the United States With Particular Reference to the Baltic States', PhD thesis, New York University, 1965; W. Hough, 'The Annexation of the Baltic States and its Effect on the Development of Law Prohibiting Forcible Seizure of Territory', *New York Law School Journal of International and Comparative Law,* 6 (1985), p. 301; K. Marek, *Identity and Continuity of States in Public International Law.* Geneva: Librarie Droz, 1968, pp. 398–416, 551–87. On Australia's strange Baltic behaviour, see below, note 71.

62 SC Res. 662 (1990) adopted on 9 August 1990, UN SCOR, 45th Year, Resolutions and Decisions, at 2, UN Doc. S/Res/662 (1990). I suppose that Australia might try to respond that the situations are different – the Security Council did not adopt such a resolution in the case of East

Timor. The answer to this is that the obligation not to recognize arises from the general law – not from the Security Council resolution. In the case of Iraq, the political forces were such that it was possible for the Security Council to remind states of their obligations under the law. And see operative para. 5 of G.A. Res. 31/53, 31 U.N. GAOR, Supp. (No.39) 125, U.N. Doc. A/31/39 (1976) in which the General Assembly (Australia abstaining): '*Rejects* the claim that East Timor has been integrated into Indonesia, inasmuch as the people of the territory have not been able to exercise freely their right to self-determination and independence'. The General Assembly spoke strongly for the international community.

63 see above, note 27.

64 UN Doc. A/C.6/SR.1502 at 227 (1974). According to the representative of Indonesia, Mr Wisnoemoerti:
'*His delegation welcomed article 5, in particular the third paragraph, [the relevant provision of the definition which was quoted earlier in the text at note 32] which reaffirmed the principle of international law according to which any territorial acquisition resulting from the threat or use of force was inadmissible and should not be recognized.*'

U.N. Doc. A/C.6/SR.1482 at 110 (1974).

65 See above, note 29.

66 In earlier writing (see above, note 3), I made the point that Indonesia's action breached the separate norm of self-determination as well as the proscription of the use of force, and both points are made in the relevant Security Council and General Assembly resolutions deploring the Indonesian military intervention. One can probably argue that international law also requires that such a denial of self-determination independently requires non-recognition also, but the point is not as developed in this form in state practice and in the literature. In view of the strength of the case concerning use of force, it is not necessary to pursue the point for the purposes of the present analysis. Portugal's case against Australia (see above, note 21), places more emphasis than the present argument on the self-determination point. See also note 82 below on self-determina-

tion and *jus cogens*.

67 Senator Evans, text at note 36, above.

68 See above, note 3.

69 See H. Blix, 'Contemporary Aspects of Recognition', *Receuil des Cours*, **130** (1970), p. 589, at 662–5.

70 'Legal Consequences for States of the Continued Presence of South Africa in Namibia (South West Africa) Notwithstanding Security Council Resolution 276 (1970)', [1971] ICJ, **16**, 56:

'*In general, the non-recognition of South Africa's administration of the Territory should not result in depriving the people of Namibia of any advantages derived from international co-operation. In particular, while official acts performed by the Government of South Africa on behalf of or concerning Namibia after the termination of the Mandate are illegal and invalid, this invalidity cannot be extended to those acts, such as, for instance, the registration of births, deaths and marriages, the effects of which can be ignored only to the detriment of the inhabitants of the Territory.*'

See to the same effect the discussion by the Privy Council in *Madzimbamuto* v. *Lardner-Burke* [1968] 3, All Eng. Rep. 561 (illegal Rhodesian regime).

71 The concession appears to have taken place as early as February 1979. See, e.g., statement by Senator Evans [Australian] *Hansard, Senate*, 18 October 1988, p. 1525. I have yet to be persuaded of the inevitability of the position that merely beginning negotiations implies or requires *de jure* recognition. I do not see why as a legal/diplomatic position Australia's negotiators could not have dealt with Indonesia insisting that they were conceding – at most – *de facto* but not *de jure* control. Plenty of negotiations have taken place over the years with the governments of the two Chinas by states which reserved their position on recognition. Much modern state practice (but not apparently Australia's) downplays the difficult distinction between *de facto* and *de jure* recognition, and indeed formal recognition in general. The distinction has always seemed to be one of degree with *de jure* coming after some significant passage of time has indicated a greater degree of permanency.

De jure recognition, because of its name, inevitably carries with it some connotation of prescriptive legitimacy. The absolutely weakest possible interpretation of the non-recognition principle is that it forbids explicitly granting *de jure* recognition. (See Blix, above, note 69 at 664: 'It is believed that this formula [in the 1970 Declaration] may be interpreted to mean that *no formal admission* may be made *of the legality* of a forcible acquisition as described.' [Emphasis in original]. This would permit some accommodation of the aggressor but make the point. Obviously, I think the obligation goes beyond that. On Australia's (shifting) recognition policy, including its unique recognition and de-recognition of the Soviet Union's *de jure* sovereignty over the Baltic states, see K. Suter, 'Australia's New Policy on Recognizing Governments', *The Australian Quarterly*, **61** (1989), p. 59.

72 I have in mind the language of the Boundary Agreement between China and Pakistan of 2 March 1963 which admits that India (and possibly the Kashmiris themselves) may have some claims to the area in question, by speaking of 'the alignment of the boundary between China's Sinkiang and the contiguous areas the defence of which is under the actual control of Pakistan'. Text in *International Legal Materials*, **2** (1963), p. 541. Article Six of the treaty reads:
'The two Parties have agreed that after the settlement of the Kashmir dispute between Pakistan and India, the sovereign authority concerned will re-open negotiations with the Government of the People's Republic of China, on the boundary, as described in Article Two of the present Agreement, of Kashmir, so as to sign a Boundary Treaty to replace the present Agreement.

Provided that in the event of that sovereign authority being Pakistan, the provisions of this Agreement and of the aforesaid protocol shall be maintained in the formal Boundary Treaty to be signed between Pakistan and the People's Republic of China.'

73 There is one other possible line of inquiry as to this aspect of the situation. The Treaty is 'provisional' pending a final agreement on the delimitation of the continental shelf. It will last, however, for a

minimum of 40 years. See the first preambular paragraph and Article 33 of the Treaty. In an article, 'Australia Rejects Portuguese Criticism of Timor Gap Treaty', in *Backgrounder*, **1**(8) (23 February 1990), p. 7, the Australian Department of Foreign Affairs and Trade emphasized this point. The Department commented:
'The treaty itself contains provisions to the effect that it will not prejudice the position of either Australia or Indonesia in respect of permanent delimitation of the continental shelf in the Zone of Cooperation. Therefore Australia does not concede that any sovereign rights over seabed resources that appertain to the land mass of East Timor in fact extend into the Zone of Cooperation.

The assertion that the people of East Timor have permanent sovereign rights over the seabed resources in the Zone of Cooperation is not accepted by Australia. Consistent with this position is the fact that Australia had never conceded, prior to 1975, any Portuguese interest in the area of seabed forming part of the Zone of Cooperation.'

In short, the interim nature of the solution is not meant as a device to protect the rights of the people of East Timor, if any. They are cut out of the deal. Again, it should have been possible to draft language which expressly protected the position of an eventually separate East Timor – even while disagreeing about what its legal rights might be – but this was not done.

74 Statement to Timor Gap Forum, see above, note 35.

75 Treaty, preambular para. 5.

76 Treaty, operative para. 24.

77 See material discussed at notes 7–12 above.

78 Brownlie, I., *Principles of Public International Law*. Oxford: Clarendon Press, 4th edn. 1990, p. 125. Brownlie refers to the Island of Palmas case (*Netherlands* v. *US*), *Reports of International Arbitral Awards*, **2** (1928), p. 829. The Arbitrator held that Spain could transfer no more territorial rights under the 1898 Treaty of Paris than she herself had. In particular, Spain could not transfer Dutch territory forming part of the Netherlands Indies (now Indonesia).

79 I have not explored this line of thought in depth into the international area but it leads quickly into two other bodies of material that at least characterize the Indonesian effort. (1) The invasion was an international crime as understood in the Nuremberg Principles, in Article 19 of the International Law Commission's draft Articles on State Responsibility, Report of the International Law Commission on the Work of its Twenty-Eighth Session, 31 UN GAOR, Supp. (No. 10) 174, UN Doc. A/31/10 (1976), and in Art. 15 of the Draft Code of Crimes Against the Peace and Security of Mankind (1991). (2) The invasion was a breach of an obligation *erga omnes*, as that concept was floated by the dicta in the ICJ's 'Barcelona Traction Judgment', [1970] ICJ 4, 32, which lists 'acts of aggression' as one of the breaches of rights which, in view of their importance, all states can be said to have a legal interest in their protection. Does this mean that some state or other legal person besides Portugal and the Timorese can enforce against Indonesia the right of East Timor not to be forcibly taken off the map? Where does this lead on a complicity argument with Australia?

80 I do not wish to overstate the distinctiveness of the two arguments – they may well be essentially alternative modes of expressing the same point.

81 Vienna Convention on the Law of Treaties, Art. 53, UN Doc.

A/CONF.39/27 (1969).

82 [1966] 2 *Year Book of the International Law Commission*, p. 247. And see the most comprehensive discussion of the topic to date, Lauri Hannikainen, *Peremptory Norms (Jus Cogens) in International Law*. Helsinki: Finnish Lawyers' Publishing Co., 1988, pp.163–4, 323–56. And see Crawford, note 61 above, at 81. The right to self-determination is listed by many scholars as a norm of *jus cogens*. See Hannikainen at 357–424. But see Crawford, note 61, above. And see GA Res. 35/118 (1980), 35 UN GAOR, Supp. (No. 48) at 21, UN Doc. A/37/48 (1981), the Plan of Action for the Full Implementation of the Declaration on the Granting of Independence to Colonial Countries and Peoples, in para. 5 of which the General Assembly:

'*Categorically rejects any agreement, arrangement or unilateral action by colonial and racist Powers which ignores, violates, denies or conflicts with the inalienable rights of peoples under colonial domination to self-determination and independence.*'

Thus the right to self-determination of the Timorese supports a separate argument for the treaty being void. While Portugal's case in the International Court, (see above, note 21), stresses the self-determination aspects of the situation, it is presented in such a way that it does not go as far as to argue the invalidity of the Timor Gap Treaty.

PART III

Views From the Inside

CHAPTER 5

The War in The Hills, 1975–85: A Fretilin Commander Remembers

Paulino Gama (Mauk Muruk)

'Solitudinem faciunt, pacem appellant'

('They make a wilderness [and] call it peace')
(Tacitus, *Agricola*, 30)

Introduction

My name is Paulino Gama. I am 39 years old, a widower and father of two children. All three of my family died at Indonesian hands – my wife had her throat cut in 1980, my children were poisoned. Thirteen other members of my family also perished. I was born in Saelari-Laga in the district Baucau, East Timor, and am currently living as a refugee in the Netherlands where I arrived from Lisbon in 1992. As a Fretilin commander, my *nom de guerre* was Mauk Muruk Ran Nakali Lemorai Teki Timor.

Between 1975 and 1985, I held the post of Operational Commander of the Timorese Resistance Forces (Falintil), and, in addition, from 1980 I was a member of the Timorese National Resistance Supreme Council – the political command of the resistance – with special responsibilities as Deputy Chief-of-Staff of Falintil and as Commander of the Red Brigade Commando. I was also *ad interim* Secretary for Defence and Security on the Fretilin Central Committee.

The Guerrilla War

After the fall of the border village of Batugadé, the last stronghold of the UDT, in mid-September 1975 at the end of the Fretilin–UDT civil war, and the beginning of the incursion of Indonesian special forces units,

Timorese nationalists of all political affiliations were provoked to a bold and obstinate resistance. It should be stressed that at this time the surviving UDT troops in East Timor joined the Fretilin-led National Resistance, and fought shoulder to shoulder against the expansionist and colonialist Indonesians, in particular the Javanese, who have today made a colony of all Indonesia.

I was at that time a Falintil Operational Commander on the border, and, since I knew a little English, I was entrusted by Nicolau Lobato (died 31 Dec. 1978), then Fretilin Vice-President, with the task of accompanying the five foreign journalists – Greg Shackleton, Malcolm Rennie, Tony Stewart, Gary Cunningham and Brian Peters – to the border, where they were subsequently killed by the Indonesians at Balibo (16 October 1975). This killing was witnessed by a number of Timorese who were subsequently shot to eliminate all trace of this hideous crime. Since I had to take the five journalists' films to Dili, I was not, in fact, present at the time of the enemy attack on Balibo during which the five journalists perished.

The Indonesian border invasion proper took place in early October 1975, after the UDT military defeat, with the occupation of Batugadé (8 October) by Indonesian troops. At that time, I was at the lightly defended forward post at Bálibo with the five journalists. After the frontier line was breached, the Indonesians eventually launched a full-scale air, sea and land invasion on 7 December 1975, when Dili, and other strategic towns such as Baucau, Suai, Viqueque, Maliana, Bobonaro, Samé and Liquiçá were all attacked. In Dili, terrible massacres of the civilian population took place: women, children, invalids, the old and infirm, and even the patients in the Central Hospital and in the Social Welfare building at Caicoli – none were spared. There were also many deaths at the harbour wharf, and in other places in Dili such as Vila-Verde, Bidau, and Taibesse.

In the face of these Indonesian atrocities and shocked by the sheer scale of the invasion, the surviving population and the Falintil units made a strategic withdrawal to the mountains in order to regroup and organize a more effective resistance. I would like to record here that, on 7 December, forces under my command freed many of our UDT and Apodeti brothers who were being held in Comarca jail and in the security police prisons in Dili, as well as four Indonesian soldiers who had been captured at Nunura near Maliana during the fighting in October 1975. This took place, despite various pressures I was under from my more radical Fretilin brothers that they should suffer a different fate. Later, in January 1976, my troops freed about 250 Timorese prisoners in Aileu and Samé in the Central Highlands. In Aileu, we were only able to save about a hundred Timorese after the military headquarters had been surrounded and the rifle unit commanded by the former Portuguese army sergeant, José da Silva, had been neutralized. These prisoners had been part of the unit commanded by Lieutenant-Colonel Rui Alberto Maggiolo Gouveia, a senior officer of the Portuguese army and Chief of Police in Dili who had sided with the UDT after their coup attempt of 11 August 1975. Unfortunately, we arrived too late.

My actions with regard to the UDT prisoners were misinterpreted by some of my more extremist Fretilin brothers, who accused me of insubordination and rebellion. I was subsequently pursued on various occasions and there were even attempts made to physically eliminate me merely because I had placed human rights and national ideals above party interests. Later, on Mt Matebian (1977–8), when we still had support bases, we captured a number of Indonesian soldiers and they remained with us as prisoners for over a year. In late 1978, when Matebian was surrounded and heavily bombarded by the Indonesians, many of our soldiers wanted these prisoners eliminated by way of reprisal for the Indonesian attacks. I firmly opposed this and eventually ordered the prisoners to leave our mountain positions and rejoin their Javanese brothers who had encircled the area. I did this out of a spirit of compassion.

Years later, after my surrender to the Indonesians in January 1985, when I was in Bali and Surabaya, I met some of these selfsame Indonesian soldiers whom we had captured in September 1977 and whom I had released in November 1978 at the time of the Matebian encirclement. One of these was a certain Lieutenant Edi of the Indonesian Marine Corps (KKO; *Korps Komando Operasi*), who, when he heard that I was in Surabaya, came in person to see me and went down on his knees in a gesture of gratitude for my having saved his life. I mention this fact to stress that we members of the East Timorese resistance are not murderers, as some people have tried to depict us, but simply nationalist soldiers dedicated to the defence of our country in the face of Indonesian invasion, occupation, and genocide. We are dedicated to upholding the fundamental principles of the UN Universal Declaration of Human Rights (1948), such as the avoidance of arbitrary violence and arrest, respect for human life, and the protection of the lives and dignity of all prisoners of war. We place special emphasis on this because, in our view, we are fighting the outdated military dictatorship of President Suharto in Jakarta, and not the Indonesian people themselves. We are, in fact, friends and brothers of the Indonesian people, and would like to join in solidarity with all Indonesian organizations which oppose the Suharto regime.

From 1975 to 1978, the majority of the surviving East Timorese population (over 425,000) were with us in the bush where they were the subjects of all manner of barbarism at Indonesian hands, ranging from bombing raids to massacres of whole communities and individual rapes and murders carried out by Javanese soldiers. This was, in fact, the most difficult phase of the resistance struggle – we simply did not have an administrative organization capable of supporting and protecting the hundreds of thousands of our fellow East Timorese brothers and sisters. This created huge obstacles for the mobility of our forces, preventing them from responding adequately to the repeated Indonesian land, sea, and air attacks. At the same time, we had to try to organize a logistical structure to remedy the food problem and the nutritional deficiencies of the sizeable civilian population. It was rare for crops to reach maturity because they were systematically destroyed by Indonesian bombardments and sabotage attacks. Springs and wells were poisoned on a number of occasions, which greatly affected the availability of clean water and caused the deaths of many people. This was the period (1978–80) of the terrible famine in East Timor which claimed so many lives, and was graphically portrayed in the pictures of emaciated men, women, and children published in various contemporary newspapers and magazines, for example *The Sydney Morning Herald* and *The Financial Times* of London, both of 2 November 1979. The distant look in the eyes of these famine victims seemed to be a bitter reproach to the world for its indifference.

The enemy seemed determined to exterminate the majority of the East Timorese civilians still in the hills with the resistance. From June to November 1978, the Indonesians launched what was known as 'Operation Total Encirclement and Annihilation'. About sixty battalions (i.e. about 40,000 troops) were deployed to surround and destroy the support bases. Biological weapons were used which caused dysentery, diarrhoea and premature deaths amongst children, as well as nerve paralysis, rheumatism, and sudden fits of madness. Amongst other weapons used was napalm, which burned everything within a range of about two hundred metres, and a high-explosive (1,000 pound) bomb which blew craters in the hard rock several metres deep and wide. These bombs caused countless deaths on Mt Matebian. On one occasion, an incendiary bomb, probably napalm, fell on a group of 27 people, who were instantly incinerated. At another time, about a hundred people, many of them women, children, and the elderly, who had taken refuge in a cave during an aerial bombardment, were entombed alive when a high-explosive bomb detonated outside and completely blocked the cave mouth. After two weeks we could no longer hear their groans. The use of napalm on East Timorese civilians was later confirmed to me by members of the Indonesian military intelligence (*Intel*).

As a result of this grievous situation, many people came down from the hills to surrender to the Indonesians in the nearest towns. But even then, the enemy had no mercy and thousands of innocent and defenceless people were butchered. In my home village of Laga, and in Uatu Karabau, Uatu Lari, Quelicai, Luro, Lospalos, and in all the areas adjacent to Mt Matebian, countless were the executions and murders at Indonesian hands. Our mothers, wives, sisters, and daughters who had surrendered, were physically abused and raped. There were also cases where men and women were flung out of helicopters and drowned in the open sea. Because of these barbaric acts, many civilians fled back to the bush, preferring to die fighting rather than be humiliated and gunned down like wild animals.

While Operation Encirclement was taking place in the mountains, the enemy continued to make many arrests and carry out executions in Dili itself. The prisons were full – the most notorious being those in Dili (Comarca), Atauro Island, Maliana, Cailaco, Aileu, Ueberec, Ainaro and Tutuala (Lospalos). It was during this extermination campaign that Nicolau Lobato, the President of Fretilin, was killed on 31 December 1978 after a six-hour gun battle in the Maubisse mountain range, 50 kilometres south of Dili. By then, nearly the whole first generation of Fretilin leaders had been wiped out.

After Lobato's death and the destruction of the support bases, the reorganization of the armed resistance became the top priority for the survivors. Work on the reorganization began early in 1979. The most important military commanders who had survived the encirclement and destruction campaign were myself, Kilik Wae Gae, Olo Gari, Nelo and Freddy. On the political side, the principal survivors were Xanana (Gusmão), Ma'Huno, Mau Hodu, Bere Malay Laka and Taxy, most of whom had eluded the Indonesians in the Ponta Leste region (at the far eastern tip of East Timor). This small group of politico-military commanders met in March 1979 at Titilari-Laivai in the central-eastern zone to analyse the causes and consequences of the military collapse, and to devise adequate measures for the reorganization of the resistance, both political and military. At this meeting we decided to create a 'National Council of Maubere Resistance' ('*Conselho Nacional da Resistência Maubere*' or CNRM), the highest organization in the resistance, which was later consolidated at the historic conference at Mabai (Lacluta) in March 1981 when Xanana Gusmão was chosen as leader. After the reorganization, the new politico-military leadership revived armed resistance throughout the whole of the national territory.

This second generation of East Timorese resistance leaders, with Xanana Gusmão at their head, completely abandoned the political radicalism and 'status quo' policy of 1975, both in its tactics and in the positions it adopted in its conduct of the national liberation struggle. As a consequence of this new political line, on 21–3 March 1983 at the village of Lariguto near Ossu in the central-eastern zone, the first negotiations took place with the Indonesians, led by Colonel Purwanto, the East Timor military commander. These negotiations resulted in a ceasefire which lasted from March to August that year.

This followed on the failure of the second Indonesian encirclement and annihilation operation known as 'Operation Security' (*Operasi Keamanan*) which took place in July–September 1981. About 17 battalions (each with around 650 men) brought from Java were used in this operation in addition to the forces stationed in East Timor. Timorese men from the age of 15 to 60 were forcibly recruited to act as 'beaters' and porters for the Indonesian army in their infamous 'fence of legs' tactics against the resistance. At Lacluta, in the mountains of Aitana, Lalini and Santo António (i.e. at the shrine of St Antony's Rock), the enemy slaughtered about four hundred Timorese men, women, and children in an incident which later became known as the 'Lacluta massacre' (September 1981). Pregnant women had their stomachs sliced open, and sharpened stakes were driven into their vaginas; young children were dashed against trees and rocks. Here the enemy did not even bother to use their guns, but killed with knives and clubs. Even household animals – chickens, dogs, and cats – did not escape their murderous rage. The group at Lacluta was caught because they did not know the area, being from the Ponta Leste region in the extreme east.

In the bush, we regularly received news of the outside world through Radio Netherlands, the Voice of America, Radio Deutsche Welle, Radio Australia, and the BBC. The stations which carried the most news on East Timor were Radio Australia and the BBC. The first foreign report I heard on the situation inside East Timor was from a church source: Fr Francisco Maria Fernandes, a refugee Timorese priest in Australia, who spoke on Radio Australia in June 1979. It was a badly-needed stimulus and source of moral support for us. Later, many other organizations and individuals sent messages of support for our cause. However, it was evident in the late 1980s that Radio Australia had been coming under pressure from the Canberra government over its reporting of Timor, perhaps because – especially since the signature of the Timor Gap Treaty on 11 December 1989 – Canberra and Jakarta have ever closer economic interests. As regards the Fretilin mission abroad led by José Ramos-Horta, we only received its communiqués from 1982 onwards. During the period 1978 to 1982, there was total silence. Even so our determination to fight the Indonesian occupiers remained unshakeable.

In 1982, the Indonesians launched a new sweep operation involving about five battalions, but this did not result in any casualties either amongst the resistance forces or the civilian population in the bush. In August 1983, however, after the breakdown of the ceasefire agreed at the March talks (with Colonel Purwanto), the enemy slaughtered over 3,000 [*sic*, see also Taylor 1991: 102, who gives a figure of 200 'burnt alive in their homes' and a further 500 survivors killed on the banks of the Bé-Tuku river] people at Kraras near Viqueque on the south coast, in reprisal for the killing of 17 Indonesian soldiers. The massacre took place on 21–2 August 1983, and was confirmed by a special resistance investigation team in September of the same year. They counted the bodies of the victims in the two large buffalo enclosures belonging to the *liurai* (local chieftain) of Uma-Tolo, Lacluta, beside the river Uétuku (Bé-Tuku), and found about 3,000 decomposing skulls. At another place, Taci-Tolu near Dili, hundreds of Timorese were shot by firing squad as a reprisal for the killing of these selfsame Indonesian soldiers. Other victims of the massacre at Taci-Tolu included the resistance team which had made contact with the Australian parliamentary delegation led by Senator Bill Morrison on the Lospalos–Baucau road east of the village of Laga on 29 July 1983. The team was twelve strong and headed by my cousin, Cancio de Sousa Gama.

On 24 January 1985, after differences with my fellow resistance comrades over the correct strategy to be adopted for the liberation of our homeland, I decided to go down from the mountains and rejoin my people in the areas under Indonesian control. I thus surrendered to the Indonesians, and, as a political prisoner, I was deported to Jakarta on 2 February 1985 where I was detained in the isolation ward of the Psychiatry Department of the Jakarta Army Hospital where I stayed until 9 September 1989. I was then cared for by several national and international humanitarian and human rights organizations, *inter alia* the International Committee of the Red Cross and the Jesuit Refugee Service, before arriving in Lisbon as a refugee on 1 October 1990.

Conclusions

East Timor must be free and independent – anything else means our extermination as a people and as a nation. We have now endured twenty years of physical and cultural ethnocide at the hands of the Indonesians. Their invasion and occupation has been characterized by an open violation of international law, a flagrant disregard for the relevant UN resolutions calling for the withdrawal of their troops, and an inexorable campaign to eliminate the identity and dignity of the people of East Timor. We Timorese, however, are more united than ever around the project of national unity embodied in the *Convergência Nacional Timorense* (CNT; 'Timorese Nationalist Convergence') which since March 1986 has brought Fretilin and the UDT back together in a united front. Furthermore, since 1987, Falintil, in the national interest, has been renamed the Armed Forces of National Liberation, thus ceasing to serve as the armed wing of a particular party (i.e. Fretilin), and turning itself into a genuinely national and non-political army. Xanana Gusmão also left the Fretilin leadership at the same time and became the head of the new 'National Council of Maubere Resistance' (*Conselho Nacional da Resistência Maubere* or CNRM), thus showing the world that the resistance is a truly national and broad-based one. Despite his arrest in November 1992 and subsequent trial (Feb.–May 1993) and imprisonment, Xanana is the figure who commands respect and consensus amongst all Timorese, of whatever political persuasion.

The most rational way to achieve a just and lasting solution to the East Timor problem is by a dialogue between the three interested parties, Indonesia, Timor, and Portugal. The last is still recognized by the UN as the administering power and can in no way be excluded from any peace agreement. Indeed, any such peace solution must uphold the right of Portugal to return to Timor as the administering power to resume and complete the process of decolonization which was so brutally and tragically aborted by the Indonesian invasion of 7 December 1975. The decolonization process could be based on Law 7/75[1] with the necessary modifications to suit the circumstances of its application.

In view of the above, I appeal to all freedom-loving countries, especially the Five Permanent Members of the Security Council – the US, Russia, Britain, France, and China – to bring pressure to bear on Indonesia to withdraw its forces. The great nations of the world cannot have a double standard for identical situations – one standard for oil-rich states like Kuwait, which was so brutally invaded by Iraq in August 1990, and another for East Timor. We, the Timorese people, are not asking for much: we are not asking the Security Council to approve the use of force to make Indonesia withdraw; rather they should bring effective political and economic pressure to bear to secure implementation of the two Security Council resolutions (384 of 22 December 1975; and 389 of 22 April 1976) which call for the total withdrawal of Indonesian armed forces and an act of self-determination for the long-suffering people of East Timor. Only then will justice be done and one of the great wrongs of the late twentieth century be set to rights.

Notes

1 This refers to the Constitutional Law of 17 July 1975 approved by the Portuguese Council of the Revolution, which set October 1976 as the date for popular elections in East Timor for a General Assembly to determine the territory's future, and the end of Portuguese control in October 1978. In order to achieve this, it provided for the establishment of a High Commissioner's Council, comprising a High Commissioner (who was to retain a casting vote) and five 'joint secretaries', two of them Portuguese nominees and three Timorese (i.e. one from UDT, Fretilin and Apodeti respectively). For further details, see Dunn, *Timor*, pp.97-8.

CHAPTER 6

The East Timor Intifada: Testimony of a Student Activist

Donaciano Gomes

A people that knows itself cannot be reduced, cannot be subjected. This is the case of the Timorese youth, and this is the fundamental problem of the war. If Indonesia thinks that by exterminating Falintil [the armed forces of the resistance] the war will end, they are wrong.

(Xanana Gusmão to Robert Domm, September 1990, quoted in *The Age*, 25 October 1990)

My name is Donaciano Gomes. I am 25 years old and I am a student. I left East Timor on 6 September 1990 and went as a refugee to Portugal where I now live. I will briefly describe here some of my own personal experiences before my departure. I pray that these will not represent the reality for East Timorese in the future.

I was six years old when East Timor was invaded by the Indonesian Armed Forces (ABRI) on 7 December 1975. At that time I was in Dili with my family. There was a football field near our house which served as an assembly point for Indonesian troops – both paratroopers who had dropped from the air over Dili, and infantry disembarking from landing craft in Dili harbour. Those Timorese who passed near this area, mainly women and children seeking refuge in the adjacent Motael Church, were killed by the Indonesians. We did not leave our house for fifteen days. When I at last ventured out, I came across bodies in the streets, often half eaten by animals. On the beach (Areia Branca) nearest to us, a number of bodies had been washed up. I helped a Timorese nurse bury many of them on the beach.

In 1983–4, when I was fourteen years old, I became directly involved in the conflict because I could no longer bear the barbarous actions of the Indonesian Armed Forces who were massacring people night and day, imprisoning them without pretext, and violating women as they pleased.

What meaning did these actions have? For me, growing up in East Timor was a deeply tragic experience.

It was in 1983–4 that I met someone who had become a member of the guerrilla resistance while living in a village. He was later captured by the Indonesian forces, subjected to terrible torture, and then sent as a political prisoner to Atauro Island. He was dead within a year. Naturally, I was influenced by these events. Who could not have been? In the history of this century, many others in Southeast Asia have also suffered appalling oppression: for example, those in the Indonesian Independence Movement had to struggle for five years (1945–9) to liberate their nation from Dutch colonialism. Our struggle is now in its twentieth year.

In May 1989 we learned that Pope John Paul II would visit East Timor that October. In that selfsame month of May I wanted to try to meet the Commander-in-Chief of the resistance, Xanana Gusmão, in order to plan a demonstration. But the Indonesian military campaigns against the resistance were so widespread that it proved impossible to meet him in person. Only through a clandestine message did he approve our plan to carry out a demonstration after the high mass was celebrated by the Pope at Taci-Tolu on 12 October.

In order to cow and intimidate the population in advance of the Pope's visit, numerous Timorese were rounded up, imprisoned and tortured. Lieutenant-Colonel Prabowo, President Suharto's son-in-law, at that time serving in East Timor, personally tortured (my friend) Idelfonso Araújo, breaking his leg and his teeth. This climate of terror, however, did not prevent the demonstration taking place at the end of the papal mass on 12 October. But immediately after the Pope had left, the forces of repression descended on us. There were many arrests: two of my friends, Jacob Xavier and Virgilio Costa, were detained at Senopati III, a commando barracks (used by the Indonesian Special Forces, *Kopassus*), and were tortured. I escaped this fate by hiding out for some nights in the woods around Dili. Knowing that the military had threatened to take my family hostage, however, I sought refuge in the residence of the Catholic Bishop of Dili, Mgr Carlos Filipe Ximenes Belo, on 26 October. There were about 38 young people there already. The head of Indonesian military intelligence and other officers tried to make us leave, but the Bishop took personal responsibility for our protection and refused to hand us over. During this visit, the Indonesian intelligence chief demanded to know my name and I shouted back '*Xanana*', a riposte which probably caused me to be singled out later for special treatment at the hands of the Indonesian military interrogators.

Some days later, after the tension had built up following demonstrations in support of us, the Indonesian military commander (Brigadier-

General Mulyadi) and officers of the East Timor Operations Command (*Kolakops*) entered the Bishop's residence and threatened to take away the Bishop if we did not come out of our own accord. We eventually came out, after the commander had promised us in front of the Bishop that we would not be tortured and that, after a short interrogation, we would all be set free. We were taken by bus to the main police station in Dili and the Bishop came with us. During the interrogations, the police were replaced by Red Beret commandos. Afterwards, the majority of my companions were indeed released. But, despite the undertakings made by the commander to Mgr Belo, several others, including myself, were taken to four different military headquarters, where we were tortured with cigarette burns and electric shocks. A dagger was stuck in my back, and I received blows to the head and gun muzzles pointed at my chest, head and in my mouth. Our tormentors apparently wanted us to accuse a particular Timorese priest of having instigated the demonstrations during the Pope's visit. The interrogation and torture went on for fifteen days.

On 6 February 1990 I was at last set free. Seven months later, on 4 September 1990, on the eve of my departure for Portugal, there was another demonstration (on the occasion of the 50th anniversary celebration of the diocese of Dili) in favour of self-determination and independence. The Indonesians responded in their usual manner, imprisoning and torturing hundreds of people. A similar situation existed in the run-up to the aborted Portuguese Parliamentary visit in November 1991, which later resulted in the Santa Cruz massacre (12 November 1991) when over two hundred died. A major military campaign was also launched to capture Xanana before that visit (Xanana was, in fact captured a year later in November 1992).

What I have seen and experienced is what all our people have witnessed and experienced over the past nineteen years as prisoners in our own land. The only way to peace is through genuine dialogue (between all three parties to the conflict, namely the Indonesians, the Portuguese and the Timorese). Otherwise, this tragic situation will continue indefinitely. The Indonesian military and the people of Indonesia should both remember their own arduous struggle against Dutch colonialism in the late 1940s. They should remember that we too, the long-suffering people of East Timor, have the same rights as they do.

CHAPTER 7

Planting a Tree in Balibo: A Journey to East Timor

Shirley Shackleton

My interest in East Timor began in October 1975 when my journalist husband, Greg Shackleton, disappeared with four colleagues in Balibo, a border town which separated Portuguese Timor from Indonesian West Timor. When Indonesia invaded East Timor on 7 December 1975, two months after my husband's disappearance, I expected the truth of what had happened in Balibo to be told to the world. As the years passed with no official explanation for Greg's apparent death, I became determined to find out the truth for myself. However, for fourteen years, I was prevented from visiting East Timor because the country was officially closed by the Indonesian authorities. In January 1989, when the country was at last 'opened', I received word from reliable sources inside East Timor that I might try to go in during the October 1989 visit by Pope John Paul II, because Indonesian military and intelligence operations would be scaled down at that time.

Frankly, I hoped I would find that the situation was not as bad as had been reported in the West. Fourteen years is a very long time to have worked consistently on something which caused me so much grief and for which there had been so little apparent change for the better. During my three-week visit, I interviewed military personnel, Indonesian tourists, Italian, Spanish, Filipino and East Timorese priests, and the Apostolic Administrator, Bishop Carlos Filipe Ximenes Belo (in office, 1983 to present). I also had the chance to talk with Indonesian school-teachers, office workers and a judge, a Western aid worker, members of the Fretilin resistance and Timorese in hiding from the authorities. In public, the Timorese people behaved as if they were afraid to speak to foreigners.

I travelled as far east as Lospalos, and as far west as Maliana and Balibo, with one-day visits to places like Dano, Ermera, Liquiçá and Gleno, where I spent a morning at the Indonesian transmigration centre. The resistance wanted me to go across the island to Viqueque in the southeast, but that journey had to be called off when it became known that Dili would be completely closed off for three days prior to the papal visit. It would have been impossible for me to explain what I was doing away in the countryside for three days without implicating others and, besides, I wanted to witness the Papal Mass for myself.

On my first day I took a bus journey with Indonesian transmigrants and, although I cannot claim to have interviewed them, what I saw of their harsh treatment at the hands of their own soldiers and military police convinced me that they are dealt with almost as badly as the *maubere* (ordinary East Timorese). They were tense, apprehensive and openly resentful once we had left the soldiers and the military police behind. When I shouted at a soldier to stop pushing us around, I received a lot of encouragement. Indeed, as soon as we left the road-block, a great deal of produce was heaped in my lap. I was to witness Timorese and Indonesian transmigrants being harassed on many similar occasions, although it did not seem to me that the latter were as frightened of the Indonesian security forces as the *maubere*.

During my three weeks in East Timor, I saw enough to convince me that great injustices are being visited on the Timorese people: they appear to live in fear and unremitting sadness, many are malnourished and walk listlessly in the dust by the side of the roads. In contrast, Indonesian civilians appear well fed and are smartly dressed. They travel, for the most part, in cars and taxis. I saw numerous military barracks. In fact, it is not an exaggeration to say that military buildings of one sort or another are to be found on almost every street and road in the territory. At a time when military operations were supposed to have been scaled down, everywhere I went I saw troops marching out of their barracks, mounting guard, taking part in exercises and standing to attention in seemingly endless military parades. I even saw workers in the fields surrounded by armed soldiers, ostensibly there to guard them from 'terrorist' attack. Although it is not unusual to see a strong military presence in other parts of Indonesia, especially Aceh and North Sumatra, Indonesians in East Timor told me it was excessive. They immediately qualified this, however, by saying that the military were 'needed' in East Timor to protect Indonesian settlers from 'primitive bandits'.

One unforgettable impression, which took me a long time to understand, was the lack of East Timorese males in their thirties and forties amongst the wider population. Those adults whom I did see, including some children, exhibited symptoms suggestive of long-term trauma, something which I am able to recognize as a trained nurse. At the same time, I saw many Timorese with missing limbs, their legs and arms having been hacked off with machetes by the Indonesian military.

I have already referred to my meetings with East Timorese political fugitives on the run from the Indonesian secret police and military. By way of illustration, I will relate here an experience by Peter Philp, author of *Journey Among the Poor*, and sometime editor of *The Advocate*, a now defunct Melbourne Catholic newspaper. During a long career in journalism, he had reported from Brazil, Chile, Colombia, Guatemala, El Salvador, Nicaragua, Ethiopia, Uganda, Zimbabwe, and the Philippines. In his view, however, the precautions of his local guides in East Timor were greater than anything he had ever experienced before, even at the height of the 'death squads' in Central America in the early 1980s. While in East Timor, he had set up an interview with a male nurse, who had been in hiding for several months, and an East Timorese priest, who was under constant harassment from the Indonesian authorities. The meeting had been arranged to take place in a large building whose owner, a highly placed Church official, had purposely absented himself in order to avoid any political complications. The male nurse began to relate how both he and his wife had been arrested and detained over a period of several months. He was describing the treatment they had received at the hands of the Indonesians – beatings, filthy cells and decomposing food. All the time he was looking at the door, jumping at every sound. Suddenly, the door was flung open and everyone in the room, including Philp, felt that their last moment had come. They jumped to their feet, expecting *Intel* (Indonesian secret police) agents to rush in. But it was just the church official: he had forgotten they were there and was in a hurry – the room was apparently a short-cut to the toilet.

The male nurse's crime was that he had written a letter of support to Bishop Belo in response to the latter's 6 February 1989 appeal to the United Nations Secretary-General, Xavier Perez de Cuellar, calling for a UN-supervised referendum on the political future of the territory. He was accused by the Indonesians of 'wanting the Portuguese to return'. When he was finally released, he was warned that he would be immediately rearrested if he became involved in any trouble of any sort. He said the subsequent pressure exerted on him, and the fear of being subjected once again to incarceration and beatings, had forced him underground. Although he did not want to desert his family and country, if someone would help him to get out, he would go like a shot. He just could not take any more.

The Timorese priest, for his part, had publicly advocated support for Bishop Belo and had incurred heavy criticism from his Indonesian brother priests, who had even gone so far as to accuse him of being 'Pre-Vatican II' in his attitudes. He gave evidence to Philp that his treatment was unusual: the more common way to discredit Timorese priests is to accuse them of not doing their pastoral work properly, or of casting aspersions on their sexual conduct. Perhaps one should consider here that these men were guilty of no crime, yet they were constrained to meet clandestinely and in great fear because they had voiced their support for a seemingly unexceptional request, a UN-supervised referendum.

Permission to travel outside Dili changed daily and, even on some of my comparatively short trips, my fellow passengers and I had to alight for repeated examination of travel documents. By May 1990, most of the road-blocks were no longer manned, but, after, Robert Domm, an Australian Trades Union lawyer, recorded an interview with Xanana Gusmão, for the Australian Broadcasting Corporation (broadcast on 27 September 1990), Timorese wrote to tell me that many repressive measures, such as the reestablishment of roadblocks, mass arrests, closure of schools, red zoning of areas (no-one allowed in or out), and arbitrary executions, were reintroduced.

In Dili, a women's project, designed to teach traditional skills, was being planned. I asked a Western aid worker about its likely effectiveness. 'The Indonesians go in for projects with high visibility and a high "success" rate,' he sighed, 'yet the good they do is minimal when you consider what they cost. They don't serve the great bulk of the people because they don't improve their basic living standards.' He repeated what many Timorese had told me, 'what concerns the Timorese most is what they will eat tomorrow'.

Two nights before the Pope was due to arrive in East Timor, while I was dining in Dili with a group of Australian journalists, General Murdani, the Indonesian Defence Minister and the man responsible for the overall planning of the bungled invasion of East Timor, approached our table and was invited to sit down. If the occasion had been a press conference, I might have stayed, but to share a meal with a man whose orders must have been sought before the murder of my husband and his four colleagues at Balibo was unthinkable. As the general sat down, I got up and quietly walked away.

After a sleepless night, I decided that I must not miss the opportunity to meet this man. As a long-time intelligence supremo, he would certainly know the truth of what had happened at Balibo. As soon as I entered the dining room for breakfast the next day, Murdani, who was eating with his party of about a dozen aides, glanced over at me. I sat down and ordered coffee. While I drank, he repeatedly turned his head in my direction. 'Ah,' I thought, 'the journalists must have told him about me.' The next time he stared at me, I said, 'General Murdani!' and walked across the room to his table exclaiming, 'I would so like an opportunity to speak with you !'

The general shook his head and mumbled something under his breath. I added, 'No journalists!' At that, he agreed to talk when he had finished his breakfast. I returned to my table. A Timorese waiter rushed over with a new pot of coffee. 'Double strength for courage!' he whispered as he served me. I learned nothing new about Balibo from the evasive general, so I suggested to Murdani that it was obvious that the Timorese people were not getting a fair deal: they do not have adequate educational facilities, certainly none of a high enough standard to enable them to work at anything but the most menial jobs and, compared with the Indonesians dwellings, the Timorese are sub-standard. At the same time, health-care is virtually non-existent and medicines in short supply. The large Indonesian army of occupation continues to behave as though it is in conquered territory, individual soldiers acting with great brutality towards the *maubere*. Needless to say, the general was not pleased. When we parted, I reminded him that if he ever discovered what had really happened at Balibo, he should tell me. He murmured that he would look into his files. All that day people asked me if I had found out anything new. Meanwhile, the Australian journalists told me that they had drunk and talked with Murdani until two o'clock the previous morning: they had told him about me, and when they asked what he would say to me, he had replied, 'I would say *nothing!*'

Just before the Papal Mass was to take place on 12 October, people were issued with thousands of red-and-white Indonesian flags (*merah putih*) and were instructed to wave them enthusiastically at all times during the ceremony. They were told that they would not be allowed in unless they had them in their hands. On the great day, I noticed few Timorese were carrying them. When I asked where the flags were, the invariable response was, 'Oh, we left them at home!' They said the numbers attending the Mass were so far below those which the authorities had expected that they had taken the chance that the Indonesians would be forced to let them in, flags or no flags. Meanwhile, Xanana had warned there would be a boycott, and had estimated Timorese attendance at not more than 100,000, far below the 400,000 the Indonesians were confidently predicting. Later, Indonesian national TV claimed there were 350,000 there, but, in fact, only about 130,000 turned up, many of them Indonesians.

At the end of the Mass, young men bearing banners started a noisy protest. Rodney Hughes, a Darwin-based reporter, told me that he had asked his Indonesian minder what was written on the banners. While looking straight at them, the man had replied, 'What banners?' That evening, Bishop Belo told me that his translation of the Pope's homily, which he had placed in a green folder on the lectern, had been substituted for an Indonesianized version during the Mass itself. He was thus forced to read this bogus text, since he had not thought to bring along a second copy of his own draft.

The day after the Mass (13 October), I travelled to the eastern part of the island with Louise Williams, Southeast Asia correspondent of the *Sydney Morning Herald* and Roy Eccleston, foreign affairs writer of the *Australian*. Rumours fly around the country at great speed, as is the case with any place where there is censorship, oppression, and foreign military occupation. When we arrived at Baucau and Lospalos, we were repeatedly approached by people who wanted to know whether it was true that only twenty students had been shot by the Indonesians at the Mass? Yet, according to the local intelligence chief, Colonel Bimo, no-one had been arrested or shot. On our return to Dili we learnt that many people had been arrested including a Spanish priest (Fr Sanchez) and several of Fr Locatelli's pupils from Fatumaca, the Salesian College near Lospalos which I was soon to visit. The Indonesians claimed to have film proving that the priest had urged his hapless choristers to take part in the demonstration. Bishop Belo and Fr Locatelli had spent two full days interceding on their behalf with the Indonesian military authorities, and when they were finally able to see the incriminating video, the priest in question was seen running towards the choir boys shouting at them to take to their heels rather than get involved in the *mêlée*. Fr Locatelli told me that many other students had been forced to go into hiding in Dili and had been without food for many days. About forty young people had taken shelter in Belo's residence, an asylum which was to afford them little real protection from the ubiquitous Indonesian *Intel*.

When I interviewed the Spanish priest after his release, he told me that though he had himself been very frightened, his main concern was for the mental state of his younger charges, the Indonesians having deliberately separated him from the children, thus intensifying their anguish in a place of filth and horror. During a subsequent visit, Mark Baker, foreign editor of the Melbourne *Age*, interviewed a youth in Dili in March 1990 who said that he had been arrested after the Mass and detained without trial for several months. He claimed that he had been starved, beaten, tortured with electric shocks and bayonet cuts (he showed Baker his scars), and kept in filthy water for twenty-four hours at a stretch. He described how many of his friends were suspended by their hands and feet from ceilings and beaten, punched in the genitals, and had their hands crushed under the legs of chairs while fat Indonesian soldiers sat interrogating them. Church sources also reported that Bishop Belo's residence had been raided and several young men taken away and imprisoned without trial for three months.

In the eastern part of the island, we spoke with many priests, and visited Fatumaca. We learned that the impressive Italian principal, Father Locatelli, teaches his students to respect the occupying forces: 'The Indonesians are our masters and are here to stay. What they want, they take!' He confirmed that he has had to put himself in front of orphans on several occasions when Indonesian soldiers have come to kill them. Many are the sons and daughters of resistance fighters, and are being cared for at Fatumaca in the absence of their parents. It is interesting to note that the existence of orphans in East Timor often indicates that the entire extended family has perished. Indeed, I know of several Timorese who claim to have lost every single member of their family: one woman could name 168 relatives whom she had lost following the Indonesian invasion.

Everywhere I went people seemed to know that Fr Locatelli had come looking for me when I first arrived in Dili, and I was regarded with affection as a result. 'When he first came to Fatumaca,' people told me, 'there were only stones. He built this college with his bare hands.' In teaching his pupils to accept Indonesian rule, he is not condoning any part of it. He made this very clear to me during the course of our conversations. Instead, he is trying, against terrible odds, to save lives. I was also told that he had been taken in for questioning and beaten up on several occasions. 'The Indonesian army will never leave,' Locatelli said, 'if Xanana dies or is captured tomorrow, they will have to invent another resistance leader because they are making so much money here.'

The Indonesian intelligence chief in East Timor, Colonel Bimo, had told me that Fretilin 'bandits' habitually burn down villages and crops. In Lospalos, civilians and priests both laughed at this, claiming Indonesian building contractors set fire to villages and houses to keep themselves in work. I was asked: 'Do you really think Xanana would destroy the very homes and livelihood of his supporters?'

On the night we stayed in Lospalos, an Indonesian soldier was shot in a gun-battle with Xanana's guerrillas near Tutuala at the extreme eastern point of the island. Next morning, we went to see the local military cemetery. Our terrified Timorese driver did not want to stop, but we prevailed on him to put up his bonnet and pretend a breakdown. Roy Eccleston then climbed on to the roof of the station wagon, and counted eight fresh graves. He had been told in Dili by soldiers on leave that they had lost eight of their comrades in skirmishes the previous week, but when he had asked the Indonesian authorities for confirmation, he was told it was a Fretilin guerrilla who had perished. Our driver was now increasingly agitated and started pulling things out of the engine to make the 'breakdown' look truly authentic. His terror reached fever pitch when a convoy of army trucks packed with fully armed Indonesian soldiers sped towards us. When eventually we had 'repaired' our motor and driven off, a small vehicle passed us with the body of the soldier who had been shot the previous night. It was making for the cemetery. Upon our return to Dili, we were again informed by the military authorities that the man killed at Tutuala had been a Fretilin 'bandit'. However, when we enquired why he was being buried in the Indonesian Military Heroes' Cemetery, there was silence.

While at Baucau and Lospalos, I met no nuns (they were still in Dili attending to matters arising from the Papal Mass), but I was frequently told by ordinary East Timorese that the local Canossian nuns are their sole medical resource, medicines being donated by the foreign nuns' families, especially that of the Mother Superior. Timorese claim that they are not treated efficiently or humanely at the Indonesian government medical centres (Puskesmas). Many people were sick as a result of the poor diet due, in part, to the Indonesian prohibition on tilling distant fields in order to prevent civilian contacts with the resistance. Tuberculosis, polio, rabies, hepatitis, cerebral malaria, leprosy, and hookworm are all rife. Gastric disorders are also endemic amongst the Timorese because of the contaminated water supplies. In Baucau, as in most other parts of the country, there used to be a plentiful water supply from local springs. But, these are now out of bounds. Now that the Indonesians have taken over the local water supplies, fresh water has to be purchased at exorbitant prices.

When we returned to Dili, I was told by many Indonesians that the younger generation of Timorese, still at school, would be graduating in 1993 and would be unable to find work. Trouble was expected. Indeed, I was warned that gangs of Indonesian and Timorese youths already went out at night to beat each other up. Parents from both communities expressed despair over the deteriorating situation. There is employment for Indonesian newcomers, apparently, but no jobs available in East Timor for the East Timorese themselves. One consequence of the high levels of unemployment are the large numbers of Timorese girls and young women forced into prostitution. In Dili, I visited a seedy market area known as Pasar Senggol Bidan Lecidere, a street filled with run-down food stalls where one can see many impoverished prostitutes, Javanese as well as Timorese. As I walked through, I was offered the sexual services of young boys and girls, and was also badgered to attend cockfights and buy drugs. Everywhere I went, I visited the local markets. The food on sale was limited, but pleasingly displayed: every tomato seemed to have been polished and placed in a careful design. But prices seemed exorbitant by Australian standards (they were probably raised because I was a foreigner).

I rarely saw Timorese or Portuguese names in relation to businesses, or in any of the government-controlled telecommunications centres, banks, and post offices. Shops, eating places, travel agencies and hotels, all seemed to be operated by Indonesians or Indonesian Chinese, with the exception of the Turismo hotel which had some local staff working for Arsénio Ramos-Horta, a well-known collaborator and brother of José Ramos-Horta, the chief foreign affairs spokesman of the Fretilin–UDT coalition.

Two independent sources gave me what I believe to be close to the truth about my husband's death. One was an Indonesian officer with whom I spoke in a Dili park. When any Indonesian asked me what I was doing in East Timor, I always answered, 'I want to go to Balibo'. When they asked why, I replied, 'because your army murdered my husband there'. No-one, apart from General Murdani, ever attempted to deny this. In fact, the officer in the park said straight out, 'The Balibo Five, I am *so* very sorry.' He remarked that, when he was in Australia for military training, everyone he had met had wanted to know what had happened at Balibo. 'It was a tragedy and a grave mistake,' he said. We talked for about fifteen minutes. Several of his best friends and brother officers had been killed in East Timor. When I asked if he knew what had actually happened at Balibo, he said, 'you would not want to know'. I assured him that, on the contrary, he would be doing me a favour by telling me the truth. After a silence, which seemed to last an eternity, he replied, 'they were immobilized before being taken into a house where they were cut with knives. Their bodies were then burnt.' I asked him why the story of their shooting had been put about and he said, 'more acceptable for Westerners'. 'They saw too much' were his last words when I asked him why on earth they had been killed at all. According to a CIA report cited in James Dunn's book, *Timor. A People Betrayed*, a massive attack had taken place along the whole border on 16 October 1975: elite Indonesian troops were ordered to wear uniforms without identifying insignia and to carry older weapons of Soviet manufacture (supplied pre-1965 to the Indonesian Army during the last years of Sukarno's 'Old Order'). This was so as not to embarrass the United States, at that time Indonesia's principal foreign arms supplier.

The Indonesian officer admitted admiration for Xanana Gusmão, and said some sections of the army were sympathetic to his cause. They did not like what they were doing, but had a job to do. When I asked why Indonesian soldiers behaved so atrociously, he replied, 'we have our fair share of thugs in uniform'.

My visit to Balibo took place on the fourteenth anniversary of my husband's death (16 October 1989). It was a miracle it was made at all because the Indonesian authorities went out of their way to make things difficult for me: both the police and military intelligence changed their minds on the morning I was due to leave and insisted that I had to have a special pass to visit Balibo. However, the men who could actually issue this pass remained studiously absent from their offices. Arsénio Ramos-Horta, who was to drive me, finally got permission, but would not say how. Later, in Balibo itself, the military police kept me in suspense for hours while they told odd anecdotes which only seemed to make sense when I realized that they were worried that, if the commemorative tree I intended to plant died, I would blame them. When I assured them that this was not the case, I was told to go ahead and plant the tree where I wanted. The sudden twilight of the tropics was descending, and I reflected that to plant the tree in darkness would just be another cover-up. So I insisted that I should be allowed to return the following morning. Next day, I was told that the whole town wanted to attend the planting ceremony. When I said everyone was welcome, permission was promptly refused. I then planted the tree alone, the military police and soldiers lounging nonchalantly nearby. As I spoke aloud the names of my husband and his four colleagues and pressed the warm earth with my hands, sprinkling Greg's favourite perfume around the roots of the tree, seemingly out of nowhere a capella choir began to sing. The police said afterwards it was only local Timorese children practising for Mass. Months later, after my return to Australia, the true significance of this ethereal music began to dawn on me: I realized that there had been no 'coincidence' at all, the singing practice had been exactly timed to coincide with the tree-planting ceremony. In this way, the people of Balibo had participated directly in the occasion despite the prohibition of the Indonesian authorities. It was another moving example of the strength of the resistance of ordinary Timorese against Indonesian rule.

Someone else who had been in Balibo at the time of Greg's death sent a message which confirmed the Indonesian officer's account of their murder. This person, who had fled the room in Dili when he realized who I was, asked one of his friends to act as an emissary on his behalf. When I asked why he had been so anxious to avoid me, his friend replied, 'Are you kidding! If the authorities knew that he had even been in the same room as you, that would have been quite enough to have had all his finger-nails pulled out.'

During the last three days of my visit, many Timorese approached me, asking me to follow them behind buildings where they told me of their suffering. I was terribly moved when I saw the severity of their wounds: some were old gunshot wounds, others were chest and head wounds. Missing limbs and fingers seemed commonplace, marks of ubiquitous

Indonesian torture. Some people merely wanted me to post letters to relatives who had escaped. The letters were stamped and I was asked to post them in Bali where they would not be censored. In those last days, many young people began to speak to me in public. When I asked if they were not taking foolhardy risks with their lives, they replied that their lives were forfeit anyway, and they would rather tell of their mistreatment than die in silence. There was a great deal of bravado and youthful boasting in their behaviour, but I saw many newly healed scars and crushed hands and feet which led me to believe that their stories of torture were not exaggerated.

I cannot help but be deeply affected by the plight of the East Timorese people. If life is as good as the Indonesians make out, why do so many, once they have decided to trust a foreigner, tell such heart-rending stories? Why, if the resistance is such a spent force, is it necessary to maintain such a large occupation force? When I finally left East Timor, I realized I had not found what I had been looking for: a reason to get on with living my life. Instead, I felt a strong commitment to tell the truth of what I had seen. I remember being told by a Spanish priest: 'If the war raging here was in Europe, it would be front page news every day.' I felt that it would be a miracle before the world could even begin to understand.

CHAPTER 8

The Catholic Church in East Timor

Robert Archer

We have nothing left to lose. We are human beings and they have treated us like insects. We will never accept them here. Even if we have to die resisting, we will resist. We have our dignity and our own identity. And God is with us.[1]

(Quoted in *CIIR News*, No.27 [October 1993], p.4)

These words, which were spoken by a woman in East Timor last year, take us some way towards understanding the Catholic Church's influence in the territory. Suffering, for the people of East Timor, is not distinct from their vision of God. It is, in fact, integral to their identity as Timorese. Challenged as deeply by the same experience of suffering, the Timorese clergy have remade their Church, once steeped in the experience of colonialism, into a church of service. The clergy achieved this momentous shift (one that amounted to adopting Vatican II) in almost complete isolation. As the people of East Timor discovered from somewhere within themselves a quite unusual strength – the foundation of their capacity to resist – the isolated diocese of East Timor uncovered a sense of mission, almost entirely by reflecting inwardly on its own experience, which has enabled it to retain – in spite of many weaknesses and contradictions – the profound loyalty of its people. This chapter records some of the elements involved in this process, though the deep spiritual journey that individual priests and Christians have made may only be guessed at and will not become known until people in East Timor are free to speak again.

Towards a New Church

Isolation was not a new experience for East Timor, of course. It was the norm under Portuguese rule. Throughout the colonial period, and formally after Rome signed a Concordat in 1940 with the Portuguese dictator Dr Salazar (in office, 1926–68), the Catholic Church was integrated within the colonial system. For much of the colonial period, the Church was the main, often the only, indication of Portuguese authority in many rural areas of East Timor. In addition, it ran most of the territory's few educational institutions and was the principal instrument for transmitting Portuguese culture. It is well known, for example, that the nationalist leaders who came to prominence in 1974–5 were almost all trained in Catholic schools or in the Catholic seminary of Nossa Senhora de Fatima just outside Dili, at Dare.[2]

This was at heart a foreign church. The majority of Timorese did not identify with it. Church statistics record that in 1970 most people were animists; less than one third were Catholics.[3] Though it is no doubt right to say that the Church defended parishioners against certain colonial abuses (in the world of commerce, for example[4]) and that individual priests were among those who resisted the dictatorships of Salazar and Caetano, it is a telling fact that, at moments of political crisis, the response of the majority of church personnel was to leave for Portugal or Australia. This happened, for example, when Japan occupied Timor during the Pacific War and again during the conflict between UDT and Fretilin in 1975.

All this changed after the Indonesian invasion. The priests and religious who remained were not able to leave. Many went with the population into the mountains to escape the Indonesian army. Their links with Portugal were severed and, influenced by the rise of nationalism in 1974–5, they were forced to reconstruct their Church amid the carnage and destruction of the war.

Their attempt to come to terms with, and then surmount, this traumatic dislocation can be tracked, very imperfectly, by comparing a small number of important documents that eventually appeared abroad. Some were intended for publication; others were not. They excited considerable local controversy, and were suppressed or disowned by the Indonesian authorities.

The Reflection of 1981

The first of these documents appeared in 1981, and reflected the nightmare and isolation of the first phase of the war between 1975 and 1980, which culminated in the death of most of Fretilin's original leadership, the defeat of Fretilin's attempt to protect territory from Indonesian occupation, and the terrible famine of 1979–80. *Reflections of the East Timorese Religious* was a private communication addressed to the members of religious orders in Indonesia. Written at a time when most assumed that resistance was at an end, it asserted with surprising prescience that:

We must all realize that the Indonesian National Army which liberated Indonesia from the colonial power in an astonishing manner will never liberate the people of East Timor from their colonial situation towards autonomy and national independence because its situation and reality are very different.

It went on to list, with precision, the abuses of the occupation:

What has taken place during these five years is most significantly: invasion, war, looting, the destruction of the indigenous population, territorial subjection, colonial exploitation, the expulsion of the indigenous population who are replaced by people from other islands, military occupation, attempts [at] mass mobilisation of people (from 12 to 55 years) to make war on each other.

However, the heart of the document describes the deepening of faith that appears to have occurred *because* of the war, both among the people and among the clergy. It is worth quoting at some length:

The people are aware that their faith comes from God whose Word takes the form of social justice. This justice derives from the justice of God in His relations with His people. This justice must be built by the people themselves based on faith and co-operation with God and with one's fellow men who are still the sacrifices of oppression. For us, living the faith without serious endeavours for the building of social justice is the same as making faith merely foreign and mystical. Creating justice together with the present Indonesian government is not possible, or not yet, although the people desire justice greatly...

The document then goes on to describe how teachers, catechists and numerous village communities had experienced a deepening of faith.

While these events have been happening, the people have developed in their efforts to become the community of God. Certainly there were such efforts earlier, but it is now more realized and strengthened because the need is felt to unite in the faith. Often we hear 'only God can make us safe'. This means: the certainty of religious standards faced with the facts of the destruction.

The *Reflection* ends by describing the shock of isolation that the Timorese clergy experienced after 1975:

Our connections with the Universal Church, with the religious and the wider world, were suddenly cut off. We are the religious of East Timor who, still together with the people, were suddenly thrown into emptiness and alienation for six years until we became the dumb Church of East Timor. Now we are more aware of the faith, that this experience was very useful because our faith was deepened and more felt in life as a gift from God. This faith says that we are still one with the Universal Christian Church [...]

[Yet]

We must also acknowledge that we have not yet understood why the Indonesian Church and the Central Roman Church have up till now not stated openly and officially their solidarity with the Church, people and religious of East Timor. Perhaps this has been the heaviest blow for us... We felt stunned by this silence which seemed to allow us to die deserted...[5]

The Statement of January 1985

A second major document appeared in January 1985, this time written by East Timor's Council of Priests. Much had changed in East Timor and in the Church during the interval; it was at this time, for example, that Xanana Gusmão reorganized the resistance movement, as Paulino Gama (Mauk Muruk) has described earlier in this volume. In 1983 the Apostolic Administrator, Mgr da Costa Lopes (in office 1977–83), was retired. Mgr Lopes was popular and widely respected because he had spoken out against abuse and had protected many individuals from repression. The decision to remove him was made over the heads of the Timorese clergy, who opposed it. He was replaced by Mgr Carlos Filipe Ximenes Belo (born 1948), a relatively young member of the Salesian Order who had been outside East Timor during the period of isolation described in the *Reflection*.[6]

The Church was also acutely short of personnel, and both Mgr Lopes and then Mgr Belo responded to this emergency by inviting Indonesian religious to work in East Timor.[7] Abroad, the situation had also evolved. Although the territory remained isolated from the outside world, several Bishops' Conferences – including those of Indonesia and Portugal – had responded to the appeal for solidarity. Most significantly, in mid-1984 the Pope formally alluded to the need to respect human rights in East Timor, when he told the incoming Indonesian Ambassador to the Vatican that, 'The Holy See continues to follow the situation in East Timor with preoccupation and with the hope that particular consideration will be given in every circumstance to the ethnic, religious and cultural identity of the people.'[8]

The 1985 *Statement* reflected these changes. Whereas the 1981 *Reflection* had been written by Timorese and foreign religious, it was signed by the Council of Priests – in effect the Timorese clergy of East Timor. Indonesian religious were not involved. The document was addressed to the Indonesian authorities and was to have been public – the first time such a formal declaration of principle had been issued in the name of the local Church. Furthermore, it was signed by Mgr Belo, who had already indicated in several remarks and letters that he was just as opposed to abuses of human rights as his predecessor.

In content, the *Statement* reflected many of the same themes as the *Reflection*, dwelling as it did on the continuing gravity of human rights abuses, the alienation of the people, the denial of self-determination, the Church's place alongside the population. In addition, however, the *Statement* argued in explicit terms that the people of East Timor faced genocide. The Council wrote:

> In East Timor, we are witnessing an upheaval of gigantic and tragic pro-
> portions in the social and cultural fabric of the Timorese people and their
> identity is threatened with death .... There is a Timorese culture that is
> made up of words, attitudes, emotions, reactions, behaviour, ways of being
> and relating to the world. It is in these things that the people recognise
> their own culture and in it their own identity.... All attempts to hinder or
> to prevent this evolution would be an attack that the people of East
> Timor, like any other people, would find intolerable.... An attempt to
> Indonesianise the Timorese people through vigorous campaigns to promote
> pancasila, through schools or the media, by alienating the people from
> their world view, means the gradual murder of Timorese culture. To kill
> the culture is to kill the people.[9]

Thus the shock and outrage against violations of rights, expressed in numerous letters and comments by Church leaders throughout the period, as well as the language adopted by John Paul II (in office, 1978 to present) to demarcate the areas of Rome's concern is here enriched by a new assertion of national identity, which parallels the emergence of political nationalism during the same period. Indonesia's response to the Statement was swift. Mgr Belo was put under acute pressure to deny his involvement with it. When he eventually did so its resonance evaporated.

The Appeal to Democracy

The 1981 *Reflection* and the 1985 *Statement* explicitly affirm the right of East Timor's people to self-determination. This has been the consistent position of the local Church. It was stated particularly clearly in a letter by Mgr Belo in December 1984:

Despite all forces against us, we continue to hold and disseminate that the only solution to the East Timor conflict is a political and diplomatic one, and this solution should include, above all, the respect for the right of a people for self-determination.... As long as this is not implemented, there will not be a peaceful solution for East Timor.[10]

Four years later, as Indonesia prepared to 'open' Timor and Xanana Gusmão had developed a new strategy for liberation that emphasized political mobilization rather than military action, Mgr Belo took up this theme again. His private letter of 6 February to the Secretary General of the UN (then, Sr Perez de Cuellar) remains of capital importance and remains unanswered to this day:

The people of Timor must be allowed to express their views on their future through a plebiscite. Hitherto the people have not been consulted. Others speak in the name of the people. Indonesia says that the people of East Timor have already chosen integration, but the people of East Timor themselves have never said this. Portugal wants time to solve the problem. And we continue to die as a people and as a nation.[11]

Mgr Belo came under great pressure to deny that he had written this letter, or withdraw what he said in it. He refused to do so and made his position even clearer by stating that he was not advocating one political solution rather than another, but affirming a basic democratic principle.

He has continued to maintain the same view, and it is now increasingly difficult to ignore. After the fall of the Berlin Wall later that year (November 1989), the most powerful states in the international community – including the United States, the European Union, and Japan – formally adopted policies that proclaim they will protect and promote democracy and human rights anywhere in the world. Since the United Nations has never recognised the legitimacy of Indonesia's 'act of integration' of 17 July 1976, Mgr Belo's appeal to the rule of law and democracy *can* only be answered by silence or assent.

At the same time, Church leaders have recognised (as did Xanana Gusmão before his arrest) that the international community is unlikely to act decisively to restore the rights of the people of East Timor. Mgr Belo is almost uniquely well-informed on this matter because he has talked with almost all of the principal figures involved in resolving the conflict, including President Suharto, Foreign Minister Alatas, commanders (*panglima*) of the Indonesian armed forces, leaders of the Timorese resistance movement, the Portuguese President, the Pope, and senior UN officials and top officials in the United States government. It is noticeable that in recent years Mgr Belo has increasingly emphasized the importance of taking a long-term political perspective, while pressing for an immediate improvement in abuses of human rights.

Interviewed by *Timor Link* in September 1993, for example, he said:

> For me, the best way to reach a peaceful and honourable solution is still the idea of a referendum... this is the only way – to ask the people if they would like to become Indonesian, Portuguese or independent. It is the only way. But living here I see that day by day we are losing the possibility of saving ourselves or of being saved. I am now suggesting the idea of a kind of status, a special status, autonomy for East Timor... because we are not prepared, we have no men, we have no infrastructure.[12]

The war cut down a generation of Timorese, the generation that would now be running the territory had East Timor's independence been recognised in 1975. As in Pol Pot's Cambodia, the attrition of educated and experienced people has been exceptionally high, and there were precious few such people to start with. The language of Mgr Belo reflects the burden of realism and the sense of responsibility that weighs upon leaders in the Church (and also leaders of the resistance movement). How is it possible, he asks, to pursue the desire for freedom, when Timor is so small and repression so vicious? How also is it possible not to do so? There is little doubt that the feeling of isolation and embitterment expressed by the religious in 1981 remains very much alive.[13]

Rome: The International Dimension

In short, during the 1980s the Catholic Church broke with its colonial past, and with the Indonesian authorities, and for the first time attached itself to the local culture, rather than the metropolitan power. At the same time, this important shift was experienced in terms of a painful isolation.

While this was so, however, the Church also benefited from an unusual and privileged relationship with Rome. Because East Timor was the subject of an international dispute, the Vatican did not attach the diocese to the Bishops' Conference of Indonesia, but administered it directly from Rome, via the Pro-Nuncio's office in Jakarta. This arrangement, which remains in force to this day (1994), meant that, throughout the occupation, the Catholic Church was the *only* local institution that communicated independently with the outside world, maintained institutional connections with an international structure, and could therefore guard for itself a certain independence from the Indonesian authorities.

As a result, during the 1980s, the Catholic Church was able, to a far greater extent than any other Timorese institution (with the possible exception of the resistance movement), to defend threatened individuals and threatened values. It has been noted that the first Apostolic

Administrator, Mgr da Costa Lopes, won great popular respect for his attempts to protect individuals from abusive treatment and his trenchant condemnation of corruption and human rights violations. Bishop Belo took up where he left off. Both prelates have had to cope with the discomfort of being exposed to political pressures from all sides: from the Indonesian authorities, who have ruthlessly worked to create an acquiescent Church; from the Vatican, which has consistently feared that too active a sympathy for East Timor might provoke a political or religious backlash against Christianity in Indonesia where there are an estimated five million Catholics; and from nationalists in East Timor, particularly the young, who would like Bishop Belo to swing the Church publicly and unequivocally behind the independence movement.

The Church has been for Timorese a source of spiritual solace in a society that has suffered profound trauma. In addition, in a world overturned by war, it represents an important element of continuity. It has a national organization, which can provide, at least to some degree, resources and services to people who would otherwise be without support. Most rare of all, it has offered a cultural space, a public place not occupied by the Indonesian authorities, a sense of inner liberty. In the words of Bishop Belo: 'The Catholic faith of the people is a kind of symbol to unite them, it is a way of expressing the fact that they are Timorese.'[14] It can be understood, given these circumstances, why so many of the public protests that have taken place since 1989 have started at, or finished at religious events or places of worship.

Church leaders are often criticized for fomenting such events. But Mgr Belo has claimed repeatedly that the Church is not, and should not be, politically partisan. He argues, however, that the Indonesian government fails to distinguish political bias from the Church's commitment to human rights and human development.[15]

A Church Divided?

Given these circumstances, it is hardly surprising that the great majority of Timorese opted for Catholicism when they were required to adopt a religion recognised by *pancasila* in the early 1980s. In the space of a few years, the proportion of nominal Catholics shot up from less than 30 per cent to more than 80 per cent of the population – from approximately 180,000 in 1970 to over half a million in 1990. This growth added to the institutional weight of the Church, which could reasonably claim to represent the views of the majority of East Timor's people. But at the same time, it imposed huge new demands on the diocese and on Church personnel which, as already noted, led Bishop Belo and his predecessor to increase very steeply the number of Indonesian priests and religious in the territory. By the end of the 1980s, when East Timor was 'opened up' (January 1989) and the Pope visited (12 October 1989), the Church's institutional structure had been transformed.

Three reasonably distinct groups can be distinguished within the clergy. There are, first of all, the Timorese. The majority are diocesan priests rather than members of religious orders. Most work in parishes south and west of Dili. Many have less access to resources and educational opportunities than members of the missionary or religious orders. There is general consent that the great majority share the nationalist views of East Timor's people.

The Indonesian clergy and religious are also a rather homogeneous group, but, by contrast with the Timorese clergy, they generally accept the Indonesian government's official analysis according to which East Timor 'consented' to join Indonesia by an act of 'self-determination' in July 1976. Many of the religious are doing important and necessary work; but only those who show real understanding of what East Timor's people have experienced appear to have been accepted by the people. Many are considered by Timorese to be 'colonizers', no different from the many officials, soldiers or traders who have made their living in East Timor since the occupation.

The third group is composed of foreign missionaries and religious. It is a highly diverse group, including Italians, Spaniards, Indians, Portuguese, Filipinos, Czechs, Slovaks, and Mexicans. An influential but declining number began their service before 1975, but many have arrived more recently to work in new missionary areas such as Suai, where the Claretians have recently established themselves. Most of the Eastern sector is in practice managed by the Salesian fathers, the order to which Mgr Belo belongs.[16] While the political views of the foreign missionaries are naturally mixed, as a group they would fall between the Indonesian and Timorese clergy. In number, approximately 31 priests were from abroad in 1991, while 32 were from Indonesia and 26 from Timor. Over one hundred sisters from eight orders are also working in East Timor.

Managing so disparate a body is no doubt one of the clergy's most challenging tasks. Nevertheless, on a wide range of matters there is much common ground about what the people of East Timor need. Development, education, health care, better communications, contact with the outside world, employment, correction of abuses would be listed by clergy of all backgrounds. On a visit to East Timor in April 1991, I found considerable pragmatism in my discussions about such matters, and open-mindedness about how such needs might be met.[17]

The critical issue is the question of self-determination. Among Timorese there is virtual unanimity that self-determination is the eventual legitimate and realizable goal. Most Indonesian clergy and religious, however, regard this aspiration as wholly unrealistic, if not illegitimate. Anything like consensus seems virtually unachievable. The gap in perceptions is very wide and, in addition, very strong emotions are naturally generated, particularly among the Timorese, who resent deeply the intolerance and lack of respect they detect among many incomers.

There is a further implication. It is that attitudes towards self-determination themselves determine the way that other issues are dealt with. They influence the way the Church works and, in the most practical ways, to whom the Church and the clergy feel accountable. The 1981 *Reflection*, for example, emphasized the Church's responsibility to serve the people, and its detachment from interests of state. The view from Indonesia would be very different. It is likely that priests and Church workers will tackle problems of development or health care and even their pastoral work in radically different ways, according to whether they believe the problems Timorese face are due to a fundamental deprivation of liberty or to backwardness and a difficulty of adaptation. Foreign priests too, for all that they may sympathize with the Timorese, will conduct their parish affairs quite differently if they privately believe that Timorese aspirations are unrealistic.

If this is true, it is clear that different sections of the Church, approaching their work from sharply different perspectives, will tend to pull the Church in different directions. This is one explanation for the sometimes contradictory or hesitant behaviour that Mgr Belo and other Church leaders have sometimes displayed. On the fundamental matter of self-determination, this is a profoundly divided Church. It should be emphasized too that, in the eyes of Timorese, it could again become a Church that is partly foreign.

Dialogue or Co-option?
Nevertheless, this is only part of the picture. For the Church is also engaged in a complex and direct relationship with the government. In the judgement of the local authorities – and no doubt Jakarta – the Catholic Church is both one of the principal obstacles to achieving full pacification, and at the same time a vital partner in the government's strategy to achieve that goal. For official integration policy relies increasingly upon the effective delivery of government services – the provision of material resources that will efface the original traumatic imposition of Indonesian rule. The institution that can most effectively persuade the public to accept the government's services – in health, education and other areas – is unquestionably the Church, which has, therefore, to be co-opted.

This conclusion emerged particularly clearly from a report that was prepared in 1990 for the provincial government of East Timor by researchers from the Gadjah Mada University, Indonesia, under the direction of Professor Mubyarto.[18] The report described the Indonesian government and the Catholic Church in terms of patronage organizations that were locked in competition with one another, but also dependent upon one another for the provision of essential resources. 'The competition between the two patrons...constitutes an integral problem for this province. As a patron, the Catholic Church controls an important resource – the people – but it lacks other resources, such as wealth and coercive power, while the Indonesian government does not have any "possession" over the people.'[19]

Substantial largesse has been offered to secure the Church's goodwill. An obvious example is the new cathedral, which was funded, among others, by gifts from the military budget and grants from central government (US $160,000 in fiscal 1994-5 alone). The Catholic Church in East Timor is learning to deal with the temptations of resource allocation at a time when the local government receives the highest budget allocation per capita in Indonesia. In this intensely political, and deeply compromised society, every gift represents a political debt and is an admission of the giver's sense of need.

Co-option is accompanied by the ever-present threat of violence. This threat is no less terrifying because, for Church leaders, it is more often indirect. The Church is, in effect, forced to help the authorities manage the false peace in East Timor, because the clergy and religious know that another massacre like that at the cemetery of Santa Cruz is always a possible consequence of failing to do so. A recent letter from Mgr Belo catches graphically the moral space in which the Church must operate. In September 1993 three junior staff from the US Congress visited Dili. As tension rose rapidly, security was tightened and young nationalists were dispersed:

> At around 6 p.m. we celebrated mass on the patio of my residence, because the number of faithful present was very high and the chapel was too small. This mass was attended by a large number of people, because there were many young people. After mass some of them went into hiding in the rooms, bathrooms and kitchen, to wait for the right time to demonstrate in front of the congressional staff. There were about 100 young people. During the day, more of them arrived. Most of them left after I asked them to do so. However, one group managed to remain hidden in the bathrooms. At 5 p.m. I myself escorted them to the door of the residence. The problem was that the house was surrounded by military, police, police informers, altogeth-

*er about 200 people. After a lot of discussion with the young people, I decid-
ed to take them personally in a truck and drop them off near their homes.
That way there was no demonstration. But when the young people were in
front of the door of my residence (about 50 of them) they were filmed by
Indonesian intelligence. The next day, 6 September, soldiers captured all
these young people and took them to their headquarters; they had not even
demonstrated before the congressional staff but were barbarously beaten and
tortured. Please pray for me, because now I have to confront two sides:....
The soldiers continue to accuse me of promoting demonstrations, and the
young people accuse me of having sold out to Indonesia because I do not
allow them to have a demonstration at my residence.*[20]

In another recent incident, after the arrest of Xanana Gusmão on 20
November 1992, the government announced that the Catholic Church
would support the government in calling upon guerrillas to surrender
and would help to receive those who surrendered. In fact, no agreement
had been made. Mgr Belo considered the report to be exceptionally
offensive and dangerous because, in 1979 and 1980, surrenderees who
had been promised an amnesty were brutally done to death after giving
themselves up.[21]

Conclusion

What has been created in East Timor is a dangerous, unstable political
environment, penetrated by informers, murky with compromise. Mgr
Belo has described East Timor as a society in which 'half the population
is paid to spy on the other half'.[22] Though power is not evenly distributed, those who determine what happens – in the army, the government,
business, the Church, even the nationalist movement – must for the present co-habit with one another, if only to protect themselves. The
Indonesian government cannot sustain control in East Timor without the
cooperation of the Church. The nationalist movement cannot secure
independence, at least in the short-term, and so must work for a future
independence by exploiting the opportunities for education and economic development that are made available by the Indonesian authorities. Even the Indonesian army's objectives do not assume that force
alone will deal with the problem. What was black-and-white is now various shades of grey. A murderous military conflict has been superseded by
a political manipulation that is almost as dangerous, at least for some of
the players, but almost invisible to the casual view.

The Indonesian authorities believe that in the long-term they can co-
opt Timorese nationalism into submission. The nationalists believe they
can play the same game longer and better and emerge in the end with a

stronger hand than their enemy. In this murderous and intricate campaign of attrition the Church will play a central role – as protector, actor, mediator, and as witness. As Bishop Belo has put it:

> The people of East Timor must be able to live in an atmosphere where they feel they have a place, that they are human beings, that they are being given attention; they must be given the freedom to be complete human beings. These conditions can be achieved if physical and material development is accompanied by human development. That's what is not yet happening here. ...People should have the freedom to move, the freedom to express their opinions. the freedom to say that there are things they do not like. There is no such democracy yet.[23]

Notes

1 Quoted by a recent visitor, in *CIIR News* (October 1993).

2 See J.S. Dunn, *Timor: A People Betrayed*. Milton, Queensland: Jacaranda Press, 1983, pp. 52–3.

3 *Pro Mundi Vita*, No. 4/1984, p. 1.

4 Mubyarto *et al.*, *East Timor: The Impact of Integration. An Indonesian Socio-Anthropological Study*. pp. 31–2.

5 *Asia Bureau Australia Newsletter*, June 1982.

6 Mgr Belo (born 1948) became a Bishop in June 1988. Though he is Timorese, Mgr Belo took the title of Bishop of Lorium, a diocese in Italy, and remains the Apostolic Administrator of East Timor. There is, to this day (1994), no Bishop of the diocese of Dili. This has enabled Rome to take account of East Timor's disputed status in the United Nations. See further reports in *Timor Link*, **15/16** (joint number) (January/February 1989).

7 The Indonesian government's policy on foreign missionaries is to allow those already working to complete their term of service, but to refuse new permits. Until the 12 November 1991 Santa Cruz massacre (in which the Indonesian authorities saw the hand of the Catholic Church), the policy was applied less rigorously in East Timor than in Indonesia proper. Nevertheless, as the number of Catholics rose, it became increasingly difficult for the diocese to staff churches and maintain its social programmes. There is even talk in Indonesia about splitting the diocese of Dili, see above, p. 16.

8 *Osservatore Romano*, (13 August 1984), p. 5, in *Pro Mundi Vita: Asia–Australasia Dossier*, No. 31, *East Timor*, **4** (1984), pp. 31–2.

9 *Timor Link*, No. 2 (June 1985).

10 Quoted in *East Timor. An International Responsibility* (London: CIIR, 1992), pp. 28–9.

11 Quoted in *I am Timorese/Je suis Timorais: Testimonies from East Timor* (London: CIIR, 1990), p. 40.

12 *Timor Link*, No. 27 (October 1993), pp. 6-7.

13 *'Seeing the extent of the tragedy of the East Timorese people…is well known throughout the world, we felt stunned by this silence which seemed to allow us to die deserted.'* See note 5.

14 Bishop Belo, interviewed in *Timor Link*, No. 27, (October 1993). See also João Frederico Boavida, 'The Fusion of Religion and Nationalism in East Timor. A Culture in the Making', MPhil thesis, Faculty of Anthropology and Geography, Oxford University, 1993.

15 *'The Church's message relates to the whole human being…. This is what is sometimes misunderstood by some people. If I speak out, they say I am engaging in politics. When I only busy myself with the sacraments, they say this is what the priests and bishops should be doing. But our duty relates to all aspects of life, in particular the moral, the ethical and the spiritual. We don't practise these things at a technical level. It is for the politicians to strive to realize the Church's view of things in practice.'* Mgr Belo, interviewed in *Matra*, August 1992, partial English translation in *Timor Link*, No. 24 (September 1992), pp. 7–8.

16 In 1991, he was one of two Timorese among more than 30 Salesians working in the territory.

17 The author visited East Timor in April 1991.

18 For full citation, see note 4 above.

19 Mubyarto *et al.*, op. cit., note 4, p. 6.

20 *Quoted in Timor Link*, No. 27 (October 1993).

21 *Timor Link*, No. 25 (March 1993). Most recently, in January 1994, Mgr Belo reported that the military had tried to force some young detainees to make incriminating political allegations against a priest, Fr Sancho Amaral; and that the military had made incriminating political allegations against three foreign missionaries – Frs Locatelli (Italian), Calleja (Spanish) and João de Deus (Portuguese) – to justify refusing them new visas. *Timor Link*, No. 28 (January 1994).

22 'Cry of a Forgotten Land', Clare Dixon, *The Tablet*, 22 November 1991.

23 Bishop Belo, interviewed in *Matra*, August 1992, (partially) reproduced in English by *Timor Link*, No. 24 (September 1992).

PART IV

Future
Scenarios

CHAPTER 9

East Timor and Indonesia: Some Implications

Benedict R. O'G. Anderson

Twenty years ago, in the autumn of 1975, my remote upstate New York university received a large group of visitors from Jakarta. At its head was General Ali Murtopo, Deputy Head of Bakin, the State Intelligence Coordinating Agency, and informal chief of Opsus (*Operasi Khusus*, Special Operations [Executive]), the Suharto government's special apparatus for black political operations. With him were General Benny Murdani, recently appointed head of G-1 (Intelligence) at Armed Forces' Headquarters; Liem Bian-Kie, a.k.a. Yusuf Wanandi, special assistant to Murtopo, key Opsus operative, specialist in American affairs, and a leading figure at the Center for Strategic and International Studies; Daud Yusuf, an Opsus economist who would soon become Minister of Education and Culture; Panglaykim, another Opsus economist of some renown; as well as various people from the Indonesian Embassy in Washington.

The purpose of the delegation's visit was not at all connected with East Timor, but because I had known Liem Bian-Kie from the time we were students together in Jakarta in 1963–4, I took the opportunity to ask him about East Timor and Jakarta's East Timor policy. With his characteristic loud laugh, he replied: 'Don't you worry. Everything is under control. The whole business will be settled in three weeks.' Twenty years have passed, and the 'business' is still unsettled. Ali Murtopo and Panglaykim are dead; General Murdani, Daud Yusuf, and Liem Bian-Kie have fallen from power. Almost all the other key people who framed Jakarta's policy in 1975 are either dead or in the political wilderness – with one central exception: President Suharto, who today is, with the exception of General Mobutu of Zaire, the longest-ruling military leader in the world. In 1975 the President was still a vigorous man of 54. In June 1995, he will turn 74, beyond the age at which his deposed predecessor Sukarno (in office 1945–67) died (June 1970). The world has changed so much in the meantime that it requires an act of imagination to think oneself back to those days. But it is necessary to do so to grasp the implications of all the changes that have since occurred – in the world at large, in Indonesia, and in East Timor itself. The contrasts may help us to think ahead more intelligently.

The World Context
Historians are already identifying 1975 as the plausible apex of Communism's strange parabola of power in the modern world. In the Soviet Union, the Brezhnev armaments' programme appeared to have created a rough parity with the military strength of the United States. The disastrous decision to intervene in Afghanistan had not yet been made, and only a few specialists guessed the magnitude of the growing internal economic crisis. In China, Mao Tse-Tung and Chou En-Lai were still alive, their prestige still largely intact. A rapprochement with the US had begun in 1972, but the People's Republic of China (PRC) and the US still had no normal diplomatic relations, and the former was still excluded from the United Nations. No one then would have believed that within four years, the PRC would launch a military invasion of its Communist neighbour Vietnam (February 1979). In Southeast Asia, the US-supported regimes of Indochina were in their death-throes; successful Communist armies rolled into Vientiane, Phnom Penh, and Saigon in March and April 1975. Finally, the stable division of Europe between Soviet and American spheres showed signs of becoming unsettled with the fall of the Salazar–Caetano fascist regime in Portugal in April 1974. In July, Colonel Vasco Gonçalves, regarded as close to the leadership of the newly legalized Portuguese Communist Party, became Prime Minister in Lisbon. In the spring of 1975, left-wing military officers and left-wing political organizations were at the peak of their power. These revolutionary changes in Western Europe precipitated the abrupt collapse of the oldest and last European empire in Africa. Independence was conceded to Guinea-Bissau in September 1974, to Mozambique in June 1975, to tiny Cape Verde in July 1975, and to Angola in November 1975. (We might pause here to note that no-one argued seriously about Cape Verde's right to independence though it is one fifth the land area of East Timor, and boasted less than half East Timor's population.)

This context is worth bearing in mind for two reasons. First, it helps to explain the policy of the United States and its allies in Europe, in Southeast Asia, and in the antipodes. In almost any other period, before or after 1975, the US would have been supportive of Portugal and its foreign policy. But in that year it was working hard, along with the Social Democratic government of West Germany in particular, to stem the leftist tide in Portugal, to remove the Gonçalves government, and to destroy the influence of the Portuguese Communist Party. At almost any other period, the US – and perhaps Japan and Australia – might have tried to restrain Suharto on East Timor. But as the rout in Indochina accelerated, it was strongly felt that the counterweight of a ferociously anti-communist Indonesia was essential. Even if the East Timorese independence movement had not been dominated by Fretilin, Washington, in those days, would have tried to accommodate Jakarta. But, insofar as Fretilin then appeared to be dominated by committed leftists cooperating with 'undesirable' elements in the Portuguese military, there seemed all the more reason to wink at, if not openly to support, Jakarta's policies. There was one further reason which we should not overlook. The alarms of the Cold War had earlier encouraged Washington to negotiate a secret arrangement with Suharto whereby American nuclear submarines could, against existing international law, pass through Indonesian waters between the Pacific and Indian Oceans without coming to the surface, where they could be monitored by Soviet satellites.

Second, in the local situation, the existing world-context had its influence both in Jakarta and in Dili. We do not really know who, in Jakarta, genuinely believed that an independent Fretilin-controlled East Timor might have provided a refuge for fleeing underground Indonesian Communists, pathetic survivors of the vast massacres of 1965–6, or been willing to invite Soviet or other Communist personnel to help strengthen the infant East Timorese state apparatus and to keep US naval activity under surveillance. But I think we can assume that at least some senior military officers and some right-wing civilian politicians, bureaucrats, journalists, and intelligence types were so convinced. Even if we assume complete cynicism, it is likely that the policy-makers understood that, politically speaking, the world context was completely favourable to their designs. To be sure, on the economic side, the situation was less auspicious. In spite of the OPEC-determined soaring of oil-prices in the autumn of 1973, the state oil company Pertamina had managed to go bankrupt (for a record US $10 billion) at the end of 1974, and foreign investment in Indonesia was still in its infancy. But Jakarta's anti-communist prestige was at its height, and it was the anti-communist card that seemed most likely to win support from the big capitalist states. At the same time, in Dili, the world-conjuncture made it plausible for ultra-leftists to argue that one could play the same cards as Angola and Mozambique had played, and that there was no special need to accommodate the anxieties of the real and honorary West. Hence what, from today's perspective, seems a certain naive optimism and even adventurism on the part of the Fretilin leadership (note especially their boycott of the Lisbon-sponsored talks between the various East Timorese groups that was held in Macao in late June 1975), seemed then a sensible view of the direction of world events and world history. Both sides seriously misread their respective situations, but in ways that in retrospect are quite easy to understand.

The Domestic Situation

The years 1974–5 were also critical from the viewpoint of Indonesian domestic politics. In January 1974, three months before the fall of the Salazarist regime in Lisbon, and three months after the spectacular fall of the Thanom–Praphat dictatorship in neighbouring Thailand, occurred the so-called Malari Affair. Climaxing several months of student protests against corruption and repression in the ruling regime, severe riots broke out in Jakarta on the occasion of Japanese Prime Minister Tanaka's state visit. According to official figures over 150 buildings were destroyed, and hundreds of people were injured. Popular riots of this kind had not happened since the collapse of the Sukarno regime in 1966, and were not to happen again until the labour disturbances in Medan over twenty years later (April 1994). Aside from the international humiliation involved, and the damage to Japanese–Indonesian relations, the other alarming aspect of the Malari Affair was that close politico-military associates of Suharto were deeply involved, in antagonistic groups, and that these conflicts were in highly visible public view. In many quarters it was being said that the struggle over the 'succession' to Suharto was under way. In the immediate aftermath of the Affair, Suharto abruptly dismissed General Sumitro, head of the Kopkamtib Internal Security Command, and General Sutopo Yuwono, head of Bakin, the State Intelligence Coordinating Agency. The ambitious Sumitro, in particular, was believed to have been encouraging students and other dissatisfied elements as part of a sort of informal electoral campaign. Sumitro's chief antagonists, General Ali Murtopo of Opsus, whom the students had denounced as a 'political pimp', and General Sudjono Humardani, presidential consultant for magic and for economic relations with Tokyo, were treated more gently, but never had the same kind of power in the presidential palace that they had before Malari. Benny Murdani, then an eager observer of the Park Chung Hee regime's consolidation in Seoul, where he had served as Chargé d'Affaires, was brought back to Jakarta to take control of military intelligence (a job which included the vital task of internal political surveillance of the military). And if this political disarray were not enough, there followed the financial disaster of the bankruptcy of the huge state oil company Pertamina, which unfolded from the last months of 1974 and culminated in February 1975. The debts accumulated by Pertamina's powerful chief, General Ibnu Sutowo, amounted to over ten billion dollars (four times the foreign debt of the Sukarno regime so often abused for its spendthrift ways) and their rene-gotiation involved protracted and humiliating bargaining with American banks and private businessmen, the American government, and interna-tional financial agencies. In many ways, then, the 'team' which had helped bring Suharto to power and to consolidate his initial dominance was falling apart.

This contest helps illuminate the development of Jakarta's East Timor policy in 1974–5. In the early stages the key actor was Ali Murtopo, who felt his power diminishing, and was eager to show Suharto that he was as effective and trustworthy as he had earlier shown himself to be in stage-managing the national elections of 1971 and the 1969 'integration' of West New Guinea (Irian Jaya), as well as in manipulating the collapse of Indonesia's political parties after 1967. Scarcely less eager were Murtopo's closest political aides, the two Chinese-Indonesian Catholics Liem Bian-Kie (Yusuf Wanandi) and Harry Tjan Silalahi, for among the student banners during Malari had been some with the words 'Hang Liem Bian-Kie!' scrawled across them. These people thought that the same methods used inside Indonesia could be deployed in the small, backward neighbouring territory of East Timor, and that success there would ensure their full return to power in Jakarta. How fortunate that events in Lisbon in April 1974 opened up so sudden and so golden an opportunity. Suharto seems initially to have been cool to the idea of mas-sive intervention, but later appeared willing to give the Opsus group a second chance. It is also likely that senior figures in the military saw cer-tain domestic opportunities for themselves in East Timor. General Panggabean, the Armed Forces Commander in Chief, had been largely marginalized by his ambitious, capable deputy, General Sumitro. He now looked for a chance to reassert himself and reassure Suharto as to the Armed Forces' unity and loyalty. Furthermore, promotions in the mili-tary had been slowed substantially since the later 1960s, and there were plenty of colonels waiting in the wings who welcomed the career possi-bilities of a little 'action'. Nor can one discount the possibility that Suharto himself, shaken by Malari and Pertamina, and aware that among the student accusations against his regime was the charge of subservience to foreign interests, saw in an aggressive stance towards East Timor an opportunity to play national hero.

Let me conclude this second section by stressing the importance of con-juncture. Had the Caetano regime in Lisbon fallen two or three years ear-lier, Indonesian intervention is much less likely to have occurred. Jakarta would not then have felt itself in crisis, Opsus would have still been busy in West New Guinea and in domestic political manipulations, the army would have been more unified, intelligence would have been under the sober and cautious Sutopo Yuwono, and Suharto himself less under siege.

The Present World Context

As we are all very much aware, today's world is utterly different from that of 1975. To borrow, perhaps unkindly, from Marx, one could say that all that was solid in 1975 has melted into air. Far the most important change has been the collapse of Stalinist communism and the ending of the Cold War. Stalin's east European empire has vanished, and the Soviet Union has disintegrated into a dozen militarily weak and economically ravaged states. Once-mighty Russia has no presence or influence in Southeast Asia. Post-Mao China is struggling with huge economic, cultural, and political problems. One outcome of this has been the effort, since 1976, to link up with the economic power of overseas Chinese capital in the Four Little Tigers (Taiwan, South Korea, Hong Kong and Singapore) and in Southeast Asia. Nothing better reveals this change than Peking's long wooing of the Suharto government which finally resulted in the renewal of normal diplomatic ties after a break of almost a quarter of a century (1967-89). The revolutionary regimes in Indochina are also in very serious crisis, although there is no point in elaborating on the reasons here. The former Portuguese colonies in Africa, ravaged by external interventions and civil conflicts, as well as economic difficulties, have been making rapid accommodations to Western capital. We might add that in the last decade the once powerful Thai, Burmese, and Malayan communist parties have been, to all intents and purposes, liquidated; and even in the Philippines the CPP–NPA is heading inexorably downhill. It was for these reasons that already, in the mid-1980s, General Benny Murdani was saying something that no top military leader had ever said before in the history of the young Republic: 'For the foreseeable future Indonesia faces no external threats.'

The ending of the Cold War and the collapse of Stalinist and Maoist communism have thus had two very important, if apparently contradictory, political implications. On the one hand, the anti-communism which underlay the legitimations of authoritarian, right-wing military regimes in the Third World, including Southeast Asia, has been rapidly losing its force. I believe this is the case even in Indonesia, where a quarter of a century has passed since the physical elimination of the Indonesian Communist Party (PKI), and where there are not the least signs of any revival – not even in overseas exile. On the other hand, all old-style left-wing revolutionary movements have lost their single most important resource – more important even than guns and organization; namely, the confidence of being at the vanguard of world history.

Of course, this change, crucial as it is, does not at all mean that economic exploitation and political oppression have diminished or that popular opposition to them has vanished. But the legitimation of this oppression has been shifting from, so to speak, the future to originary pasts. The
signs of this change were becoming evident soon after Jakarta's invasion
of East Timor – along three axes. First, originary religion, as exemplified
by the astonishing success of Khomeini's Islamic revolution in Iran at the
end of the 1970s, and the spread of so-called fundamentalist Muslim and
Christian movements in many parts of the Third World. Second, originary human rights, as exemplified by the steep climb in Amnesty
International's world prestige, the spread of organizations like the Watch
Committees' legislative enactments such as the Fraser Amendment, and
third, originary nationalism, visible now throughout the old European
Socialist bloc, but also in a new contesting of the early post-World War
II ex-colonial nation-state order. One might say this tendency got visibly
under way just two months before the fall of the Caetano regime, when
Pakistan was forced to recognize the independence of Bangladesh. Since
then, however, one can observe both the complete lack of effective
opposition to the reunification of Germany, the near partition of Sri
Lanka, the pressure on Peking with regard to Tibet, the negotiations
between Morocco and Polisario, Eritrea's independence, the triumph of
black majority rule in South Africa, and so on.

These movements differ from the older Communist-led movements
in one other very significant way. Although they are inspired, to varying
degrees, by world ideas – revived Islam, revived Christianity, the rights
of human beings everywhere, self-determination – and often have external allies, they are also more visibly locally rooted. The Bangsa Moro in
the Philippines may get help from Libya or Sabah, and may feel itself part
of a more confident world of Islam, but their struggle is a provincial one,
without substantial ambitions beyond Mindanao and Sulu. It is very difficult to imagine seriously a world-wide Islamic, human rights, or
nationalist conspiracy, in the way that a 'Communist conspiracy' could
plausibly be imagined between 1920 and 1980. This change lessens the
chances of such movements gaining substantial external military support,
but also puts a premium on different forms of struggle. It also lessens the
chances of repressive regimes successfully externalizing their enemies and
calling on international allies for assistance. Thus from both sides pressures are building for a more accommodationist style of conflict – perhaps what we hear so much of now as 'democratization' – by authoritarian regimes, and by oppositions. We can look at such contrastive cases as
right-wing South Africa and left-wing Nicaragua, but also Sri Lanka,
Mali, South Korea, and so on. Even more striking has been the attention

given to the Kurds in justification for the Gulf War, and the new forms of pressure exerted to finally resolve the Palestinian question in the aftermath of the September 1993 Rabin-Arafat agreement.

At a tangent to all this is the spectacular change in the world economic order, notably America's emergence as the world's largest debtor nation, the decline of the dollar, the rise of the yen bloc, and the economic successes of East and Southeast Asia. The speed with which capital now moves around the globe, combined with the end of the Cold War, means that ambitious regimes, including that in Jakarta, are having to adapt their style of rule. International capital is interested in stability for purposes of investment, but this is often a stability threatened as much by repressive regimes as by opposition to them. Since there are now very few regimes or movements which are explicitly opposed to capital and capitalism, regimes and oppositions are not as violently juxtaposed in capital's eyes as they often were in the Cold War era. This can mean more pressure on regimes than on oppositions. For example, the assassination of two Japanese businessmen in Manila is not very difficult to arrange, but the shock effect in Japan may be substantial. Japanese capital's response is more likely to be to withdraw, or to urge political responsiveness, than to urge greater repression by the Manila government.

The Present Local Context

As mentioned earlier, Suharto is among the longest-ruling non-royal heads of state in the world. In Asia only the ailing Deng Xiaoping goes back further. One by one, the generals who helped him to power have died off, gone into quiet opposition, or have been removed from effective influence. His eminence now is a deliberately lonely one. You would have to be close to forty years old today in Indonesia to have any memory of a non-Suharto regime, and the majority of Indonesians are under thirty. Such durable regimes almost always have a contradictory quality – in the short run they offer powerful guarantees of stability, but in the longer run they delay normal generational turnover, they encourage administrative sclerosis and rigid thinking, and they dam up pressures for change and other dissatisfactions.

In most ways, the Indonesian political system has not changed since the days of the invasion of East Timor. But this system now sits over a society which the regime's own developmental success has profoundly transformed. Indonesia is by no means a rich country, but it is much richer than it was eighteen years ago (per capita GDP now stands at US $680, five times what it was in the early 1970s), and a substantial middle class has come into being which is not confined to the capital city, but has components in all the regional capitals, many small towns, and even in some parts of the countryside. It is a conservative middle class, but it is not, I think, a frightened one, and it would like now to have a political role commensurate with its economic influence. Its way of life is the way of life of businessmen, its world that of bargains, deals, tax evasions, informal monopolies, managerial seminars, and trips overseas. It does not have any substantial interest in Suharto's pre-1975 'security state', and does not have much sympathy with the repressions that as much as anything have spawned the recent violence in Aceh, as well as the long-standing resistances in West New Guinea and East Timor. Many of its younger members are uncomfortable with Indonesia's international image. Businessmen dislike, or are envious of, the Suharto family's greedy monopolism; lawyers dislike the government's profound contempt for law; many provinces dislike the financial–administrative arrangements whereby, even when richly endowed by nature, they are made financially dependent on the centre. Students and intellectuals dislike the boring nature of the press and the dreariness of university life. More important, there is less and less feeling that all of this is necessary, or that it is what the outside world actually wants.

How Does All This Relate to the East Timor Question?
Up to the end of the 1980s, the Indonesian government seemed confident that its long-standing policies for the territory could be advantageously pursued with only minor cosmetic changes here and there. Thus, the resistance was less and less described as 'Communist,' and more and more as 'a small residual group of bandits' in the remoter countryside. After January 1989, somewhat greater access to East Timor was granted to tourists, journalists, and human rights agencies.

What the government did not understand was that its policies were astonishingly similar to those of the later Netherlands–Indies colonial regime and were bound, in the long run, to have parallel consequences. In the two decades between 1900 and 1920, the Dutch educated far more natives than they had done in the three previous centuries of their presence in the archipelago; they systematically invested large sums in 'development', especially in communications, transport, and infrastructure; and they created an elaborate police apparatus for surveillance and repression. Precisely out of the nexus between these transformations was born an Indonesian nationalism that ended Dutch rule in 1949. In East Timor, during the 1980s, the same explosive mixture of education, development, and repression was steadily deepening and widening East Timorese nationalism, especially among the young. The Timorese Catholic church has massively expanded its membership and increasingly voices the aspirations of this nationalism. And the resistance has moved out of the hills into the capital city of Dili, the population of which has increased almost tenfold since the last days of Portuguese rule.

Out of this juncture of unchanging policy and vastly changed conditions came the world notorious 12 November 1991 'Dili Massacre' of unarmed nationalist youngsters – too young to remember the Portuguese era, and in every way the products of Indonesian occupation.

Jakarta was caught completely off guard both by the tragedy itself and by its national and international consequences. President Suharto was forced to engage in the humiliating dismissal (in fact transfer) of the two generals with the most direct formal responsibility for East Timor, and thereby exacerbated growing army antagonism to his long rule. Jakarta's record on human rights has come under ever sharper scrutiny in the United Nations and its agencies, as well as in the advanced industrial countries. The Suharto government can no longer rely on unconditional support in Washington and Tokyo. When the famed guerrilla leader Xanana Gusmão was finally captured on 20 November 1992, there was no possibility that he would be summarily killed like his predecessor Nicolau Lobato (1952–78); he had to be tried in a court of law with international observers present some of the time, and to be sentenced to life imprisonment rather than the execution visited on so many former Indonesian Communist leaders. Furthermore, Jakarta was compelled to reopen negotiations, under UN auspices, with Portugal on the future of East Timor. Another sign of the vast changes since 1975 when Portugal was a weak, isolated, and divided country; by 1986 it had become a full member of the European Community, with veto power over the Community's foreign policies, enjoying rapidly growing prosperity and internal political unity.

In Indonesia itself, the Dili Massacre resulted in unprecedented news coverage of East Timor, and the first public signs, however cautiously expressed, of disillusionment with government policy. There is every reason to believe that this disillusionment will spread, not least because in the 1990s younger-generation Indonesians are more and more acquainted with East Timorese, who are both fluent in Indonesian and yet completely reject being Indonesian, in the same way that in the 1920s intelligent Dutchmen were meeting young Indonesians fluent in Dutch who completely rejected Dutch rule.

At another level the anomalies of Indonesia's domination of East Timor are becoming ever more visible in the present post-communist and post-Cold War era. In ASEAN, Jakarta has the most cordial relations with Brunei and Singapore, micro-states far smaller than East Timor. At the United Nations, Jakarta has been quick to build political and economic ties with some of the new states emerging from the former Soviet

Union. Lastly, having voted in the General Assembly against Saddam Hussein's attempted annexation of Kuwait, it has substantially undermined its own international defence of its annexation of East Timor.

CHAPTER 10

Towards A Just Peace

Pat Walsh

In 1991, the Australian Council for Overseas Aid published *East Timor: Towards a Just Peace in the 1990s*.[1] Written by three veteran East Timor watchers, this short monograph sought to rekindle concern in the issue following the 1991 Gulf War in which the United Nations authorized military intervention to reverse Iraq's annexation of Kuwait.

The interest of the authors lay not in advocating similar action in East Timor but in reminding the US and countries like Australia, which enthusiastically committed troops to the US-led *Operation Desert Storm*, of their abandonment of the East Timorese, who theoretically enjoyed the same UN endorsed right of self-determination and the right to inter-national protection from aggression as the people of Kuwait. More importantly, the authors sought to address the argument that the situation was irreversible, that nothing could be done for East Timor at this late hour. They argued that changes in the international environment follow-ing the end of the Cold War and offers by the East Timorese resistance to negotiate with Indonesia opened up important new possibilities that should be fully explored in the interests of a lasting peace which would benefit both the East Timorese and Indonesia.

What has been the fate of these hopes and strategies for peace in the intervening years? Is a just peace that takes account of the legitimate aspi-rations of the East Timorese people still possible? What is needed to keep the process alive?

Most of the factors that favoured the case for peace in 1991 are still in place in 1994. These include continued conflict and human rights abuse in East Timor arising from East Timorese aspirations for self-determination and independence, strong concern over East Timor in many countries, renewed attention to the issue at various levels in the UN, including the Secretary-General's office, an international context conducive to an Indonesian reappraisal of its relations with East Timor, the absence of any external or internal threat to Indonesia from Communism, and the offer of the East Timorese resistance to engage in talks without preconditions under UN auspices.

In some notable instances these factors have strengthened significantly in the early 1990s. Indeed, it is arguable that Indonesia has experienced more pressure on the issue since 1991 than at any period since the late 1970s.

A single event has been primarily responsible for this. On 12 November 1991, Indonesian troops gunned down defenceless demonstrators at the Santa Cruz cemetery in Dili as tensions between the East Timorese and the military peaked following the cancellation of a long awaited UN-backed Portuguese Parliamentary visit to the disputed territory. The shooting was witnessed by foreign observers from a number of countries and filmed, ensuring widespread publicity. The tragedy galvanized whole new sectors of public opinion around the issue, sharply increased scrutiny and criticism of Indonesia's behaviour in East Timor and provided unprecedented visual evidence of East Timorese opposition to Jakarta's rule. Over two years later, images of the massacre and claims about what happened continue to appear in magazines and on television (most recently in John Pilger's *Death of a Nation: The East Timor Conspiracy*, 28 February 1994) and to dominate discussions on East Timor in forums such as the UN Commission on Human Rights. Described as an 'aberration' in some quarters, Santa Cruz has, in fact, become a paradigm for the whole East Timor saga. Like the 1976 Soweto massacre in South Africa, it may yet prove to be a turning point in East Timor's history.

US attention to the issue has also increased significantly following the arrival of Bill Clinton in the White House in January 1993, just over a year after Santa Cruz. The Clinton Administration is giving higher priority to human rights than the Bush Administration and both the President and Vice-President Al Gore have expressed concern over East Timor. The US spearheaded a vote against Indonesia in the UN Commission on Human Rights in March 1993 and in July 1993 President Clinton met with Indonesia's President Suharto in Tokyo and passed on a letter from forty-three US Senators urging him to facilitate 'serious negotiations…in pursuit of the self-determination of the East Timorese people.'

The US Congress has been active on the issue for many years and has taken other initiatives in 1993 including stressing the linkage between US arms sales/training and human rights. What is noteworthy now is the increased level of cooperation between the legislature and the executive, and the stronger emphasis placed by Congress on the need for a UN-sponsored process leading to a lasting settlement. A letter to President Clinton of 15 November 1993 signed by thirty-seven Senators urged him to 'raise our concerns with President Suharto [during the November 1994 APEC Summit in Jakarta] and reiterate the need for an authentic long-term solution to the Timor struggle under the auspices of the United Nations.' The letter concluded, 'Such a solution should be "in pursuit of the right of self-determination" for East Timor, as endorsed by the US Senate in a November 1991 resolution.' This represents an important shift of emphasis within Congress which has put the Administration on the spot. The debate and policy focus on East Timor must be moved on from an exclusive preoccupation with human rights to the wider context of peace and justice. It should also be recognized that these developments have not occurred in a vacuum. They have been facilitated by a range of activists, editorials writers, NGOs, churches and intellectuals who have taken up the issue since Santa Cruz and added their voices to the small band of advocates who have been active over many years.

Concern in Japan, which provides by far the largest part of Indonesia's bilateral aid, has also grown. In December 1991, the Diet Members' Forum on East Timor persuaded 262 Diet members to sign a petition calling for a review of Japanese aid to Indonesia. In September 1992, 143 Diet members, in a joint action with the US Congress, petitioned the UN Secretary-General to be more active on East Timor. Although the Japanese government continues to be cautious on the issue, ex-Prime Minister Miyazawa raised concerns about East Timor with President Suharto when he visited Indonesia in January 1993.

Portugal's role should also be emphasized. Indonesia and Australia are at pains to minimize Portugal's credibility on the question by insisting that Portugal 'abandoned' East Timor in 1975 and, in the words of Australian Prime Minister Paul Keating, has been 'the world's worst colonial ruler'. However, its role cannot be so easily dismissed. Supported by strong public sentiment and led since 1986 by Mário Soares, a President with a deep personal commitment to the East Timor question, Portugal has been more active in recent years than at any point since 1975. It is currently challenging Australia's signature of the Timor Gap Treaty in the International Court of Justice, which largely explains Australia's hostility, and is an active advocate of East Timorese self-determination within UN forums and the European Union. While Portugal's economic and strategic influence is small, its diplomatic role on the Timor issue is critical. In the absence of a genuine act of self-determination in East Timor, the UN continues to regard Portugal as the *de facto* 'administering power'. This makes it a key player in UN efforts to resolve the issue and it is, in fact, an interlocutor with Indonesia in UN sponsored talks on the matter. What this means to the issue can be better grasped if one compares Portugal's constructive engagement with its former colony with Holland's abandonment in the early 1960s of its former colony, West Irian, now discarded and languishing as the Indonesian province of Irian Jaya.

Given that external pressure on Indonesia has increased since the Santa Cruz débâcle, what effect has this had on the search for a durable settlement?

Talks between Indonesia and Portugal, mandated by the UN General Assembly in 1982, were broken off shortly before the Dili massacre and did not resume until September 1992. Since then, the Portuguese Foreign Minister, José Manuel Durão Barroso and his Indonesia counterpart, Ali Alatas, have met four times with UN Secretary-General Boutros Boutros-Ghali. These meetings were in New York in December 1992, Rome in April 1993, New York in September 1993, and Geneva in May 1994. A fifth round took place in Geneva in January 1995. In the same context, the Secretary-General's Senior Political Adviser, the Peruvian diplomat Alvaro de Soto, has held a number of meetings with the UN ambassadors of Portugal and Indonesia and with representatives of a number of East Timorese political parties and organizations.

Little has been made public about the content and outcome of these meetings. After the December 1992 meeting, the Portuguese Foreign Minister stated that the two sides were '180 degrees apart'. Indonesia is said to have rejected proposals by Portugal that there be a UN presence in East Timor and that East Timorese representatives be included in the UN sponsored talks.

The next two rounds of talks yielded some small signs of progress. Given the differences between the two sides regarding the political status of East Timor, the talks focused on possible confidence building measures. As the UN Secretary-General put it in his report to the 1994 UN Commission on Human Rights, it was hoped that 'confidence-building measures…could be undertaken by Indonesia and Portugal with a view to creating a more conducive atmosphere for a discussion at a later stage of the core issues concerning the political future of East Timor.'

US Secretary of State Warren Christopher wrote to the two Foreign Ministers ahead of the September 1993 talks urging them to do more to reach agreement. That meeting agreed on seven points of which the most important were: respect for the full spectrum of human rights in East Timor, less confrontation, access by UN humanitarian and human rights organizations, UN consultations with all parties before the 1994 round, and exchange visits by journalists and personalities.

Some of these undertakings have been acted on. In accordance with the agreement to lower the political temperature, the 1994 UN resolution on East Timor adopted by the UN Commission on Human Rights was agreed to by consensus, thus avoiding a bruising vote like the previous year. It was also considerably milder in content and language. As agreed, UN consultations also took place: two senior political officers from the UN Secretariat in New York visited Indonesia, East Timor, Portugal and Australia in January 1994 and conducted wide-ranging consultations with the Portuguese and Indonesian governments, and with leading East Timorese, including the gaoled East Timorese leader Xanana Gusmão, Bishop Belo and the indigenous East Timorese clergy. Visits to East Timor by journalists have also taken place, although it is understood that some foreign correspondents, in particular, were critical of attempts to manipulate them and restrict their access to East Timorese activists.

There were also some small signs of progress in the May 1994 round, particularly in the agreement to broaden the consultation process. In addition to UN consultations with the parties, efforts will now be made to encourage 'intra-Timorese dialogue', and Portugal and Indonesia both undertook 'to meet with leading East Timorese supporters and opponents of integration respectively'.[2] This would appear to represent a significant concession on the part of Indonesia, although it should be noted that the Indonesian Foreign Minister, Ali Alatas, later ruled out consulting with Xanana Gusmão or 'any other Fretilin activists such as Ramos-Horta'.[3]

On the fundamental issue of respect for human rights, however, there has been little progress. Although Indonesia allowed the UN Special Rapporteur on Extra-Judicial, Summary or Arbitrary Executions, Bacré Waly N'Diaye of Senegal, access to visit East Timor from 7–11 July 1994, similar access for human rights organizations like Amnesty International continues to be denied and frequent reports of human rights abuse continue to be received.[4] In addition to visits by the UN and bodies like Amnesty International, other specific measures should be considered if internationally-accepted human rights standards are to be upheld in East Timor. Such measures could include the placement of UN human rights monitors on the ground in East Timor charged with responsibilities to investigate and report publically on human rights violations and to provide training and education in human rights issues. The UN might also seek agreement between the parties to the talks on which human rights are of foremost concern in East Timor and on concrete indicators against which progress in respect for these rights can be measured on the ground in East Timor. One minimum indicator of how serious the Indonesian government is about halting human rights abuse in East Timor would be to replace the current practice of virtual impunity for the Indonesian security forces with an appropriate system of punishment of the perpetrators of abuse.

In addition to the UN visit referred to above, there have been at least three other UN visits to East Timor since the Dili massacre, though no reports have yet been made public. Two of these were undertaken by the Kenyan Attorney-General, Amos Wako, as a personal envoy for the Secretary-General, to report on the human rights situation and to meet with key East Timorese, including the Catholic Bishop of East Timor, Mgr Belo, and Xanana Gusmão, then on trial for 'rebellion and conspiracy'. Following the latter meeting, Xanana used his defence speech to denounce the Indonesian occupation and repeated his earlier call for talks under UN auspices and the holding of a referendum.[5] The third visit was undertaken by an observer from the UN Secretariat who attended the final stages of the Xanana Gusmão trial in May 1993.

It would appear, then, that after years of neglect, the issue is back on the UN agenda and is receiving high-level attention. This represents some progress in the search for peace and should be welcomed, though from the point of view of the East Timorese, these steps forward must seem painfully slow and minimal. After all, nearly twenty years have elapsed since 1975 when the first of two Security Council resolutions and eight General Assembly resolutions were adopted affirming East Timor's right to self-determination and calling on Indonesia to immediately withdraw its troops. What the Secretary-General calls 'the core issues concerning the political future of East Timor' are also still to be resolved and they are certain to test the political will and diplomatic skills of all involved.

It is here that the settlement proposals from the East Timorese side are of such vital importance. Two main East Timorese settlement proposals are on the table. One comes from the National Council of Maubere Resistance (CNRM), the umbrella body representing mainstream East Timorese opinion both inside and outside East Timor, and was presented by CNRM's Special Representative, José Ramos-Horta, to the Human Rights Sub-Committee of the European Parliament in April 1992.

In summary, this proposal calls for a ceasefire and the immediate release of all political prisoners, following which Indonesia would reduce its troops in East Timor to 1000 within two years and allow UN agencies to operate there. Following this two-year period, the government of the territory would be accountable to an elected provincial assembly, with Indonesia retaining sovereignty and control of foreign policy. A referendum, with independence as one option, would he held after either five years or ten years of this arrangement, that is, either seven or twelve years after the ceasefire. Indonesia would have the option of making the initial five-year period into a ten-year one.

The plan, which is generous towards Indonesia, has been widely publicized. Although particular aspects may be further modified and refined, its broad thrust is supported by the East Timorese resistance, including UDT and Fretilin, and Church circles in East Timor. In addition to the European Parliament, it has also been presented to bodies such as the US Council on Foreign Relations and the UN Decolonization Committee.

A second East Timorese proposal put forward in February 1993 by Bishop Belo, the head of the majority Catholic Church in East Timor (which is administered by the Vatican because of East Timor's disputed status), contains much less detail. It calls for a 'special status' for East Timor, involving autonomy within Indonesia which would begin with the cultural and religious fields and then extend to the economic and political realms. The Bishop has referred to Puerto Rico's relationship to the US, and that of Madeira and the Azores to Portugal, as possible models for East Timor's relationship with Indonesia. It is not clear whether he sees arrangements of this sort as permanent or as an intermediate or pre-referendum possibility, as is the case with the CNRM proposal. Whatever his view, he is clearly on record as insisting on a UN conducted referendum for East Timor and would appear to believe that the CNRM must be party to any political settlement.

Another critical issue is who will be involved in the process and at what point. East Timorese views must be fully taken into account by the UN, both to comply with its own resolutions supporting self-determination and because East Timorese cooperation is essential for a durable outcome. But process and content are not the same thing. Insistence on direct East Timorese participation, at least in the earlier delicate stages, may be counterproductive, and parallel consultations, as are now happening, may be wiser.

Whatever the preferred course of action, Indonesia will have to negotiate with people who are widely supported by the East Timorese and who can be depended on to make any arrangement stick, particularly if a settlement involving compromises with Indonesia is agreed to. Xanana Gusmão, seen by some as East Timor's Nelson Mandela, is an obvious candidate. The gifted and charismatic leader, in whose fate the UN Secretary-General has taken a close personal interest, is widely revered by the East Timorese for his patriotic defence of East Timorese interests. Whether or not he is released from prison in Jakarta, where he is serving a twenty-year gaol term, may well be the clearest signal of Jakarta's intentions on the future of East Timor.

Other possible negotiators are Bishop Carlos Belo and Mário Carrascalão, East Timor's governor between 1982 and 1992, who has recently been appointed Indonesia's ambassador to Rumania. As Herb

Feith has observed, 'Happily, these three: Xanana the guerrilla leader, Belo the cleric and Carrascalão the agricultural engineer, whose ten years as governor gave him a detailed familiarity with Jakarta politics, have a good deal of trust and respect for each other. An agreement from which the three of them emerge in positions of authority and influence would be likely to be widely acceptable.'[6] It might also be useful to consider a role for ASEAN in addition to that of the UN, both in terms of facilitating the talks process and providing long-term guarantees to ensure durability. The foreign policies of the East Timorese political parties favour future membership of ASEAN.

Is Indonesia likely to respond positively to settlement proposals like these? No clear cut answer can be given, but the signals are not encouraging. According to Herb Feith, there are two schools of thought. Those who believe a change of policy is in the pipeline point to the need to do away with the embarrassment that East Timor persistently creates, if Indonesia is to improve its standing in the international community. They also argue that President Suharto, now in his sixth term, has sufficient influence over the military to make concessions on East Timor. His statements in July 1993 that East Timor was a burden and that Indonesia had incorporated the territory because the East Timorese had invited its intervention, have been seen by some as an indication of a coming change of policy.[7]

The other school of thought see no hard evidence that the President believes his Timor policies have failed. No senior government figure has indicated that an alternative to the status quo is being considered. On the contrary, the appointment of hardliners to key positions in East Timor following the Santa Cruz massacre indicated precisely the opposite, namely an official belief that concessions do not work and that a relaxation of military discipline encourages dissidence and is a recipe for instability. They admit that international concern over East Timor has strengthened, but believe this must be balanced against Suharto's growing international influence, economically and politically, through his chairmanship of the Non-Aligned Movement (NAM) and the Asia Pacific Economic Cooperation (APEC) forum. Others, like Australia's Foreign Minister Senator Gareth Evans, argue that Indonesia would risk fragmentation if Jakarta were to make concessions to the Timorese and that too many Indonesian soldiers have died in East Timor to make withdrawal politically feasible. Indonesia's development investment in East Timor is also seen as a tangible sign they intend to stay.

Indonesia has sought to wrest the initiative from the East Timorese resistance by initiating its own 'peace process'. This has taken the form of 'reconciliation talks' involving East Timorese described as pro-integrationist and anti-integrationist, supported by President Suharto particularly through the active participation of his eldest daughter Siti Hardiyanti Rukmana (Mbak Tutut) and the Indonesian Ambassador in London, J.E. Habibie, a younger brother of Research and Technology Minister, Ir. B.J. Habibie. A first meeting was held outside London (near Cambridge) in December 1993, and a second took place in Chepstow (South Wales) on 29 September–1 October 1994. The key interlocutors were Abílio Araújo, the former head of Fretilin outside East Timor, and Francisco Lopes da Cruz, President Suharto's Roving Ambassador on East Timor Affairs and an erstwhile leader of the UDT (*União Democrática Timorense*). Others attending included the former Fretilin President, Xavier do Amaral (in office, 1974–7), a man very much under the control of the Indonesian military since his capture in 1978, José Gonçalves, the son of the pro-integrationist *liurai* of Atsabe, Guilherme Gonçalves (second Governor of East Timor, 1977–82), and Rogério Lobato, another ex-Fretilin member and brother of Nicolau Lobato (killed in action, 31 December 1978), whose recent career has been marked more by opportunism than principle. It is understood that a representative from the UN Secretariat in New York, Tamrat Samuel, was present at the Chepstow talks which suggests that the Portuguese may have given their approval. Little is known of the objectives or content of these meetings, but they have been presented by the principals as consistent with the confidence-building measures sought by the UN, especially the point made in the May 1994 communiqué which spoke of the Secretary-General 'encouraging dialogue amongst the East Timorese', and 'facilitating an *all-inclusive* [author's italics] intra-Timorese' exchange of views. The process and its major participants, however, have little support amongst East Timorese: the CNRM and both East Timorese political parties (UDT and Fretilin) have considered the initiative as an Indonesian manoeuvre designed to divide the East Timorese and subvert the UN process, and Bishop Belo has said that he saw no point in negotiations which did not include 'Ramos-Horta and his colleagues'. It also smacks strongly of internecine political rivalries in East Timor itself since it is known that Ambassador Lopes da Cruz and his ex-UDT circle resent the way in which the present Governor, Abílio Soares (in office, 1992 to present), has promoted his own Apodeti allies within the present East Timorese administration. Furthermore, Fretilin can hardly said to have been properly represented, since Abílio Araújo was expelled from the party in 1993 for corruption and abuse of power.[8]

Though there are now some encouraging signs of hope, the prospects for peace in East Timor are at best long term. To achieve this at least six conditions will have to be met. First, Indonesia will have to cease playing diplomatic games and recognise that it is in a difficult, if not untenable, position and that changes of policy will have to be made to accommodate both international concern and East Timorese attitudes. The issue has been a running sore for twenty years and shows no signs of going away. The East Timorese remain deeply dissatisfied, fearful and resentful. Development, Jakarta's best card, in which it has invested so heavily and trumpets as a form of anti-colonial 'liberation', is neo-colonialism to the East Timorese and poorly administered.[9] There is no basis for reconciliation in the current situation: the Timorese and Jakarta are poles apart. Second, international pressure will have to continue at both community and official levels, including in Asia (now more sensitized to the issue following the furore over the May/June 1994 Manila Conference), but policies will need to be developed to focus more directly on a long-term peace process in which the East Timorese themselves participate. An effective human rights policy must include a strategy for peace. Third, international action on East Timor will have to be more cooperative and mutually supportive, particularly of the efforts of the UN Secretary-General, Boutros Boutros-Ghali. Australia, for example, should cease its cheap and opportunistic attacks on both the Portuguese and on US policy and work in cooperation with them. Fourth, the content of the CNRM Peace Plan and the fact that anti-integrationist East Timorese are prepared to negotiate will both need to be more widely publicized and discussed in Indonesia. This applies particularly to the emerging Indonesian democracy movement which, through the efforts of East Timorese and Indonesian researchers like Dr. George Aditjondro[10] and others, is becoming better informed on the issue and more understanding of why the East Timorese feel the way they do about the Republic. Indonesians should know, for example, that East Timorese leaders have no intention of subverting or dismembering Indonesia. Fifth, continuing ethno-nationalist demands in other parts of the world, such as Kashmir, the Kurdish areas of Turkey and Iraq, Palestine and Tibet, to mention only a few, will benefit East Timor by keeping issues of self-determination and imperatives for new political arrangements firmly on the international agenda. The sixth condition can be met only by the East Timorese people themselves. In principle, their right of self-determination is inalienable and non-forfeitable. In practice, however, the ultimate exercise of this right will depend upon the depth of their tenacity and the keenness of their hunger for justice, a hunger which, they must insist, only an act of genuine free choice will assuage.

Notes

1 Scott, David, Feith, Herb and Walsh, Pat, *East Timor: Towards a Just Peace in the 1990s*. Melbourne: Australian Council for Overseas Aid, 1991.

2 Boutros-Ghali, Boutros, *Statement on the Question of East Timor*. Geneva: United Nations, 6 May 1994.

3 See Department of Foreign Affairs, Republic of Indonesia, 'Statement by the Minister for Foreign Affairs of Indonesia on East Timor', Jakarta, 26 August 1994. Despite Alatas's statement, he did meet informally with José Ramos-Horta and other anti-integrationist Timorese leaders (José Belo, João Carrascalão and Abílio Araújo) in New York on 6 October 1994, see Ted Morello, 'Flirting with the Enemy: Foreign Minister Meets East Timor Separatists', *FEER*, 20 October 1994, p.21. On the wider changes currently being considered in Indonesia's East Timor policy, see John McBeth, 'Change in the Wind: Jakarta may be Rethinking Its Timor Policy', *FEER*, 6 October 1994, pp.26-8.

4 See the AI reports for 1994 listed in the Bibliography below, especially *Indonesia & East Timor. Power and Impunity: Human Rights under the New Order*. London: Amnesty International, 28 September 1994, pp. 29–31, pp. 50–4, pp. 69–71, and pp. 83–6.

5 See 'Xanana's Defence Statement', *Inside Indonesia*, No. 35 (June 1993).

6 Feith, Herb, *The East Timor Issue Since the Capture of Xanana Gusmão*. Fitzroy Victoria: East Timor Talks Campaign, 1993.

7 See further John McBeth, 'Change in the Wind: Jakarta may be Rethinking its Timor Policy', *FEER*, 6 October. 1994, pp. 26–8.

8 For a more optimistic view of these talks, see Jill Jolliffe, 'The London Talks: A Second Opinion', *Timor Link*, No.30 (September 1994), pp. 4–5.

9 Mubyarto, Loekman Soetrisno *et al.*, *East Timor: The Impact of Integration. An Indonesian Socio-Anthropological Study*, ed. Pat Walsh. Northcote (Australia): Indonesian Resources and Information Program [IRIP], 1991; Aditjondro, G.J., 'Prospek Pembangunan Timor Timur Sesudah Penangkapan Xanana Gusmão', *Dian Ekonomi*, 2 (1992-93); *ibid*., 'From Memo to Tutuala. A Kaleidoscope of Environmental Problems in East Timor', in Herb Feith *et al.* (eds), *East Timor. An Indonesian Intellectual Speaks Out*. Canberra: ACFOA Development Dossier No.33, 1994; and Saldhanha, José Mariano da Sousa, *Ekonomi-Politik Pembangunan Timor Timur*. Jakarta: Pustaka Sinar Harapan, 1994.

10 Aditjondro, George, *East Timor: An Indonesian Intellectual Speaks Out*. ed. Herb Feith, Emma Baulch and Pat Walsh. ACFOA Development Dossier No.33, Canberra: Australian Council for Overseas Aid, 1994. As of the time of writing (October 1994), Aditjondro is under investigation by the Yogyakarta police for speaking out on matters relating to the presidential succession and the democratization process in Indonesia at a seminar at the Universitas Islam Indonesia (UII) in Yogyakarta on 11 August 1994. He has since (January 1995) taken leave of absence from his Indonesian university (Universitas Kristen Satya Wacana, Salatiga) and gone to the Murdoch University, Perth, Western Australia for a six month sabbatical.

PART V

Dimensions of Domination: An East Timor Colloquy

Dimensions of Domination: An East Timor Colloquy

(Social Science Research Council Workshop on East Timor, American University, Washington DC, 25–6 April 1991) edited by G. Carter Bentley

Participants (in order of appearance)

Sanford Unger – Moderator, Dean, School of Communications, American University, Washington DC, USA.

James Dunn – Foreign Affairs Columnist; former Australian Consul-General in Portuguese Timor.

Dr John G. Taylor – Principal Lecturer, South Bank University, London.

José Ramos-Horta – Director, Diplomacy Training Program, Faculty of Laws, University of New South Wales, Australia.

Prof. Elizabeth Traube – Professor of Anthropology, Wesleyan University, USA.

Prof. Benedict R. O'G. Anderson – Professor of Government, Director, Modern Indonesia Project, Cornell University, USA.

Alan Nairn – US journalist.

Sidney Jones – Executive Director, Asia Watch, New York, USA.

Rt. Rev. Paul Moore – Episcopal Bishop of New York (retired).

Harold W. Maynard – Lt Col, US Air Force (retired).

Amy Goodman – Producer, Pacifica Radio, USA.

Pat Walsh – Director, Human Rights Program, Australian Council for Overseas Aid.

Geoffrey Robinson – Head of Research for Island Southeast Asia, Amnesty International, London.

Martin Rendon – US Congressional Aide to Rep. Tony Hall (D-Ohio).

Fr Reinaldo Cardoso – Catholic priest, formerly assigned to East Timor, now domiciled in USA (Rhode Island).

George Benson – Oil industry consultant, US Army (retired).

Professor Mubyarto – Professor and Director, Center for Rural and Regional Development Studies, Gadjah Mada University, Yogyakarta, Indonesia.

Colonel Luhud Panjaitan – Special Forces, ABRI (*Angkatan Bersenjata Republik Indonesia*, Armed Forces of the Republic of Indonesia).

USSD1 – US State Department official.

Donaciano Gomes – East Timorese refugee.

João Ramos Pinto – Portuguese Embassy, Washington, DC

USSD 2 – US State Department official.

Robert Archer – Christian Aid, London, England.

(25 April 1991)

Unger: It has been suggested that the circumstances in East Timor are the result of Portuguese colonialism. Mr Dunn?

Dunn: When, in 1974, Portugal declared its colonies to be self-governing territories, it was doing what it had been pressed to do by the international community, including Western countries, for more than ten years. When Portugal got into very tough circumstances and appealed to us for help, we had a responsibility to give that help. Portugal appealed to Australia for help based on its commitment to implement a plan of decolonization. In the circumstances, it was a compelling request and deserved a positive response. Canberra's reaction was totally unsympathetic and, I suggest, cynical because that was not the outcome people in government wanted at that time.

Unger: Mr Dunn, I have never heard Portugal portrayed as a benign colonial power. Angola, Mozambique, and her other colonies in Africa were very harshly treated. I suppose some people find retrospective comfort from the role of the Portuguese at the end, but what was the contribution of the Portuguese [to Timor] historically?

Dunn: Well, it was a very undeveloped country and a very poor country, but it was also a little disturbed country. As the Timorese have often said, the Portuguese didn't impose themselves on the Timorese communities. The Portuguese presence was uncontested by the Timorese people. In contrast to Timor today, which has never had less than 10,000 [Indonesian] troops, the Portuguese never had more than 1,500. It was not a severe colonial rule, even though it was not an acceptable form of colonial rule. By 1974, things had changed quite a lot. There were more schools than have been suggested and there were more hospitals. There were twenty-two Portuguese doctors in Timor and there was a well equipped hospital in Dili. Incidentally, a Red Cross official who went back there a year after the invasion found most of the up-to-date equipment had disappeared.

Taylor: I think that people have been relatively tolerant of the Portuguese. During three hundred years of the Portuguese presence there were long rebellions; they're very well documented. A second point relates to the role of the Portuguese in the 1970s, particularly after the April [1974] coup. There were many meetings between Portuguese government officials and the Indonesians. At these meetings the Portuguese stated very clearly that an independent East Timor was impossible. There were moments when they could clearly have argued against [the Indonesian position]. When they withdrew [from East Timor] in 1975 during the UDT coup attempt, they didn't have to do that either. At every stage, they went along with what was suggested by the Indonesians, so the way they are being portrayed seems to me to be rather strange to put it mildly.

Unger: Mr Ramos-Horta, I wonder if you would like to comment on what Mr Taylor said about Portuguese complicity in these final stages.

Ramos-Horta: In Portugal, there were some people in favour of the integration of East Timor into Indonesia. These were President [Francisco da] Costa Gomes [in office April 1974 – June 1976] and the Prime Minister [Vasco dos Santos Gonçalves, in office 1974–5]. Why Costa Gomes and Vasco Gonçalves? Costa Gomes and Vasco were the pro-Moscow elements in Portugal. If you look into Indonesia's relationship with the Soviet Union and the Soviet Union's strategic views of Southeast Asia, you can understand. For Indonesia, the Soviet Union was never the threat in Southeast Asia, the threat was China. The pro-Moscow elements in Portugal, like Vasco Gonçalves and Costa Gomes, thought that East Timor would be better off with Indonesia. Costa Gomes today doesn't deny these views. On the other hand, the Portuguese team that was dispatched to Timor by the Armed Forces Movement, led by Governor [Mário] Lemos Pires [in office 13 November 1974 – 7 December 1975], were very serious. They were people of integrity. Lemos Pires was a conservative military officer, highly decorated, having served in the United States before he went to East Timor, so he was not pro-Moscow or pro-China. On arriving in Timor they saw that the majority of the people in Timor opposed integration with Indonesia. They realized that the views held in Lisbon by Costa Gomes and Vasco Gonçalves were utterly unfair. So they decided to carry out the process of decolonization in all fairness, to all three parties. There were many instances when all three parties accused them of favouring one over another, which tended only to prove that they tried to be as neutral as possible. Despite the shortcomings of the Armed Forces Movement in Timor, they were doing an excellent job. Local elections had started throughout Timor [in July 1975], in preparation for the referendum which was due to take place in 1976. However, Indonesia, through the Center for Strategic and International Studies [and its Director] Yusuf Wanandi [a.k.a. Liem Bian-Kie], through [Armed Forces Commander] Maradean Panggabean, and Benny Murdani [then Assistant Director of Army Intelligence], orchestrated a campaign in Timor to destabilize the country, to undermine the process of decolonization, to weaken the Portuguese presence. It was a multi-faceted, multi-pronged campaign. Through *Antara*, the [Indonesian] news agency, they planted false stories internationally about instability in Timor, stories about a Vietnamese general landing in the south to train threatening forces, about four Chinese generals arriving in Timor, precisely to create this *mise en scène* to justify an intervention. Whatever instability was created in Timor during that period of 1974–5 was solely of Indonesia's making. It was part and parcel of [Ali Murtopo's] 'Operation Komodo'. Of course, Portugal, with very limited resources in Timor, could not counter it. On many occasions I talked to the Portuguese information officer, Captain Ramos, who told me that the Indonesians were doing this in Balibo; the Indonesians are doing this in Atsabe; they have landed one hundred com-

mandos across the border. That was in November–December 1974. So Indonesia was deeply involved in Timor way before the invasion. As early as November–December 1974, there were already Indonesian [military] operatives inside East Timor.

Unger: Dr Traube, do you have anything you might want to say about the role of the Portuguese?

Traube: Yes. I just wanted to say that a phrase I've usually used to characterize Portuguese colonialism on Timor is 'benign neglect'. During the first centuries you really have to talk about a colonial presence rather than colonial rule. What you had was a handful of Portuguese colonizers trying to defend themselves from the Dutch on the one hand and against a mestizo trading class, Portuguese speaking but of different ethnicity, on the other. Even after colonial rule was tightened and rationalized, which didn't take place until the turn of the century, Portuguese attention remained focused on the African colonies, with the result that, if there wasn't a whole lot of development, there was also less overt exploitation on Timor. These were the conditions for the kinds of ideological legitimations of colonial rule that were common among Timorese peoples, not only the Mambai of whom I spoke [in my paper].

The other point I wanted to make is that if anything would have radicalized Mambai it was the Portuguese administration's abandonment of Timor in the midst of the civil fighting. That was precisely what people feared. They sensed that their younger brothers weren't going to play their proper role, that they were going to bolt. It's those conditions that would have broken the ideology that I have described. At that point it would have become clear that all cards were on the table and I can imagine Mambai being drawn into radical forms of action.

Anderson: One of the things I think is not brought up enough is the fact that, from the summer of 1974, when Vasco Gonçalves became the Prime Minister of Portugal, this government was widely regarded as threatening to break the post-1950s balance in Europe. The Portuguese Communist Party had reemerged from underground and was imagined to be much more influential than it turned out to be. Costa Gomes and Vasco Gonçalves both were thought to be close to the Party. This was a government, therefore, which was under very heavy suspicion and pressure from the United States. It's the one time, in modern European history, when a government in Western Europe was not only under suspicion, but was being [actively] undermined [by the US]. It seems to me that if decolonization had started under the Caetano regime [1968–74], if it hadn't been under this particular [post-1974 leftist] government, the United States and the other powers might well have listened to Portugal or been willing to encourage Portugal to behave better.

Dunn: Certainly, the government of Portugal was regarded with suspicion by the United States and its allies, but it was clear to everybody that the Portuguese wanted to get rid of East Timor. I believe, as far as the Portuguese role was concerned, the important time in terms of heading off the invasion was the civil war period [11–31 August 1975]. Obviously, the Portuguese retreat to Atauro [on 26 August 1975] was really quite crucial, but Almeida Santos [Dr António de Almeida Santos, Portuguese Minister for Overseas Territories] made a proposal to the Australian government after the civil war that a peacekeeping force be sent into East Timor, involving Malaysia, the Philippines, Australia, and one other country. Prime Minister Whitlam rejected it out of hand, yet I thought it was a very constructive proposal. I believe that Fretilin might have accepted it. And it is one thing that might have stopped what was to transpire a few months later.

Nairn: I was in East Timor last year and, although many people there were quite critical of the Portuguese, they also said that the Indonesians, by comparison, made the Portuguese look good. There is really no comparison in terms of the death toll between the two occupations.

I want to pose two brief questions to the panel. One is on the food situation in East Timor prior to the invasion, whether there was hunger among the population in this period? Second, could they give more detail on the role of the United States in this period, since politically that is more relevant even than the role of the Portuguese?

Unger: The food situation before the events of 1975, and the role of the United States. Mr Dunn.

Dunn: Yes. I was, at that time, leader of a humanitarian aid mission sent by the Council of Churches [Australian Council for Overseas Aid, ACFOA], Catholic Relief, and other bodies. The food situation in East Timor during the Fretilin interregnum was becoming serious, partly because of a blockade which had been imposed by Indonesia. We did get one shipload of food in with great difficulty. Once there the distribution of food was fairly done. During this Fretilin interregnum [August–December 1975], there was no vacuum. The Fretilin administration was short on professionals, but it was an orderly administration. There was little looting. Whatever food there was was distributed equitably. The aid agencies travelled in any part of East Timor they wanted to go to. The International Red Cross were [also] very active. They used to give Fretilin lectures on the treatment of their UDT prisoners. We found that the prisoners were getting more food than the local population! Yes, the food situation was becoming difficult, but Timor in normal circumstances could feed itself and it would only have been a matter of time [before this was achieved].

Ramos-Horta: The fact is that the International Committee of the Red Cross, from early September till December 6 [1975] had a presence in East Timor. It was able to travel extensively throughout the country, to visit every Fretilin prison. One need only read the 1975 report of ICRC [dated] October 1975, where they acknowledge full Fretilin cooperation in discharging their mission in Timor, in contrast with what happened after 1975 where for four years [1976–80] the ICRC was not allowed to enter East Timor. Even today

[1991] its presence is extremely [restricted].

Traube: Prior to 1974, the Timorese had functioning subsistence economies that were producing for the needs of the population including surpluses for ritual exchange. There were growing ecological problems in certain areas from a pattern of over-cultivation, not allowing fields enough time to fallow. There was the beginning of what could have become serious erosion, a situation much more pronounced on the western [Indonesian] part of the island, where widespread cattle farming had produced what has been described as 'the Timor problem'. The ecological situation [there] was [indeed] a matter of concern.

Jones: I'd like to put the human rights situation in East Timor in some perspective by looking at human rights elsewhere in Indonesia. Everything that Alan [Nairn] says about what is happening in East Timor could be said almost word for word about what was going on in Aceh from July to November 1990 when I visited briefly. There are a number of other parallels as well. Reports of arrests and torture smuggled out of East Timor are really no different from what you read happening to activists with the OPM [Organisasi Papua Merdeka, Free Papua Movement] in Irian Jaya or people who belong to the Usroh [family-based fundamentalist] group of Muslim activists in Central Java. The reports of torture from people arrested after demonstrations in Dili are no different from the reports of torture, not only from people accused of subversion but also from common criminal suspects in Jakarta jails. The methods that are used to break up demonstrations, for example the one following the Pope's visit [on 12 October 1989] or the September 4 [1990] demonstration in Dili, should be looked at in conjunction with the demonstration in Yogyakarta after the verdict was announced in the case of [Bambang] Isti Nugroho, a young lab assistant [in September 1989]. That again was a mass street demonstration which was broken up forcibly by the Indonesian security forces.

I think there are two things going

on here. One is a gradual institutionalization of the security force mechanisms in East Timor, parallel with what is happening elsewhere [in Indonesia]. The police and military bureaucracy is more entrenched now than it has been before. Also we may be getting what you might call a 'Timorization' of insurgencies taking place elsewhere in Indonesia. What is happening in Aceh with the repression of the Aceh Merdeka guerrilla movement [1989–93] may be drawing on the experiences of the military in East Timor.

To continue the comparison, look at human rights abuses that have taken place in East Timor and see how they compare with others in Indonesia. One particularly interesting question is to look at the whole area of arrests and political trials. For a long time suspected Fretilin activists were either sent into exile and imprisonment on Atauro Island or just held in detention without trial. They were eventually brought to trial beginning in 1983. The trials are significant in that the Indonesians became willing to say publicly that there was a major conflict involved and that they had evidence that they could bring before an Indonesian court. No one suggested that the trials were fair, but, by bringing these people before judicial proceedings, the Indonesians were acknowledging an end to the chaotic period of the guerrilla conflict [1975–80]. It was also a way of identifying individual leaders and charging them with specific actions in connection with the insurgency. These people were not charged with subversion but were charged with being involved in a 'separatist' movement.

This shift in tactics paralleled what happened in the early 1970s with the decision of the Indonesian government to bring some of the category A prisoners – people who had been suspected of [direct] involvement in the 1965 ['Communist'] coup attempt – to trial. That again was an acknowledgment by the Indonesians that the situation was 'under control'. In terms of the appearance to the outside world, it worked as a way of saying things are better now.

An interesting ramification concerns how the United States now regards the people who were tried during that period and who now face execution in Indonesian prisons. The United States' position was that it was far better for these people to be brought to trial than to just sit in jail. When some of these people have come up to be executed, the United States government has not opposed the executions, partly because they feel it's hypocritical given that capital punishment exists in this country, but also partly because these people had a trial and [US officials] don't want to go back and examine whether those trials were fair.

A second phase started in about 1987 when the Indonesians started releasing large numbers of prisoners from East Timorese jails. This again was a symbolic gesture, because most of these people had served the majority of their sentences. Some were released a few months before their sentences had expired. These releases, however, gave the Indonesians two things. First, they gave them credibility with the international community, in that they were letting these political prisoners out of jail. Second, they reduced the number of political prisoners who were left in East Timorese jails. It was almost an admission of the role of international pressure, because [when] you keep political prisoners in jail for long periods of time, you create a focus around which international pressure can be mobilized. If you release large numbers of such prisoners, the international criticism gets more muted.

After most of the prisoners were released by 1989, we began to see a pattern which you find in Irian Jaya, for example, of arrests and short-term detentions of large numbers of people. In Irian Jaya, if an incident that is linked to the OPM [Organisasi Papua Merdeka] occurs, massive arrests take place. Most people are held for a couple of days and then released, but once someone is arrested, he becomes much more susceptible to arrest the next time an incident occurs. You get a gradually widening pool of people who are rounded up for arrest and detention. This pattern has emerged in East Timor now. It is much more frequent to get large numbers of people arrested for very brief periods than to get people arrested, brought to trial, and sentenced. Short-term detention represents an admission of much more widespread social unrest. The conflict in East Timor has changed over the past two and a half years from primarily a guerrilla conflict to more of an *intifada* with more widespread and less focused social unrest. I think the pattern of arrest and detention reflects that.

If we look at Aceh, on the northern tip of Sumatra, we're beginning to see what East Timor was going through in the early 1980s. Following a period of terror [in Aceh] during the summer of 1990, of an intensity not seen in East Timor since 1983 or 1984 [or following the 12 November 1991 Santa Cruz massacre], people now are being brought to trial. Again, it's an acknowledgment that the Indonesians have things under control. They can afford to bring people to trial, to have their pictures in the newspapers, have stories about them. They even acknowledged for the first time that it was a political movement rather than a criminal movement. I think if Aceh goes the way of East Timor you may soon have the pattern reemerging of massive short-term arrests and detentions.

Unger: Thank you Sidney. Reverend Moore, we come to you next.

Moore: My wife, Brenda, and I visited East Timor a little over a year ago [1990]. The atmosphere of fear was much greater than any I had encountered elsewhere. Our first visit was with Monsignor Belo [Carlos Filipe Ximenes Belo, Apostolic Administrator of East Timor, 1983 to the present], and even though I had a letter of introduction from Father Cardoso, and even though I was a bishop, though the wrong kind of bishop perhaps (Anglican not Roman), for the first ten minutes Bishop Belo didn't utter a word and I sensed that he was afraid of us. We encountered that fear right across the board. I've visited Nicaragua, South Africa, Vietnam, and

Soviet Russia over the years, but I have never ever encountered the kind of repression that I encountered in East Timor. We were followed when we were there. Everyone we spoke to was interviewed by the secret police or the military after they spoke to us. When we had conversations with people they made a point of our going where we couldn't be heard so that we could have confidentiality. I gather that since then conditions haven't changed that much. Mr [Hugh] O'Shaughnessy's report in the London *Observer* [7 April 1991, 'Secret Killing of a Nation'] speaks of the conditions there now, and he said that conditions are far worse than anything he has encountered in Latin America over twenty-five years as a journalist. The point is that the situation there is intensely cruel, and gets worse [in my view] all the time.

A few words about the United States' role...we are all aware of the fact that the night before the [Indonesian] invasion [7 December 1975], Secretary Kissinger and President Ford were with President Suharto. A document that came out in *The Nation* [Mark Hertsgaard, 'The Secret Life of Henry Kissinger', 29 October 1990] a few months ago verified that Kissinger encouraged or at least blessed the invasion. Eighty to ninety per cent of the arms used were from the United States. I think we are guilty of this atrocity and therefore we, as United States citizens, should be intent in trying to redress the wrongs.

In recent years, there has been a certain amount of interest in East Timor on the part of members of our government. Quite recently, Representative Tony Hall [D-Ohio] circulated a letter to the President and the State Department on the subject of East Timor which was signed by a majority [223 members] of the House of Representatives [November 1990]. We hope there will be a similar letter in the Senate very soon. There is a growing concern in the Congress of the United States about the people of East Timor. This is enormously important. If our President [George Bush, in office,

1988–92] intends to have a 'New World Order', the basic principle of which is the integrity and sovereignty of nations, and refuses to recognize the indignity of the occupation of East Timor, the hypocrisy of it is so blatant that sooner or later it is going to undermine his leadership. East Timor is no different from Kuwait in terms of morality and international law.

Even if we set aside the issue of self-determination, there are disturbing signs that the United States is trying to downplay the human rights crisis that now exists in East Timor. I had a phone call from a member of the State Department recently describing a visit that a member of the Embassy staff in Jakarta had paid to East Timor. He said that things were much more tranquil, that human rights problems had subsided. There were still problems in terms of the people not wanting to be occupied, but it really was a much better situation. Within three days, I got a letter from a Timorese exile in Portugal documenting forty or fifty cases of torture and disappearance which had taken place recently, in December 1990 for the most part. The point is that even though there may be a momentary lull in this kind of thing, it is not subsiding.

I am impressed but also apprehensive about the young people of East Timor. I am afraid that if the *intifada* kind of resistance that is going on now in the cities continues, the Indonesians will finally decide to wipe them out like the Chinese did in the Tiananmen Square massacre [4 June 1989]. I think this is a real possibility, and I think it is one of the reasons we must continue to bring the situation to the attention of our Congresses and State Departments and our Presidents and Prime Ministers. Unless the searchlight of the world is on East Timor, this situation is going to intensify and perhaps even reach the crisis proportions it did in China. I feel there should be a high level of cooperation amongst our governments, which I do not see the signs of yet, and a much greater effort than before to try to persuade Indonesia to change its policy.

Ramos-Horta: What happens in East

Timor and what happens in Indonesia seem to fit into a pattern of human rights violations throughout the Third World. We in the Third World can be proud of having some of the worst unelected beasts in human history, people like Idi Amin, Mobutu, Pinochet, Marcos, Suharto, Benny Murdani, and the others. East Timor, unfortunately, is not an exception. It is a typical case of Third World regimes, Third World attitudes toward our own people. How can people, with impunity, in Indonesia, in Zaire, and elsewhere, deny human beings their right to self-determination, their right to security, to life? Sometimes I almost cry when I go to Paris and meet Indonesians in Paris who have been denied their right to live in their own country, to see their families, [in exile] for more than twenty years. How can I comprehend, understand a regime that is trying to execute somebody who has already been tortured, denied the light, denied air, for fifteen or seventeen years? If we want to blame the West, we can do so, because it is the shortsightedness and the hypocrisy and the guns from the West that have enabled these regimes to pursue policies that deny human beings their basic life. I stand for independence for East Timor because I believe in human freedom and in human dignity. I would not conceive of independence for East Timor where East Timor's leaders would do exactly what Indonesia's leaders are doing. What is the meaning of independence? For an elite to take over, to rob the people and stash away the money in Switzerland, the US, and elsewhere? It is sheer hypocrisy that debases the Third World. That is how I put in context the problem of East Timor.

Unger: I want to ask if there are any comments from the audience.

Nairn: There are two key facts to remember about East Timor. First, if you look at it in proportion to the population, this has been the worst holocaust in the world [in] the past twenty or thirty years. The only real counterpart was Cambodia and in proportion to the population it appears it was somewhat worse in East Timor. The second

basic fact is that this may be the most totalitarian area in the world in terms of incessant army surveillance and control and constant threats of torture and death. The various moves that Indonesia makes to hold occasional trials are window-dressing, of no real importance to the Timorese. For those concerned about human rights, you have to look at what is happening and not how it is packaged, and what is happening in Timor is certainly grave. Finally, I'd say that for Americans, the key question is what is the government of the United States doing and what role has the US government played? As was pointed out, Ford and Kissinger were there right before the invasion. As the invasion happened, Kissinger was asked for comment and he said the US 'understood' the Indonesian position. Vice-President Walter Mondale visited Jakarta in 1978 and personally telephoned back to Washington to expedite a shipment of planes [OV-10 Bronco counter-insurgency bombers; and A-4E McDonnell Douglas Skyhawk bombers] which the Indonesians used in their bombing and strafing of people who were fleeing in the hills [in 1978–9]. Ninety per cent of the arms used in the invasion came from the US and the basic policy of support continues to this day. That is the key fact for Americans to think about.

Unger: Alan, I just want to know if you have insight into why you were permitted to enter and spend two weeks in East Timor.

Nairn: Well, for about a year and a half now [i.e. since January 1989], there has been open travel there. You just get on the plane and go there.

Unger: So once you have a visa to Indonesia you don't need special permission to go to East Timor?

Nairn: Right. I've heard that since then there have been various restrictions, so it really depends on when you go. Sometimes foreigners coming in have not been able to go out to the countryside. So it depends on when you happen to arrive. Overall, the policy of opening up East Timor was part of an effort to improve Indonesia's image internationally.

Maynard: I'm Hal Maynard, currently of United Engineers, formerly a military attaché in Jakarta and formerly a student at the Staff College [Sekolah Staf dan Komando Angkatan Darat, SESKOAD] in Bandung. I have been twice to East Timor and travelled around extensively and what you describe I did not see. If you ask government officials, whether they're American officials from the State Department, the CIA, or AID [ie USAID, US Government Overseas Aid Program], or Department of Defense, or Australian government officials, or Japanese government officials, or French and German, by and large they do not see what you have described. Now, there are several things that might be going on. Number one is that they're imbeciles; number two is that they're insensitive; or number three, maybe it's an elephant and each one of us has a different part of the elephant that we are describing. My question for you is, if all the things you describe have been taking place and this is the greatest holocaust in this century by proportion, why is it that so many governments are ignoring it?

Jones: I think that two parts of what you say are probably true. I do think that there are many different sides of Timor that people see. People who work for development agencies, for example, tend to see schools and hospitals and roads and things like that. People who work on human rights questions do see questions of torture. That is their business, to look for that and to find it. I also think that, to some extent, there has been a successful packaging of the issue. While the level of human rights abuse is certainly lower now than it was in the 1983–4 period, there are still major abuses going on now. However, because we are not able to focus on long-term prisoners and because we do not see mass executions, there is less willingness to see the much less pronounced kind of repression that exists now. I think that holding trials has been successful in portraying a return to the rule of law.

Moore: The occupation by Indonesia has not yet been recognized by any international body. That is a fact. Why other nations aren't concerned, I think, is flat out geopolitics. It is not to our advantage in the United States to irritate Indonesia. I don't think we feel East Timor is important enough to put any chips on the table. I think this is probably also true of Japan, whose investment [in Indonesia] is far greater than ours. Certainly it's true of Australia, which doesn't want to give up the mineral resources of the Timor Gap. I don't think it's very mysterious why the nations of the world have not come to the rescue of East Timor.

Nairn: A couple of points. The reason the US declines to officially recognize and speak the truth about what is happening in East Timor is the same reason it doesn't tell the truth about what is happening in Guatemala and El Salvador and other countries around the world. The US will selectively stand up for law and human rights when it is to its political advantage, as in Kuwait, but in far more cases it will violate those same laws and principles when it feels it's to its political advantage. It's routine politics. I was a little surprised when I spoke to current US officials with responsibility in this area and asked what they had to say about what I observed in East Timor. I expected them to say that things are getting much better, but they didn't say that. Instead, they basically acknowledged what I said, but dismissed Timor as an issue. What they wanted to talk about was the growing US business relationship with Indonesia and the fact that Indonesia is opening up markets for things like US software and video cassettes and various semi-marginal interests for which the US feels it is advantageous to push Timor to the side.

It is also the case that within Indonesia the army has gone to great lengths to cover up what is happening from those who visited. If the visitors are US officials, however, then there is no need for that kind of deception because people see the US as allies of the Indonesian army. If they fear the Indonesian army, then they will naturally be circumspect in what they say [to US officials]. It is not a matter of subjectivity and point of view when it comes to finding [human] rights violations in a place like Timor. It is a documented fact by any objective standards, that they have been much much worse there than almost any place else in the world.

Goodman: I think that there are two reasons why you [Mr Maynard] would not see what we saw. One is that you represent a business working with the Indonesian government in Timor (*sic*). Who you travel with will make a big difference as to who will come up to you and talk. Speaking Portuguese or Spanish [also] makes a big difference, because then you're speaking to Timorese as opposed to Indonesians.

I also have a question for anyone on the panel, and that is how you think the media has covered the situation in East Timor? This also might address your concern of why the rest of the world doesn't seem to notice.

Jones: I think East Timor has been covered abominably by the Western press. I think the Australians have done, probably, a better job than the American papers, but it has partly to do with the fact of sheer ignorance and the fact that there is usually one Bangkok-based reporter covering that entire area. I think there is an appalling lack of good coverage not just on East Timor but on Indonesia and on Southeast Asia more generally, with the possible exception of Cambodia and Vietnam, because that area is of more strategic interest.

Unger: In some respects, it is remarkable that editorials [about East Timor] continue to surface in many newspapers, since there is very little new reporting and very few people bother to travel there. I think when you look at the number of crises and tragedies and problems in the world that are competing for coverage, even leaving aside the unattractive question of compassion fatigue, it is actually remarkable that people come back with some regularity.

Nairn: If the standard is major events, then East Timor should have been one of the best known stories of the world of the past fifteen years. After all, what are events? Events are massacres; events are a dramatic exodus of people who are starving in the hills; events are bombers swooping in. When these events happen in places like Cambodia, when repression is happening to demonstrators in Tiananmen Square, we hear all about them. We are bombarded with them. Cambodia is a good example, because it was happening at roughly the same time [i.e., 1975–8]. Access to the refugees who had the information was actually in some ways easier with the Timorese refugees than with the Cambodians, yet we were bombarded with information about the Cambodia genocide and not the one in Timor. I think the basic reason is because the press tends to defer to Washington and to let Washington set the agenda. If Washington is talking about it, the press in turn talks about it. If they don't, the press doesn't.

Walsh: I want to say a word in defence of the press. It has been an incredibly difficult story to cover, particularly before the territory was opened up in [January] 1989. Indonesia is very skilled at managing the media in its own country and has been very skilled at managing the international media in relation to East Timor. It has been particularly important for Indonesia to keep it off TV. The reason that we have done something about the Kurds in Iraq, for instance, is that the issue was headlined night after night on the news around the world and political decision-makers could not resist the pressure imposed upon them. There has been no TV coverage of East Timor, none at all, by Indonesia or by the western media. It is simply not permitted. So East Timor doesn't exist as an issue.

From the Australian point of view, Indonesia is the fifth biggest country in the world, leader of ASEAN [Association of South-East Asian Nations], candidate to lead the Non-Aligned Movement, a very important country to Australia, strategically and diplomatically. Do you know how many journalists we have based in Indonesia? One. The reason there is only one there is that Indonesia doesn't allow more than one. The national broadcaster in Australia, the ABC [Australian Broadcasting Corporation], is not allowed in there. I could go through a whole range of people who are not permitted in there. An *Age* journalist went into East Timor in February with the parliamentary delegation, but his visit was very strictly controlled. I might add that he was banned from Indonesia following that visit. We have the Australian Defence Minister in Indonesia right this minute. Quincy Murdoch, this same journalist, was forbidden to go to Indonesia to cover his visit, so you can see the problems.

Robinson: The discussion of monitoring and access to information about human rights is, of course, very interesting to Amnesty International. I just want to make two points which suggest some of the problems in getting accurate information about human rights in East Timor. The first has to do with the fact that the act of monitoring, gathering, and disseminating such information is regarded as a subversive act in Indonesia. If I had time I would quote from an Army intelligence document dated 9 February 1991 which suggests that people who are engaged in these acts, not only in East Timor but elsewhere in Indonesia, are being monitored currently by Indonesian Army Intelligence. The people mentioned in this document as being under surveillance for monitoring human rights activity and for discussing the question of East Timor's independence are, among others, foreign journalists, tourists, and students who have contact with East Timorese. There can be little doubt, after reading a document like this, about why there is difficulty with getting accurate information. If people are going to be imprisoned or harassed or tortured for carrying out human rights investigations, then they will be disinclined to do so. The second point I should like to make with respect to Amnesty International's own position is this: Amnesty International has repeatedly requested the Indonesian authorities for access both to East Timor and Indonesia and has repeatedly been either ignored or, more politely, denied. We have been told curtly that as members of the European Community we are entitled to visit as tourists for two months. We don't wish to go to East Timor and

to visit Indonesia as tourists. We wish to go to monitor human rights violations and to discuss with the government and relevant officials what can be done about them. We have also written numerous letters to Indonesian government and military authorities requesting information, for example, about the punishment that was handed down to the killers of Candido Amaral. Answers are not forthcoming.

Rendon: I'd like to talk about the history of Congressional activity regarding East Timor and the current Congressional interest in the subject. Congressional activity on the East Timor tragedy dates back more than fifteen years, to the period immediately following the December 1975 invasion when then Representative Tom Harkin [D-Iowa] sponsored an unsuccessful amendment to reduce US military aid to Indonesia because of the invasion. In 1977, then Representative Donald Fraser [D-Minnesota] began a series of four Congressional hearings that examined questions of Indonesian use of American-supplied military equipment in the East Timor conflict and a host of legal and human rights issues. State Department testimony at one of those hearings brought out the fact that roughly ninety per cent of the arms available to the Indonesian armed forces at the time of the 1975 invasion were of United States origin. High-ranking Indonesian officials confirmed this assessment.

Another four Congressional hearings were held on the Timor issue from 1979 to 1982, and in 1989, the Chairman of the Senate Foreign Relations Committee, Senator Claiborne Pell [D-Rhode Island], devoted considerable time in the confirmation hearing of US Ambassador to Indonesia John Monjo to questions regarding East Timor. Last November [1990], Representative Tony Hall [D-Ohio], who has been concerned about the Timor issue since his election to Congress twelve years ago, led a group of 223 House members, a majority of that body, who wrote to Secretary of State Baker raising a variety of human rights and humanitarian issues and calling for a just and peaceful settlement. Thus, there is a history of consistent effort in the Congress on this matter. The feeling exists in Congress that the Timor question is an issue that will not go away.

How best to summarize the basis of this concern? One must begin with the series of Congressional hearings in 1977–8 and the events that followed. At the hearings, members of Congress were assured by various government representatives that whatever major human rights problems had taken place in East Timor, these problems were largely in the past – that is, had taken place in early 1976 for the most part. A Congressional delegation that was allowed to visit East Timor in May 1977 saw throngs of smiling people carrying signs praising then President Jimmy Carter [in office, 1976–81] and no visible traces of conflict, a pattern that has been repeated over the years in various forms. There was, however, a cautionary note struck in at least one of the reports of the Congressional visitors, which noted that they had been unable to meet with specific individuals or bring independent interpreters. John P. Salzburg, then on the staff of the Subcommittee on Human Rights and International Organizations, stated that he had been followed by Indonesian personnel wherever he went in East Timor. For these reasons, the validity of the May 1977 visit was questioned by Chairman Fraser, who continued to pursue the issue.

By the latter part of 1978, it was evident that earlier testimony in Congress and the aforementioned visit had presented a highly selective view of the realities of East Timor, as first-hand accounts of large-scale starvation, attributable in good measure to Indonesian military action, emerged. But this was not the worst of it: by late 1979 independent authorities were stating openly that the Timor situation was worse than Biafra and potentially as serious as Cambodia. No less an authority than then Indonesian Foreign Minister Mochtar [Kusumaatmadja, in office

1978–88] added that the Timor situation might have been worse than Cambodia.

It was then, in 1979, that Representative Hall, newly elected to Congress, became involved in Congressional efforts on the Timor issue, with special regard for the humanitarian emergency that existed at the time. Representative Hall, it should be noted, is Chairman of the House Select Committee on Hunger, a position he has held since 1989. A key interest of Representative Hall's is the use of food as a weapon in situations of armed conflict. I will not go into detail about the Timor situation as independent authorities saw it in 1979, but there were two elements which stood out: first, the scale of the humanitarian emergency, and second, shared American responsibility for this human tragedy, through weapons shipments and other means, as summarized by the commentator Morton Kondracke in an influential article ['Another Cambodia'] in the *New Republic* on November 3 1979.

A sense of responsibility to continue efforts to assist East Timor took hold during this period. Also during this period, an increasingly effective network of American secular and religious groups stepped up their efforts to inform the American public on various aspects of the Timor situation, efforts that continue to the present. As knowledge of the Timor issue has been spread by this network, through the media and organizations such as Amnesty International, Congressional support has steadily increased for humanitarian efforts, on human rights, and for a just and peaceful settlement of the ongoing conflict in East Timor. Representative Hall believes that strong efforts should be made wherever possible to resolve armed conflict, and East Timor is obviously no exception.

In the earliest days of Congressional involvement on the Timor issue, there was a strong sense of the need to defend a small territory of scarcely more than 680,000 people from being swallowed by a nation with a population of more than two hundred times that number. The humanitarian emergency of 1978–80 gave compelling evidence of the need for continued monitoring of the situation. And while responsible independent accounts indicate that the human rights and humanitarian concerns have changed since the darkest days of the mid- to late-1970s, there is little doubt that severe problems in these areas and others remain outstanding. As recently as April 7 1991, an extensive article in *The Observer* of London [Hugh O'Shaughnessy, 'Secret Killing of a Nation'] made it clear that whatever talk there may be of improvement in the situation, such evaluations are only relative. Many other independent investigators essentially have reached the same conclusion.

In 1977, when Representative Fraser began his hearings on the East Timor situation, he also held hearings on the fate of other small and endangered nations. Doubtless these hearings appeared exotic and marginal to at least some observers at the time. Since then, however, the world has witnessed the Vietnamese invasion of Cambodia [December 1978], the Soviet invasion of Afghanistan [January 1980], the Argentine invasion of the Falklands [April 1982], and, most notably, the Iraqi invasion of Kuwait [August 1990]. One can easily draw distinctions between and among these various invasions and their consequences, and the East Timor situation. Nonetheless, there have been comparisons made, in several cases, between Kuwait and East Timor, such as in a *New York Times* editorial of December 7 1990.

Comparisons have been made on numerous occasions with the other countries cited above, especially with regard to Cambodia. Taken together, these comparisons have helped draw attention to the case of East Timor, both in Congress and elsewhere.

One can argue about the validity of these comparisons. One can argue about differences that may exist. Certainly, from the official Indonesian point of view, such comparisons are unfair, if not insulting. But to many well-placed

observers in legislatures, the news media, and a host of other respected institutions, the similarities are more troubling and important than the differences. Add this fact to the long history of American as well as international interest and East Timor ends up with a special claim on Congressional attention.

It must be stressed that the US Congress is hardly alone in its concern over East Timor. Parliamentary groups throughout the world have been active on the question for some time. The European Parliament has issued a number of strong resolutions in recent years. The Japanese Diet has become increasingly committed in its work on East Timor. On another level, the European Economic Community [now European Union] presented a strong statement to the United Nations Commission on Human Rights in Geneva on February 27 [1991].

In short, activities on the Timor issue are truly widespread. They are obviously not a peculiarity of the US Congress, and should be seen for what they are, an understandable reaction to a tragedy a large body of international opinion finds unacceptable.

What will come next for East Timor? The pace of change in international events in recent times makes speculation rather a hazardous pursuit. Nonetheless, there are signs of hope, as world trends have tended toward changes that not long ago seemed impossible. In the US Congress, one can safely predict that there will be growing activity on various aspects of the Timor issue. This is an important human rights question among a broad-based, bipartisan group on Capitol Hill, and there should be no misjudgement about the seriousness of this endeavour.

Maynard: I just retired after twenty-three years in the US Armed Forces. You will not find me anti-military. I spent five years in Indonesia [1982–7]. I only spent seven days in East Timor, so you will forgive me if my impressions of East Timor are exactly that, impressionistic and vignettes, but I'd like to share a number of them with you.

First, coming back from a recent trip in 1989 I was surprised to receive a cable coming out of Portugal about a Portuguese press story about my presence in East Timor. According to the story, we had gone there with a group of six Air Force officers to advise the Indonesian Air Force on how to use OV-10s to bomb Fretilin. The facts are there were five of us. I was from the Air Force; there was one from the Army; there were three civilians. We were there overnight. None of us knows anything about OV-10s. The story was generated by two Australian journalists who were checking out of the hotel as we were checking into the hotel lobby. That is all they saw of us. To find this relayed back through Australian sources, and Australian sources quoted in Portugal, was personally distressing. What I am telling you is, they got the facts wrong. I suspect that many times what we hear from East Timor about human rights violations is a case of they got the facts wrong. I'm not telling you that human rights violations don't take place. But they have to be very carefully checked.

Another impression is of the tremendous economic development across East Timor. I don't think even those who cry correctly about human rights violations in East Timor can deny that the roads have been dramatically improved, there are television stations where there were none before, along with the stores, and the marketplaces, and the rest of that. I remind you that, even though we talk about political rights, we also have to accept the Latin American theories that you can't have a lot of political freedom unless you have a certain economic base to start with. That is something that the Indonesian government has been successful in bringing to East Timor. Now, in an absolute sense, are they poor? Of course, it is [one of] the poorest part[s] of Indonesia. If you compare it with Jakarta, of course they are poor. If you compare what the Indonesian government has done in the economic development of East Timor with West Timor, or with Savu, or with Flores, of Sumba, or Sumbawa, or Irian

Jaya, or the entire eastern part of the country, the government has done a remarkable job.

My impressions of the people were not impressions of fear. My impressions were very similar to what I noticed elsewhere in Indonesia, great curiosity about the foreigners, great shyness, great deference. There was a great desire to better their lot in life.

I also came back with negative impressions, and I'll share some of those with you. We were toured around [Lospalos] by the Bupati [District Administrator], whom, I am convinced, knew he had been reincarnated as a local rajah. He had his big car; there was no speed limit for him. The pigs and chickens had to get out of the way and I swear that if a child had stepped into the street he probably would not have paid much more attention to him. He lived in a grand palace and he had lots of servants and he was very happy. I was negatively impressed by that. I was also negatively impressed in Iliomar, which was the only one of a dozen places I visited in East Timor where I found the populace to be genuinely sullen; not upset, not violent, not angry, but just sullen. They weren't very happy to be there and to be in our presence and when we left, the local police official begged for a ride in the helicopter to get out of that place. It is the poorest part of a rather poor region in East Timor.

Finally, a negative impression from the Lautem area, which has had noteworthy development, has a brand new pier, has economic development. The local military official asked who, among a crowd of approximately two hundred people assembled there, had been to Dili, and it turned out that absolutely nobody from this village in Lautem had ever been to Dili, even though there was good paved road all the way. So he said he would get a bus and two trucks, and would take as many as could be carried to the big city to see what the rest of Indonesia, or at least East Timor, is all about. That was a good impression. However, I went to the side of the crowd in the back and there was a Land

Rover. I take a double look at Land Rovers, being an old intelligence officer, and I found a very close-cropped young man in civilian clothes, with very large muscles, standing carefully by his Land Rover, and when I approached he snapped a little bit to attention wondering who I was, and I noticed there was an M-16 inside and a PRC-77 radio in the back. I had run into the Indonesian Armed Forces, and specifically Special Forces [*Kopassandha/Kopassus*] troops before. I was a little upset by the fact that they felt that I needed a bodyguard in obviously a very happy part of the island. The things that most impressed me negatively about that whole image was the fact that he had an absolutely gargantuan gold ring. Now I know the impression it had on me, and I can tell you it had a very similar sort of impression on the local natives. So I am telling you, at the very least, that the Indonesian armed forces have a PR problem.

Next, how does ABRI [*Angkatan Bersenjata Republik Indonesia*, i.e. Indonesian Armed Forces] view its role? I have often been told that 'we ABRI officers believe that we could wipe out the problem in East Timor, in the sense of Fretilin opposition, and could pacify the population of the countryside, if given the task. However, to do so would require such force that we would, in the process of wiping out that opposition, violate our own set of values and, by the way, draw down great international condemnation.' The second thing is that ABRI views its operations in East Timor as a burden on itself, not as an opportunity to rape, pillage, and plunder. It is a burden on the people who have to go out there; it's a burden on the budget. Now there is a flip side to that ABRI view. Some people say it is a good training ground where we take out a young lieutenant and show him a combat situation. So it is not entirely a negative, but predominantly it is a burden on the Armed Forces. Another impression along that line relates to what you can expect from a new commander there. After he has been there thirty days or sixty days, he

knows he's only got nine months left to make his mark, to get his promotion. Young lieutenants or young captains are inclined to do excessively courageous things by their own standards to make a name for themselves. They are going to find Xanana, personally. They are going to personally behead him. To do that they are going to find someone who knows and find out the information, regardless of what it takes. Now, it's an obligation on the armed forces commanders, of course, to contain that within the bounds of propriety.

Finally, how are you going to improve the human rights situation in East Timor? I would suggest that first you have to ask yourself a question. Is it more likely to be improved by being internationalized and publicized, which I think is the primary axiom under which most of the people in the room are working, or is it more likely to be improved by locally addressing local problems? When we talk about the Indonesians, I encourage you to judge them by their own value system, and not by the words and value system we use. A handout is available just outside the door, which is the *pancasila* and the *saptamarga* ['seven paths'], the soldier's oath, but, more importantly, a breakdown of the *pancasila* into what they call thirty-six 'pearls'. Now, if you want to judge the Indonesian armed forces or the Indonesian government, go to the thirty-six pearls, where it says, 'We're going to develop an attitude of consideration for others; we're not going to be high-handed with other people; we are going to uphold humanitarian values; we are going to have the courage to defend truth and justice; we're going to give precedence to the interest of the state over society.' It is not individual human rights that are most important for the *pancasila* or for the ideology; it is societal values and societal welfare, the good of the group as opposed to the good of the individuals. I'll just give you one more, where it says, 'One nation, an Indonesian nation, and one country.' If you start off with the proposition that East Timor should be independent, you have fundamentally violated their assumption that East Timor is now and forever will be part of Indonesia. If your real purpose in life is not to set up an autonomous government but in fact to improve the welfare of the people there, I would suggest the way to do it is to look, within the context of the current government, how things could be improved.

My suggestion on how to approach the Indonesian armed forces is to go straight through the front door, tell them who you are, what you want, what the limits of your questions are, where you want to go, how long you want to be there. That has always to me been the most successful. Number two, is to remember that you are a guest in somebody else's house. The guest can come in and plead and convince and argue. The guest in someone else's house does not ransack the drawers, does not go in through the basement, does not publicize the diaries. If you are in Indonesia, you are still a guest in Indonesia.

The last point I'd like to make is that when you criticize the Indonesian government or the Indonesian armed forces, you've got to make sure you're not putting them in a situation where they are damned if they do and damned if they don't. For example, earlier today we had a discussion about the Wanandis [Yusuf Wanandi, a.k.a. Liem Bian-Kie, and his brothers Marcus Wanandi, a Jesuit priest in East Timor, and Sofyan Wanandi, involved in tourist development in Baucau] doing business in East Timor. If you want development in East Timor, how do you get it? If the government doesn't have enough capital, you invite private enterprise in. If you invite private enterprise, and the government can get the Wanandis into East Timor, then do you criticize them for the fact that they are involved in doing business in East Timor? You can't have it both ways. Along the same lines, if Amnesty International is going to go into East Timor, are you going to go in there as judges, as guests, as observers? I think very few of us would be inclined to invite people into our own home in our own country if, when they come

through the door, we know we are under the inquisition. If you start in with that approach I think it's going to fail in the end.

Robinson: There is a rather lengthy history to the relationship between Amnesty International and the government of Indonesia. The last time Amnesty International was permitted to visit Indonesia was in the late 1970s. There have been repeated requests, as I mentioned earlier, for a visit since that time. On a number of occasions in the last two years, Amnesty International has had face to face meetings with the Foreign Minister Ali Alatas and we have, on a number of occasions, been assured that our requests to visit Indonesia and East Timor are being seriously considered. In those meetings we emphasized that our intention in visiting Indonesia was to find out through direct talks what in fact the position of the Indonesian government is, and on Amnesty's part to explain clearly our concerns, both in Indonesia and generally, to describe our methods of work, to describe international human rights standards; in other words to communicate, not through the media and not indirectly through fora like this, but directly in the interest of mutual understanding. I think it is probably five times in the last two years that we have raised with the Indonesian government authorities our desire for this kind of communication. On each occasion we have been told by the foreign minister that he is in agreement, but that the Indonesian military, and particularly Indonesian military intelligence, are not. We've tried very hard to go through the front door with the legitimate government of Indonesia by speaking as we do, in most cases, with foreign ministers where possible. We've welcomed the efforts of the foreign minister [Ali Alatas] to speak with us, but we feel frustrated by the fact that, when speaking to the foreign minister, we are effectively being told that we are not speaking with the government. So I would simply say that our interest is genuine. We would go to East Timor as we go to most countries, with an interest in finding out what is going on, but particularly in this case, in order to smooth the lines of communication, to explain what it is that we do and to find out precisely what the Indonesian government, and the military, understand by human rights, in order to put an end to this communication through the media.

Unger: Are there other comments from the audience?

Dunn: Colonel Maynard, having myself been a diplomat and having travelled with service attachés, I have to say that we are conditioned by our views of the situation by our government's policies. Certainly, in the case of Australia, which had already recognized East Timor as part of Indonesia [in January 1978 (*de facto*) and February 1979 (*de jure*)], it is inconceivable that one of our attachés or diplomats would come out publicly and talk about the kind of [human rights] violations that would have made that earlier decision absolute nonsense and unacceptable. I really think that your presentation is extraordinary. Last year [1990] an Australian brigadier went [to East Timor] and he found extensive monitoring of [his] movements, controls throughout the island, and also everywhere he went – he had been one of the commanders there during the Second World War – the Timorese were saying this is not what we want, we don't want Australia with Indonesia, we want an act of self-determination. It may be that the Timorese would approach you differently because the Timorese are traditionally very sensitive about talking to diplomats.

One last point. You mentioned having an escort. In the bad Portuguese days, as some would describe them, never once did I travel anywhere in East Timor with an escort, and often I drove myself.

Cardoso: I have to correct something Mr Archer said about the Church and Salazar. The big trick of Salazar was to convince the people that we [priests] are with the state. Some bishops and priests were with the state, but the major part of the priests were not with the state. We were with the people.

What is at stake here is not the development of East Timor. It is not the roads, the TVs, the gold, or the silver. It's the people. Give the people the opportunity to live in peace, to go back to their own places. The people of East Timor were displaced from the mountains, from their villages. You go to Ainaro, you go to Baucau, you go to Balibo, you go to Maliana, you go to Queliquai, you go to Maubisse, you go to all these places. Where are the people of those villages, who formed those districts? They have been displaced by war, by occupation.

Many people try to direct attention [away] from the problem of East Timor because a lot of things are at stake there, economically speaking. Nobody is talking about the oil in Timor. It is a secret.

Unger: Does anyone on the panel want to comment.

Maynard: We have an expert on Indonesian oil in the audience. I wonder if he could comment on that issue.

Benson: My name is George Benson and I am now a private consultant. I spent thirty-one years in the US Army. Nine years in Indonesia. Twenty years with Pertamina. Father [Cardoso], as far as I know, there have been no wells drilled anywhere in Timor. The water in the [Timor] Gap is very deep and there have been no wells drilled there. In the oil business, until you drill a well and the oil or the gas comes up that pipe, you do not have any large amounts of gas or oil. The geology onshore in Timor is not promising. There is some possibility of oil in the famous [Timor] Gap, but it is very deep and the possibility of that coming up in any reasonable time I think is very slight.

Ramos-Horta: For the past fifteen or sixteen years I have met UN officials, diplomats from various countries, and they all zealously defend their regimes or defend their business interests. It's quite natural. Business people are not in the world to be philanthropic, to care for human rights. So I don't take issue with various statements with regard to East Timor. I would like only to say that one day, back in East Timor, when I can get near the graves of my brothers and sisters – I don't even know where three of them are buried. One sister, who was seventeen years old at that time, was blown up with twenty other kids by a Bronco aircraft. A brother, fourteen years old, was blown up by a helicopter gunship in 1977. Another brother, Nuno, was executed on the spot when he was captured. One day, when I can find their graves, I will say to them, 'You idiots, you were not there because you were not seen. No one saw you killed, so wake up!' That same thing will have to be addressed to thousands of Timorese, to entire families who were wiped out, families that no longer exist, not one single soul; villages that no longer exist. I was born and grew up in the mountains. Frequently, I ask refugees in Australia and Portugal, 'How is Pualata?' 'Pualata does not exist.' 'How is Bariki?' 'Bariki does not exist. No one lives in Bariki today.' And on and on. We will say to them, 'But you did not disappear. You are not dead. You were not killed. You were not tortured, because no one saw you. The oil men who came here, the US diplomats who came here, the Third World diplomats who came here, they did not see you. They did not see you killed, so you are not dead. You are alive.'

Taylor: We seem to be in a bit of an impasse. I think it is undoubtedly the case that the Indonesian government has spent incredible amounts of money in East Timor building roads and so on. On the other hand I don't think you can deny that there are a substantial number of East Timorese who are completely alienated from the Indonesian attempt to incorporate East Timor. Given that we accept that there is an attempt to develop, which doesn't seem to be working particularly well for those for whom it is supposed to be working, and they are alienated from it, then under what conditions can Indonesia successfully incorporate East Timor? Under what conditions can real development occur in East Timor?

Unger: Under what circumstances can Indonesia effectively incorporate East Timor? Does it require a change in Indonesia or in East Timor, or in international circumstances, or whatever?

Professor Anderson, perhaps you will want to address yourself to this.

Anderson: This reminds me of the basic miscalculation that this all started out with. In the fall of 1975, I asked Yusuf Wanandi [Director of the Centre for Strategic and International Studies, CSIS], Liem Bian-Kie as he was then known, 'Well, what's going on in Timor? What are you going to do?' and he said, 'Oh, it's all taken care of. It'll all be over in three weeks.' I think he really believed that this would be a very simple operation and there would be no real resistance. What's really impressive about what has happened since then is that every kind of powerful pressure has been put on the East Timorese. You ask yourself, why have the foreigners been kept out of East Timor? It seems to me that the hope was that in those years [1976–89], something could be created, some kind of change in attitude, some kind of development, that would produce a situation that would be satisfactory. I think all the evidence, conversions to the Catholic Church, the *intifada*-like character of what happens when the Pope and other people come, suggests that the policy has basically failed. What has to change now is not the people of Timor. What has to change now is the policy of the Indonesian government. I'm really suggesting that Suharto is getting very near the end of his time. Indonesia is changing. The world is changing, and it seems to me that at some point the regime or the government has got to recognize that this policy has failed. What do you do after that? I think it is much better if Indonesia tries to make a sensible adjustment now, and not simply go on bluffing and saying, well, next year, next year, next year it's going to be all right. It isn't going to be all right.

Mubyarto: Even as an Indonesian, I cannot pretend to know East Timor much better than everyone else attending this session. When I went there three times and I sent three of our assistants to stay with the villagers in Ermera and Maubisse for one month, they needed interpreters to talk to the local people, the local people who do not speak

Indonesian. So when we came back and we wrote a report about our findings on the situation in East Timor [see Bibliography, *Impact of Integration*], we confessed that we don't think we can present the real inner feelings of the people of East Timor. When Indonesia became independent in 1945, I think it took fourteen years, up to 1959, before Indonesia really became one. So fourteen years for East Timor is not really long enough to settle the situation.

Every one of us who comes here this morning, I think, has only a partial understanding of what is the whole situation in East Timor. I do not pretend to know about the whole situation. It is not easy to find facts about East Timor. If the question is under what condition East Timor will develop according to the wishes of the East Timorese, nobody now can answer, because the problem has so many different aspects.

Unger: Mr Maynard.

Maynard: I think with East Timor, there are many people who want to speak [about] what is good for the people. I accept at face value the pastor's comments that the priests speak for the people. But Golkar [Golongan Karya, Indonesian Government Party] thinks it speaks for the people. ABRI thinks it speaks for the people. The [US] AID mission in the embassy [in Jakarta] thinks it speaks for the people. Asia Watch speaks for the people. Everybody has a different view of what the will of the people is. I think in the discourse on the East Timor issue, one of the most helpful things would be to differentiate that question, what is good for the people, from the separate question of who should be in charge. I think the time has come to put the question of East Timor sovereignty behind us and to put the 1975 events behind us and address what is good for the people, recognizing that many people think that they carry the flag of the people and that probably all of them have some part of the truth.

Goodman: Who speaks for the people? We have to say the people speak for the people. Saying that we have to put the issue of integration behind [us] is a way of speaking for the people, and possibly not saying what they want. Colonel Maynard, I have three questions for you. The first is, why were you there? The second question is, what languages do you speak? And the third question is, whose helicopter did you travel in?

Maynard: The first question is why we were there? It was a delegation from the Department of Defense which was there overnight, basically to see what was East Timor which we keep hearing about in intelligence reports coming out of Southeast Asia. Since I was the only one in the delegation who had actually set foot in that territory, we took five other people. At least they got a ride around, in an ABRI helicopter, by the way, to see what does the countryside look like, what are the problems of communications, where are the highways working etc. That was the purpose and it was just an overnight trip. The answer to the second question is, though I have studied German, Thai, and French, I speak only Indonesian, and when I was in East Timor I could speak English or I could speak Indonesian. I can't speak Portuguese except to say I don't speak Portuguese. To answer the last question, we went in an ABRI helicopter, absolutely no doubt about that.

Goodman: I expect the answers to the last two questions dictated what you heard. Speaking Indonesian and English told people where you were coming from, and certainly the helicopter let them know where you were coming from. Maybe many of us don't know what's going on completely in East Timor because there has been a complete blackout, but to suggest that you might know coming in as you did is a real problem.

Maynard: There is a tremendous liability in travelling in an ABRI helicopter if you want to speak to the people. There is, however, one advantage, and that is that ABRI said, 'Look, we have got the helicopter all day. You tell us where you want to go and where you want to set down. We aren't afraid to put this helicopter down anywhere.' Now, it turned out that during that day, the pilots were afraid two times, both up in the mountains where there were big thunderheads and down draughts and I have to accept their word that this was not a safe place for a helicopter. There was an advantage in that we got to go to a lot of places of our choosing when we wanted to go. I was not there in a private capacity. It was clear we were with the government and with the armed forces, but by the same token we got to see a lot that we would not have seen from another perspective.

Goodman: I think what you got to see is that built-up infrastructure. You can see the infrastructure from the sky, but when you come down, what can you hear from the people when you come in an ABRI helicopter?

Maynard: The economic conditions are obvious. I would also point out that there is a tremendous inclination of Indonesian government officials to keep statistics on absolutely everything. Whether they are correct is a separate question, but they keep these statistics and they believe them. It is a different issue from sitting down in a village that is two kilometres from the nearest road and asking people who do not speak Indonesian, much less English, how the conditions of their life have changed. I accept that. But the way I look at that is philosophically back to the Indian elephant. We've got one elephant here. Maybe I've only got a tail or maybe I'm only holding on to an ear. Maybe you feel the oppression of the foot of the elephant sitting on your chest. But it's still one elephant, and I guess we have to improve the communications in order to describe exactly what it is. I don't deny the validity of your impressions or the sources of your information. I ask you to double-check them, as I would expect you to ask me to double-check mine. But I don't think that my impressions are any less valid than yours. Flying over East Timor in a helicopter is very different than sitting down in a village. I give you that. But it is the same elephant.

Panjaitan: I spent three years in [East Timor] and I have been there several times besides. I am from North Sumatra, a little bit different from Pak Mubyarto. I am Batak. I am a Protestant, so the way I talk is different from Pak Mubyarto. As a previous speaker said, we cannot pretend that we know everything about that area. It is the same also in other parts of Indonesia. As you know, it is a large country, [with] more than 13,000 islands, local languages, 360 types [ethnic groups], and four main religions. It's really very hard to govern that country. We have problems in Irian Jaya; we have problems in East Timor; we have problems in Jakarta, in Central Java, in Aceh, and elsewhere. The most important thing I believe is the will of the government to solve the problem. That is the question you have to ask; whether the Indonesian government has the will to solve problems in any part of Indonesia, in Aceh, in Jakarta, in Central Java, in my home town in Sumatra, and also in East Timor. If I compare development in East Timor and in my home town, [on] Lake Toba, to be honest I [am] jealous. How come in East Timor [conditions are] better than in my home town right now? We realize that the government is trying very hard to solve the problem in that area. What I saw in East Timor the first time I was there around fifteen years ago, was very sad. The people were very poor. The people had very little education. I saw the efforts of the government to build the infrastructure of that island. They spent a lot of money and a lot of effort to do so.

Maybe I can talk with Sidney about human rights. From which point of view do you look at human rights? A friend told me, the greatest good for the greatest number. I believe that applies in East Timor as well as in Jakarta, as well as in this country.

I love that island. To express it I adopted one Timorese as my child. I sent him to high school. I teach him as my child, equal to my children. You can see him if you come to Jakarta. I love him, and I have a very good relation with his father. I send him frequently to his home village just next to Matebian Mountain. They love me there very much. I never ever have a problem over there. With the Timorese people, I just walk with them. I say, I trust you, you trust me. There are a lot of good things in East Timor. I don't want to deny some bad things happen over there, the same as happen in this and every country. So let's talk about the future. Do you want us to do something to make it better faster? Maybe you have some ideas. Let us discuss them. But we cannot discuss about the referendum, whatever you call it, because it is some years past. I don't have any capacity to discuss it. If you talk about what we have to do in that island, then I think the Indonesian government will be very happy to accept that.

Ramos-Horta: Professor Mubyarto asked what are the interests of the people? What [do] the people really want? I would say that the movement I represent, Fretilin, certainly does not represent the entire people of East Timor, nor does the Timorese Democratic Union [UDT]. It may be that in local elections Fretilin might even lose. Who knows?

I think there is a way for all of us to get out of this problem, by first accepting the very reasonable proposal put forward by Xanana Gusmão [the East Timorese resistance leader and President of Fretilin, since 1980]. That is for a round table conference without preconditions, where all options would be discussed. Xanana has proposed that, and it was backed up by more than half the members of the US Congress. It has been backed up by the European Parliament, by the Council of Europe, by the Japanese Diet, and many other national parliaments. And, I believe, Indonesia should in the true spirit of brotherhood sit down and try to find a solution to this problem.

Nairn: Colonel Maynard, are you saying that the best way to reflect the will of the people is not to have the election?

Maynard: No, I didn't say that.

Nairn: Well, it seems you are saying let the current situation stand. You say the Indonesian government believes they have resolved the situation. We all agree here, even though we disagree on other things, that they have resolved the situation by sending in troops, and by all accounts more than 100,000, maybe 200,000 people have been killed and there are still many thousands of troops occupying Timor. That's the way they have resolved the situation. Why is having a free election not the best way to answer the question about the will of the people?

Maynard: What I'm saying is my impression, with the exception of sullen people in Iliomar, was that the people were very happy. So my impression is that the people are happy with the Indonesian government as opposed to a viable alternative, of which I see none. All I see you putting the East Timor people through is many months or years of misery if you want to open this to some sort of international plebiscite. And that's why I suggest we should not drag in the question of who is sovereign in East Timor. I accept that the Jakarta government is sovereign in East Timor. It is a separate question how to improve the conditions of the people.

Nairn: Why not let the Timorese people decide both questions? Let them decide what is the best course to improve their own lot, and also let them decide the question of sovereignty. Shouldn't the only relevant thing be what the Timorese think?

Maynard: Again, I go back to what I said. Do you want to internationalize the problem or do you want to localize it?

Nairn: Localize it. Let the Timorese decide, quite locally.

Maynard: You are obviously advocating an international plebiscite with outside observers on the question of the sovereignty of the Indonesian government. My proposition is that if you want to communicate and really improve the interests of the people that are there, let's deal from the script that the Indonesian government is already working from. I have already accepted that East Timor is part of Indonesia. For me it is not a question. The question then becomes, are they upholding humanitarian values? Are they not being highhanded? Are they developing the country with consideration for others? Those are questions I would prefer to address.

Unger: Professor Anderson has asked to address a question to Professor Mubyarto.

Anderson: We have been talking a good deal about the attitudes of the Timorese people and, to a certain extent, also the attitudes of the Indonesian government. I was very struck by one thing we have not discussed. That is, how do ordinary Indonesians think about this issue, so far as you know? Do people think it would be an absolute national tragedy if the Timorese became like Brunei or became like Singapore or like Sarawak, or do they say, well, sure, why not, what's the big deal? I'd like to have some sense of how much Timor is integrated into the national consciousness of ordinary people.

Mubyarto: Once upon a time, a group of [Timorese] MTT people – Mersa Tenggara Timoria – caused a lot of headaches for the governor and the deputy governor because they crossed the border into Sabah [Malaysia] without the necessary documents. They were being paid very low wages. The deputy governor went to Sabah and was told that they have to accept the facts that they are uneducated, they are poor, and not very diligent workers. I happened to meet the deputy governor, Mr Puki, in the airport of Ujung Pandang at that time. He said, 'Well, after all, they are part of Indonesia, part of our Indonesian people. Whatever they are, we have to fight for better wages for our poor people.' Maybe the Indonesian government even now feels it is more a burden for Indonesia to have East Timor become part of Indonesia, but whether it was the right decision in 1976 or not, it is a fact that now East Timor has already become part of the Republic of Indonesia.

Anderson: Let me push that question a little bit further, and give you another example, which suggests that these facts somehow don't always stay facts. One of the most surprising developments in the last two or three years in the Soviet Union has been the position taken by Boris Yeltsin and many of his associates. What they see is that some of the republics of the old Soviet Union are a burden. He has now offered to make treaties with Georgia, with Latvia, Lithuania, Estonia, and the CIS saying we can have quite new relationships. So a 'fact' that was established in 1940, when Stalin took control of [the Baltic States] has turned out fifty years later not to be a 'fact.' A new relationship is already emerging. Do you think it is possible that the situation could evolve over the next few years, where something quite similar could happen? There is no reason why Timor and Indonesia couldn't be perfectly friendly neighboring powers in the way that Russia and Estonia eventually will be too. What would stop that? If tomorrow, for example, the Indonesian government said, 'We've decided the policy wasn't very good. We should change it. We'd like to have a new relationship with East Timor,' do you think there would be hundreds of thousands of Indonesians on the streets saying, 'Suharto, Suharto don't do that. Please don't do that!'

Mubyarto: I would like to refer to 1957, when Sumatra thought Java was a burden to Indonesia, because Java was becoming a Communist centre and was so poor that Java became a symbol of poverty. Now, the picture is reversed, because now Java is becoming the symbol of prosperity, and now Sumatra is poorer than Java, according to the data of the 1987 census. I don't think I can give an answer that supposes this will happen, because I think Indonesians believe in *pancasila*, becoming one country, an integrated country. I don't believe that Indonesia ten years from now will become like Russia, like the [former] Soviet Union.

Unger: I think Professor Anderson poses an interesting point that we should take up further tomorrow morning when we are talking about scenarios for the future.

(26 April 1991)

Unger: Good morning. The Social Science Research Council has received a letter from Florentino Sarmento, an East Timorese who works in the Indonesian administration in Dili [and heads the East Timor Agricultural

Development Program, ETADEP], and I have been asked to read excerpts from his letter, dated April 12 [1991], before we begin our session this morning. Mr Sarmento writes,

'I deeply regret that due to various circumstances, I will not be able to participate in this rare and wonderful event to provide inputs from an insider's perspective or a native Timorese who has been working as a development worker for the past ten years. I am mostly interested to provide some information on two panels out of four as requested. The two I have chosen are 'Implications of the Conflict' and 'Scenarios for the Future of East Timor' [which is our subject for this morning]. Unfortunately, I will not be able to participate in the workshop, so allow me to express very shortly some of my views in this letter.

The real problem for East Timor is the state of extreme poverty that affects more than 90% of the population and, under such condition[s] of poverty, people hardly question what should be the color of their flag. All other problems are mostly tailored simply to mask the real burden of this shameful poverty. The other very crucial problem is the severe shortage of skilled or educated Timorese. Qualified and more skilled people from other islands come to East Timor and mostly they are the ones who can profit from the opportunities opening up here both in the government or private sectors. Another very sad situation is the paradoxical attitude of the people in governments in the western countries during the past sixteen years. They continue to pour huge amounts of money to Indonesia to strengthen their economic and political interests. All this financial assistance or bilateral projects are kept far away from the East Timorese, since it is still internationally under dispute. As [a] result, the job opportunities and development can only take place in other parts of Indonesia. The position of the government is stronger and the already poor Timorese become weaker and poorer.

I personally think the time has come when those who claim to help the East Timorese should update their information and reevaluate their actions. Otherwise they will continue to hurt the poor people they claim to help. Very sincerely, Florentino C. Sarmento.'

Mubyarto: It is interesting that almost all the speakers since yesterday refused to speak of the integration of East Timor into Indonesia, but always call it the 1975 invasion. I believe that the government and people of Indonesia sincerely considered integration the best solution for the East Timorese in 1975. But even if we feel integration is the right solution for the East Timorese and for the Indonesian people as a whole, still we must recognize that integration itself creates many social and political problems for all concerned. The problem we are facing in East Timor is not only [one of] economic development, but also [a] social, political, and moral [problem]. The East Timorese, indeed the whole Indonesian community in East Timor, are currently in transition, a transition to a new society. It is not an easy transition, but many of us in Indonesia, both in the government as well as outside the government, are willing to help. Father Villorno, rector of academic affairs of the Universitas Timur Timor, a staff member of the Faculty of Agriculture, Gadjah Mada University, has organized university programmes to train the future leaders of East Timor. Gadjah Mada University, my university, is currently helping to supply lecturers to the University of East Timor.

It is misleading to hear that the present situation of East Timor is a military problem only, a problem created by the Indonesian Army. Up to December 1989, there were problems of communication between the Army leaders, the Church, and the governor. Now, since the abolition of *Koopskam* [Komando Operasi Keamanan Timor Timur, Security Operations Command, East Timor], the situation has much improved. In April 1990, when I met Monsignor Belo, he had just returned from briefing the incoming military personnel to be assigned in East Timor. This kind of exercise had never happened before. The military are now engaged in territorial assignments to help people restore rural areas through agricultural activities. In the future the students of the University of East Timor will go, for their practical work, to the rural areas together with the military engaged in territorial activities. Still,

Governor Mário Carrascalão [in office 1982–92], on behalf of the people of East Timor, frequently talks openly about the many malpractices of economic development in East Timor. He frequently suggests, most recently at the University of Atma Jaya, the Catholic University of Yogyakarta, and also at Satya Wacana Christian University in Salatiga, that we should not [talk of] economic development *in* East Timor, but economic development *of* East Timor. He criticizes especially the handling of education, which we discussed also in our [1990] Gadjah Mada report. We need special education in East Timor, so that people become capable of social and political development for themselves. This criticism has been widely publicized in [the] Indonesian media and shows that the people of Indonesia are serious in solving the problem of the Indonesian people in East Timor, the same problems experienced by the Dayak in Kalimantan, the Irianese in Irian Jaya, all the peoples of Eastern Indonesia. To conclude, there are many problems ahead of us, but the problems will be solved, not by East Timorese alone, but with the help of their Indonesian brothers under the guidance of the *pancasila* ideology.

Ramos-Horta: We have heard a number of statements concerning the human rights situation in East Timor. There were conflicting assessments of the situation. We heard people who visited that territory working for reputable organizations. We heard journalists; we heard businessmen; we heard our brother, the colonel, and currently a student at the American University. Very importantly we heard my compatriot, Donaciano Gomes, from East Timor. He represents the present and the future of East Timor. Donaciano Gomes speaks for a generation who were born just before the invasion [in 1975] and grew up during the past fifteen years of Indonesian occupation [see above 'The East Timor Intifada: Testimony of a Student Activist']. There are hundreds, thousands like him in East Timor, in Indonesia. There are hundreds of them in Portugal and in Australia. They are a

force, a reality that Indonesia has to reckon with. As we witness changes around the world, the dismantling of the military pacts, democratization throughout the world, improved communications between East Timor and the rest of the world, I believe that it has become impossibly difficult for Indonesia to simply silence the current generation.

As Clausewitz says, war is the continuation of politics by other means. Indonesia, by entering East Timor in 1975 sought to achieve political ends through military means. But Clausewitz also said that negotiations come about when parties to a conflict realize that the costs for both sides are too high. For the East Timorese, they have been enormous[ly] high. Whether we attribute all the blame to the Indonesian Army, or to famine caused by drought, or we attribute it to the resistance forces, the undeniable fact is that thousands and thousands of people were killed or died in East Timor. For the Indonesian side there have been some costs also in soldiers killed in East Timor. It has also cost Indonesia [dear] politically and diplomatically.

Isn't it time for Indonesia to think realistically, seriously, soberly about finding a solution? Xanana Gusmão, the resistance leader of East Timor, has made a proposal which I referred to yesterday, a round-table conference without preconditions where we will discuss all possible options. One option, with which Xanana agrees, is to start without discussing the issue of sovereignty. Let us deal instead with some concrete issues, for instance, reducing Indonesian military forces in East Timor to the minimum necessary and setting up an independent human rights commission under the leadership of the Catholic Church. This commission would report directly to the Prosecutor-General of Indonesia, to the Speaker of the Assembly in [Jakarta]. It would be assisted by the United Nations Human Rights Commission Advisory Services. There should be genuine free elections in East Timor for a local assembly – I am not yet talking about challenging the sovereignty issue, but local elections for a genuinely local parliament – where East Timorese are elected without having to vote for Golkar [Golongan Karya, Indonesian Government Party] or other parties by force. Let the Timorese form their own parties because, after all, Indonesia claims that it is a democracy. These are some concrete steps which would show Indonesia's good faith, honesty, courage in dealing with the problem, would enhance confidence, trust, and would probably heal some of the wounds of the past fifteen years. As [the] situation in Indonesia also changes [and] democratizes, I believe that army officers and other officials who are charged with human rights abuses in East Timor must be brought to trial. People cannot just go on with impunity killing others, be it in East Timor, in Irian Jaya, in Jakarta, or elsewhere. This would, I believe, enhance the credibility of Indonesia in East Timor, and would pave the way for a final settlement.

Anderson: The change that you describe as 'democratization' implies a willingness on the part of the government to permit a more open electoral process than what goes on now. But there is one big imponderable which I'd like you to address, and this is censorship in the media. Indonesians as a whole are extremely poorly informed about East Timor. Now what seems to me would be a very important change is an opening up of the mass media, at least the newspapers and magazines. There is going to be enormous pressure for this, and it seems to me that a whole lot of things that have not been allowed to be discussed, of which East Timor is only one – issues about land, for example, issues about the way development is working, environmental questions, and so forth – these will become matters of more general debate. My question, therefore, is what do you think is likely to come out of a situation where the whole realm of public discussion in Indonesia changes in character? What sort of consequences is this likely to have, and in which directions with regard to the East Timor situation? It seems to me there are two obvious pos-

sibilities. One is that, by bringing the broader public into the debate, the flexibility of a government would actually lessen. Right now, if Suharto tomorrow decided to give East Timor back to the Timorese, he probably could do it. Such is his power and such is his degree of control over the mass media. It is possible that under freer conditions, public pressures might actually increase on the government to take a hard[er] position. Alternatively, it may be that the opening up of public discussion and the more full realization of what the problems are, might create pressure to work out some civilized and intelligent long-term resolution to the problem. So what are the likely consequences of the democratization of the mass media?

Unger: John Taylor, do you want to go first?

Taylor: It's rather difficult to hypothesize. What strikes me is that the situation could be dramatically improved in East Timor by a relatively small policy change, a greater degree of autonomy, a Timorization. Given that this is quite easy to achieve, why on earth doesn't the regime do that? It would stop having to spend so much money and gain some international prestige by doing it. Why don't they do it? I think it is because the present regime has invested so much in it, it is a question of national honour. If you have a change of regime, and people were more well-informed, how would they react to it? One way of answering is to ask how Indonesians who oppose the government, and who are relatively well-informed, react now. When you explain what has happened and what government positions are, their reaction is, 'Yes, you're right. It *is* a problem, but how is it different from the rest of Indonesia, because in other parts of Indonesia people face the same problems?' Then you say, 'Well, these problems could be improved by a change in policy.' They say, 'Well, how about for other areas of Indonesia as well?' So it opens up a whole area of discussion, which even for a regime which was more democratic might be a bit of a problem, because in some ways it questions the status of existing areas of

Indonesia. If people become more well-informed, other issues open up as well. For that reason, I find this question difficult to answer.

Unger: Professor Mubyarto, your thoughts on the likely effects of an opening of the media, and also perhaps on some of the measures mentioned by Mr Ramos-Horta.

Mubyarto: Last month [March 1991], maybe you read the news about the establishment of Forum Demokrasi by Abdurrahman Wahid together with some friends. There was reaction pro and against, but the fact that the Forum Demokrasi, 'Democratic Forum', was established by non-government people like Abdurrahman before the general election next year [April 1992] is important. There is a general feeling in Indonesia that we need more democracy in many [areas], but I don't think you want to separate East Timor from the others because this problem of democracy really could be applied to many issues. The news about East Timor, the news about Aceh, the news about what happened in Lampung [March 1989] – I don't see the difference, that East Timor is the least publicized or not allowed to be publicized. I think the situation is the same concerning all issues.

I mentioned the publication of criticism by Governor Carrascalão himself. I think there is no evidence that the government has a policy against publishing about the problem of East Timor. The mass media in Indonesia publicize it very widely.

The current 'Go East' policy in the [current] Fifth Five Year Plan [Repelita V, 1989/90–1994/5] has been strongly associated with solving the problem of East Timor. Every day we talk about how to improve the conditions in the eastern part of Indonesia. The 'Go East' policy symbolizes the goal of equitable development, while till now development has been concentrated on Sumatra, Java, and Bali. Since Repelita V, the government has realized the importance of developing other parts, Kalimantan, Nusatenggara Barat, Nusatenggara Timur, Maluku, Irian [Jaya], and Sulawesi. So I think there is

nothing special about East Timor. It's the same. Everyone feels that we need more democracy, less censorship for all issues.

Unger: Does anyone else want to comment on this particular point?

Taylor: What you're saying is essentially what the current people in the NGO [Non-Governmental Organization] movement would say. But there is obviously a sense in which East Timor is different, because it has had such a totally different historical experience. It was an area outside Indonesia which was colonized by Indonesia and it's been brutal and everybody resents it. There's no real rule of law in East Timor. Refugees say the main problem is that you don't know where you stand. They execute justice on the spot. They take you out and they deal with you in that way. That's what makes East Timor so different from other parts of Indonesia. There's no way in which the East Timorese are ever going to accept integration until the situation reaches at least the level of the rule of law which exists in other parts of Indonesia.

José Ramos-Horta has said what people in East Timor are prepared to do in order to come to an agreement with the Indonesians. What we don't hear is what the Indonesian government is prepared to do to improve the situation. That's the crucial issue. Until the Indonesian government can actually do something to improve the situation, there is no possibility of an agreement or a rapprochement.

Ramos-Horta: I would like to add that often regimes do not seize on opportunities to initiate change in policies and, when they do, it is often too little, too late. Indonesia has already wasted a number of opportunities to redress the situation in East Timor. As much as we have been prepared to bend backwards to accommodate Indonesia, we are not going to relent in our efforts to achieve what we want. It was not imaginable for many people a few years ago that Portugal would take the steps that it has taken today. I remember, in Canberra, talking with Foreign Minister Gareth Evans, just [last] December [1990]. He basically dismissed Portuguese threats to take the case of the Timor Gap Treaty [of 11 December 1989] to the International Court of Justice. He considered it a bluff. When in February [1991], Portugal lodged a complaint under the compulsory jurisdiction clause, Australia was caught by surprise. For Portugal this is a great crusade. Not one single politician in Portugal disagrees with current government policies. Some even demand tougher action. So it is advisable for Indonesia now to seize these opportunities and begin serious negotiations towards a solution. As Xanana Gusmão emphasizes, and again I emphasize, a round-table conference without preconditions would be the best first step to discussing a solution to the problem. Do not think we are going to give up easily.

Unger: If this is a great crusade for Portugal, how much support can it get, not just in the European Community, but in the United States?

Moore: I'd like to know how much difference it would make if, indeed, the United States did change.

USSD 1: I would like to address the questions which have been raised about US policy and possibilities for change. It seems to me that from very early on in this whole thing, the United States has accepted that East Timor was part of Indonesia, and I do not see that that is likely to change. I think that the focus of the policy has been on trying to improve the conditions for the people within East Timor, initially by arguing for access for the ICRC [International Committee of the Red Cross] and other organizations for getting food in to help in a very bad situation and by continuing monitoring of the human rights situation. There are obviously questions about how much influence this would have. I myself do not see that the government of Indonesia will change its policy on Timor being part of Indonesia. I think, therefore, that, rather than trying to recreate a situation that might have been influenced fifteen years ago, it is probably more realistic to work on improving the situation for people in East Timor and in Indonesia as a whole,

and I think the thrust of most American aid policies are in that direction.

I would like to make one comment about Henry Kissinger's 'blessing' of the invasion. I was not part of the US government at that time, have no inside information on what went on, and hold no particular regard for Mr Kissinger, I might add. I do think from what I have heard from other people that, in fact, the timing of the Indonesian invasion [7 December 1975] was related to the visit because they felt, had they invaded before, the visit might have been cancelled, so that, rather than being a 'blessing', the invasion was put off for some time until the high-level visitors had left. I would end by saying the fact that several of us from the Department of State have come today to listen to what people have to say and to get different points of view is an indication that we do take seriously the concerns of people such as Bishop Moore and others who have visited East Timor. We would like to be open to these views, but we also, as diplomats and government people, are forced to deal with realities, not with ideals, and that sometimes puts us in an awkward situation.

Unger: Your statement raises several questions. First of all, I am wondering whether your comment about Secretary Kissinger's visit is not a technicality. It may have caused postponement of the invasion, but presumably there was considerable intelligence, there were briefings, and he and President Ford would have been in a position to say we don't think you ought to do this, if they had chosen to do so. Isn't that right?

USSD 1: I haven't seen the documents so I have no idea what was in their briefings. As a practitioner of *realpolitik*, it may well have been Kissinger's view to accept what seemed inevitable. On the other hand, it may well have been that this was not discussed. It certainly would not have been in Indonesia's interest to bring it up.

Unger: You said it seems unlikely Indonesian policy is going to change any time soon and therefore the United States is dealing with that as a reality, but we have in the last twenty years some remarkable examples of policy changes. Two that come to my mind are Anwar Sadat going to Jerusalem [in 1978], which was unthinkable until he said he wanted to do it, and some of the things that have happened in eastern Europe [since November 1989]. President Gorbachev did things that no-one might have expected and people had to move quickly when those changes began. So that's why I ask about the United States being prepared to play a more active mediating role or to take a more active interest in the question.

USSD 1: I was impressed by Ben [Anderson's] giving us a new context and trying to look at things in that [way]. On the other hand, I'm also basically a 'Sulawesi' person and am familiar with the 'Sulawesi' solution [i.e. the solution ending the Permesta Rebellion (1958–61) in North Sulawesi, involving a ceasefire combined with amnesty arrangements, and an honourable part for rebels in the post-rebellion settlement]. It seems to me, from what information we have on the situation on East Timor, that there is less resistance to Indonesian rule than there was a number of years ago. People are not happy about the Indonesians being there, perhaps, but the letter that came in from the young man who has made his peace with the Indonesian government, saying the best way to advance the interests of the people is through working with the Indonesians – that seems to be a theme. I don't think conditions in East Timor are such that they would convince us there is a totally new situation there. I would like to raise a question concerning Portuguese policy. I notice Mr Ramos-Horta calls this a 'crusade' for Portugal. There are several things that concern me about that. In this, I should say I am not reflecting my government's position. It is not anything that has been discussed within the Department of State. One is that we have had indications that in 1975 the Portuguese government was quite prepared to see East Timor become part of Indonesia. The second is an historical and, in a sense, contemporary question about Portugal. Why was Goa not a crusade? What is

the Portuguese position on Macau? What makes Timor so special that it is a crusade for Portugal?

Ramos-Horta: As I said, concerning 1975, Vasco Gonçalves and Costa Gomes both were pro-Moscow elements and they were the ones who favoured East Timor becoming part of Indonesia, because the Portuguese Communist Party was subservient to the Soviet Union and because the Soviet Union had very close relations with Indonesia. Concerning Macao, Macao was always part of China. It was only administered by Portugal. It is going to be handed over to China in 1999. The situation is very different from East Timor historically. East Timor never was part of the Dutch East Indies. It has been the scale of human rights violations in East Timor and information that has filtered to Portugal from refugees and accounts from newspapers around the world. Countless sources have fuelled the agony of Portugal and made the entire nation angry with what is going on and [with] Portuguese indifference for many years. We were critical of Portugal for not doing anything until after 1986. That again has to do with the fact that there were so many changes in government in thirteen years. There was no stability in the foreign policy establishment. Finally, President Mário Soares was elected in [March] 1986 and democracy was consolidated in Portugal. The economy is doing well. They now have greater self-confidence and pride, and a tremendous sense of responsibility. It is ironic that Indonesia, which in the 1960s condemned Portugal for its colonial policies in Africa, is now on the receiving end of criticism in the Special Committee on Decolonization. It is Portugal, a colonial power, that is fighting for the rights of a colony, instead of Indonesia, a Third World country.

Unger: John Taylor has asked to reply.

Taylor: It seems that, according to the logic of [the State Department], you should have supported Saddam Hussein's invasion of Kuwait [in August 1990]. Indonesia invaded East Timor, which had declared its independence. That's the inescapable logic of your position, and I find it stunning.

Nairn: To amplify on the last point, I think the statement the State Department's representative has just made shows that the things that President Bush [in office 1988–92] and [Secretary of State] James Baker said about US policy regarding Kuwait were not sincere. James Baker at one point made a very dramatic statement where he said, 'We believe, and it is US policy, that large powerful countries should not be permitted to invade small weak countries and get away with it.' President Bush said on at least three occasions that Saddam Hussein should be put on trial before a 'Nuremberg' tribunal for crimes against humanity. Now, these were very reasonable and noble statements, but the statement of the State Department representative shows that, in fact, these are not the guiding principles of US policy. They were invoked in the case of Iraq because it happened to be at that moment politically convenient for the State Department.

Beyond that, it's not as if the US is simply observing what Indonesia is doing in East Timor and has to make a judgement about it. The United States is a participant and a perpetrator. I think the best way to put that in perspective is to imagine that the situation were different, that the day before the invasion, Brezhnev visited Jakarta and, with his top foreign affairs advisor, sat down with Suharto. As the troops went in and invaded Dili, Brezhnev and his advisor were then asked for comment about the invasion and they stated that they 'understood' the Indonesian position and that Indonesia had legitimate security interests to protect – these were the public statements made by President Ford and Henry Kissinger after the invasion – and that after that, as the Indonesians continued to prosecute their campaign, the Soviets sent in the planes essential for them to conduct their bombing and strafing raids and so on, and over the years the Soviet Union continued to be the principal arms supplier to Indonesia. Someone here would be laughed at if they got up and said,

'Well, the Soviet Union is in a difficult position regarding Indonesia; the degree of their influence is uncertain; they're an observer looking on trying to help the situation.' Obviously we wouldn't look at it that way.

The remark about a diminution in resistance in East Timor strikes me as fantasy from what I saw there. I wonder if Donaciano Gomes could comment on that since he is someone who was tortured and who has had many of his friends killed because of their resistance, and if he could talk about what has been happening in recent months in terms of resistance.

Gomes: [translated from Portuguese] I'm going to give you a brief introduction to the present situation in East Timor. The State Department representative said that the situation in East Timor has improved a lot and that is a big lie. Important nations in this world would rather that the public not find out what actually is happening in East Timor, but we, the sons of East Timor, can say what the present reality in East Timor is. As long as Indonesian soldiers are in East Timor, human rights are going to be violated, and they will continue to be violated as long as these soldiers are there. I want very much that interested governments will not support Indonesia in continuing to kill women, children, and old people in East Timor.

Walsh: My question is directed to Professor Mubyarto. He stated that many people in the room had read the Gadjah Mada study on East Timor. It is my impression that the Gadjah Mada report has not had such circulation, either within Indonesia – for example, within NGO circles – or internationally. Very few people are aware of it, even though it was published in March 1990 [in Yogyakarta] and is now over twelve months old [see Bibliography, subsequently published in Australia by the Indonesian Resources and Information Program (IRIP) in December 1991]. I think that is a great shame because my reading of the report is that it is a very sensitive, constructive document. It makes a lot of important recommendations that the American administration, the Australian government, and others who say continually that they are concerned about the situation in East Timor, could well take up. For that reason, I think it is important that the document is better understood. For example, it says that it is important that the number of the military in Timor be significantly reduced. It recommends that the economic monopolies in East Timor be terminated. It recommends that people be allowed to return to their original villages and way of life, that the resettlement policy, which has been such a central feature of the Indonesian administration of East Timor over the last fifteen years, be radically revised. It recommends a meaningful role for the young educated East Timorese in policy-making and in decision-making in East Timor. It recommends a similar role for the very central institution of the Catholic Church in East Timor and a devolution of power from the centre in Jakarta to the provincial government in East Timor. These seem to me to be major considerations and deserving of study and possibly being picked up in the policies of governments like Australia, Indonesia, the European Community, and so on. For those reasons, the report is important. My question to Professor Mubyarto is, what is the status of the report in Indonesia at the moment? Is it in any way a public document? Has it been discussed in various fora? More precisely, what has been the ABRI reaction to the recommendations and the general thrust of the report?

Mubyarto: The seminar which was supposed to be held in Dili in March [*sic* 19 April 1990] changed from a public seminar into a closed seminar attended by representatives from the governor's office and also ABRI representatives from Jakarta.

What is the status of the report? The report now is given to those who ask for the report. We don't publish it as a book, but we give it to anyone from Indonesia who asks for the report. Within ABRI it has been considered a very accurate report. [Major-]General Sintong Panjaitan of Udayana [Military

Command] in Bali [dismissed February 1992] has instructed all his officers to read it, but it is another thing to discuss it in an open seminar. It is true that we have recommended reducing the armed personnel in Dili and I think it has been done. We recommended abolishing the coffee monopoly and establishing an export association in Dili. We have recommended that villagers be allowed to return to their old places rather than being kept in the settlements set up by the government. We recommended that the youth be allowed to establish associations, like the Catholic Student Association, because then they would have more room for discussion. Finally, about the devolution of central power, at one point, we were thinking about giving full autonomy to East Timor, comparable to what was given to Irian Jaya in the late 1960s. As John mentioned earlier, the fact that the history of East Timor is so different from the rest of Indonesia gives a lot of room to give special autonomy to the province of East Timor.

Ramos Pinto: My name is Ramos Pinto from the embassy of Portugal. I am answering the question that the official from the State Department asked on the interests of the Portuguese government on the question of Timor. There are several UN resolutions that consider Portugal the administering power of Timor so that we have a responsibility to assure its right to self-determination. Besides that, it is written in the Portuguese constitution itself that the President and the government have an obligation to assure that the people of Timor exercise their right of self-determination. That is the reason the Portuguese government is committed to it. This is a question of national consensus in Portugal. All the parties, from the Christian Democrats to the Communists, the Social Democrats and the Socialists, they all agree with this. There are no divisions among the political parties in Portugal about this question.

Unger: And [the] other question about why the feelings are stronger about East Timor than about Macau and Goa?

Ramos Pinto: As Ramos-Horta said, Macau was never a colony. Macau is [recognized as] Chinese territory under Portuguese Administration. By [the] agreement between Portugal and the Peoples' Republic of China (1987) it was decided that Macau will become a special administrative region of the PRC in 1999. So it is a totally different situation. The question of Macau is not and has never been a colonial situation. Furthermore, Macau is not considered by the UN as a non self-governing territory as Timor is.

Unger: And reaching back to Goa in the [early] 1960s?

Ramos Pinto: Was there any resolution of the United Nations condemning the integration of Goa into India? We had a revolution in Portugal and one of the first declarations after the revolution was that we would grant independence to our colonies. That was something the international community was demanding from Portugal for a long time.

Traube: I wanted to make a comment on the question of determining popular attitudes toward the Indonesian regime. I want to emphasize that peasant resistance to state power rarely takes the form of direct and open defiance for the simple reason that, when such acts of protest do occur, they are almost inevitably crushed. At the same time, neither the decline in open resistance to Indonesia nor the deference that people may show to authorities in public situations should be interpreted as signs of general acquiescence or popular support for the regime. To get access to popular feelings requires access to those private, backstage situations, the 'hidden transcript' as James Scott calls it, those situations in which the powerless are more likely to speak their minds, to criticize those in power. I suggest that in the present situation on Timor we need to keep in mind that language is critical to whether one has access to those sorts of situations. Indonesian, as the language of the powerful, is likely to be an obstacle. I spent two years on Timor speaking Mambai and some Tetum and it still took me a good eight months before Mambai confided to me the resentments

they felt against the Portuguese at that time. Therefore, it seems to me that the fact that journalists have been able, in a few weeks using Portuguese and English, to hear so many accounts of deep bitterness toward the Indonesians is a very clear index of the strength and depth of popular feeling.

Unger: It seems relevant in that regard to ask whether the US embassy in Jakarta has Portuguese speakers who go out to East Timor?

USSD 2: To my knowledge we do not have Portuguese speakers who go there. Nearly all of the people who go there speak Bahasa Indonesia when appropriate. It is usually Bahasa and English that are used.

Unger: The point is that, not being Portuguese speakers, they might have a barrier from finding out the feeling of the people.

USSD 2: That is possible. Using the two languages that we tend to use there, we try to speak with as many people from as many different groupings as we can and attempt to learn what they have learned through their long experience there, and then attempt to report back as objectively as we can.

Goodman: This is a question for the State Department spokesperson. Do we just consider the level of resistance, or do we also consider the level of atrocity? In the case of Kuwait, the Sheik [Jaber al-Ahmed al-Jaber al-Sabah, 13th Amir, r. 1977 to the present] fled as did the Kuwaiti soldiers. As for the level of resistance, quoting from Hugh O'Shaughnessy's article ['Secret Killing of a Nation'] from the *Observer* [7 April 1991], 'After fifteen years of occupation by Indonesian troops and deaths of perhaps 200,000 people, one-third of the Timorese population, sixty-year-olds are resigned to a life of terror. Five-year-olds are petrified. The young, however, are frightened but defiant.' My question to you is, what evidence do you have that the resistance is down? When was the last time a State Department representative went there to talk with people? What is your criterion for information? Where do you get your evidence?

USSD 1: First of all, I am not a State

Department spokesperson. I do work for the State Department, but I am not representing them as an official today. The last time an embassy person was there was in March this year [1991]. I can let Larry [Dinger] give you more details. He was one of the people who went while assigned to Jakarta. We try to have people go four times a year. We talk not just to government officials but also to people who have been there for considerable lengths of time. We try to draw on the knowledge of people who live in that community. We realize that there are inevitably gaps and inadequacies but I wonder, when we are talking about language, how widely is Portuguese spoken? The level of education during the colonial period was relatively low, so the number who were educated to speak Portuguese, I would think, is relatively small.

Unger: You would concede, though, that it would be useful to have someone go who spoke Portuguese?

USSD 1: I concede it would be useful. It would be useful to have people speaking far more languages than we are able to cope with in the State Department, considering the number of officers we have now. We are not saying that we are going to Timorese speaking Indonesian, though there are Timorese who do understand Indonesian. A lot of the people we speak to could be foreigners.

Nairn: Language, while it has some importance, is I think beside the point when it comes to the State Department. I mean, that is much too subtle. First of all, within the past two years, we have seen a series of mass demonstrations which were unheard of previously in Timor. You have had hundreds of people coming out and being tortured afterwards because they participated in demonstrations. One demonstration [17 January 1990] was sparked by the presence of the US ambassador [John Monjo]. You don't have to speak the language to see the people demonstrating in the streets. Just this past December [*sic*, September 1990], there was a mass demonstration on a religious occasion [i.e. pro-independence protests on the occasion of the 50th anniversary

celebration of the diocese of Dili]. The reason that the State Department is not able to see this in Timor is, I think, that it is simply a matter of policy. The US did not want to speak the truth and so they didn't. As someone who has spent a lot of time in some of the more repressive places in the world, in the Middle East and Central America for instance, I can tell you that, by simply walking into Timor and walking around, it assaults you, it surrounds you. You immediately see that you are in the midst of a police state. People accost you when they have the chance and, providing you don't have an Indonesian army officer accompanying you or you don't fly in in an Indonesian helicopter or are not giving off some other overt sign of officialdom, try to tell their story. You don't have to speak Tetum. You don't even have to speak Portuguese. You could go in there, I think as Bishop Moore said, speaking English. You could simply observe with your eyes, if you happened to be there during one of the demonstrations. These are palpable facts and there is nothing subtle about it. The State Department won't acknowledge it because it is US policy not to acknowledge it.

Unger: Colonel Panjaitan, I wonder if you would like to address some of these questions that have accumulated for you. Perhaps you would like to start by talking about the security on the occasion of the Pope's visit [12 October 1989], which was raised before.

Panjaitan: I was right on that spot during the visit of the Pope. A very clear policy in my country is that everyone is allowed to express their feelings as long as they do it in the right way. So when I was in Timor together with the Pope, as soon as we landed at the airport, some Timorese friends told me that a small number of people might demonstrate during the ceremony. I said, 'Well, this is a Catholic ceremony, so I think it is very bad if they demonstrate during the ceremony, because it will disturb the ceremony itself.' But I said, 'Well, if they want to do it, they can do it.' My job at that time was just to protect the Pope. At the ceremony, we walked with the Pope among the crowd of around 200,000 people [*sic*, see Shirley Shackleton, 'Planting a Tree in Balibo: A Journey to East Timor' above]. Nothing happened. The Pope went to his car. Suddenly around ten or fifteen people began shouting about the Indonesian government. I made sure that the Pope got to his car safely and then I went to the crowd and said, 'What happened?' And they said, 'We don't like Indonesia', or something like that. 'Okay,' I said, 'You can act like this, but it is not necessary here. You can do that anywhere, because you are allowed to express your feelings. This is a democracy, but of course this is not America. This is not like Western countries. We have rule[s] of the game.' Nothing happened at that time. I guarantee it, because I was there. Some other Timorese, who did not agree with this demonstration, started a fight. They threw a folding chair among them. I said, 'This is dangerous for me because I don't want to be hurt by both sides.' So I said, 'Look, you have to solve this. Calm down.' I think [Donaciano] Gomes was there because I was right on the spot. Nothing happened and then I left and went back to the aircraft and then we flew back to Jakarta. So I didn't see this big problem during the Pope's visit to Dili. Maybe some people try to glamorize this small thing. There were around 200,000 people. If the majority of the people didn't like Indonesia, it was a very good opportunity to have an uprising, but most of the people, they just don't care. It is very good proof that the majority of the people like the integration with Indonesia.

The number of troops, as recommended by Pak Mubyarto, has been reduced significantly. There used to be around ten battalions [i.e. approximately 8,000 men]; now they are going down to six territorial battalions. In East Timor we trained the local people to defend their own villages. So we reduced the number of troops. Of course, we cannot say that all the Indonesian troops will be removed from that area, because each province has two territorial battalions to defend it.

Anywhere you go in Indonesia, it is the same pattern. So there is no specific treatment for East Timor.

The second thing you see now is the government policy of opening East Timor to anyone who wants to go there, so long as you are not going to interfere [in] our internal problems. As a tourist, fine, you can go there. You can talk to anybody.

About language, the majority of the people over there speak Bahasa Indonesia now. Maybe some educated people speak Portuguese, but if you go to the village, stay in the village, they will speak Bahasa Indonesia or maybe Tetum. In Dili, lots can speak Portuguese, as in Jakarta, the old generation can speak Dutch.

Horta (translator): Excuse me. The old generation?

Panjaitan: Yes, the old generation.

Horta: Donaciano was four [*sic*, six] years old [at the time of the Indonesian invasion in December 1975]!

Archer: I'd like to say that I felt for some of the last half hour a sense of frustration because, having worked for quite a long time on East Timor and having just been there [April 1991], I find the whole debate very unrealistic. At no point anywhere did I find anyone who denied that a principal obstacle to the effective integration of East Timor within Indonesia was the fact that a substantial portion of the Timorese population was still resistant to it. I think that what José Ramos-Horta said at the beginning is extremely important to remember as we close. There have been several attempts over a period of years to integrate East Timor and there was a point, I believe, when the Indonesian authorities recognized that, because of the difficulties at the beginning, the older people were likely to be very resistant. The crucial fact is, and I assume this is accepted by all parties within East Timor, that the younger generation have in large numbers decided not to accept Indonesian rule, but to oppose it, to be nationalist in their approach. If the governments of Europe, the American government, the governments of Asia, and the Indonesian government, do not recognize that, this is nonsense. The professor's report, by implication, accepts it, and any serious observer understands this. The problem is not to quibble about the numbers or to talk about the proportions. It is as arid a discussion as to discuss the number of dead, which preoccupied public debate for a number of years. Let us admit that thousands have died. And let us admit that many, many Timorese still oppose Indonesian rule. The problem of policy is how do you deal with that? It is the principal problem facing the Indonesian authorities in East Timor. It is the principal fact facing the Church in East Timor. It is the principal fact facing anyone who tries to look responsibly at the future of the territory. I do think we should stop quibbling about the detail of how many and accept the fundamental facts which I believe all principled parties in this dispute privately agree on.

Unger: Thank you, Mr Archer. I have been asked to say that the Social Science Research Council wants to thank everyone for participating in this workshop on East Timor. It is hoped that a learning process and a dialogue will continue on all sides of this very important issue. Thank you very much.

PART VI

East Timor: A Bibliography, 1970–94

East Timor: A Bibliography, 1970–1994

compiled by Sue Rabbitt Roff
with the assistance of Peter Carey and Wendy Lambourne

This bibliography is an unannotated listing of publications, and some unpublished works, on East Timor from the period 1970 to 1994. It includes items in English, Dutch, French, Danish, German, Indonesian, Japanese, Norwegian, Portuguese, Russian, Spanish, and Swedish, and covers political, sociological, anthropological, historical, economic, legal and scientific aspects. No area or language has been deliberately excluded. However, a conscious decision was made not to include newspaper or newsletter articles except for some pieces judged to be of special significance, for example those by the Australian lawyer, Robert Domm, who met with Xanana Gusmão in September 1990, and Hugh O'Shaughnessy, whose special reports in the *Observer* helped to draw attention to East Timor at a critical time in the early 1990s.

While aiming to be comprehensive, the bibliography does not claim to be exhaustive nor perfectly complete. Rather, it is intended as a checklist of items to be used as a research tool. We hope it will have an organic existence and will, in time, be amended and grow through the contributions of others working in the field of East Timor studies.

Acknowledgements
The publication of this bibliography would not have been possible without the assistance of researchers and writers with expertise on East Timor who offered additions and corrections to the original list compiled by Sue Roff. In addition to the substantial contributions made by the leading bibliographer of East Timor, Kevin Sherlock, the present editor, Peter Carey, and Wendy Lambourne of the Peace Research Centre in Canberra, others to whom acknowledgement is due include Carmel Budiardjo, Roger Clark, Herb Feith, Liz Gardiner, Charles Scheiner, John Taylor and Pat Walsh.

The following bibliographies were also consulted for items to include in this bibliography: Andrew McClean (compiler), *Security, Arms Control, and Conflict Reduction in East Asia and the Pacific: A Bibliography, 1980-1991*, Bibliographies and Indexes in Law and Political Science No. 19, Westport, CT: Greenwood Press, 1993; Ian Rowland (compiler), *Timor: Including the Islands of Roti and Ndao*, World Bibliographical Series Vol. 142, Oxford: Clio Press, 1992; and Kevin Sherlock, *A Bibliography of Timor: Including East (Formerly Portuguese) Timor, West (Formerly Dutch) Timor and the Island of Roti*, Canberra: Research School of Pacific Studies, Australian National University, 1980. A substantial part of the present bibliography (covering the period 1970-1993) has already been published by the Peace Research Centre of the Research School of Pacific Studies (Australian National University, Canberra; see the listing under Roff in the present Bibliography).

Key to Location Symbols

The location of rare books and pamphlets, where known, is identified according to the following legend:

A: Centrale Bibliotheek, Koninklijk Instituut Voor de Tropen, Amsterdam

C: Columbia University, New York

K: Koninklijk Instituut, Leiden

Y: Yale University, New Haven, Connecticut

A Paz é Possível em Timor Leste, *see* Paz é Possível em Timor Leste, A.

Aarons, M. and R. Domm, *East Timor: A Western Made Tragedy*. Sydney: Left Book Club, 1992.

Aarse, R., 'Le Jeu de l'Indonésie et des États-Unis dans l'Île de Timor' [The game of Indonesia and the United States in the island of Timor], *Le Monde Diplomatique* (Paris), **23**(264)(March 1976).

Adil, Hilman, 'The Problem of East Timor in the Context of Indonesian Australian Relations', *World Review*, **17** (October 1978).

Aditjondro, G.J., 'Prospek Pembangunan Timor Timur Sesudah Penangkapan Xanana Gusmão' [The prospects for development in East Timor after the arrest of Xanana Gusmão], *Dian Ekonomi*, **2** (1992–3).

—, 'From Memo to Tutuala. A Kaleidoscope of Environmental Problems in East Timor', in Herb Feith, Emma Baulch and Pat Walsh (eds.), *East Timor. An Indonesian Intellectual Speaks Out*, ACFOA Development Dossier No. 33. Canberra: Australian Council for Overseas Aid, 1994.

— (ed. Herb Feith, Emma Baulch and Pat Walsh), *East Timor. An Indonesian Intellectual Speaks Out*, ACFOA Development Dossier No. 33. Canberra: Australian Council for Overseas Aid, 1994.

Aldeia, F.A., *Na Hora do Arranque .... Discurso proferido na abertura solene da Assembleia Legislativa e da Junta Consultiva de Timor, no dia 29 de maio de 1973, em Díli* [Time to move ahead .... Speech given at the solemn opening of the Legislative Assembly and Consultative Board of Timor, 29 May 1973, in Díli]. Lisbon: Agência-Geral do Ultramar, 1973.

—, *Por um Timor Melhor – Para um Portugal Maior, Discurso proferido na abertura solene da Assembleia Legislativa de Timor, no dia 30 de Abril de 1974, em Dili* [For a better Timor – Towards a greater Portugal. Speech given at the solemn opening of the Legislative Assembly of Timor, 30 April 1974, in Dili]. Dili: Imprensa Nacional de Timor, 1974.

Alkatiri, M., 'East Timor: Survival and Resistance', *Kommentar* (Stockholm), (February 1982).

Amnesty International, *East Timor: Statement of Amnesty International's Concerns in East Timor.* London: Amnesty International, 29 April 1980.

—, *East Timor: List of Timorese who have 'Disappeared' after Surrender to or Capture by Indonesian Occupation Forces in East Timor.* London: Amnesty International, 9 June 1980.

—, *Indonesia/East Timor: Update on Amnesty International's Concerns in Indonesia and East Timor.* London: Amnesty International, 30 April 1981.

—, *East Timor: Recent Allegations of Continuing Human Rights Violations.* London: Amnesty International, 4 February 1982.

—, *East Timor: Amnesty International's Concerns in East Timor,* London: Amnesty International, 28 September 1982.

—, *East Timor: Statement of AI's Concerns in East Timor.* London: Amnesty International, 9 August 1983.

—, *East Timor: Amnesty International Statement on East Timor to the United Nations Special Committee on Decolonization.* London: Amnesty International, 12 September 1983.

—, *East Timor: Statement on East Timor.* London: Amnesty International, 3 August 1984.

—, *East Timor: Amnesty International Statement on East Timor to the United Nations Special Committee on Decolonization.* London: Amnesty International, 20 August 1984.

—, *East Timor: Statement on the Human Rights Situation.* London: Amnesty International, 28 February 1985.

—, *East Timor: AI's Written Statement to the 41st Session of the UN Commission on Human Rights on the Situation of Human Rights in East Timor.* London: Amnesty International, 28 February 1985

—, *East Timor: Some Individual Cases of Concern to Amnesty International in East Timor.* London: Amnesty International, 14 May 1985.

—, *East Timor: Violations of Human Rights, Extrajudicial Executions, 'Disappearances', Torture and Political Imprisonment.* London: Amnesty International, 1985.

—, *East Timor: Human Rights in East Timor.* London: Amnesty International, 26 June 1985.

—, *East Timor: Amnesty International Statement on East Timor to the United Nations Special Committee on Decolonization (8 August 1985).* London: Amnesty International, 30 August 1985.

—, *East Timor: Unfair Trials and Possible Torture in East Timor.* London: Amnesty International, December 1985.

—, *East Timor: East Timorese Political Prisoner Detained in Jakarta.* London: Amnesty International, July 1986.

—, *East Timor: Statement of Amnesty International to the United Nations Special Committee on Decolonization.* London: Amnesty International, 15 August 1986,

—, *East Timor: 'Disappearances' in East Timor since August 1983: Update.* London: Amnesty International, March 1987.

—, *Indonesia/East Timor: Summary of Amnesty International Concerns in Indonesia and East Timor.* London: Amnesty International, April 1987.

—, *East Timor: Statement by Amnesty International to the United Nations Special Committee on Decolonization.* London: Amnesty International, 13 August 1987.

—, *East Timor: Releases of Political Prisoners.* London: Amnesty International, October 1987.

—, *Indonesia/East Timor: Further Releases of Political Prisoners*. London: Amnesty International, November 1987.

—, *Indonesia/East Timor: Additional Information on the Release of Political Prisoners*. London: Amnesty International, January 1988.

—, *Indonesia/East Timor. Allegations of Torture*. London: Amnesty International, March 1988.

—, *Indonesia/East Timor: Unfair Trials and Further Releases of Political Prisoners*. London: Amnesty International, April 1988.

—, *Indonesia/East Timor: Summary of AI's Concerns in Indonesia and East Timor*. London: Amnesty International, May 1988.

—, *East Timor: Statement to the United Nations Special Committee on Decolonization*. London: Amnesty International, August 1988.

—, *East Timor: Amnesty International Statement to the United Nations Special Committee on Decolonization*. London: Amnesty International, August 1989.

—, *East Timor: Short-Term Detention and Ill-Treatment*. London: Amnesty International, January 1990.

—, *Indonesia/East Timor: A Summary of AI's Concerns*. London: Amnesty International, 1990.

—, *East Timor: Amnesty International Statement to the United Nations Special Committee on Decolonization*. London: Amnesty International, August 1990.

—, *East Timor: Update on Human Rights Concerns Since August 1990*. London: Amnesty International, January 1991.

—, *East Timor: Amnesty International Statement to the United Nations Special Committee on Decolonization, August 1991*. London: Amnesty International, 1991.

—, *Indonesia/East Timor: AI Appalled at Massacre, Calls for Impartial Inquiry*. London: Amnesty International, 14 November 1991.

—, *East Timor: The Santa Cruz Massacre*. London: Amnesty International, 1991.

—, *East Timor: After the Massacre*. London: Amnesty International, 1991.

—, *Indonesia/East Timor: AI Urges Rigorous Standards for International Enquiry into Massacre*. London: Amnesty International, 3 December 1991 [press statement].

—, *East Timor: Violations Continue and Doubts Remain Over Official Inquiry*. London: Amnesty International, 9 January 1992 [press statement].

—, *Indonesia/East Timor – Santa Cruz: The Government Response*. London: Amnesty International, 6 February 1992.

—, *Indonesia/East Timor: Human Rights Protesters Charged with Subversion*. London: Amnesty International, 27 March 1992 [press statement].

—, *Indonesia/East Timor: Human Rights Activists Convicted of Subversion*. London: Amnesty International, 27 May 1992 [press statement].

—, *Indonesia/East Timor: Fernando de Araújo – Prisoner of Conscience*. London: Amnesty International, May 1992.

—, *Indonesia/East Timor: The Suppression of Dissent*. London: Amnesty International, July 1992.

—, *East Timor: 'In Accordance with the Law'. Statement before the United Nations Special Committee on Decolonization*. London: Amnesty International, July 1992.

—, *Amnesty International Refused Access to East Timor for Anniversary of Santa Cruz Massacre*. London: Amnesty International, 6 November 1992 [press statement].

—, *Indonesia/East Timor: Amnesty International Fears Further Deterioration of Human Rights Situation*. London: Amnesty International, 9 November 1992 [press statement].

—, *Indonesia/East Timor, A New Order? Human Rights in 1992*. London: Amnesty International, February 1993.

—, *East Timor: Xanana Trial a Travesty of Justice*. London: Amnesty International, 21 May 1993 [press statement].

—, *Indonesia/East Timor: Seven East Timorese Seek Asylum*. London: Amnesty International, 23 June 1993.

—, *Indonesia/East Timor: Seven East Timorese Still in Danger*. London: Amnesty International, July 1993.

—, *East Timor: Unfair Political Trial of Xanana Gusmão*. London: Amnesty International, July 1993.

—, *East Timor: State of Fear. Statement before the United Nations Special Committee on Decolonization*. London: Amnesty International, 13 July 1993.

—, *Indonesia & East Timor: Fact and Fiction – Implementing the Recommendations of the UN Commission on Human Rights*. London: Amnesty International, 16 February 1994.

—, *East Timor: Who is to Blame? Statement Before the UN Special Committee on Decolonization*. London: Amnesty International, 13 July 1994.

—, *East Timor: Protestors Beaten, Detained and 'Disappeared'*. London: Amnesty International, August 1994.

—, *Indonesia & East Timor. Power and Impunity. Human Rights under the New Order*. London: Amnesty International, 28 September 1994.

—, *Indonesia: 'Operation Cleansing' – Human Rights and APEC*. London: Amnesty International, November 1994.

—, *Indonesia & East Timor. The 12 November Protests*. London: Amnesty International, 15 November 1994.

—, *Indonesia & East Timor: Update on 12 November Protests*, London: Amnesty International, 23 November 1994.

Amnesty International USA, *Human Rights Concerns in Indonesia/East Timor. Statement Before the Senate Foreign Relations Committee, February 21 1991*. Washington, DC, 1991 [mimeograph].

'An Uneven Chorus of Condemnation: International Reactions', *Inside Indonesia*. 29 (December 1991).

Anderson, B.R.O'G., 'Ten Years After Integration', *Inside Indonesia*. 9 (December 1986).

—, 'The Importance of Liberating Indonesia from East Timor', address to the Universidade Católica, Oporto (Portugal), (27 May 1992).

—, 'On Being Valiant for Truth', *Asian Studies Review*, **16**(1) (July 1992).

—, 'Imagining "East Timor"', *Arena Magazine* (Melbourne), **4** (April–May 1993).

Anderson, D., 'Independence for East Timor', *IPA Review*. **45**(2) (1992).

Andris, V. Balmaks, 'The Influence of East Timor on Australia's Relationship with Indonesia', MA thesis, Deakin University (Geelong, Victoria), 1993.

Apodeti, see *Associação Popular Democrática Timorense*.

Araújo, A. de, 'East Timor: Fretilin Speaks', *Tricontinental* (Havana), **49–50** (1976).

—, *Timor Leste: Os Loricos Voltaram a Cantar* [East Timor: The Loricos Sing Again]. Lisbon: Edição do Autor, 1977.

—, J. Jolliffe and B. Reece, *Timorese Elites*. Canberra: CIET, 1975.

Araújo, R., 'Reminiscences of East Timor', *Nieman Reports*, **47**(3) (Fall 1993).

Arndt, H. W., 'Timor: Expediency or Principle?', *Quadrant* (Sydney), **106**(20) (May 1976).

—, 'Timor: Vendetta Against Indonesia', *Quadrant* (Sydney), **23**(13–17) (December 1979) [reprinted without the notes and with some omissions in: *The Bulletin*, 18 December 1979].

Asia Watch [post-March 1994, Human Rights Watch/Asia], *Human Rights in Indonesia and East Timor: An Asia Watch Report*, ed. D.F. Orentlicher. New York: Asia Watch Committee, 1988. *See also* Jones S.

—, *Human Rights in Indonesia and East Timor*. New York: Asia Watch, March 1989.

—, *Injustice, Persecution and Eviction: A Human Rights Update on Indonesia & East Timor*. New York: Asia Watch, March 1990.

—, *East Timor: The November 12 Massacre and its Aftermath*. New York: Asia Watch, December 1991.

—, *East Timor: Asia Watch Criticizes Commission Report*. New York: Asia Watch, January 1992.

—, *Anatomy of Press Censorship in Indonesia: The Case of Jakarta-Jakarta and the Dili Massacre*. New York: Asia Watch, April 1992.

—, *Deception and Harassment of East Timorese Workers*. New York: Asia Watch, May 1992.

—, *East Timor: The Courts-Martial*. New York: Asia Watch, June 1992.

—, *Charges & Rebuttals Over Labor Rights Practices*. New York: Asia Watch, January 1993.

—, 'Remembering History in East Timor: The Trial of Xanana Gusmão and a Follow-up to the Dili Massacre', *AsiaWatch* (New York), **5**(8) (April 1993).

—, *The Limits of Openness. Human Rights in Indonesia and East Timor*. New York: Human Rights Watch, September 1994.

Associação Popular Democrática Timorense (Apodeti) Dili: Apodeti, 1974. [political manifesto of the Apodeti Party including a short biography of its chairman, Arnaldo dos Reis Araújo]. **K**

Atta, D. van, *see* Van Atta, D.

Auburn, F.M., and V.L. Forbes, 'The Timor Gap Zone of Co-operation', *Boundary Briefing,* No.9, International Boundaries Research Unit. Durham, UK: University of Durham, 1991.

—, D. Ong and V.L. Forbes, *Dispute Resolution and the Timor Gap Treaty*, IOCPS Occasional Paper No. 35. Perth: Indian Ocean Centre for Peace Studies, University of Western Australia, 1994.

Australia, Department of Foreign Affairs and Trade, *Treaty between Australia and the Republic of Indonesia on the Zone of Cooperation in an Area between the Indonesian Province of East Timor and Northern Australia (Timor Gap Treaty)*. Australian Treaty Series No. 9. Canberra: Department of Foreign Affairs and Trade, 1991.

—, Joint Standing Committee on Foreign Affairs, Defence and Trade, *A Review of Australia's Efforts to Promote and Protect Human Rights*. Canberra: Australian Government Publishing Service, December 1992.

—, Joint Standing Committee on Foreign Affairs, Defence and Trade, *Australia's Relations with Indonesia*. Canberra: Australian Government Publishing Service, November 1993.

—, Senate Standing Committee on Foreign Affairs and Defence, *Hearings on East Timor, May–October 1982*. Canberra: Australian Government Publishing Service, 1982.

—, Senate Standing Committee on Foreign Affairs and Defence, *Report of the Inquiry into the Human Rights and Conditions of the People of East Timor*. (Chairman, Senator Gordon D. McIntosh). Canberra: Australian Government Publishing Service, 1983.

—, *Official Report of the Australian Parliamentary Delegation to East Timor* ('The Morrison Report'). Canberra: Australian Government Publishing Service, 1983.

Australia–East Timor Association Newsletter. Melbourne: Australia–East Timor Association, 1975– [quarterly newsletter].

Australia–East Timor Association, *East Timor: Betrayed But Not Beaten*, Vol. 1: 1975–83; Vol. 2: 1983–9. Melbourne: Australia–East Timor Association, 1983, 1989.

—, *The Hidden War: The Struggle for Justice at Home and Abroad*. Melbourne: Australia–East Timor Association, 1989.

'Australia Rejects Portuguese Criticism of Timor Gap Treaty', *Backgrounder* (Canberra), **1**(8) (23 February 1990).

Australian Council for Overseas Aid, *Report on Visit to East Timor for the ACFOA Timor Task Force*. Canberra: ACFOA, November 1975.

—, *Aid and East Timor*. Canberra: ACFOA, 1979.

—, *East Timor Today*, ACFOA Development Dossier No. 1. Canberra: ACFOA, 1980.

—, 'Notes Towards a Critique of [the] Report of the ACFOA-initiated East Timor Commission of Enquiry', ACFOA East Timor Sub-Committee, Canberra, 1981.

—, *Dossier on East Timor* [containing 26 documents, with eye-witness accounts from students in East Timor]. Canberra: ACFOA, 1982.

—, *Credibility Gap – Australia and the Timor Gap Treaty*, ACFOA Development Dossier No. 28. Canberra: ACFOA, 1990. *See also* Stepan, S.

—, *East Timor: Keeping the Flame of Freedom Alive*, ACFOA Development Dossier No. 29. Canberra: ACFOA, 1991.

—, *East Timor: Towards a Just Peace in the 1990s.* Canberra: ACFOA, 1991.

—, *From Memo to Tutuala. A Kaleidoscope of Environmental Problems in East Timor*, ACFOA Development Dossier No. 33. Canberra: ACFOA, 1994. *See also* Aditjondro, G.J.

Azis, I. J., 'Key Issues in Indonesian Regional Development', in Hal Hill (ed.), *Unity and Diversity: Regional Economic Development in Indonesia Since 1970.* Singapore: Oxford University Press, 1989.

Badan Koordinasi Penanaman Modal Daerah Timor Timur (East Timor Regional Investment Board), *Profil Investasi Daerah Timor Timur* [Profile of investment in the East Timor region]. Dili: BKPMD, 1987.

—, *Potensi Daerah Timor Timur* (The potential of the East Timor region). Dili: BKPMD, 1987.

—, *Regional Investment Chart of East Timor.* Dili: BKPMD, 1989.

Bagwell, S., and E. Himmelreich, 'The Roger East Story', *New Journalist*, **32** (May 1979).

Bappeda Tingkat 1 dan Kantor Statistik Propinsi Timor Timur, *Pendapatan Regional Provinsi Timor Timur 1981–1984 – Tabel Pokok-Pokok* [Regional income (levels) in the province of East Timor, 1981–1984 – Key Tables]. Dili: Bappeda Tk1 dan Kantor Statistik Tim-Tim, 1986.

—, *Indikator Kesejahteraan Rakyat Propinsi Timor Timur 1986* [Welfare indicators of the inhabitants of the province of East Timor 1986]. Dili: Bappeda Tk1 dan Kantor Statistik Propinsi Timor Timur, 1988.

—, *Pendapatan Regional Propinsi Timor Timur 1983-1989* [Regional income (levels) in the province of East Timor 1983-1989]. Dili: Bappeda Tk1 dan Kantor Statistik Tim-Tim, 1991.

—, *Pendapatan Regional Propinsi Timor Timur 1983-1990* [Regional income (levels) in the province of East Timor, 1983-1990]. Dili: Bappeda Tk1 dan Kantor Statistik Tim-Tim, 1992

—, *Timor Timur Dalam Angka, 1990*]East Timor in the statistics, 1990]. Dili: Bappeda Tk1 dan Kantor Statistik Propinsi Timor Timur, 1992.

—, and Universitas Kristen Satya Wacana, *Evaluasi Repelita Keempat Daerah 1984/1985 – 1988/1989 Propinsi Daerah Tingkat I Timor Timur* [Evaluation of the fourth five-year regional development plan 1984/1985 – 1988/1989 for the first-level (regional) province of East Timor]. Salatiga: Universitas Kristen Satya Wacana, 1988.

Barata, F. T., 'Timor: Da Ocupação Japonesa à Ocupação Indonésia' [Timor: From the Japanese occupation to the Indonesian occupation]. *Independência*, **5** (1987).

Barbedo de Magalhães, *see* Magalhães, A. Barbedo de.

Barclay, G. St.J., 'Problems in Australian Foreign Policy', *Australian Journal of Politics and History*, **39** (2-3) (1993).

Barrento, A.M., 'A Crise de Timor' [The Timor crisis], *Revista Militar* (Lisbon), **1** (January 1988).

Barreto, J. L., *The Timor Drama: Portugal and East Timor April 1974 – December 1975.* Lisbon: Timor Newsletter, 1982.

Barreto, S. (ed.), *Tebe. Colectânea de Canções Populares de Timor Leste* [Tebe. A collection of popular songs from East Timor]. Lisbon: Fundação Austronésia Borja da Costa, 1987.

Bartlett, J. W., 'Blood on Our Hands', *On the Issues*, **25** (Winter 1992).

Bartu, F., 'East Timor: Bloody Past, Anguished Present', *Swiss Review of World Affairs*, **40**(3) (June 1990).

Baseline Survey Timor-Timur, *Profil Perekonomian Timor-Timur* [Economic profile of East Timor]. Bandung: Bank Indonesia dan Lembaga Manajemen FE-UNPAD, 1988.

Bele, A., 'Suku Bunaq di Pedalaman Timor' [The Bunaq tribe in the interior of Timor]. *Hidup*, **46**(28) (12 July 1992).

Bell, I., *et al.*, *East Timor: Betrayed But Not Beaten. The Ongoing Struggle for Independence in East Timor, 1975–83*. Melbourne: AETA, 1983.

—, *East Timor: The Hidden Wars. The Struggle for Justice at Home and Abroad*. Melbourne: AETA, 1989.

Belo, Mgr Carlos Filipe Ximenes, *see* Indonesia, Bishops Conference of *and* Tolomundu.

Bergin, A., 'The Australian–Indonesian Timor Gap Maritime Boundary Agreement', *International Journal of Estuarine and Coastal Law*, **5**(4) (1990).

Berry, R.F., and G.A. Jenner, 'Basalt Geochemistry as a Test of the Tectonic Models of Timor', *Journal of the Geological Society* (London), **139**(5) (1982).

Berthe, L., *Bei Gua: Itinéraire des Ancêtres. Mythes des Bunaq de Timor* [Bei Gua: The Journey of the Ancestors. The Myths of the Bunaq of Timor]. Paris: Centre National de la Recherche Scientifique, 1972.

Bewley, G., 'Timor Before December 1975', *Northern Perspective*, **15**(1) (1992).

Biro Pusat Statistik (Jakarta), *Kantor Statistik Timor Timur: Bahan Masukan Rapat Koordinasi Antar Departemen Urusan Timor Timur Biro Pusat Statistik Jakarta* [East Timor statistical office: Input data for the inter-departmental coordination meeting on East Timor affairs, Central Bureau for Statistics, Jakarta]. Jakarta: Biro Pusat Statistik, 1987.

—, *Pendapatan Regional Propinsi-Propinsi di Indonesia 1983-1986 Bagian II* [Regional income in the provinces of Indonesia 1983–1986, second part]. Jakarta: Biro Pusat Statistik, 1989 [covers East Timor].

—, *Statistik Indonesia 1990* [Indonesian statistics, 1990]. Jakarta: Biro Pusat Statistik, 1991 [includes statistics on East Timor].

—, *Indikator Kesejahteraan Rakyat 1991* (Public welfare indicators, 1991). Jakarta: Badan Pusat Statistik, 1992 [includes indicators for East Timor].

Bizarro, V.M., 'Estrutura Económica de Timor' [The economic structure of Timor]. *Boletim Trimestral do Banco Nacional Ultramarino* (Lisbon), **97**(2-27) (January–March 1974).

Bizot, J., *The Forgotten Cause of East Timor's Rights to Self-Determination. A Report to the Parliamentary Human Rights Group*. London: Parliamentary Human Rights Group, 1987. *See also* Great Britain.

Black, L., 'Australian Foreign Policy Towards East Timor', BA (Hons) thesis, Arts Faculty, Adelaide University, 1977.

Blaskett, B., and Loong Wong, 'Towards Resolution of Internal Conflict in Indonesia: West Papua, East Timor and the International Order', *Interdisciplinary Peace Research*, **4**(1), May–June 1992.

Boavida, João Frederico, 'The Fusion of Religion and Nationalism in East Timor: A Culture in the Making', MPhil thesis, Faculty of Anthropology and Geography, Oxford University, 1993.

Bonner, Raymond, 'A Reporter At Large: The New Order II', *The New Yorker* (New York), (13 June 1988).

Borja da Costa, F. (ed. Jill Jolliffe), *Revolutionary Poems in the Struggle against Colonialism. Timorese Nationalist Verse* [*Poesias Revolucionárias na Luta Contra o Colonialismo*], trans. James J. Fox, Mary Ireland and Elizabeth Traube. Sydney: Wild and Woolley, 1976. *See also Coral*.

Brandão, C.C., *Funo (Guerra em Timor)* [Funu. War in Timor]. Lisbon: Perspectivas e Realidades, 1987 [originally published in Oporto: Edições 'AOV', 1946] [deals with East Timor during World War II].

Bretes, M. da G., *Timor entre Invasores, 1941-45* [Timor between the invaders, 1941-45]. Lisbon: Livros Horizonte, 1989.

Bridgeman, J.C., *East Timor: A Case Study of Law of the Sea Conflicts*. New York: Ocean Education Project of the Methodist Mission to the United Nations, 1977.

Briére, E., and S. Gage, *The Indonesian Kit: A Study Kit*. Vancouver: East Timor Alert Network, 1991.

—, *see also* Retbøll, T.

British Campaign for an Independent East Timor, *Integration Never! East Timor's Struggle Against Indonesian Aggression*. London: British Campaign for an Independent East Timor, 1981. **A**

Brito, F.G. de, *Tata-Mai-Lau: Timor contra o Japão* [Tata-Mai-Lau: Timor against Japan]. Lisbon: Iniciativas Editoriais, 1977.

Browning, M.A., and S. Vitka, 'East Timor and Diplomatic Pragmatism', *Southeast Asia Chronicle*, **94** (June 1984).

Bruce, R.H., *US Response to the East Timor Massacre: Historical Grounds for Scepticism about a Suggested Remedy*, IOCPS Briefing Paper No. 4. Nedlands, Western Australia: Indian Ocean Centre for Peace Studies, University of Western Australia, 1992.

Brunton, 'The Timor Gap', *Arena*, **75** (1986).

Budhisantoso, S., 'Lingkungan Alam dan Potensi Penduduk di Timor Timur' [The natural environment and the potential of the people of East Timor]. *Berita Antropologi*, **11**(36) (1980).

—, 'Kehidupan Ekonomi Penduduk di Timor Timur' [The economic life of the people of East Timor]. *Berita Antropologi*, **11**(36) (1980).

Budiardjo, C., and Liem Soei Liong, *The War Against East Timor*. London: Zed Books, 1984. *See also* Liem.

Bunge, F.M. (ed.), *Indonesia: A Country Study*. Washington, DC: Army Department Headquarters (American University Foreign Area Studies), 4th ed., 1983.

Burgel, H., 'East Timor', *Medicine and War*, **9**(2) (1993).

Burke, A., 'The Sad Story of East Timor. A Case Study in Foreign Policy in the Australian Press', MA thesis, Faculty of Humanities and Social Sciences, Sydney University of Technology, 1990.

Burmester, H., 'The Timor Gap Treaty', *Australian Mining and Petroleum Law Association Yearbook*. Melbourne: AMPLA, 1990.

—, 'The Zone of Co-operation Between Australia and Indonesia: A Preliminary Outline with Particular Relevance to Applicable Law', in H. Fox (ed.), *Joint Development of Offshore Oil and Gas*, Vol. 2. London: British Institute of International and Comparative Law, 1990.

Burns, P., 'East Timor? Timor Timur? Or Timor Leste?', *Kabar Seberang*, **15** (July 1985).

Burnett, P. (a.k.a P. Carey), 'From Decolonisation to Destruction: The Tragedy of East Timor', *Times Literary Supplement*, (16 December 1983).

Caldwell, M., and E. Utrecht, *Indonesia: An Alternative History*. Sydney: Alternative Publishing Cooperative, 1979.

Callinan, B.J., *Independent Company: The Australian Army in Portuguese Timor, 1941–43*. Melbourne: Heinemann, 1984 [originally published in 1953, same place and publisher, as *Independent Company: The 2/2 and 2/4 Australian Independent Companies in Portuguese Timor, 1941–1943*].

Campagnolo, H., *Fataluku I: Rélations et Choix: Introduction Méthodologique à la Description d'une Langue 'Non Austronésienne' de Timor Oriental* [Fatuluku I: Relations and choice: A methodological introduction to a description of a 'non-Austronesian' language in East Timor] (Langues et Civilisations de l'Asie du Sud-est et du Monde Insulindien No.5). Paris: Société d'Études Linguistiques et Anthropologiques de France (SELAF), 1979.

—, 'La Langue des Fataluku de Lórehe (Timor Portugais)' [The language of the Fataluku of Lórehe (Portuguese Timor)], PhD thesis, Paris: Université Réné Descartes, 1973.

Capell, A., 'People and Languages of Timor', in A. Capell (ed.), *Linguistic Papers, I: General. II: Indonesia and New Guinea* (Oceania Linguistic Monograph No.15). Sydney: Sydney University, 1972 [originally published in *Oceania*, **14**(3) (March 1944), **14**(4) (June 1944), and **15**(1) (September 1944)].

—, 'Portuguese Timor: Two More Non-Austronesian Languages', in A. Capell (ed.), *Linguistic Papers, I: General. II: Indonesia and New Guinea* (Oceania Linguistic Monograph No.15). Sydney: University of Sydney, 1972.

Capizzi, E., H. Hill, and D. Macey, 'Fretilin and the Struggle for Independence in East Timor', *Race and Class* (London), **17**(4) (1976).

Cardoso, A.P. Silva, M. Mayer Gonçalves, and E. Daehnhardt, *Fertilidade dos Solos de Timor: Esboço de uma Carta de Pontos* [The fertility of the soils in Timor: sketch of a map of [key] points]. 'Comunicações' da Missão de Estudos Agronómicos do Ultramar No. 85. Lisbon: MEAU, 1974. **A**

Cardoso, G.F., 'Peristiwa Berdarah Santa Cruz: Implikasi Model Pembangunan' [The bloody event of Santa Cruz: Its implications for development models], *Veritas*. Dili: Universitas Timor Timur, **1**(4) (1991–2).

Carey, P., 'A Land Where No-one Laughs', *Times Literary Supplement*, (27 February 1987).

—, *see also* Burnett, P., Cox, Steve *and* Retbøll, T.

Carlos, R.P., *Eu Fui ao Fim de Portugal* [I went to the end of Portugal]. Queluz: Liberal, 1977 [3rd ed. Lisbon: Universitária Editora, 1993].

Carvalho, J. dos Santos, *Vida e Morte em Timor durante a Segunda Guerra Mundial* [Life and death in Timor during the Second World War]. Lisbon: Livraria Portugal, 1972.

Carvalho Branco, J.D.A., 'A Ordem de São Domingos e as Origens de Timor' [The Order of Saint Dominic and the Origins of Timor], *Independência*, **5** (1987).

Cascais, A.M. Cravo, *Timor. Quem é o Culpado?* [Timor. Who is guilty?]. Braga: Braga Editora, 1977.

Casimiro, J. Kao Tai, 'East Timor', *Habitat Australia*, **20**(2) (April 1992).

Catholic Commission for Justice and Peace, *East Timor, A Forgotten People*, CCJP Issues No. 10. Sydney: CCJP, 1987.

Catholic Institute for International Relations, *East Timor*. London: CIIR, 1985. **A**

—, *Timor Link*, London: CIIR, 1985– [quarterly newsletter].

—, *East Timor: A Christian Reflection/Timor Oriental: Une Réflexion Chrétienne*. London: CIIR, 1987.

—, *I am Timorese/Je suis Timorais: Testimonies from East Timor*. London: CIIR, 1990 [a set of ten refugee testimonies].

—, *East Timor: An International Responsibility*. London: CIIR, 1992.

Centre for Strategic and International Studies, *Integrasi Timor Timur* [The integration of East Timor]. Jakarta: Biro Informasi dan Data, 1983. **C**

—, *Pra-integrasi Timor Timur* [Pre-integration in East Timor]. Jakarta: Biro Informasi dan Data, 1983. **C**

—, *Diplomasi tentang Timor Timur* [Diplomacy on East Timor]. Jakarta: Biro Informasi dan Data, 1984. **C**

—, *Pembangunan Timor Timur* [Development in East Timor]. Jakarta: Biro Informasi dan Data, Jakarta 1984. **C**

—, 'Satu Dasawarsa Timor Timur' [One Decade of Timor Timur], *Analisa* (Jakarta), 1986.

Centro de Documentação Científica Ultramarina, *Pesquisas ou Estudos em Curso dos Organismos da Junta de Investigações do Ultramar* [Research or on-going studies of the organization of the Committee of Investigations of Overseas (Areas)] Lisbon: Centro de Documentação Científica Ultramarina, 1973.

Chamberlain, M. (ed.), *East Timor International Conference: Report.* New York: Clergy and Laity Concerned, 1981.

Chinkin, C.M., 'The Law and Ethics of Recognition: Cambodia and Timor', in P. Keal (ed.), *Ethics and Australian Foreign Policy.* Sydney: Allen & Unwin with Canberra: Department of International Relations, Australian National University, 1992.

Chomsky, N., *East Timor and the Western Democracies*, Spokesman Pamphlet No. 67. Nottingham: Spokesman Books, 1979.

—, 'Indonesia in East Timor: Terror, Massacre and Starvation', *Arena* (Melbourne), **54** (1979).

—, *Towards a New Cold War: Essays on the Current Crisis and How We Got There.* New York: Pantheon Books, 1982 [pp. 337–48 refer to the US and East Timor].

—, 'A Curtain of Ignorance', *Southeast Asia Chronicle*, (August 1980) [reprinted in N. Chomsky, *Towards a New Cold War.* New York: Pantheon, 1982].

—, in James Peck (ed.), *The Chomsky Reader*, New York: Pantheon, 1987.

—, *Deterring Democracy.* London: Verso, 1991.

—, *see also* Retbøll, T.

—, and E. S. Herman, 'Benign Terror: East Timor', *Bulletin of Concerned Asian Scholars*, **11**(2) (April–June 1979).

—, *The Political Economy of Human Rights. Volume I: The Washington Connection and Third World Fascism.* Nottingham: Spokesman Books, and Boston: South End Press, 1979.

Christian Conference of Asia/World Council of Churches, *Not By Bread Alone*, report on a Visit to East Timor by an Ecumenical Delegation Representing the Christian Conference of Asia and the World Council of Churches, 16–19 April 1992.

Christian Consultation on East Timor, *East Timor – A Christian Reflection.* Lisbon, February 1987.

Christian Movement for Peace, *East Timor – No Development without Justice.* Brussels: CMP, 1989.

'The Church in East Timor: Friend of the People', *Japan Missionary Bulletin*, **47**(2) (Summer 1993).

Cinatti, R., *Motivos Artísticos Timorenses e a sua Integração* [Timorese artistic motifs and their integration]. Lisbon: Instituto de Investigação Científica Tropical, Museu de Etnologia, 1987.

——, L. de Almeida and S. Mendes, *Arquitectura Timorense* [Timorese architecture]. Lisbon: Instituto de Investigação Científica Tropical, Museu de Etnologia, 1987.

Clamagirand, B., 'The Social Organization of the Ema of Timor', in J. J. Fox (ed.), *The Flow of Life: Essays on Eastern Indonesia.* Cambridge, MA: Harvard University Press, 1980. *See also* Renard-Clamagirand, B.

Clarence-Smith, W.G., *The Third Portuguese Empire, 1825–1975. A Study in Economic Imperialism.* Manchester: Manchester University Press, 1985.

—, 'Planters and Smallholders in Portuguese Timor in the Nineteenth and Twentieth Centuries', *Indonesia Circle*, **57** (March 1992).

Clark, R.S. 'The "Decolonization" of East Timor and the United Nations Norms on Self-Determination and Aggression', *The Yale Journal of World Public Order* (New Haven, CT), **7**(1) (1980).

—, 'Does the Genocide Convention Go Far Enough? Some Thoughts on the Nature of Criminal Genocide in the Context of Indonesia's Invasion of East Timor', *Ohio Northern University Law Review*, **8**(2) (1981).

—, 'East Timor and International Law', *Mennesker og Rettigheter* (Oslo), **2**(1) (1984).

—, 'Timor Gap: The Legality of the "Treaty on the Zone of Cooperation in an Area between the Indonesian Province of East Timor and Northern Australia"', *Pace Yearbook of International Law*, **4**(69) (1992).

—, 'Some International Law Aspects of the East Timor Affair', *Leiden Journal of International Law*, **5**(2) (1992), reprinted as 'The East Timor Affair in International Law', *Camões Center Quarterly*, **4**(25) (1992–3).

Clarke, R., 'Indonesia's Genocide in E[ast] Timor: Australian Government Complicity Exposed', *Direct Action*, **9** (8 November 1979).

Cluysenaer, M.W.F., 'Waar Ligt de Grens? Gezagsuitbreiding op Timor ten tijde van de Onthoudingspolitiek, 1840–1860' [Where lies the border? Extension of [Dutch] authority in Timor at the time of the non-intervention policy, 1840–1860]. MA thesis, 's-Gravenhage, 1983 [deals with the 1859 boundary agreement].

Colebatch, H., 'Impressions of Timor, 1973', *Quadrant* (Sydney), **36**(12) (December 1992).

Collier, W. L., and S. Tjakrawerdaja, *Problems and Prospects of Increasing Cattle Exports From Nusa Tenggara Timur Province.* Jakarta: Agro Economic Survey, 1974. **A**

Commissão para os Direitos do Povo Maubere [The Commission for the Maubere People's Rights], *Timor Leste* [pre-1994, *Informação Timor Leste* (East Timor Information)]. Lisbon: Comissão para os Direitos do Povo Maubere, 1985–87 [irregular newsletter], 1987-[monthly newsletter].

Commissie Justitia et Pax Nederland, *East Timor, The Most Important Developments Since (Mid) 1983.* 's-Gravenhage: Justitia et Pax, 1986.

—, *Oost-Timor: De Ontwikkelingen vanaf 1975* [East Timor: The developments from 1975]. 's-Gravenhage: Justitia et Pax, 1984.

Committee to Protect Journalists, *In the Censor's Shadow. Journalism in Suharto's Indonesia, With an Update on the Massacre in Dili, East Timor, November 12, 1991.* New York, NY: The Committee [to Protect Journalists], 1992.

—, *Oost-Timor: Een Vergeten Eiland: Samengesteld op Basis van het Rapport 'Oost-Timor: De Ontwikkelingen vanaf 1975'* [East Timor: A Forgotten Island: Composed on the basis of the report: East Timor: The developments from 1975]. The Hague: Justitia et Pax, 1984.

Communion of Churches in Indonesia, *East Timor – A Bird's Eye View.* Jakarta: Communion of Churches in Indonesia (PGI), 1988.

'Conflict in Timor', *Pacific Research and World Empire Telegram*, **7**(1) (Nov–Dec 1975). **Y**

Constitution of the Democratic Republic of East Timor, *see* East Timor, Democratic Republic of.

Cook, C., 'The Australia–Indonesia Maritime Boundary', in *Australia's Offshore Maritime Interests*, Occasional Papers in Maritime Affairs No. 3. Canberra: Australian Centre for Maritime Studies, 1985.

—, 'Filling the Gap: Delimiting the Australia-Indonesia Maritime Boundary', *Australian Yearbook of International Law*, **10** (1987).

Cooley, F.L., 'Revival in Timor', *Southeast Asia Journal of Theology*, **14**(2)(1973) [deals mainly with the Protestant Church in West Timor].

Coral: Revista da Fundação Austronésia Borja da Costa (Lisbon), **1** (December 1991); **2** (September 1992).

Corner, L., 'East and West Nusa Tenggara: Isolation and Poverty', in Hal Hill (ed.), *Unity and Diversity: Regional Economic Development in Indonesia Since 1970.* Singapore: Oxford University Press, 1989.

Costa, C., 'Timorese Refugee on Indonesian Operations in East Timor since 1975', *Tapol Bulletin* (The Indonesia Human Rights Campaign), No. 86 (April 1988), No. 87 (June 1988), No. 88 (August 1988).

Costa, F. Borja da, *see* Borja da Costa, F.

Cox, Steve, (with P. Carey), *Generations of Resistance: East Timor*. London: Cassell, 1995.

—, *see also* Retbøll, T.

Cravo, J., *Foi Timor* [This was Timor]. Lisbon: Edições Pluma, 1976.

Crawford, R. and P. Dayanidhi, 'East Timor: A Study in Decolonization', *India Quarterly* (New Delhi), **33**(4) (1977).

Cronau, P., 'New East Timorese Leader [Konis Santana]', *Inside Indonesia*, **34** (March 1993).

Cullen, P., 'Australia's Policy on Timor', *Pacific Defense Reporter*, **4** (October 1977).

Cummings, J., S. Forsyth, J. Noble, A. Samagalski and T. Wheeler, *Indonesia: A Travel Survival Kit*. Hawthorn, Australia and Berkeley, CA: Lonely Planet, 1990.

Dagg, C., 'Human Rights and Aid. A Canadian Perspective', *Indonesian Quarterly* (Jakarta), **21**(1) (1993) [deals with East Timor in the context of Canadian aid to Indonesia in the New Order period].

Dalrymple, F.R., 'East Timor: Visit by Australian Ambassador', *Australian Foreign Affairs Record*, **55**(7) (July 1984).

Dalton, B., *Indonesia Handbook*. Chico, CA: Moon Publications, 1991.

Davidson, K., 'Portuguese Colonisation of Timor: The Final Stage, 1859–1912', PhD thesis, University of New South Wales (Sydney), 1993.

'Death in Dili', *Inside Indonesia*, 29 (December 1991), [collection of articles on the 12 November 1991 Santa Cruz massacre in Dili].

Defert, G., *Timor Oriental* [East Timor], Volume 1 (Étude Monographique), Volume 2 (Années 1974–5), Volume 3 (Évolutions Contemporaines). Mémoires de Maîtrise et de DEA. Paris: Université de Paris, 1988–9.

—, *Timor Est: Le Génocide Oublié. Droit d'un Peuple et Raisons d'États* [East Timor: The forgotten genocide. The right of a people and reasons of state]. Paris: Éditions L'Harmattan, Collection Recherches Asiatiques, 1992.

—, 'Timor Est, "Vu d'Indonésie"' [East Timor seen from Indonesia], *Archipel*, **46** (1993).

—, 'La Lente Agonie de Timor-Est' [The slow agony of East Timor], *Pol-Internat*, (Summer 1994).

Departemen Dalam Negeri, Republik Indonesia (Ministry of the Interior, Republic of Indonesia), *Laporan Akhir Penelitian dan Pengembangan Pemerintahan Timor Timur 1979/1980: Menentukan Identitas 'Desa' di Timor Timur, Suatu Studi Sosio-Kulturil* [Final research and development report on the administration of East Timor 1979/1980: Establishing the identity of the 'village' in East Timor; A socio-cultural study]. Jakarta: Badan Penelitian dan Pengembangan (Departemen Dalam Negeri, RI), 1981.

—, *Susunan Organisasi dan Tatakerja Propinsi Daerah Tingkat I Timor Timur Sampai dengan Tahun 1984* [Organization and structure of the first-level regional province of East Timor up to and including 1984]. Jakarta: Sekretariat Koordinasi Antar Departemen Urusan Timor Timur (Departemen Dalam Negeri, RI), 1984.

—, *Ikhtisar Daftar Isian Proyek-Proyek Pembangunan Timor Timur, Tahun Anggaran 1984/1985* [Synopsis of the inventory of development projects in East Timor for fiscal year 1984–85]. Jakarta: Sekretariat-Jenderal Koordinasi Urusan Timor Timur (Departemen Dalam Negeri, RI), 1984.

—, *Penyusunan Rencana Struktur Tata Ruang Propinsi Dati Timor Timur* [Structural plan for the use of space in the first-level province of East Timor]. Jakarta: Proyek Peningkatan Pendayagunaan Rencana Ruang dan Pembinaan Pembangunan Daerah Tahun Anggaran 1991/1992 (Departemen Dalam Negeri, RI), 1992.

Departemen Kehakiman, Republik Indonesia (Ministry of Justice, Republic of Indonesia), *Laporan Penelitian dan Pengembangan Pemerintahan Timor Timur: Struktur, Kultur dan Birokrasi Formil di Timor Timur* [Research and development report on the administration of East Timor: Structure, culture and formal bureaucracy in East Timor]. Jakarta: Departemen Kehakiman RI, 1980/81.

—, *Laporan Pembangunan Daerah Timor Timur* [Development report on the East Timor region]. Jakarta: Departemen Kehakiman, RI, 1987.

Departemen Luar Negeri, Republik Indonesia (Ministry of Foreign Affairs, Republic of Indonesia), *Penjelasan Menteri Luar Negeri RI dalam Pembicaraan Tingkat III atas RUU [Rancangan Undang-Undang] tentang Celah Timur di Komisi I DPR-RI* [Clarification of the Minister of Foreign Affairs of the R(epublic of) I(ndonesia) in the third-level discussions of the draft legislation concerning the Timor Gap in the First Committee of the D(ewan) P(erwakilan) R(akyat)-R(epublik) I(ndonesia) (Peoples' Consultative Assembly of the Republic of Indonesia)]. Jakarta: Departemen Luar Negeri, 1990.

—, *Keterangan Pemerintah RI di Hadapan Sidang Paripurna DPR-RI tentang Pengesahan Perjanjian antara Republik Indonesia dan Australia mengenai Zona Kerjasama di Wilayah antara Propinsi Timor Timur dan Australia Utara* [Clarification of the Government of the R(epublic of) I(ndonesia) before the plenary session of the D(ewan) P(erwakilan) R(akyat)-R(epublik) I(ndonesia) (Peoples' Consultative Assembly of the Republic of Indonesia) concerning the ratification of the treaty between the Republic of Indonesia and Australia on the zone of cooperation in an area between the province of East Timor and Northern Australia]. Jakarta: Departemen Luar Negeri, 1990.

Dias, J.A. Travassos Santos, 'Reconhecimento Nosoparasitológico Veterinário em Timor' [Veterinary Nosoparasitological Survey in Timor], *Garcia de Orta, Série Zoologia* (Lisbon), **15**(2) (1988) [based on research carried out in 1973].

Dirdjasusanto, A., 'A Visit to East Timor', *Social Survey*, **29** (February 1980).

Dijk, C. van, 'East Timor (I)', *Review of Indonesian and Malayan Affairs* (Sydney), **10**(1) (1976).

Dirdja, S.J.A., 'Timor Timur: Beberapa Pengalaman dan Pemikiran' (East Timor: Some experiences and thoughts), *Inter-Nos* [Indonesian Jesuit periodical], **23**(2) (April-June 1979).

Dixon, C., 'Cry of a Forgotten Land', *Catholic Herald*, (22 November 1991).

Dixon, G., *Indonesian Ports: An Atlas-Gazetteer*. Townsville: James Cook University of North Queensland, 1985.

Doig, C.D. (comp.), *A History of the 2nd Independent Company and 2/2 Commando Squadron*. Trafalgar (Victoria): Valley Word Processing Service, 1986.

Domm, R., 'Report from the Mountains of East Timor: Interview with Resistance Guerilla Commander, Shanana Gusmão', Australian Broadcasting Corporation, 'Background Briefing', (28–30 October 1990) [partly published in *The Age*, (25 October 1990); and *Sydney Morning Herald*. (25 October 1990)].

—, 'Xanana Face to Face: Interview with East Timorese Guerrilla Leader', *Inside Indonesia*, **25** (December 1990).

Duarte, J.B., *Ainda Timor* [Still Timor]. Lisbon: Gatimor – Gabinete dos Estudos de Timor, 1981.

—, *Timor: Ritos e Mitos Ataúros* [Timor: Rites and myths of Atauro (Island)]. Lisbon: Ministério de Educação, Instituto de Cultura e Língua Portuguesa, 1984.

—, *Em Terras de Timor* [In lands of Timor]. Lisboa: Edição do Autor, 1987.

—, *Timor – Jeremiada* [Timor – Lamentation]. Odivelas: Pentaedro, 1988.

—, *Timor: Um Grito* [Timor: A cry]. Lisbon: Pentaedro, 1988.

—, *Vocabulário Ataúro–Português, Português–Ataúro* (Atauro–Portuguese, Portuguese–Atauro Vocabulary). n.p.: Instituto Português do Oriente, n.d. (? 1993).

Dunn, J. S., *Portuguese Timor Before and After the Coup: Options for the Future*. Canberra: Parliamentary Library Legislative Research Service, 1974.

—, 'Portuguese Timor – The Independence Movement from Coalition to Conflict', *Dyason House Papers* (Melbourne), **2**(1) (1975).

—, *The Timor Story*. Canberra: Parliamentary Library Legislative Research Service, 1976.

—, *The Timor Affair – From Civil War to Invasion by Indonesia*. Canberra: Parliamentary Library Legislative Research Service, 1976.

—, *East Timor – From Portuguese Colonialism to Indonesian Incorporation*. Canberra: Parliamentary Library Legislative Research Service, 1977.

—, *The East Timor Situation: Report on Talks with Timorese Refugees in Portugal*. Canberra: Parliamentary Library Legislative Research Service, 1977.

—, 'The Timor Affair in International Perspective', *World Review*, **17** (October 1978).

—, *Notes on the Current Situation in East Timor*. Canberra: Parliamentary Library Legislative Research Service, 1979.

—, *East Timor: Reports on the Situation in 1980–1*. Canberra: Parliamentary Library Legislative Research Service, 1981.

—, *Timor: A People Betrayed*. Milton, Queensland: Jacaranda Press, 1983.

—, 'Behind the Gloss', *Australian Society*, **7**(12) (December 1988); **8**(1) (January 1989).

—, 'East Timor: A Sorry Saga', *The Bulletin*, **114** (22 December 1992).

—, 'Alatas Misrepresenting Timor', *Inside Indonesia*, **36** (September 1993).

—, *see also* Retbøll, T.

Durieux, A., 'De l'Évolution de Divers Territoires de l'Ancien Outre-Mer Portugais' [On the evolution of various territories of the ex-Portuguese overseas (empire)], *Bulletin des Séances de l'Académie des Sciences d'Outre-Mer*, **26**(3) (1980).

Eason, R., and L. Hubbard, 'East Timor: Struggles and Aspirations', *Arena* (Melbourne), **64** (1983).

East, Roger, *Independence or Death! East Timor's Border War*. Sydney: CIET, 1976.

East Timor, Democratic Republic of, *Constituição da República Democrática de Timor Leste* [Constitution of the Democratic Republic of East Timor]. Lisbon: Edições Comité 28 de Novembro, n.d. (? 1976).

East Timor, Provincial Government of, *East Timor Develops*. Dili: Provincial Government of East Timor, 1984 [2nd revised edn, 1985].

—, *Rencana Pembangunan Lima Tahun Kelima 1989/1990 – 1993/1994* [The fifth five-year development plan, 1989/1990 – 1993/1994]. Dili: Pemda Tim-Tim (Provincial Government of East Timor), 1989.

—, *Neraca Kependudukan dan Lingkungan Hidup Daerah* [Balance sheet of population and living environment in the (East Timor) region]. Dili: Pemda Tim-Tim (Provincial Government of East Timor), 1989.

—, *Pola Dasar Pembangunan Daerah Kabupaten Daerah Tingkat II Lautem* [Basic patterns of regional development in the second-level regency of Lautem]. Dili: Pemda Tim-Tim (Provincial Government of East Timor), 1989.

—, *Pola Dasar Pembangunan Daerah Kabupaten Daerah Tingkat II Baucau* [Basic patterns of regional development in the second-level regency of Baucau]. Dili: Pemda Tim-Tim (Provincial Government of East Timor), 1989.

—, *Pola Dasar Pembangunan Daerah Kabupaten Daerah Tingkat II Viqueque* [Basic patterns of regional development in the second-level regency of Viqueque]. Dili: Pemda Tim-Tim (Provincial Government of East Timor), 1989.

—, *13 Tahun Propinsi Timor Timur Membangun* [13 years of the province of East Timor's development]. Dili: Pemda Tim-Tim (Provincial Government of East Timor), 1990.

—, *East Timor Strives for a Better Future.* Dili: Provincial Government of East Timor, 1990.

—, *Laporan Bupati Kepala Daerah Tingkat II Manufahi pada Rakerda antara Gupernur KDH Tk I Timor Timur dengan para Tugub dan Bupati KDH Tk.II se-Propinsi Timor Timur* [Report of the Bupati (and) Regional Head of the second-level district of Manufahi to the R(apat) K(erja) D(aerah) (regional working meeting) between the Governor and the Tugub (Pembantu Gupernur/Assistant Governors) and KDH Tk II (Kepala Daerah Tingkat II/second-level regional heads) of the Province of East Timor]. Dili: Pemda Tim-Tim (Provincial Government of East Timor), 1991.

—, *East Timor's Potentials Profile in 1991*, Dili: Pemda Tim-Tim (Provincial Government of East Timor), 1991. *See also* 'Bappeda Tingkat I dan Kantor Statistik Propinsi Timur Timor', 'Kantor Wilayah Departemen Perdagangan Propinsi Timur Timor', *and* 'Kantor Statistik Propinsi Timur Timor'.

'East Timor', *Indonesia Reports*, **53** (1991).

'East Timor: A Backgrounder', *Pacific Issues* (Auckland), **11** (May 1992).

'East Timor and Self-Determination', *The Review of the International Commission of Jurists*, **32** (June 1984).

'East Timor: Back on the Agenda', *Pacific Islands Monthly*, **62**(1) (January 1992).

'East Timor: "Betrayal" by the South Pacific', *Pacific Islands Monthly*, **62**(1) (January 1992).

'East Timor. Beyond Hunger', *Southeast Asia Chronicle* (Berkeley, CA), **74** (1980) [analysis of 1979-80 famine].

'The East Timor Dilemma', *Pacific Islands Monthly*, **62**(10) (October 1992).

'East Timor: Eyewitness Account Before UN Commission of Human Rights, February 1992', *Disarming Times*, **17**(2) (April 1992).

'East Timor: From the Portuguese Pan into the Indonesian Fire', *Pacific Islands Monthly*, **62**(1) (January 1992).

'East Timor (Portugal v. Australia)', *Hague Yearbook of International Law*, **5** (1992).

'East Timor, Sweet Seventeen', *Indonesia Magazine*, **24**(3) (1993).

'East Timor: Unfinished Business', *Southeast Asia Chronicle,* (Berkeley, CA), **94** (June 1984).

East Timor and Pacific Report (formerly *East Timor Report*). Canberra: Campaign for an Independent East Timor, 1979–.

East Timor Infomation Bulletin. London: British Campaign for an Independent East Timor, 1975–9 [bi-monthly].

East Timor International Conference Report, ed. Michael Chamberlain. New York City, October 1980.

East Timor Ireland Solidarity Campaign, *East Timor. An International Responsibility.* Dublin: East Timor Ireland Solidarity Campaign, 1994.

East Timor News/Bulletin of the East Timor News Agency, see Freney, D.

East Timor News. Lisbon: Peace is Possible in East Timor, Committee for the Rights of the Maubere People, 1987– [monthly newsletter; also published in Portuguese [since 1982], *see Em Timor Leste, a Paz é Possível*].

East Timor and Pacific Report (formerly: *East Timor Report*). Canberra, 1982–5.

East Timor Talks Campaign, *Santa Cruz Massacre, Selected Articles from the Australian and International Press*. Fitzroy, Victoria: East Timor Talks Campaign, December 1991. *See also* Scott, D.

—, *The Missing Peace. Newsletter of the East Timor Talks Campaign.* Fitzroy, Victoria: East Timor Talks Campaign, 1992– [regular newsletter]. *See also* Feith, H.

East Timor Update (Bulletin of the East Timor Human Rights Committee, Syracuse [USA]). Syracuse: East Timor Human Rights Committee, 1978–81 [irregular newsletter].

Elliott, P.D., 'The East Timor Dispute', *The International and Comparative Law Quarterly* (London), **27**(1) (January 1978).

Em Timor Leste, a Paz é Possível [Peace is possible in East Timor], Lisbon: Em Timor Leste, a Paz é Possível, 1982– [regular bi-monthly newsletter in Portuguese, English and French].

'The End of Colonialism by the Year 2000', *Aide-Mémoire: East Timor Diplomatic and Intelligence Digest*, **1** (July 1990).

Enterrem meu Coração no Ramelau [Bury my heart on Ramelau]. Luanda: União dos Escritores Angolanos, 1982 [collection of traditional and contemporary East Timorese poetry].

Ernste, B., 'De Kwestie Oost-Timor: Dekolonisatie of Annexatie?' [The East Timor Question: Decolonization or Annexation?], *Internationale Spectator*, **41**(10) (October 1987).

Escarameia, P., *Formation of Concepts Under International Law: Subsumption Under Self-Determination in the Case of East Timor*. Lisbon: Fundação Oriente, 1993.

—, 'O Que e a Autodeterminacão? Análise Crítica do Conceito na sua Aplicação ao Caso de Timor', *Pol-Internacional* (Lisbon), **1**(65-110) nos 7-8 (1993) [Portuguese publication of 'The Meaning of Self-Determination and the Case of East Timor', unpublished paper presented at the CIIR/ICJ Conference on 'Indonesia's Occupation of East Timor: Legal Questions', London, 5–6 December 1992].

Esmara, H., 'Prospek Pembangunan Daerah Timor Timur' [Prospects for development of the region (province) of East Timor], *Prisma*, **8**(7) (1979).

European Parliament (Brussels), *Report by the Political Commission of the European Parliament on East Timor*, Ien van den Heuvel (*rapporteur*), 1 July 1988.

Evans, Grant, 'Eastern (Portuguese) Timor: Independence or Oppression?', Melbourne: Australian Union of Students, February 1975 [reprinted as 'Portuguese Timor', *New Left Review*, **91** (May–June 1975)].

—, 'Timor', *Intervention*, **5** (July 1975).

Evans, Gareth, *Making Australian Foreign Policy*, Australian Fabian Society Pamphlet No. 50. Leichardt, NSW: Pluto Press, 1989.

—, Press Briefing on East Timor, transcript, 26 November 1991.

—, *see also* Sen, K.

Feith, H., 'New Hope For East Timor: From Creative Constitution Mongering Elsewhere', *Prospek* (Yogyakarta), **3**(2) (1990).

—, 'East Timor: After the Dili Massacre', *Pacific Research* (Canberra), Peace Research Centre, Australian National University, **5**(1) (February 1992).

—, 'East Timor: The Opening Up, the Crackdown and the Possibility of a Durable Settlement', in H. Crouch and Hal Hill (eds), *Indonesia Assessment 1992: Political Perspectives on the 1990s*, Political and Social Change Monograph 17. Canberra: Australian National University, 1992.

—, 'New Moves for Peace in East Timor: José Ramos-Horta's Proposals', *Inside Indonesia*, **31** (June 1992).

—, 'Conflict in East Timor', *Peace Review*, **4**(2) (Summer 1992).

—, *The East Timor Issue Since the Capture of Xanana Gusmão*. Fitzroy, Victoria: East Timor Talks Campaign, 1993.

Fiedler, H., 'Hans Albrecht von Plüskow als Oberhaupt van Timor. Geschichte eines kleinen Kantors der VOC, 1758-1761', *De Indische Navorscher*, **4**(2) (1991), 67-71; **4**(3), 126-34; **4**(4), 179-84 [first published in *Deutsche Wacht: Zeitschrift für Handels-und Kolonialpolitik, Volkswirtschaft und Völkerrecht* in 1931, these articles give an account of the political and economic history of Timor in 1760-61, and daily life on the island during a period of conflict between the Dutch and the Portuguese].

Figge, K., 'Ost-Timor: Fern, Unbekannt, Vergessen' (East Timor: Far Away, Unknown, Forgotten), *Vereinte-Nationen*, **29**(4) (1981).

Fitzgerald, R., 'East Timor: "Shame of the World"', *World Review*, **27**(1) (March 1988).

Flanagan, P., 'East Timor: The Crime of Silence', *Arena* (Melbourne), **55** (1980).

Fletcher, R., 'Portuguese Timor's Growth Points to Heightened Trade', *Overseas Trading* (Canberra), **26**(15) (August 1974).

Fonseca, J.M. da, *Comissão em Timor* [Commission in Timor]. Guarda: Tip. Véritas, 1976.

Fonteyne, J.P.L., 'The Portuguese Timor Gap Litigation Before the International Court of Justice: A Brief Appraisal of Australia's Position', *Australian Journal of International Affairs*, **45**(2) (November 1991).

Forbes, A., *Unbeaten Tracks in Islands of the Far East: Experiences of a Naturalist's Wife in the 1880s*. Singapore: Oxford University Press, 1987 [originally published as *Insulinde* by William Blackwood & Sons (London), 1887].

Forbes, H.O., *A Naturalist's Wanderings in the Eastern Archipelago*. Singapore: Oxford University Press, 1989 [originally published by Harper & Brothers (New York), 1885] [Part 6 refers to East Timor].

Forman, S., 'Descent, Alliance and Exchange: Ideology Among the Makassae of East Timor', in J.J. Fox (ed.), *The Flow of Life: Essays on Eastern Indonesia*. Cambridge, MA: Harvard University Press, 1980.

—, 'East Timor: Exchange and Political Hierarchy at the Time of the European Discoveries', in K. Hutterer (ed.), *Economic Exchange and Social Interaction in Southeast Asia*. Ann Arbor, Michigan: Center for South and Southeast Asian Studies, University of Michigan, 1978.

Forsyth, W.D., 'Timor...II: The World of Dr. Evatt', *New Guinea and Australia, The Pacific and Southeast Asia*, 10:1 (1975). *See also* Ranck, S.

Fox, J. J., *Harvest of the Palm: Ecological Change in Eastern Indonesia*. Cambridge, MA: Harvard University Press, 1977.

—, *The Flow of Life: Essays on Eastern Indonesia*. Cambridge, MA: Harvard University Press, 1980.

—, 'The Great Lord Rests at the Centre: The Paradox of Powerlessness in European–Timorese Relations', *Canberra Anthropology*, **5**(2) (1982).

—, 'Southeast Asian Religions: Insular Cultures', in M. Eliade (ed.), *Encyclopedia of Religion*, Vol. 13. New York: Macmillan, 1986.

—, 'The Historical Consequences of Changing Patterns of Livelihood on Timor', in D. Wade-Marshall and P. Loveday (eds), *Northern Australia: Progress and Prospects. Volume 1: Contemporary Issues in Development*, Darwin: Australian National University, North Australian Research Unit, 1988 [mainly deals with West Timor].

Francillon, G., 'Incursions upon Wehali: A Modern History of an Ancient Empire', in J. J. Fox (ed.), *The Flow of Life: Essays on Eastern Indonesia*. Cambridge, MA: Harvard University Press, 1980.

Franck, T., and P. Hoffman, 'The Right of Self-Determination in Very Small Places', *International Law and Politics*, **8** (1976).

Franke, R.W., *East Timor: The Hidden War*, 2nd edn. New York: East Timor Defense Committee, 1976.

—, 'Bibliography: East Timor', *Bulletin of Concerned Asian Scholars*, **11** (April–June 1979).

—, 'East Timor: The Responsibility of the United States', *Bulletin of Concerned Asian Scholars* (Charlemont, MA), **15**(2) (April–June 1983).

Freches, José, *Les Portugais en Asie: Alexandre de Rhodes et la Filière Portugaise*, Arquivos do Centro Cultural Português, Fundação Calouste Gulbenkian, Vol.4. Paris, 1972 [pp. 536–48 refer to East Timor].

Frederico, J. (pseud.), 'Refugee Voices: A Well-Founded Fear of Being Persecuted?', *Journal of Refugee Studies*, **4**(1) (1991), pp. 82–92.

Freitas, J.M.C. de, *Fretilin Massacres: Testimonies of the Survivors from Fretilin Massacres*. Singapore: Usaha, 1982. **A**

Freney, D., 'East Timor: The Modest Revolution', *Australian Left Review*, **48** (September 1975).

—, *Timor: Freedom Caught Between the Powers*. Nottingham: Spokesman Books, 1975.

—, 'Guerilla War in East Timor', *Australian Left Review* (Sydney), **52** (1976). **Y**

—, 'Resistance, Revolution and Liberation: The East Timor People's Struggle for National Liberation', *Australian Left Review*, **70** (August 1979).

—, 'A Reply to Prof. Arndt: An Apologist who can't get his Facts Straight', *East Timor News* (Winter 1982).

—, 'A Reply to Peter Hastings: A Sophisticated Apologist for Suharto's Genocide', *East Timor News*. (Winter 1982).

—, 'Fretilin has Returned from Near Annihilation to Pose a Serious Threat to the Indonesian Occupation', *Southeast Asia Chronicle*, **94** (1984).

—, 'East Timor: Briefings', *Australian Left Review*, **93** (Spring 1985).

—, *A Map of Days: Life on the Left*. Port Melbourne: William Heinemann Australia, 1991.

— (ed.), *East Timor News. Bulletin of the East Timor News Agency*. Sydney: East Timor News Agency, 1979–85.

Fretilin External Delegation, *East Timor: Indonesia's Vietnam*. New York: Department of External Relations of Fretilin, May 1977.

—, *Fretilin Conquers the Right to Dialogue*. Lisbon, 1983.

Freidberg, C., 'Repérage et Découpage du Temps chez les Bunaq du Centre de Timor' [The Marking and Division of time amongst the Bunaq of the Centre of Timor], *Archipel* (Paris), **6** (1973).

—, 'Agricultures Timoraises' [Timorese Agriculture], *Études Rurales* (Paris), **53–6** (1974).

—, 'Espaces Bunaq' [Bunaq space], in *L'Homme, Hier et Aujourd'hui*. Paris: Éditions Cujas, 1974.

—, 'Sur l'Agriculture Timoraise et ses Possibilités de Développement' [On Timorese agriculture and its development possibilities] [review of J.K. Metzner's *Man and Environment in Eastern Timor*, see Metzner, J.K.], *Journal d'Agriculture Tropicale et Botanique Appliquée*, **26**(1) (1979).

'From Santa Cruz to Jakarta: Timorese Protest in Jalan Thamrin', *Inside Indonesia*, **29** (December 1991).

Fry, K.L., 'An Exercise in Self-Justification', *The Bulletin* (Sydney), (20 April 1982) [deals with Whitlam and the Timor debate in Australia].

—, 'East Timor: Ten Years On', *Arena* (Melbourne), **72** (1985).

—, and A. Gietzelt, 'Report on a Visit to Portuguese Timor', Canberra (November 1975) [mimeograph].

Fuhrman, J., 'East Timor: An Intractable Problem', *New Zealand International Review*, **18**(1) (January 1993).

Fundação Oriente, *Povos de Timor, Povo de Timor – Vida, Aliança, Morte* (Peoples of Timor, people of Timor – life, alliance, death). Lisbon: Fundação Oriente, Instituto de Investigação Científica Tropical, 1989.

Fundação de Relações Internacionais, A Paz é Possível em Timor Leste, Comissão para os Direitos do Povo Maubere, Pascoela Barreto, *Feto Rai Timor. Mulheres de Timor* [Feto Rai Timor. Women of Timor]. Lisbon: Fundação de Relações Internacionais *et al.*, 1991.

Gadjah Mada University, *Menentukan Identitas Desa di Timor Timur: Suatu Studi Sosio-Kulturil* [Determining the identity of the village in East Timor: A socio-cultural study]. Yogyakarta: Gadjah Mada University, 1980.

—, *Struktur, Kultur dan Birokrasi Formal di Timor Timur* [Structure, culture and formal bureaucracy in East Timor]. Yogyakarta: Gadjah Mada University, 1980.

Garcia, J.S., and J. Carvalho Cardoso, 'Os Solos de Timor' [The soils of Timor], *Garcia de Orta, Série Estação Agronómica,* (Lisbon), **12**(5–18) (1985).

—, *Os Solos de Timor* [The soils of Timor], Memórias da Junta de Investigações Científicas do Ultramar, Segunda Série No. 64. Lisbon: Junta de Investigações Científicas do Ultramar, 1978.

Gardiner, L., 'East Timor: Self-Determination?', MA thesis, Dept. of Government and Administration (Faculty of Economics), University of Sydney, February 1993.

Gath, S., *Australia–Indonesia Maritime Boundary: The Timor Gap.* Canberra: Australian Parliamentary Library Legislative Branch Research Paper, 17 December 1985.

Gault-Williams, M., 'Funu – Liberation War – Continues in East Timor', *Bulletin of Concerned Asian Scholars,* **22**(3) (July 1990).

George, A., *East Timor and the Shaming of the West.* London: Tapol Publications, 1985.

'Getting Away with Murder: The Dili Massacre Courts Martial', *Inside Indonesia,* **31** (June 1992).

Glover, E., 'Mollusca in Indonesian Archaeological Research', *Indonesia Circle,* **40** (June 1986) [mollusc evidence from cave sites in East Timor and Sulawesi].

Glover, I.C., 'Prehistoric Research in Timor', in D.J. Mulvaney and J. Golson (eds), *Aboriginal Man and Environment in Australia.* Canberra: Australian National University Press, 1971.

—, 'Excavations in Timor: A Study of Economic Change and Cultural Continuity in Prehistory', PhD thesis, Australian National University, 1972.

Gonçalves, M.M., 'Aspectos das Actividades Agrárias em Timor Oriental' [Aspects of agrarian activities in Eastern Timor], *Revista de Ciências Agrárias* (Lisbon), **12**(2) (1989).

—, M.L. Rodrigues, and E. Daenhardt, *Estudos sobre o Café de Timor* [Studies on coffee from Timor]. Lisbon: Missão de Estudos Agronómicos do Ultramar, 1976.

—, 'Estudos sobre o Café de Timor. I – A *Hemileia vastatrix* B & Br. no Território e o Melhoramento da Cafeicultura face à Doença' [Studies on coffee from Timor. I – The *Hemileia vastatrix* B & Br. in the territory and the improvement of coffee-growing in regard to the reduction of the incidence of the disease], *Estudos sobre o Café de Timor.* Lisbon: Missão de Estudos Agronómicos do Ultramar, 1976.

—, 'Estudos sobre o Café de Timor. II – Nota sobre as Possibilidades de Produção do "Híbrido de Timor" no seu Habitat Natural' [Studies on Coffee from Timor. II – Note on the yield possibilities of "Híbrido de Timor" in its natural habitat], *Estudos sobre o Café de Timor.* Lisbon: Missão de Estudos Agronómicos do Ultramar, 1976.

—, 'Estudos sobre o Café de Timor. III – Evolução de Exportação de Café em 1947/74 e sua Previsão para 1975/77' [Studies on coffee from Timor. III – Growth of coffee exports during 1947/74 and forecast for 1975/77], *Estudos sobre o Café de Timor.* Lisbon: Missão de Estudos Agronómicos do Ultramar, 1976.

Goto, Takao, 'Higashi Timor Funso to Osutoraria no Taio' [The East Timor Problem and Australian Foreign Policy], *Osutoraria Kenkyu Kiyo,* **5** (December 1979) [deals with the period 1974-1976].

Grade, E.A. de Carvalho, and Mello Sales, 'Timor 73 – Panorâmica do Ensino' [Timor 73 – Panorama of Teaching], *Revista Militar* (Lisbon), **25**(4) (April 1973).

Gray, A., 'The People of East Timor and their Struggle for Survival', in T. Retbøll (ed.), *East Timor: The Struggle Continues,* IWGIA Document 50. Copenhagen: International Work Group for Indigenous Affairs, 1984.

Great Britain, House of Commons (Parliamentary Human Rights Group), *Letter from the Parliamentary Human Rights Group in Britain to the UN Secretary-General.* London: House of Commons, 10 August 1984.

—, *Hearing on East Timor. The Santa Cruz Massacre.* London: House of Commons, 17 December 1991.

—, *see also* Bizot, J.

Guan, K.C., 'The Historical Roots of Indonesian Irredentism', *Asian Studies*, **8**(1) (April 1970).

Gunn, G. C., *Wartime Portuguese Timor: The Azores Connection*. Clayton, Victoria: Monash University, Centre for Southeast Asian Studies, 1988. C

—, (with Jefferson Lee), *A Critical View of Western Journalism and Scholarship on East Timor*. Manila: Journal of Contemporary Asia Publishers, 1994. *See also* Lee, Jefferson.

Gusmão, Xanana, 'Portugal's Inadequacy. Two Post-Massacre Letters from Xanana Gusmao [Gusmão]', *Inside Indonesia*, **39** (December 1991).

—, 'Viva Timor Leste! Xanana's Defence Statement' [trans. TAPOL], *Inside Indonesia*, **35** (June 1993).

—, *Timor Leste. Um Povo, Uma Pátria* [East Timor. A People, A Country]. Lisbon: Ediçoes Colibri, 1994.

—, *see also* Domm, R.

Guterres, F. da C., 'Profil Konversi di Timor Timur: Case Study di Desa Santa Cruz' [A profile of land title change in East Timor: A case study of the village of Santa Cruz], MA thesis, Faculty of Law, Satya Wacana Christian University, Salatiga, 1991.

Guterres, J.M.A., 'A Timorese Speaks to Australians', *Arena* (Melbourne), **63** (1983).

—, 'Refugee Politics – Timorese in Exile', BA (Hons.) thesis, Victoria University of Technology (Melbourne), 1992.

Hadi Soesastro, M., *see* Soesastro, M. Hadi.

Hamilton, J., 'Timorese Situation Remains a Mystery', *West Australian*, 22 September 1983 [deals with the visit of Australian politicians Bill Morrison and Senator Gordon McIntosh to East Timor in late July 1983.

Ham, A.P. van den, 'Development Cooperation and Human Rights: [The] Indonesian-Dutch Aid Controversy', *Asian Survey*, **33**(5) (1993) [deals with the Indonesian-Dutch dispute in March 1992 over aid conditionality and East Timor].

Hastings, P., 'The Timor Problem – I', *Australian Outlook* (Canberra), **29**(1) (April 1975)

—, 'The Timor Problem – II: Some Australian Attitudes, 1903–1941', *Australian Outlook* (Canberra), **29**(2) (August 1975).

—, 'The Timor Problem – III: Some Australian Attitudes, 1941–1950', *Australian Outlook* (Canberra), **29**(3) (December 1975).

—, 'Timor and West Irian: The Reasons Why', in J.A.C. Mackie (ed.) *Indonesia: The Making of a Nation*. Canberra: Australian National University, Research School of Pacific Studies, 1980.

Herrera, J., *The Vigil*. Hobart: J. Herrera, 1988.

Hertsgaard, M., 'The Secret Life of Henry Kissinger', *The Nation*, (29 October 1990).

—, and J. Williamson, 'Arms and the Man', *New Statesman and Society*, **3** (2 November 1990) [deals with Henry Kissinger and US policy towards Indonesia and Angola in 1975 as revealed in a secret document].

Hicks, D., 'Eastern Tetum' and 'Timor-Roti', in F. M. LeBar (ed.), *Ethnic Groups of Insular Southeast Asia, Vol. 1: Indonesia, Andaman Islands and Madagascar*. New Haven: Human Relations Area Files Press, 1972.

—, 'The Cairui and Uai Ma'a of Timor', *Anthropos*, **68** (1973).

—, 'The Caraubalo Tetum', *Garcia da Orta, Série de Antropologia*, **1**(1–2) (1973).

—, 'Laver la Jambe du Buffle: Un Rite Tetum' [Washing the leg of the buffalo: A Tetum Ritual], *L'Homme*, **14**(1) (1974).

—, 'La Compensation Matrimoniale chez les Tetum' [Bride wealth amongst the Tetum], *L'Homme*, **15**(3–4) (1975).

—, *Tetum Ghosts and Kin: Fieldwork in an Indonesian Community*. Palo Alto: Mayfield, 1976.

—, 'Structural Analysis in Anthropology: Case Studies from Indonesia and Brazil', *Studia Instituti Anthropos* **30** (1978).

—, 'A Transitional Relationship Terminology of Asymmetric Prescriptive Alliance among the Makassai of Eastern Indonesia', *Sociologus*, **33**(1) (1983).

—, 'Unachieved Syncretism: The Local-Level Political System in Portuguese Timor, 1966–1967', *Anthropos* (Freiburg), **78** (1983).

—, *A Maternal Religion: The Role of Women in Tetum Myth and Ritual*. Dekalb: Northern Illinois University, Center for Southeast Asian Studies, 1984.

—, 'Conjonction Féminine et Disjonction Masculine chez les Tetum (Timor, Indonésie Orientale)' [Female union and male disunion amongst the Tetum (Timor, Eastern Indonesia)], *L'Homme*, **25**(2) (1985).

—, 'Space, Motion and Symbol in Tetum Religion', in R. S. Kipp and S. Rodgers (eds), *Indonesian Religions in Transition*. Tucson: University of Arizona Press, 1987.

—, 'Tetum Descent', *Anthropos*, **82**(1–3) (1987).

—, 'Literary Masks and Metaphysical Truths: Intimations from Timor', *American Anthropologist*, **90**(4) (1988).

—, 'Mythos und Ritual: Eine Fallstudie aus Timor' [Myth and ritual: A case study from Timor], in Karl-Heinz Kohl (ed.), *Mythen im Kontext: Ethnologische Perspektiven* [Myths in context: Ethnological perspectives]. Frankfurt-am-Main: Ed. Qumran im Campus-Verlag, 1993.

Hidayat, 'Peluang dan Tantangan Pengembangan Sumberdaya Manusia Tim Tim bagi Penciptaan Lapangan Kerja' [Opportunities and challenges of human resource development in East Timor for job creation], seminar paper given at the Impettu Seminar, Jabotabek, 1992.

Hill, D. and K. Sen, 'How Jakarta saw the Massacre', *Inside Indonesia*, **29** (December 1991).

Hill, Hal, and A. Weidemann, 'Regional Development in Indonesia: Patterns and Issues', in Hal Hill (ed.), *Unity and Diversity: Regional Economic Development in Indonesia Since 1970*. Singapore: Oxford University Press, 1989.

Hill, Helen, 'Australia and Portuguese Timor: Between Principles and Pragmatism', in R. Scott and J. Richardson (eds), *The First Thousand Days of Labor*, Volume I. Canberra: Australasian Political Studies Association, 1975.

—, *The Timor Story*, 2nd edn, Fitzroy, Victoria: Timor Information Service, 1976.

—, 'Newest Minority: The East Timorese', in G. Ashworth (ed.), *World Minorities I*. Sunbury, England: Quartermaine House and Minority Rights Group, 1977.

—, 'Timor: The Politics of Conscience', *Arena* (Melbourne), **46** (1977).

—, 'Fretilin: The Origins, Ideologies and Strategies of a Nationalist Movement in East Timor', MA thesis, Monash University, 1978.

Hiorth, F., 'Ost-Timors Uheldige Skjebne' [East Timor's unfortunate fate], *Mennesker og Rettigheter* (Oslo), **2**(1) (1984).

—, *Timor: Past and Present*, South-East Asian Monographs, No. 17. Townsville, Queensland: James Cook University of North Queensland, 1985.

—, 'Scandinavia and East Timor', *Indonesia Reports*, **14** (1986).

—, 'East Timor 1985–1991', *Kabar Seberang*, **23** (1992).

Hoadley, J.S., *The Future of Portuguese Timor: Dilemmas and Opportunities*, Occasional Paper No. 27, Institute of Southeast Asian Studies, University of Singapore, 1975.

—, 'Portuguese Timor and Regional Stability', *Southeast Asian Spectrum* (Bangkok), **3**(4) (July 1975).

—, 'East Timor: Civil War – Causes and Consequences', *Southeast Asian Affairs*, Institute of Southeast Asian Studies, University of Singapore, 1976.

—, 'New Zealand's Response to the East Timor Controversy', *New Zealand International Review*, **1**(6) (1976).

—, 'Indonesia's Annexation of East Timor: Political, Administrative and Developmental Initiatives', *Southeast Asian Affairs* (Singapore), 1977.

Hodge, E., 'The Impact of the ABC on Australian–Indonesian Relations since Timor', *Australian Journal of International Affairs*, **45**(1) (May 1991).

Hoffman, J., 'Australia and East Timor', *Journal of Australian Studies*, **2** (1977).

Hope Royal Commission, 'On the Hope Royal Commission's Report on Australian Spying in East Timor', *The National Times*, (15 March 1981).

Horne, J., 'East Timor, Australia and the United Nations', MA thesis, Australian National University (Canberra), 1977.

Horta, A. Ramos-, *The Eyewitness: Bitter Moments in East Timor Jungles*. Singapore: Usaha Quality Printers, 1981.

Horta, J. Ramos-, *East Timor Speaks: The Report of Mr José Ramos Horta, Minister for External Relations in the Democratic Republic of East Timor, to the United Nations Decolonisation Committee (Committee of 24) on September 8, 1976*. Sydney: Campaign for Independent East Timor, 1976.

—, 'East Timor: Decolonization Unfinished. A Case Study in International Law', MA thesis, Antioch University, New York 1984.

—, *Funu: The Unfinished Saga of East Timor*. Trenton, New Jersey: Red Sea Press, 1987.

—, 'Is a Political Settlement Possible?', (interview), *Inside Indonesia*, **10** (April 1987).

—, 'Peace Plan for East Timor', speech to the European Parliament, Brussels, 1992.

—, *see also* Retbøll, T.

Hull, G.S., *East Timor: Just a Political Question?*. North Sydney: Australian Catholic Social Justice Council, 1992.

—, *Mai Kolia Tetum. A Course in Tetum-Praça, The Lingua Franca of East Timor*. Sydney: Australian Catholic Relief and Australian Catholic Social Justice Council, 1993.

Human Rights Watch/Asia, *see* Asia Watch.

Hutterer, K.L. (ed.), *Economic Exchange and Social Interaction in Southeast Asia: Perspectives from Prehistory, History, and Ethnography*, Michigan Papers on Southeast Asia, 13. Ann Arbor: Center for South and Southeast Asian Studies, University of Michigan, 1978.

Hyland, T., 'US Scholar Tips Dramatic Change in Indonesian View of East Timor', *The Missing Peace* [Newsletter of the East Timor Talks Campaign], **4** (September 1992).

IDOC (International Documentation Centre), *East Timor*, IDOC (Rome), **18**(1) (1987).

'If Only I was a Free Person: An East Timorese Appeal', *Inside Indonesia*, **33** (December 1992).

'Indonesia and East Timor', *Church and Society*, **84**(6) (July 1994).

Indonesia, Bishops Conference of, 'Letter to the Apostolic Administrator of the Diocese of Dili, Mgr. Carlos Filipe [Ximenes] Belo and to the Priests, Brothers and Sisters of the Diocese of Dili'. Jakarta, 17 November 1983 [press release].

Indonesia Publications, 'Briefing Book: East Timor'. Maryland, USA: Indonesia Publications, 1988 [covers period 1984–6].

Indonesia, Republic of, *Government Statements on the East-Timor Question*. Jakarta: Department of Information, February 1976 [covers period 4–23 December 1975]. **Y**

—, *The Question of Portuguese Timor*. Jakarta: Department of Information, 1975. **Y**

—, *Decolonization in East Timor*. Jakarta: Department of Foreign Affairs, 1976.

—, *The Process of Decolonization in East Timor*. Jakarta: Department of Information, 1976. **Y**

—, *Newspaper Articles on East Timor*. Jakarta: Department of Information, 1977.

—, *To Build a Better Tomorrow in East Timor*. Jakarta: Department of Information, 1979.

—, *The Province of East Timor: Development in Progress*. Jakarta: Departments of Foreign Affairs and Information, 1981.

—, *East Timor After Integration*. Jakarta: Department of Information, 1983. **A**

—, *East Timor After Integration*, 2nd edn, Jakarta: Department of Foreign Affairs, 1984.

—, *East Timor Today*. Jakarta: Department of Information, 1984.

—, *Religious Life in East Timor*. New York: Permanent Mission of the Republic of Indonesia to the United Nations, 1985.

—, *East Timor: A Decade of Development*. Jakarta: Department of Foreign Affairs, 1986.

—, *The Process of Decolonization in East Timor*. Jakarta: Department of Information, 1987.

—, *Facts About East Timor*. Jakarta: House of Representatives, 1989.

—, *East Timor Strives for a Better Future*. Jakarta: Public Relations Bureau, 1990.

—, *Laporan Komisi Penyelidik Nasional Peristiwa/Insiden 12 Nopember 1991 di Dili* [Report of the National Commission of Enquiry into the 12 November affair/incident in Dili]. Jakarta: Department of Information, 1991.

—, *East Timor: Building for the Future: Issues and Perspectives*. Jakarta: Department of Foreign Affairs, 1992.

— *see also* Departemen Dalam Negeri, Departemen Kehakiman *and* Departemen Luar Negeri.

Indro Tjahjono, *see* Interrogation of an Activist.

Inside Indonesia, Northcote (Australia), 1983–present [quarterly].

International Commission of Jurists, *Tragedy in East Timor, Report on the Trials in Dili and Jakarta*. Geneva: International Commission of Jurists, October 1992.

International Committee of the Red Cross, *Report of Activities of the International Committee of the Red Cross Medical Team in East Timor from August 30 to September 4, 1975*, September 1975 [mimeograph]. **Y**

International Federation for East Timor, *The UN and East Timor… Why Won't the System Work?* Hiroshima: IFET, 1993.

International Work Group for Indigenous Affairs (Copenhagen), *see* Retbøll, T.

'Interrogation of an Activist: Interview with Indro Tjahjono', *Inside Indonesia*, **29** (December 1991).

Iugo-Vostochnaya Aziia na Rubezhe 70–80–kh godov (Tendentsii Problemy Razvitiia) [Southeast Asia on the threshhold of the 1970s (and) 1980s (Trends in development problems)] [contains a chapter by N.A. Tolmachev on the arrangement of political forces in East Timor in the late 1970s and early 1980s (pp. 127–36)]. Moscow: Nauka [Publishing House], 1984. *See also* Tolmachev, N.A.

'The Jaelani Official Inquiry', *Inside Indonesia*, **29** (December 1991).

Janz, J.G., and K.S. Chung, 'Filiaríase Linfática em Timor Leste' [Lymphatic Filariasis in East Timor], *Anais do Instituto de Higiene e Medicina Tropical* (Lisbon), **5**(1–4) (1977–8).

Jardine, M. 'The Secret Sacrifice of East Timor', *Christianity and Crisis*, **53**(1) (February 1993).

Jolliffe, J., *Report from East Timor*. Canberra: Australian National University Students Association, 1975.

—, 'A New Independence Struggle right on our Doorstep', *Development News Digest* (Canberra), **13** (June 1975).

—, 'The Peace in Timor', *Development News Digest* (Canberra), **15** (March 1976).

—, 'Timor: A Year of Struggle', *Arena* (Melbourne), **44–5** (1976).

—, *East Timor: Nationalism and Colonialism*. St. Lucia, Queensland: University of Queensland Press, 1978.

—, 'Rough Notes Towards an Analysis of the Military Situation in East Timor. Based on Documents Smuggled to Lisbon'. Lisbon: Timor Newsletter Occasional Report, 1986.

—, *Timor, Terra Sangrenta* [Timor, bloody land]. Lisbon: Editora O Jornal, 1989.

Jones, S., *Injustice, Persecution, Eviction: A Human Rights Update on Indonesia and East Timor*. New York: Asia Watch, 1990. *See also* Asia Watch.

Jouve, E., *Un Tribunal pour les Peuples* [A peoples' tribunal] [pp. 227–57 deals with East Timor]. Paris: Berger Levrault, 1983.

Kameo, D., *Strategi dan Kebijakan Pembangunan di Propinsi Timor Timur, Fakta dan Prospek* [Development strategies and skills in the province of East Timor: Facts and prospects]. Salatiga: Universitas Kristen Satya Wacana, 1991.

Kantor Wilayah Departemen Perdagangan Propinsi Timor Timur, *Statistik Perdagangan Tahun 1989* (East Timor) trade statistics for the year 1989]. Dili: Kanwil [Kantor Wilayah] Depag [Departemen Perdagangan], 1990.

—, *Laporan Tahunan 1990* (Annual Reports for 1990). Dili: Kanwil [Kantor Wilayah] Depag [Departemen Perdagangan], 1991.

Kantor Statistik Propinsi Timor Timur, *Baucau Dalam Angka 1989* [Baucau in the 1989 figures]. Baucau: Kantor Statistik Kabupaten Baucau, 1990.

—, *Lautem Dalam Angka 1989*]Lautem in the 1989 Figures]. Lautem: Kantor Statistik Kabupaten Lautem, 1990.

—, *Ermera Dalam Angka 1989* [Ermera in the 1989 Figures]. Ermera: Kantor Statistik Kabupaten Ermera, 1990.

—, *Penduduk Timor Timur Hasil Sensus Penduduk 1990* [The Population of East Timor – The results of the 1990 population census]. Dili: Kantor Statistik Tim-Tim, 1991.

—, *Baucau Dalam Angka 1991* [Baucau in the 1991 Figures]. Baucau: Kantor Statistik Kabupaten Baucau, 1991.

—, *Penduduk Propinsi Timor Timur, Hasil Registrasi Penduduk* [The population of the province of East Timor, The results of the registration of inhabitants]. Dili: Kantor Statistik Tim-Tim, 1991.

—, *Statistik Angkatan Kerja 1991* (Employment Statistics for 1991). Dili: Kantor Statistik Tim-Tim, 1991.

Kartodirdjo, S., 'Religious and Economic Aspects of Portuguese–Indonesian Relations 1509–1641', *Studia*, **29**(1970).

Keesings Reference Publications, *Border and Territorial Disputes*. [pp. 329–36 deals with Indonesia and Portugal], 2nd edn. Harlow: Longman, 1987.

King, P., 'The Koala, the Komodo and Conflict Resolution: A New Agenda for Australia's Relations with Indonesia', in R. H. Bruce (ed.), *Prospects for Peace: Changes in the Indian Ocean Region*, IOCPS Monograph No. 1. Perth, WA: Indian Ocean Centre for Peace Studies, University of Western Australia, and Canberra: Australian Institute of International Affairs, 1992.

—, 'Breaking Deadlocks – Peace-Making Opportunities for Australia in East Timor, West Papua, and Papua New Guinea', in K. Clements (ed.), *Peace and Security in the Asia Pacific Region: Post-Cold War Problems and Prospects*. Tokyo: United Nations University Press, and Palmerston North, NZ: Dunmore Press, 1993.

Klinken, G. van, 'Jakarta after the Santa Cruz Massacre', *Inside Indonesia*, **30** (March 1992).

Kohen, A.S., 'US Diplomacy and Human Rights: The Cruel Case of Indonesia', *The Nation*. (26 November 1977) [offprint issued as *Human Rights in Indonesia*].

—, 'Invitation to a Massacre in East Timor: The US Involvement', *The Nation*, (7 February 1981).

—, 'Massacre on Prime Time: Making an Issue of East Timor', *The Nation*, (10 February 1992).

—, and J. Taylor, *An Act of Genocide: Indonesia's Invasion of East Timor*. London: Tapol Books, 1979.

—, and R. Quance, 'The Politics of Starvation', *Inquiry* (New York), (18 February 1980).

Komitee Indonesie, *Oost Timor: De Soldaat van Maubere Schreeuwt om Recht* [East Timor: The Soldier of the Maubere (People) Cries for Justice]. Amsterdam: Komitee Indonesie, 1977. **A**

—, *Honger in Oost Timor: Drie Documenten over de Indonesische Militaire Strategie op Oost Timor* [Hunger in East Timor: Three documents concerning Indonesian Military Strategy in East Timor]. Amsterdam: Komitee Indonesie, 1979. **A**

—, *Oost Timor: Holocaust in het Geniep*, International Congress on East Timor, Amsterdam, 27-28 September 1980 [also published in English as *East Timor: Holocaust on the Sly*].

—, *Oost Timor Tribunaal* [East Timor Tribunal]. Amsterdam: Komitee Indonesie, 1981. **A**

—, *Oost Timor: Westerse Medeplichtigheid aan Volkenmoord* [East Timor: Western complicity in genocide]. Amsterdam: Komitee Indonesie, 1982. **A**

—, *Oost Timor Schreeuwt… Nederland Medeplichtig* [East Timor cries out… The Netherlands an accomplice]. Amsterdam: Komitee Indonesie, 1984. **A**

—, *Wind Ademt in Zijn Eentje: Poezie uit Indonesië, Oost Timor en Nederland* [The wind blows by itself: Poetry from Indonesia, East Timor and the Netherlands]. Amsterdam: Herv. st. Jeugd-en Jongerenwerk, 1984. **A**

Kondracke, M., 'Another Cambodia', *The New Republic*, (3 November 1979).

'Konversi Hukum Hak Tanah' [Conversion of land right law], *Kompas*, (30 November 1989).

'The Kooijmans Report: UN Findings on Torture in Indonesia', *Inside Indonesia*, **30** (March 1992) [deals with East Timor].

Kristiadi, 'The Decolonization of East Timor: A Historical Review', *Indonesian Quarterly*, **14**(4) (1986).

Kroef, J.M. van der, 'Indonesia and East Timor: The Politics of Phased Annexation', *Solidarity*, **10**(5–6) (1976).

—, 'Patterns of Conflict in Eastern Indonesia', *Conflict Studies*, **79** (January 1977).

—, 'Regional Disturbances in Eastern Indonesia', *Conflict Studies*, **79** (1977).

—, 'East Timor: The Problem and the Human Rights Polemic (I)', *Asian Thought and Society*, **7**(21) (November 1982).

—, 'East Timor: The Problem and the Human Rights Polemic (II)', *Asian Thought and Society*, **8**(22–3) (March 1983).

Kusumaatmadja, Mochtar, *Perjanjian Indonesia-Australia di Celah Timor/Indonesiaa-Australia Joint Cooperation Zone South of East Timor (The Timor Gap)*. Bandung: Pusat Studi Wawasan Nusantara, Hukum dan Pembangunan, 1990.

Lambourne, W., 'Australian Foreign Policy Towards Indonesia and East Timor: Realpolitik, Ethics and the National Interest', MA (International Relations) research essay, Research School of Pacific Studies, Australian National University, Canberra, March 1992.

Lapian, A. B., and Abdurachman, P., 'Sejarah Timor Timur' [History of East Timor], *Berita Antropologi*, **11**(36) (1980).

Larsson, B. (ed.), *Det Grymma Spelet: Sveriges Roll i Indonesiens Folkmoord i Östtimor 1975-1985* [The sinister game: Sweden's role in Indonesia's genocide in East Timor, 1975-1985]. Stockholm: Østtimor-Komiteen, 1985.

Lawless, R., 'The Indonesian Takeover of East Timor', *Asian Survey* (Berkeley), **16**(10) (October 1976).

Lawson, Y., 'East Timor: Roots Continue to Grow (A Provisional Analysis of Changes in Foreign Domination and the Continuing Struggle for Freedom and Independence)', University of Amsterdam, August 1989 [manuscript].

Lazarowitz, T.F., 'The Makassai: Complementary Dualism in Timor', PhD thesis, State University of New York, Stony Brook, 1980.

Leadbeater, M., 'East Timor: An Unprecedented Opportunity for International Action', *Peacelink*, **102** (April 1992).

LeBar, F. M., *Ethnic Groups of Insular Southeast Asia*. New Haven, CT: Human Relations Area Files, 1972–5 [section on Timor and neighbouring island of Roti by D. Hicks and J. Fox in Volume I: Indonesia, Andaman Islands and Madagascar, 1972].

Lee, Jefferson, 'The Dili Massacre and Aftermath', in J.C. Gunn, *A Critical View of Western Journalism and Scholarship on East Timor*, Manila: Journal of Contemporary Asia Publishers, 1994.

Leeuwrijk, J.H.J., 'Een Zilveren Distinctief uit Timor', *Antiek* **27**(2) (1992), pp.82–83 [deals with a silver walking stick button belonging to Nai Cobit Tabenu, *liurai* of Tabeno in Timor].

—, 'Twee Koloniale Aquarellen: J.A. Pavaricini op Timor in 1756', *Antiek*, **26**(10) (1992), pp.484–91 [deals with the diplomatic mission of J.A. Pavaricini (1710–71), *opperkoopman* (senior merchant) of the Dutch East India Company (VOC) to Timor in 1756].

Legal Issues Arising from the East Timor Conflict, 20 and 21 March 1992. Kensington, NSW: University of New South Wales, Faculty of Law, 1992.

Leifer, M., 'Indonesia and the Incorporation of East Timor', *The World Today* (London), **32**(9) (September 1976).

—, *Indonesia's Foreign Policy*. London: George Allen and Unwin, 1983.

Leite, P. Pinto, *East Timor: To Be Liberated or To Be Exterminated, That Is the Question*. Amsterdam: Komitee Indonesie, 1989. **A**

—, *Oost Timor: De Westelijk Sahara van Zuidoost Azië* [East Timor. The Western Sahara of Southeast Asia]. Leiden, 1988.

Lewis, N., *An Empire of the East. Travels in Indonesia*. London: Jonathan Cape, 1993 [contains a section on East Timor, pp. 83–140].

—, 'A Most Sinister War', *Independent on Sunday*, (8 March 1994).

Liberato, C. dos S.O., *Quando Timor foi Notícia: Memórias* [When Timor was news: Memoirs]. Braga: Editoria Pax, 1972.

Liechty, C. Philip, 'How Indonesia Engulfed East Timor', *The Washington Post*, (6 January 1992).

Liem Soei Liong, 'Indonesian Colonialism in the Pacific', in D. Robie (ed.), *Tu Galala: Social Change in the Pacific*. Wellington: Bridget Williams Books and Annandale: Pluto Press Australia, 1992. *See also* Budiardjo and Liem Soei Liong.

Light, M., 'Forlorn and Forgotten: The Sad Plight of East Timor', *Harvard International Review*, **14**(3) (Spring 1992).

Livesley, K. P., 'The Timor Gap Treaty – An Update', *Australian Mining and Petroleum Association Bulletin*, **10**(4) (1991).

Lobato, N., *Fretilin é a Liberdade do Povo em Marcha. Discursos* [Fretilin and the freedom of a people on the march. Speeches]. Lisbon: Edições Comité 28 de Novembro, n.d.

Lobato, R., 'How East Timor Fights On', *Australian Left Review*, **57** (1977).

Lolly, 'Arabica Berwajah Robusta: Tinjauan Politik Perkopian di Timor Timur' [The strong face of Arabica (Robusta): The political economy of coffee in East Timor], *Dian Ekonomi*, **2** (1992–3).

Lovard, K., 'Reporting East Timor', *Inside Indonesia*, **18** (April 1989).

Ludwig, K., and K. Horta, *Osttimor – Das Vergessene Sterben: Indonesischer Völkermord unter Ausschluss der Weltöffentlichkeit* [East Timor – The forgotten dying: Indonesian genocide concealed from world publicity]. Göttingen: Gesellschaft für bedrohte Völker, 1985.

Lumb, R.D., 'The Delimitation of Maritime Boundaries in the Timor Sea', *Australian Yearbook of International Law*, **7** (1981).

Macey, D., 'Recent Developments in East Timor', *Race and Class* (London), **18**(1) (Summer 1976).

Machetzki, R., 'Osttimor: Eine Nachbetrachtung' [East Timor: A look backwards], *Sudostasien-Aktuell*, **11** (May 1992).

Magalhães, A. Barbedo de, *Timor Leste: Mensagem aos Vivos* [East Timor: Message to the living]. Limiar, Oporto: Oporto University, 1983.

—, *East Timor: Indonesian Occupation and Genocide*. Oporto: President's Office, Oporto University, 1992.

—, *East Timor: Land of Hope*, trans. Susan Pérez Castillo. Oporto: President's Office, Oporto University, 1992.

—, *see also* Retbøll, T.

Maloney, G. J., 'Australia-Indonesia Timor Gap Zone of Cooperation Treaty: A New Official Petroleum Regime', *Journal of Energy and Natural Resources*, **8**(128) (1990).

Martin-Schiller, B., Joanne Hale and Pauline Wilson, *Review of the East Timor Agricultural Development Project (Etadep) USAID/Indonesia*. Dili: Catholic Relief Services, 1987. *See also* Metzner, J and F. Rumawas.

Masinambouw, E., 'Bahasa-Bahasa di Timor Timur' [Languages in East Timor], *Berita Antropologi*, **11**(36) (1980).

Matos, A. T. de, *Timor Português, 1515–1769: Contribuição para a sua História* [Portuguese Timor, 1515–1769: A Contribution to its History]. Lisbon: Faculdade de Letras da Universidade de Lisboa, Instituto Histórico Infante Dom Henrique, 1974.

—, 'Timor and Portuguese Trade in the Orient during the 18th Century', in A.T. de Matos and L.F.F.R. Thomaz (eds.), *As Relações entre a Índia Portuguesa, a Ásia de Sudeste e o Extremo Oriente: Actas do VI Seminário Internacional de História Indo–Portuguesa*. Macao and Lisbon, 1993.

Matra, *see* Tolomundu. Muchlis Dj.

May, B., *The Indonesian Tragedy*. London: Routledge & Kegan Paul, 1978.

McDonald, H., 'Death at Balibo', *National Times* (Australia), **21–24, 26, 28–32** (1-7 July 1979) [deals with the death of the five Western journalists at Balibo on 16 October 1975].

—, 'War and Diplomacy: The Timor Case', in H. McDonald, *Suharto's Indonesia*. Melbourne: Fontana, 1980.

McIntosh, G., 'East Timor: The Inside Story', *Inside Indonesia*, **10** (April 1987).

McIntyre, K.G., *The Secret Discovery of Australia*. Sydney: Picador, 1982 [revised and abridged edition first published by Souvenir Press (London), 1977].

—, *A Descoberta Secreta da Austrália* [The secret discovery of Australia]. Macao: Fundação Oriente, Centro de Estudos Marítimos de Macau, 1989.

McMillan, A., *Death in Dili*. Sydney: Hodder & Stoughton (Australia) and Sceptre Books, 1992.

'Menuju Kemandirian Pangan' [Towards self-sufficiency in food), *Kompas*, (1 December 1989) [deals with East Timor].

Metzner, J.K., *Man and Environment in Eastern Timor: A Geo-Ecological Analysis of the Baucau-Viqueque Area as a Possible Basis for Regional Planning*. Canberra: Development Studies Centre, Australian National University, 1977.

—, and F. Rumawas, *Evaluation Report of Yayasan ETADEP* (East Timor Agricultural Development Project Foundation). Dili: Province of East Timor, June 1991. *See also* Martin-Schiller, B. *et al.*

Miller, G., 'Contribution to a Bibliography of the Timor Crisis: Material in the A.N.U. Library', *Southeast Asian Research Materials Group Newsletter*, **9** (October 1977).

Mills, A., 'The Timor Gap Treaty: More Paper for the Cracks or a Foundation for the Wall?', *Inside Indonesia*, **22** (March 1990).

Missionair Centrum, *Oost Timor: De Vergeten Volkenmoord* [East Timor: The forgotten genocide]. Heerlen: Missionair Centrum, 1983.

Mo, T., *The Redundancy of Courage*. London: Chatto & Windus, 1991 [paperback edition by Vintage Books (London), 1992].

Moloney, G. J., 'Australian–Indonesian Timor Gap Zone of Cooperation Treaty: A New Offshore Petroleum Regime', *Journal of Energy and Natural Resources Law*, **8**(2) (1990).

Montealegre, F., *Background Information on Indonesia: The Invasion of East Timor and US Military Assistance*. Washington, DC: Institute for Policy Studies, 1982.

Moreira, A., *O Drama de Timor: Relatório da O.N.U. sobre a Descolonização* [The Timor drama: UN report of the decolonization]. Lisbon: Intervenção, 1977.

Morlanes, T.F., 'East Timorese Ethno-Nationalism: A Search for an Identity–Cultural and Political Self-Determination', PhD thesis, Department of Anthropology and Sociology, University of Queensland (Darwin), 1991.

Morris, C., *Ai Knananuk ho ai knanoik nousi Rai Timur – Rai nousi lafaek dukur. Verse and Legends from Timor, the Land of the Sleeping Crocodile*. Victoria: H.C. Morris, 1984.

—, *A Traveller's Dictionary in Tetun–English and English–Tetun from the Land of the Sleeping Crocodile East Timor*. Frankston, Australia: Baba Dook Books, 1992.

—, *Tetun–English Dictionary*. Canberra: Australian National University, Department of Linguistics, Research School of Pacific Studies, 1984.

Mubyarto *et al.*, Pat Walsh, (ed.), *East Timor: The Impact of Integration. An Indonesian Socio-Anthropological Study*. Yogyakarta: Gadjah Mada University, Research Centre for Village and Regional Development, published by Indonesian Resources and Information Program (IRIP), Northcote (Australia), December 1991.

Muller, K, (ed. D. Pickell), *East of Bali: From Lombok to Timor*. Berkeley, CA and Singapore: Periplus, 1991.

Munster, G. J., 'East Timor: From Beginning to End', in G. J. Munster, *Secrets of State*. Sydney: Angus and Robertson, 1982.

—, *Secrets of State: A Detailed Assessment of the Book they Banned*. London: Walsh & Munster, 1982.

—, and R. Walsh, (eds.), *Documents on Australian Defence and Foreign Policy, 1968–75*. Sydney: Walsh & Munster, 1980.

'Murdani's Dili Speech: Don't Dream, or else …', *Inside Indonesia*, **23** (June 1990).

Museum of Modern Art, Oxford, 'East Timor 1974–1992. Years of Silence: Images of Resistance' (1 November–13 December 1992) [exhibition catalogue].

Nairn, A., 'Colonizing East Timor: Indonesia and Australia's Oil Drilling Plans', *Multinational Monitor*, **12**(11–14) (July–August 1991) [republished in *Beacon*, February 1992].

—, 'The Talk of the Town: Notes and Comment', *The New Yorker* (December 1991).

National Council of the Churches of Christ in the USA, *The Question of East Timor*. New York: NCCC/USA, 1987.

National Press Club (Washington, DC), 'Verbatim of a Press Meeting of Indonesian Foreign Minister Ali Alatas at the National Press Club, Washington, DC, February 20 1992', Washington, DC: National Press Club, 1992.

Nelson, P., 'The Whitlam Years: Australia's Foreign Policy 1972-1975', *Cabbages and Kings*, **16** (1988).

Neonbasu, G., *Keadilan dan Perdamaian di Diosis Dili, Timor Timur: Dalam Terang Ajaran Resmi Gereja Katolik* [Justice and peace in the diocese of Dili, East Timor: In the light of the official teachings of the Catholic Church]. Dili: Komisi Komunikasi Sosial Diosis Dili, 1992.

Nettheim, G., 'Human Rights and East Timor. International Law and International Politics', paper presented at the CIIR/ICJ Conference on 'Indonesia's Occupation of East Timor: Legal Questions', London, 5–6 December 1992.

Nichterlein, S., 'East Timor in Washington: A View from New York'. Washington, 1977 [typescript photocopy].

—, 'The Struggle for East Timor – Prelude to Invasion', *Journal of Contemporary Asia* (Manila), **7**(4) (1977).

—, 'Australia: Courtier or Courtesan? The Timor Issue Revisited', *Australian Outlook* (Canberra), **36**(1) (April 1982).

Nicol, B., *Timor: The Stillborn Nation.* Melbourne, Victoria: Visa and Widescope International Publishers, 1978.

'No Place for Tourists: East Timor Observed', *Arena* (Melbourne), **90** (Autumn 1990).

Noor, Machmuddin *et al.*, *Lahirnya Propinsi Timor-Timur* [The birth of the province of Timor Timur (East Timor)]. Jakarta: Badan Penerbitan Republik Indonesia, 1977.

Nortier, J.J., 'De Guerrilla op Timor (Maart 1942 tot 1943)' [The Guerilla war in Timor, March 1942–(February) 1943], *Mededelingen van de Sectie Krijgsgeschiedenis van de Koninklijke Landmacht*, **1**(1) (1978).

—, *De Japanse Aanval op Nederlands-Indië* [The Japanese attack on the Netherlands-Indies], Volume I. Rotterdam: Ad. Donker, 1988 [deals with both East and West Timor in early 1942].

Oliveira, C. M. G. R. de, 'Dili: Panorama de uma Sociedade' [Dili: Panorama of a Society], *Boletim da Sociedade de Geografia de Lisboa*, **89**(1–3) (1971).

Onorato, W. T., and M. J., Valencia, 'International Cooperation for Petroleum Development: The Timor Gap Treaty', *Foreign Investment Law Journal* (International Centre for Settlement of Investment Disputes), **5**(1) (Spring 1990).

Orentlicher, D.F., *see* Asia Watch.

O'Shaughnessy, Hugh, 'Secret Killing of a Nation', *The Observer* (London), (7 April 1991).

—, 'Jakarta's Spider Web of Oppression', *The Observer* (London), (30 May 1993).

—, *East Timor. Getting Away with Murder?* London: British Coalition for East Timor, 1994.

Östtimor Information (Newsletter of the Swedish East Timor Committee). Stockholm: Östtimorkommittén [irregular].

Pardo, J., 'El Problema de Timor-Este' [The problem of East Timor], *Cuadernos de Debate Político* (Madrid: Iepala), **2**(1984).

Patji, A. R., 'Pasar dan Integrasi di Timor Timur' [The market and national integration in East Timor], *Masyarakat Indonesia*, **14**(3) (December 1987).

Paz é Possível em Timor Leste, A, *Droits et Libertés Religieuses au Timor Oriental.* Lisbon: A Paz é Possível em Timor Leste, 1985.

—, *The Church in East Timor.* Lisbon: A Paz é Possível em Timor Leste, May 1986.

—, *East Timor: Repression and Resistance, A Review of the 15th Year of Indonesian Occupation.* Lisbon: A Paz é Possível em Timor Leste, 1991.

—, *East Timor: The Santa Cruz Massacre /Timor Oriental: Massacre de Santa Cruz.* Lisbon: A Paz é Possível em Timor Leste, February 1992.

—, *East Timor After Santa Cruz: Indonesia and the International Order.* Lisbon: A Paz é Possível em Timor Leste, 1993.

Pélissier, R., 'A Propos de Quelques Livres Récents sur le Timor Oriental' [Regarding some recent books on East Timor], *Afrique et l'Asie Modernes*, **133** (1982) [reprinted in full in *Du Sahara à Timor: 700 Livres Analysés (1980–1990) sur l'Afrique et l'Insulinde ex-Ibériques* (1991), see below].

—, *Du Sahara à Timor: 700 Livres Analysés (1980–1990) sur l'Afrique et l'Insulinde ex-Ibériques* [From the Sahara to Timor: An analysis of 700 books (1980–1990) on Africa and the ex-Iberian Insulinde (Indonesian Archipelago)]. Orgeval, France: Pélissier, 1991.

Penberthy G., 'Bismarck's Ghost over Human Rights', *Time Australia*, **6**(48) (2 December 1991) [deals with the 12 November 1991 Dili Massacre and Australian-Indonesian relations].

Peters, G. W., *Indonesia Revival: Focus on Timor.* Grand Rapids: Zondervan, 1974. **A**

Picken, M., 'The Betrayed People', *New York Review of Books,* (4 December 1986).

Pilger, John, 'Britain's Dirty Secrets in Indonesia', *New Statesman & Society*, (11 February 1994).

—, 'East Timor: The Secret Slaughter', *The Guardian Weekend*, (12 February 1994).

—, 'On Her Majesty's Bloody Service', *New Statesman & Society*, (18 February 1994).

— (ed.), 'East Timor: The Silence and the Betrayal', *New Internationalist*, **253** (March 1994).

—, 'Suharto's Friends Deal with Death', *New Statesman & Society*, (4 March 1994).

—, 'Blood on the Hands of the Mates', *New Statesman & Society*, (11 March 1994).

— (ed.), 'East Timor: The Silence and the Betrayal', *New Internationalist*, **253** (March 1994) [collection of nine articles on Indonesia's occupation of East Timor and the international response by Carmel Budiardjo, James Dunn, Mark Curtis, Fatima Gusmão, and Max Lane].

—, 'A Voice that Shames those Silent on Timor', *New Statesman & Society*, (8 April 1994) [deals with Indonesian academic Dr George Aditjondro].

—, 'Journey to East Timor: The Land of the Dead', *The Nation*, **258**(16) (25 April 1994).

—, 'Inside the Ministry of Propaganda', *New Statesman and Society*, (29 April 1994) [deals with the British Foreign Office's denials of Indonesia's human rights abuses].

—, 'Suharto's List', *New Statesman & Society*, (29 April 1994).

—, 'True Brits, True to Mass Murderers', *New Statesman & Society*, (3 June 1994).

—, 'East Timor', *The Age* (Melbourne), (6 June 1994).

—, 'Bishop Belo Cries Out for Justice in East Timor', *The Age* (Melbourne), (15 July 1994).

—, 'Bishop Belo Accuses the West', *New Statesman & Society*, (15 July 1994).

—, *Distant Voices*. London: Vintage, 1994 [chapter 6 deals with East Timor].

—, 'How Suharto Faked the Truth', *New Statesman & Society*, (29 July 1994).

—, 'Deathly Silence of the Diplomats', *The Guardian*, (12 October 1994) [review of Amnesty International, *Indonesia & East Timor. Power and Impunity. Human Rights under the New Order.*, q.v.].

—, 'East Timor Rises Up', *New Statesman & Society*, (25 November 1994).

—, *see also* Retbøll, T.

Pinto Leite, *see* Leite, P. Pinto.

Pires, M.L., *Descolonização de Timor: Missão Impossível?* [Decolonization of Timor: Mission impossible?]. Lisbon: Círculo de Leitores/Publicações Dom Quixote, 1991. *See also* Portugal, Presidência do Conselho de Ministros (M.L. Pires).

Portugal, Presidência do Conselho de Ministros, (M. L. Pires), *Relatórios da Descolonização de Timor I: Relatório do Governor de Timor (período de 13 de Novembro de 1974 a 7 de Dezembro de 1975)* [Reports on the decolonization of Timor I: Report(s) of the Governor of Timor (for the period 13 December 1974 to 7 December 1975)]. Lisbon: Presidência do Conselho de Ministros, 1981. *See also* Pires, M.L.

—, (F.A. Riscado, P. Vicente, J. Goulão de Melo, C.S.C. Pecorelli), *Relatórios da Descolonização de Timor II: Relatório da Comissão de Análise e Esclarecimento do Processo de Descolonização de Timor* [Reports on the decolonization of Timor II: Report of the Commission for the Analysis and Clarification of the Process of Decolonization in Timor]. Lisbon: Presidência do Conselho de Ministros, 1981.

—, *Estado Maior das Forças Armadas, Relatório de Timor (1977)* [Armed Forces Headquarters, Report on Timor 1977]. Lisbon: Presidência do Conselho de Ministros, 1981.

Portugal, Parliament, *Report Presented by the Eventual Commission for the Following-Up of the Situation in East Timor.* Lisbon, 1986.

Prescott, J. R. V., 'Maritime Boundary Agreements: Australia–Indonesia and Australia–Solomon Islands', *Marine Policy Reports*. New York: Taylor & Francis, 1989.

—, H. J. Collier, and D. F. Prescott, *Frontiers of Asia and Southeast Asia.* Melbourne: Melbourne University Press, 1977.

Pro Mundi Vita, *East Timor,* Dossier No. 4. Brussels: Pro Mundi Vita, 1984.

Properjohn, T.J., 'The Attitude of the Indonesian Army to Indonesia's Three Overseas Campaigns', *Defence Force Journal* (Canberra), **48** (September–October 1984) [deals with West Irian, *Konfrontasi* with Malaysia, and East Timor].

'Punishing the Victims: Heavy Sentences for East Timorese Protestors', *Inside Indonesia,* **31** (June 1992).

Quinn, K.M., 'East Timor, Indonesia and US Policy', *US Department of State Dispatch,* **3**(11) (16 March 1992).

Radja Haba, L., *Tot Vrijheid Geroepen: Een Studie van de Christelijke Evangelische Kerk in Timor in Relatie tot haar Omgeving* [Called to Freedom: A study of the Christian evangelical church in Timor in relation to her environment]. published by the author, Oegstgeest: L. Radja Haba, 1975 [mainly deals with West Timor]. **A**

Ramos-Horta, *see* Horta, A. Ramos, *and* Horta, J. Ramos.

Ranck, S., 'Recent Rural–Urban Immigration to Dili, Portuguese Timor – A Focus on the Use of Household, Kinship and Social Networks', MA thesis, Macquarie University (Sydney), 1977.

Ranck, S., 'Timor – 1: No Changes Overnight', *New Guinea and Australia, the Pacific and South-East Asia,* **10**(1) (1975). *See also* Forsyth, W.D.

Raper, M., 'Timor: The Dragon and the Mouse', *Development News Digest* (Canberra), **17** (August 1976).

Reid, A., 'Report on a Visit to Dili', *Asian Studies Review,* **15**(2) (November 1991).

—, 'What Can We Do about East Timor?', *Uniya,* (Autumn 1992).

Relic, P.D., 'Take East Timor', *Independent School,* **53**(2) (Winter, 1994).

Renard-Clamagirand, B., *Marobo: Une Société Ema de Timor* [Marobo: An Ema society of Timor]. (Langues et Civilisations de l'Asie du Sud-est et du Monde Insulindien No.12). Paris: Société d'Études Linguistiques et Anthropologiques de France (SELAF), 1982. **A**. *See also* Clamagirand, B.

Republic of Indonesia, *see* Indonesia, Republic of.

Retbøll, T., 'East Timor and Indonesia', *Bulletin of Concerned Asian Scholars,* **15**(2) (April–June 1983).

— (ed.), *East Timor, Indonesia and the Western Democracies: A Collection of Documents,* IWGIA Document No. 40. Copenhagen: International Work Group for Indigenous Affairs, 1980.

— (ed.), *East Timor: The Struggle Continues,* IWGIA Document No. 50. Copenhagen: International Work Group for Indigenous Affairs, 1984.

—, 'The East Timor Conflict and Western Response', *Bulletin of Concerned Asian Scholars,* **19**(1) (January 1987).

— (ed.), 'Øst-Timor: Kan 200,000 Mennesker Bare Dø?' [East Timor: Can 200,000 people just simply die], *Kontakt* (Copenhagen), **3** (November 1994) [special number on East Timor with articles by Elaine Briére, Peter Carey, Noam Chomsky, Steve Cox, James Dunn, José Ramos-Horta, Matthew Jardine, António Barbedo de Magalhães, John Pilger, Michael Emin Salla, and Charles Scheiner].

Richardson, J.L., 'Problems of Australian Foreign Policy, January–June 1976', *Australian Journal of Politics and History,* **22** (December 1977).

Rigaud, F., 'East Timor and Western Sahara: A Comparative View', Paper presented at the CIIR/ICJ Conference on 'Indonesia's Occupation of East Timor: Legal Questions', London, 5–6 December 1992.

Robie, D., *Blood on Their Banner: Nationalist Struggles in the South Pacific.* Sydney: Pluto Press, 1989.

Robison, R., *Indonesia: The Rise of Capital*. Southeast Asia Publications Series (Canberra) No. 13. Sydney: Allen & Unwin for the Asian Studies Association of Australia, 1986 [reprinted by Zed Books (London) and Pluto Press (Sydney), 1991].

Rocha, C.V. da, *Timor: A Occupação Japonesa durante a Segunda Guerra Mundial* [Timor: The Japanese Occupation during the Second World War]. Lisbon: Sociedade Histórica da Independência de Portugal, 1994.

Rocha, N., *Timor Timur: 27a Província da Indonésia* [East Timor: 27th province of Indonesia]. Lisbon: Nova Nórdica, 1987.

Rodgers, P., 'Indonesia Disenchanted with Australia over Timor', *National Times* (Australia), (14–20 January 1979).

—, 'The Fate of Roger East', *National Times* (Australia), (14–20 October 1979).

—, 'Reporting the Horror on our Doorstep: How the Australian Media "Exposed" the Timor Tragedy', *New Journalist*, **34** (December 1979).

—, 'Timor Census Raises Doubts', *National Times* (Australia), (15–21 February 1981) [deals with the first official Indonesian census in East Timor].

Rodrigues, M. A. R., 'Da Campanha de 1726 às Pedras de Cailaco' [From the 1726 campaign to the stones of Cailaco], *Independência*, **5** (1987).

Roff, S. R., *Timor's Anschluss: Indonesian and Australian Policy in East Timor, 1974–76*. Lewiston, NY: The Edwin Mellen Press, 1992.

—, *East Timor: A Bibliography, 1970–1993*, Working Paper No. 148 of the Peace Research Centre, Research School of Pacific Studies (Australian National University). Canberra: Peace Research Centre, 1994.

Roger, M., *Timor Oriental, Hier la Colonisation Portugaise, Aujourd'hui la Résistance à l'Aggression Indonésienne* [East Timor, yesterday Portuguese colonialism, today resistance to Indonesian aggression]. Paris: Éditions L'Harmattan, 1976.

Rowland, I. (compiler), *Timor: Including the islands of Roti and Ndao*, World Bibliographical Series Vol. 142. Oxford: Clio Press, 1992.

Ryan, P, *Timor: A Traveller's Guide*. Darwin: Paul Ryan, 1993 [pp. 79–111 deal specifically with East Timor].

Saldanha, J.M. de Sousa, *Profil Ekonomi Regional Timor Timur*. Salatiga: Universitas Kristen Satya Wacana, 1988.

—, 'Perekonomian Timor Timur: Profil dan Prospek' [The East Timor Economy: Profile and Prospects], *Analisis CSIS*, **20**(2) (1991).

—, *Ekonomi Politik Pembangunan Timor Timur* (The Political Economy of Development in East Timor). Jakarta: Pustaka Sinar Harapan, 1994.

Salla, M.E., 'East Timor's Clandestine Resistance to Indonesian Integration', *Social Alternatives*, **13**(1) (April 1994).

—, *see also* Retbøll, T.

—, 'East Timor: The Struggle for Self-Determination', *Pacific Research*, **7**(2) (May 1994).

'The Santa Cruz Massacre: Eyewitness Accounts', *Inside Indonesia*, **29** (December 1991).

Santamaria, B.A., 'Australian Catholic Relief: The Truth about the Timor Story', *News Weekly* (24 February 1982). *See also* Scarrabelotti, G. below.

Santos, C., 'Victory in Timor', *Development News Digest* (Canberra), **15** (March 1976).

Scarrabelotti, G., 'Whitlam Accuses ACR [Australian Catholic Relief] and CCJP [Catholic Commission for Justice and Peace] over Timor Allegations', *Catholic Weekly*, (23 May 1982). *See also* Santamaria, B.A., above.

Scheiner, C., 'East Timor Update', *Bulletin of Concerned Asian Scholars*, **25**(1) (1993).

—, *see also* Retbøll, T.

Schiller, *see* Martin-Schiller, B.

Schirato, A., 'Disaster and Scandal: The Dili Massacre', *Antithesis* (Melbourne), **6**(1) (1992).

Schulte Nordholt, H. G., *The Political System of the Atoni of Timor*. The Hague: Martinus Nijhoff, 1971.

Scobbie, I., 'The East Timor Case: The Implications of Procedure for Litigation Strategy', *Oil and Gas Law and Taxation Review*, **273** (1991).

—, 'The Presence of an Absent Third: Procedural Aspects of the East Timor Case', paper presented at the CIIR/ICJ Conference on 'Indonesia's Occupation of East Timor: Legal Questions', London, 5–6 December 1992.

Scott, D., 'East Timor: The Case for Talks without Preconditions', *Australian Jewish Democrat*, **2**(4) (Autumn 1992).

—, *Ten Days in East Timor and the Case for Talks*. Fitzroy, Victoria: East Timor Talks Campaign, September 1994.

Scott-Findlay, J., and F.S. Smith, 'A Timor Experience in War and Civilian Trauma', *The Medical Journal of Australia*, **2** (17 July 1976).

'The Secret War in East Timor', *Inside Indonesia*, **14** (April 1988).

'Sejarah Misi di Timor Timur' [History of (Christian) missions in East Timor], *Majalah Hidup* (Jakarta), **30–31** (July 1988).

Sen, K, 'Bridge-Building – Using an Indonesian Design: Politics and Human Rights: Interview with Foreign Minister [Gareth] Evans', *Inside Indonesia*, **22** (March 1990).

Senate Standing Committee on Foreign Affairs and Defence, *see* Australia.

Shackleton, S., 'Whitlam and the Timor Debate: Truth Buried with the Bodies', *The Bulletin* (Sydney), 20 April 1982 [deals with the Australian Government cover-up over East Timor and the death of the five Western journalists at Balibo on 16 October 1975].

—, 'Planting a Tree in Balibo: A Study in Cross-Cultural Relations', *Island Magazine* (October 1990).

Sharp, N., 'West Irian, East Timor – Papua New Guinea...?', *Arena* (Melbourne), **61** (1982).

Shearer, I.A., 'Australia and the International Court of Justice', *Australian Law Journal*, **67**(4) (April 1993) [deals *inter alia* with the 'Timor Gap' case between Portugal and Australia at the ICJ].

Shenon, Philip, 'Dili Journal', *New York Times* (International edition), 24 April 1993.

Sherlock, K.P. (compiler), *Gazeteer of East Timor*. Darwin, 1977 [photocopies] [based on the 1:500,000 map 'Província de Timor' published by JIU, Lisbon, in the 1960s]. **A**

—, *A Bibliography of Timor: Including East (Formerly Portuguese) Timor, West (Formerly Dutch) Timor and the Island of Roti*. Canberra: Research School of Pacific Studies, Australian National University, 1980.

—, 'The Timor Collection', Darwin, 1982 [typescript] [list of holdings on East Timor]. **A**

—, *East Timor: Liurais and Chefes de Suco; Indigenous Authorities in 1952*. Darwin: Kevin Sherlock, 1983.

—, 'Timor During World Wars I and II: Some Notes on Sources', *Kabar Seberang*, **19–20** (1988).

Shimada, I., *Higeki-No-Shima – Higashi Chimóru. Sonoshizen To Hitobito* [Island of tragedy – East Timor. Its nature and people]. Tokyo: Tsukiji Shokan Co., 1990.

Sidell, S., 'The United States and Genocide in East Timor', *Journal of Contemporary Asia* (Manila), **11**(1) (1981).

Siebeck, C.A., 'Die Annexion Portugiesisch-Timors durch Indonesien' [The annexation of Portuguese Timor by Indonesia], *Internationales Asienforum*, **9**(1–2) (1978).

Simpson, G., 'Judging the East Timor Dispute: Self-Determination at the International Court of Justice', *Hastings International and Comparative Law Review*, **17**(2) (Winter 1994).

Smart, A., 'The Timor Gap Zone of Co-operation Treaty', in D. Anderson (ed.), *Australia and Indonesia: A Partnership in the Making*. Sydney: Pacific Security Research Institute, 1991 [originally published in *The APEA Australian Petroleum Exploration Association Journal* [1990]).

Soboleva, E.S., *Etnicheskiy Sostav Portugalskogo Timora XVI–XX vv. Istoriko-Etnograficheskoe Issledovanie* [The ethnic composition of Portuguese Timor from the 16th to the 20th century. An historical-ethnographic study]. Moscow Akademiya Nauk SSSR (Moscow: USSR Academy of Sciences), 1991.

Soekanto (comp.), *Integrasi: Kebulatan Tekad Rakyat Timor Timur* [Integration: The determined will of the people of East Timor]. Jakarta: Yayasan Parikesit, 1976.

Soesastro, M. Hadi, 'The Economy of East Timor: To Open or Not to Open', *Indonesian Quarterly* (Jakarta), **16**(3) (1988).

—, 'East Timor: Questions of Economic Viability', in Hal Hill (ed.), *Unity and Diversity: Regional Economic Development in Indonesia Since 1970*. Singapore: Oxford University Press, 1989.

—, *Ekonomi Timor Timur*. Jakarta: Centre for Strategic and International Studies, 1989.

—, 'Pembangunan Ekonomi Timor Timur: Tantangan bagi Penciptaan Lapangan Kerja dan Peningkatan Pendapatan Penduduk' [The development of East Timor's economy: The challenges of job creation and raising the income levels of the (local) population], *Analisis CSIS*, **21**(5) (1992).

Spence, Bill, 'East Timor: The Genocide Next Door', *Reconstruction*, **1** (March 1994).

Stahl, Max (pseud.), 'Massacre among the Graves', *Independent on Sunday*, (17 November 1991).

—, 'Procession of Death', *Observer Magazine*, (23 February 1992).

—, 'Indonesians fed "Death Pills" to Wounded', *Sunday Times*, (13 February 1994).

—, 'Timor-Oriental, Défaite Politique pour Djakarta: Une Armée contre un Peuple Insoumis', *Monde Diplomatique*, **41**(26) (April 1994).

Stepan, S., *Credibility Gap: Australia and [The] Timor Gap Treaty*, ACFOA Development Dossier No. 28. Canberra: Australian Council for Overseas Aid, 1990.

—, and D. Wilde, 'The Treaty between Australia and the Republic of Indonesia on the Zone of Cooperation in an Area between the Indonesian Province of East Timor and Northern Australia', *Melanesian Law Journal*, **18** (1990).

—, 'Portugal's Action in the International Court of Justice Against Australia Concerning the Timor Gap Treaty', *Melbourne University Law Review*, **18**(4) (December 1992).

Stichting Door de Eeuwen Trouw, *Bericht van Timor: De Strijd Gaat door...* [News from Timor: The struggle continues....], publication of the Secretariat of the Stichting Door de Eeuwen Trouw. Groningen: Stichtig Door de Eeuwen Trouw, 1977. **A**

Suara Rakyat Maubere [The voice of the Maubere (East Timorese) people], ed. Raziku Amin. Yogyakarta, 1994– [Indonesian-language newsletter on East Timor].

Suara Timor Timur [The voice of East Timor], ed. Irawan Saptono, pub. Salvador Ximenes Soares, Dili, Feb. 1993– [East Timor's only Indonesian-language daily newspaper with an estimated circulation 3,500 in 1994].

Suparlan, P., 'Kebudayaan Timor' [Timorese culture], in Koentjaraningrat (ed.), *Manusia dan Kebudayaan di Indonesia* [People and culture in Indonesia]. Jakarta: Djambatan, 1971 [mainly about West Timor].

—, 'Orang Timor Timur' [The people of East Timor], *Berita Antropologi*, **11**(36) (1980).

Suprihanto, R.B., *Tatabahasa Kelas Kata Bahasa Tetum* [Grammar and linguistic classification of the Tetum language]. n.p.: privately printed, 1992.

Suter, K. D., 'The Conquest of East Timor', *Contemporary Review* (London/New York), **232**(1346) (March 1978).

—, 'International Law and East Timor', *Dyason House Papers*, **5**(2) (December 1978).

—, 'Oil in Troubled Waters: The Implications of the Timor Gap Agreement', *Inside Indonesia*. (17 December 1988) [later reprinted in *Maritime Studies*, **46** (May-June 1989)].

—, *West Irian, East Timor and Indonesia*, Minority Rights Group Report No. 42. London: Minority Rights Group, 1979 [2nd edn published under the title, *East Timor and West Irian*, 1982].

—, 'Australia All at Sea Over East Timor', *National Outlook*, **6**(8) (August 1984).

—, 'East Timor: The International Dimension', *Unity* (Canberra), **26** (May 1992).

—, 'East Timor: A War with No Winners', *Current Affairs Bulletin*, **69**(7) (December 1992).

—, 'Timor Gap Treaty: The Continuing Controversy', *Marine Policy*, **7**(4) (July 1993).

Suwondo, Ketut, *Kerangka Acuan Perencanaan Program Pengembangan Kesejahteraan Masyarakat Pulau Atauro Timor Timur, Suatu Hasil Studi Penjajagan tentang Pengembangan Kesejahteraan Masyarakat Pulau Atauro* [Frame of reference for the design of a programme for the welfare development of the people of the island of Atauro, East Timor: Report of a preliminary assessment study concerning the welfare development of the people of the island of Atauro]. Salatiga: Lembaga Pengabdian Masyarakat, Universitas Kristen Satya Wacana, 1990.

Sword, K., 'Treading Carefully in East Timor', *Arena* (Melbourne), **93** (Summer 1990).

— (ed.), 'The Face of a Drowning Man', *New Internationalist* (Oxford), (April 1992).

—, and P. Walsh, *'Opening Up': Travellers' Impressions of East Timor, 1989-1991*, Melbourne: Australia East Timor Association, 1991.

Sylvan, F., (ill. by A. P. Domingues), *Cantolenda Maubere. Hananuknanoik Maubere. The Legends of the Mauberes.* Lisbon: Fundação Austronésia Borja da Costa, 1988 [trilingual publication in Portuguese, Tetum and English].

—, *A Voz Fagueira de Oan Timor. Poesia* [The gentle voice of an Oan Timor (Son of Timor). Poetry]. Lisbon: Edições Colibri, 1993.

Tanter, R., 'The Military Situation in East Timor', *Pacific Research Studies*, **8**(2) (January–February 1977).

TAPOL (The British Campaign for the Defence of Political Prisoners and Human Rights in Indonesia; post-1986, The Indonesia Human Rights Campaign), *Tapol Bulletin*. London: TAPOL, 1973– [bimonthly newsletter].

TAPOL (The Indonesia Human Rights Campaign), *Exchange of Messages with Fretilin* [Commander Xanana Gusmão with Lord Avebury, Chair of the Parliamentary Human Rights Group, and Carmel Budiardjo, TAPOL Organising Secretary], TAPOL Occasional Report No. 1. London: TAPOL, 1985.

—, *UDT–Fretilin Joint Statement*, TAPOL Occasional Report No. 2. London: TAPOL, 1986.

—, *Statement on East Timor to the UN Committee of 24, August 1986*, TAPOL Occasional Report No. 4. London: TAPOL, 1986.

—, *The 1987 Indonesian Election in East Timor* [an analysis written by TAPOL], TAPOL Occasional Report No. 5. London: TAPOL, 1987.

—, *[TAPOL] Statement on East Timor to the UN Committee of 24, August 1987*, TAPOL Occasional Report No. 6. London: TAPOL, 1987.

—, *[TAPOL] Statement on East Timor to the UN Committee of 24, August 1988*, TAPOL Occasional Report No. 9. London: TAPOL, 1988.

—, *East Timor: Statement to the UN Decolonisation Committee, New York, August 1989*, TAPOL Occasional Report No. 11. London: TAPOL, 1989.

—, *TAPOL Statement to the UN Decolonisation Committee, August 1990*, TAPOL Occasional Report No. 13. London: TAPOL, 1990.

—, *East Timor: United Nations Resolutions, 1975–1982*, TAPOL Occasional Report No. 14. London: TAPOL, 1991.

—, *TAPOL Statement to the UN Decolonisation Committee, August 1991*, TAPOL Occasional Report No. 15. London: TAPOL, 1991.

—, *The Killing Fields of East Timor: Comment and Analysis in the British Press*, [Nov/Dec 1991], TAPOL Occasional Report No. 17. London: TAPOL, 1991.

—, *TAPOL Statement to the UN Decolonisation Committee, July 1992*, TAPOL Occasional Report No. 19. London: TAPOL, 1992.

—, *State of War: The Diary of Ines Serra Lopes in East Timor, Feb 1993*, TAPOL Occasional Report No. 21. London: TAPOL, 1993.

—, *TAPOL Statement to the UN Decolonisation Committee, July 1993*, TAPOL Occasional Report No. 22. London: TAPOL, 1993.

—, *A Report on the Condition of East Timorese Political Prisoners, October 1993*, TAPOL Occasional Report No. 23. London: TAPOL, 1993.

Taylor, J.G., *The Indonesian Occupation of East Timor 1974–1989: A Chronology*. London: Catholic Institute for International Relations with the Refugee Studies Programme, Oxford University, 1990.

—, *Indonesia's Forgotten War: The Hidden History of East Timor*. London: Zed Books and Sydney: Pluto Press, 1991.

—, 'The Emergence of a Nationalist Movement in East Timor', in R.H. Barnes, A. Gray and B. Kingsbury (eds.), *Indigenous Peoples of Asia*, Association of Asian Studies, Monograph No. 48. Ann Arbor: University of Michigan, 1994.

Telkamp, G. J., 'The Economic Structure of an Outpost in the Outer Islands in the Indonesian Archipelago: Portuguese Timor, 1850–1975', in F. van Anrooij *et al.* (eds), *Between People and Statistics: Essays on Modern Indonesian History Presented to P. Creutzberg*. The Hague: Martinus Nijhoff, 1979.

Thatcher, P., 'The Timor-born in Exile in Australia', MA thesis, Department of Anthropology and Sociology, Monash University (Clayton), 1992.

Thomaz, L. F. F. R., 'Timor: Notas Histórico-Linguísticas' [Timor: Historico-linguistic notes], *Portugaliae Historica* (Lisbon), 2 (1974).

—, 'O Problema Económico de Timor' [The economic problem of Timor], *Revista Militar* (Lisbon), 26(8–9) (August–September 1974).

—, *O Problema Político de Timor* [The political problem of Timor]. Braga, Portugal: Editora Pax, 1975.

—, 'O Afluxo ao Meio Urbano no Timor Português' [The flow to the urban environment in Portuguese Timor], *Revista da Faculdade de Letras* (Lisbon), Série IV, 1 (1976–7).

—, *Timor, Autópsia de Uma Tragédia* [Timor, autopsy of a tragedy]. Lisbon: DIG/Livro, 1977.

—, 'The Formation of Tetum-Praça, Vehicular Language of East Timor', in N. Phillips and K. Anwar (eds), *Papers on Indonesian Languages and Literatures, Cahiers d'Archipel* (Paris), 13 (1981).

Thoyib, M. (ed.), *Khasanah Budaya Timor Timur* [Characteristics of East Timor culture]. Jakarta: Taman Mini Indonesia Indah, 1985. A

Tiffen, R., 'Process and Picture: East Timor', in *The News from Southeast Asia: The Sociology of Newsmaking*. Singapore: Institute of Southeast Asian Studies, 1978.

'The Timor Gap Treaty', *Harvard International Law Journal*, 32(2) (Spring 1991).

Timor Information Service. Melbourne: Timor Information Service, 1975-83. *See also* Waddingham, J.

Timor Informations. Paris: Association de Solidarité avec Timor, 1975–present [irregular newsletter].

Timor Newsletter. Lisbon: 1980–2 (monthly), 1982–4 (bi-monthly).

Todd, H., 'Death in East Timor', *Asian Wall Street Journal*, (25 November 1991), [reprinted as 'A Son's Death in East Timor', *The Wall Street Journal*, (3 December 1991)].

Tolmachev, N.A., 'Rol'etnisekogo Faktora v Obsuzhdenii Problemy Zapadnogo Iriana in Vostochnogo Timora v OON' [The role of the ethnic factor in the discussion of the problems of West Irian (and) East Timor at the UN], *Istoricheskaya Dinamika Rasavoii Etnicheskoi Differentsiatsii Naseleniia Azii* [The historical dynamic of the racial-ethnic differentiation of the population of Asia]. Moskva [Moscow]: Nauka [Publishing House], 1987. *See also* Iugo-Vostochnaya.

Tolomundu, Muchlis Dj. 'Kami Ingin Lebih Bebas. Uskup Belo, Integrasi, Insiden 12 November dan ABRI' [We want more freedom. Bishop Belo, Integration, the 12 November (1991) Incident and ABRI (Indonesian Armed Forces)], *Matra* (August 1992) [partially published in English translation as 'Interview with Bishop Belo of Dili', *Inside Indonesia*, 32 (December 1992)].

Toohey, B., 'Timor – Cat Among the Pigeons', *Pacific Defence Reporter*, 2(1) (March 1975).

Tornquist, O., and H. Amahorseja, *Öst-Timor: Det Glomda Kriget* [East Timor: The Forgotten War]. Stockholm: Östtimor-kommittén, 1981.

Traill, J., and K. Rivett, 'A Bid for Peace in East Timor', *Quadrant* 27 (April 1983).

Traube, E. G., 'Ritual Exchange Among the Mambai of East Timor: Gifts of Life and Death', PhD thesis, Harvard University, 1977.

—, 'Affines and the Dead: Mambai Rituals of Alliance', *Bijdragen tot de Taal-, Land- en Volkenkunde*, 136(1) (1980).

—, 'Mambai Rituals of Black and White', in J. J. Fox (ed.), *The Flow of Life: Essays on Eastern Indonesia*. Cambridge, MA: Harvard University Press, 1980.

—, 'Cultural Notes on East Timor', New York, 1984 [manuscript].

—, *Cosmology and Social Life: Ritual Exchange Among the Mambai of East Timor*. Chicago: University of Chicago Press, 1986.

—, 'Obligations to the Source: Complementarity and Hierarchy in an Eastern Indonesian Society', in D. Maybury-Lewis and U. Almagor (eds.), *The Attraction of Opposites: Thought and Society in the Dualistic Mode*. Ann Arbor: University of Michigan Press, 1989.

'Travelling in East Timor with Eyes and Ears Open', *Inside Indonesia*, 20 (October 1989).

Tully, W., 'Whitlam, Timor and Indonesia's Coup: An Apologist for Aggression', *Southern Cross*, 46 (August 1975).

—, 'A Further Contribution to a Bibliography on East Timor: A Multi-Media Survey, 1975–78', *Southeast Asian Research Materials Group Newsletter*, 11 (October 1978).

—, 'The Timor Connection: Ford to Reagan via the Ombai-Wetar Straits', *Bowyang* (Canberra), 8 (1983).

Turner, M., *Telling. East Timor: Personal Testimonies, 1942–1992*. Kensington: New South Wales University Press, 1992.

Twomey, P. D., 'Australia, the United States and the East Timor Controversy: A Thesis in Political Science', MA thesis, Pennsylvania State University, May 1984.

United Nations, Department of Political Affairs, Trusteeship and Decolonization, *East Timor*, Decolonization No. 7. New York: United Nations, 1976.

United States, House of Representatives, *Human Rights in East Timor and the Question of the Use of US Equipment by the Indonesian Armed Forces* (Hearing before the Subcommittees on International Organization and on Asian and Pacific Affairs of the Committee on International Relations). Washington, DC: House of Representatives, Ninety-fifth Congress, First Session: US Government Printing Office, 23 March 1977.

—, *Human Rights in East Timor* (Hearings before the Subcommittees on International Organization and on Asian and Pacific Affairs of the Committee on International Relations). Washington, DC: House of Representatives, 95th Congress, First Session: US Government Printing Office, 28 June and 19 July 1977.

—, *Famine Relief for East Timor* (Hearing before the Subcommittees on International Organization and on Asian and Pacific Affairs of the Committee on International Relations). Washington, DC: House of Representatives, 96th Congress, First Session: US Government Printing Office, 4 December 1979.

—, *Recent Developments in East Timor* (Hearing before the Subcommittee on Asian and Pacific Affairs of the Committee on Foreign Affairs). Washington, DC: House of Representatives, 97th Congress, Second Session: US Government Printing Office, 14 September 1982.

United States, Senate, *Crisis in East Timor and U.S. Policy toward Indonesia* (Hearings before the Senate Committee on Foreign Relations). Washington, DC: United States Senate, 102nd Congress, Second Session: US Government Printing Office, 27 February and 6 March 1992.

Uniting Church (Australia), *The Uniting Church and East Timor*. Melbourne: Uniting Church in Australia, Social Responsibility and Justice Committee, 1987.

—, *The Church and East Timor*. Melbourne: Uniting Church in Australia, Social Responsibility and Justice Committee, 1988.

Universitas Kristen Indonesia, *Propinsi Timor Timur, Menyongsong Masa Depan: Rekaman Seminar Pembangunan Timor Timur* (The province of East Timor, preparing for the future: record of a seminar on the development of East Timor). Jakarta: Universitas Kristen Indonesia, 1990.

Universitas Kristen Satya Wacana, *Usulan Tindak Lanjut Kerjasama Universitas Kristen Satya Wacana dan Pemerintah Daerah Propinsi Timor Timur* (Proposition for the continuation of the cooperation between Satya Wacana Christian University [Salatiga] and the regional government of the province of East Timor). Salatiga: Universitas Kristen Satya Wacana, 1987.

University of New South Wales, Faculty of Law, *Legal Issues Arising from the East Timor Conflict, 20 & 21 March 1992*. Kensington, NSW: University of New South Wales, 1992.

Usman, A., 'The Timor Gap in the Delimitation of the Continental Shelf Boundary between Indonesia and Australia', *Indonesian Quarterly*, **14**(3) (July 1986).

Utrecht, E., *United States of Indonesia? The Pentagon and the Generals*. Greensborough, Victoria: Sharp, 1976.

Valencia, M., *Southeast Asian Seas: Oil Under Troubled Waters. Hydrocarbon Potential, Jurisdictional Issues, and International Relations*. Singapore and New York: Oxford University Press, 1985.

Van Atta, D., and Toohey, B., 'The Timor Papers', *National Times* (Australia), (30 May–5 June and 6–13 June 1982). [reprinted in B. Toohey and M. Wilkinson (eds), *The Book of Leaks*, London: Angus & Robertson, 1987].

Vasconcellos, J., *Timor: Imperativo de Consciência* (Timor: The imperative of conscience). Lisbon: Produce, 1992.

Vikør, L.R., 'Den Glomde Krigen på Aust-Timor' (The Forgotten War in East Timor), *Syn og Segn* (Oslo), **84**(10) (1978).

—, *Aust-Timor-En Nasjou under Jerngrep.* (East Timor. A nation under the jackboot). Oslo: Cappelens, Miniserie, 1994.

Villiers, J., 'As Derradeiras do Mundo: The Dominican Missions and the Sandalwood Trade in the Lesser Sunda Islands in the Sixteenth and Seventeenth Centuries', in *II. Seminário Internacional de História Indo-Portuguesa*. Lisbon, 1985, pp.573–86.

—,'The Vanishing Sandalwood of Portuguese Timor', *Itinerario* (Leiden), **18**(2) (1994), pp.86–96.

Viviani, N., 'Australians and the East Timor Issue', *Australian Outlook* (Canberra), **30**(2) (August 1976).

—, 'Australians and the East Timor Issue: II', *Australian Outlook* (Canberra), **32**(3) (December 1978).

Waddingham, J., 'Timor: Indonesian Power over Humanitarian Aid', *Arena* (Melbourne), **53** (1979).

—, 'Resistance in Timor: Through the "Fence of Legs" ', *Arena* (Melbourne), **59** (1981).

—, 'East Timor: The Questions and the Cover-Up', *Arena* (Melbourne), **61** (1982).

—, 'East Timor: Offending the Junta', *Arena* (Melbourne), **67** (1984).

— (ed.), *Timor Information Service*. Melbourne: November 1975-1983 [regular newsletter].

—, P. Walsh, and B. Armstrong, *Het International Rode Kruis in Oost Timor* (The International [Committee of the] Red Cross in East Timor). Amsterdam: Komitee Indonesie, 1979. **A**

Walsh, P., 'Indonesia in Timor: Cruel People Devoid of Love and Morality', *Arena* (Melbourne), **57** (1981).

—, 'Australia's Support for Indonesia's Takeover of East Timor', Testimony before the Permanent Peoples' Tribunal, Lisbon, 1981.

—, 'Church May Hold the Key to Timor's Future', *National Outlook*, (January 1982).

—, 'Timor Report: Whitlam and Hastings Observed', *Arena* (Melbourne), **60** (1982) [report on a visit to East Timor in March 1982].

—, 'Timor People Support the Church in its Opposition to Indonesian Takeover', *National Outlook*, (November 1982).

—, 'Fretilin: The Struggle Continues', *Arena* (Melbourne), **65** (1983).

—, 'ALP Conference: Requiem for Timor?', *Inside Indonesia*, **3** (October 1984).

—, 'The Pope Rides the Indonesian Rapids without Rocking the Boat', *National Outlook*, **11**(10) (January 1990).

—, 'Timor Gap: Oil Poured on Bloodied Waters', *Arena* (Melbourne), **90** (Autumn 1990).

—, 'Peace in East Timor: A Long Shot', *Disarming Times*, **17**(1) (February 1992) [also published under a slightly different title in *Arena* (Sydney), **98** (1992)].

Weatherbee, D.E., *The Situation in East Timor*. Columbia: University of South Carolina, Institute of International Studies, Occasional Paper No. 1, 1980.

—, 'The Indonesianization of East Timor', *Contemporary Southeast Asia* (Institute of Southeast Asian Studies, University of Singapore), **3**(1) (June 1981).

Webb, P., *The Church in the Sandalwood Islands, 1960-1980*. Townsville: James Cook University of North Queensland, 1980 [mainly deals with West Timor].

—, *Palms and the Cross: Socio-Economic Development in Nusatenggara*, Townsville, Centre for Southeast Asian Studies, James Cook University of North Queensland, 1986 [some references to pre-1975 East Timor].

Webster, D., 'And What is Stopping the U.N.?', *Peace Magazine*, **8**(3) (May/June 1992).

Wheeldon, J., 'East Timor: Foreign Affairs', *Quadrant* (Sydney), **27** (May 1983).

—, 'The "Finlandisation" of Australia and the Occupation of East Timor', *Quadrant* (Sydney), **28**(9) (September 1984).

White, K., 'Varied Tensions are Growing in Timor', *Northern Territory News*, (21 January 1974).

Whitlam, E. G., 'Australia, Indonesia and Europe's Empires', *Australian Outlook* (Canberra), **34**(1) (April 1980).

—, 'Indonesia and Australia: Political Aspects', in J. A. C. Mackie (ed.), *Indonesia: The Making of a Nation*. Canberra: Australian National University, Research School of Pacific Studies, 1980.

—, 'Gough Whitlam: The Truth about Timor', *The Bulletin*, (30 March 1982).

—, *The Whitlam Government 1972–1975*. Ringwood, Victoria: Viking Penguin, 1985 [chap. 8 deals with Indonesia and East Timor].

Wilheim, E., 'Australia-Indonesia Sea-Bed Boundary Negotiations: Proposals for a Joint Development Zone in the "Timor Gap" ', *Natural Resources Journal*, **29**(3) (1989).

Wilson, A.K., *Travelling Through Timor*. Mareeba (Queensland): Pinevale Publications, 1992 [pp.1-37 refer to East Timor].

'Winner Takes All: Indonesianising East Timor's Land-Title System', *Inside Indonesia*, **26** (March 1991).

Wong, L. and B. Blaskett, 'Towards [a] Resolution of Internal Conflict in Indonesia: West Papua, East Timor and the International Order', *Interdisciplinary Peace Research*, **4**(1) (May–June 1992).

Woods, T., 'Propaganda: Press, Policy and East Timor. The Australian Press and its Reporting of Australian Policy regarding East Timor', MA thesis, University of Canberra, 1992.

Woolcott, R., 'Myths and Realities in our Approach to Indonesia', *Sydney Papers*, **4**(3) (Winter 1992) [publication of an address to the Sydney Institute, 26 May 1992].

Wray, Christopher C. H., *Timor 1942: Australian Commandos at War with the Japanese*. Melbourne: Century Hutchison Australia, 1987 [paperback edition, Mandarin Australia (Port Melbourne), 1990].

Yen, A., 'Under the Cover of Darkness: The East Timor Plight in the Sub-Commission', SIT, Geneva, 13 May 1991, International Service for Human Rights, Geneva.

Young, P. L., 'The Timor Issue in Australia-Indonesia-Papua New Guinea Relations', *Asian Defence Journal* (Kuala Lumpur), **10**(83) (October 1983).

Zable, A., 'East Timor: The People and the Struggle', *Arena* (Melbourne), **50** (1978).

East Timor: Contemporary History A Chronology of the Main Events since 1974

John G. Taylor

1974

Apr 25 The Armed Forces Movement (AFM) coup in Lisbon leads to the overthrow of the Caetano regime.

May 5 The governor of East Timor issues a proclamation for the establishing of political parties.

May 11 The *União Democrática Timorense* (Timorese Democratic Union, UDT) is founded.

May 12 The *Associação Social Democrata Timorense* (Association of Timorese Social Democrats, ASDT) is formed.

May 27 The *Associação Popular Democrática Timorense* (Timorese Popular Democratic Association, Apodeti) is formed.

Jun 17 Following a meeting in Jakarta between Indonesia's Foreign Minister, Adam Malik, and ASDT's representative, Jose Ramos-Horta, Malik writes to Horta assuring him that Indonesia supports independence for East Timor.

Sep 6 Australian Prime Minister Gough Whitlam meets President Suharto in Wonosobo, a resort town in Central Java, and agrees that the eventual integration of East Timor into the Indonesian Republic is inevitable.

Sept 12 ASDT becomes the *Frente Revolucionária de Timor-Leste Independente* (Fretilin).

Oct 14 General Ali Murtopo, head of the Indonesian Government's Special Operations Executive (Operasi Khusus, Opsus), visits Lisbon and has secret talks with leaders of the AFM. *Operasi*

Komodo, the Indonesian Government's plan to annex East Timor, is launched the same day.

Nov 25 Colonel Lemos Pires is appointed as the new governor of East Timor.

Dec Fretilin begins its anti-illiteracy programmes and starts to set up co-operatives.

1975

Jan 20 A coalition is formed between the UDT and Fretilin parties.

Jan 31 The Portuguese Government's National Council for Decolonization rejects the idea of internationalizing the East Timor issue.

Feb 18 The Indonesian military carries out a simulated invasion of East Timor in Lampung, South Sumatra.

Mar Elections begin in East Timor, supervised by the Decolonization Committee of the Portuguese parliament.

May 26 The UDT withdraws from its coalition arrangement with Fretilin.

Jun 26 Two days of talks begin in Macao between the Portuguese Government and East Timor's political parties. The Indonesian Government is allowed to send observers to the talks. For this reason, Fretilin refuses to attend.

Jul 1 Constitutional Law 7/75 is passed in Lisbon, setting October 1976 as the date for popular elections for a General Assembly to determine East Timor's future. Colonial control is set to end in October 1978.

Jul 29 The results of the elections for local

councils are announced: Fretilin candidates gain 55 per cent of the popular vote.

Aug 11 After a meeting in Jakarta with Indonesia's leading generals, the UDT leadership launches a coup in Dili to wrest power from the Portuguese and halt the growing popularity of Fretilin.

Aug 27 The Portuguese governor and administration withdraw from Dili to the island of Atauro offshore.

Sep 24 UDT forces retreat into West (Indonesian) Timor, leaving Fretilin in control of East Timor.

Oct 6 Indonesian troops attack Batugadé, a border town in East Timor.

Oct 16 Two Australian, one New Zealand and two British journalists are killed by Indonesian troops in the East Timorese border village of Balibo.

Nov 28 Fretilin declares East Timor an independent state.

Nov 29 In the presence of leaders of the UDT and Apodeti in Kupang, West (Indonesian) Timor, Adam Malik signs a declaration formally integrating East Timor into Indonesia.

Dec 7 Indonesian forces invade East Timor.

Dec 22 The UN Security Council calls on Indonesia to withdraw its armed forces from East Timor.

Dec 25 Indonesia is estimated by Australian intelligence to be deploying 15-20,000 troops in East Timor.

1976

Jan 13 Following its occupation of Dili, Baucau and the border region, the Indonesian military establishes a 'Provisional Government' formed from Apodeti and UDT members. This body invites Indonesia to proclaim its sovereignty over East Timor.

Feb 14 Lopes da Cruz, President of the Provisional Government and former UDT leader, claims that 60,000 East Timorese have been killed since the Indonesian invasion.

Apr 3 A revolt by UDT members in Dili is suppressed by the Indonesian military.

Apr 22 The UN Security Council again calls on Indonesia to withdraw. It receives a report from a special envoy of the UN Secretary-General, who visited

Indonesian-held areas in February. The envoy, Winspeare Guicciardi, states that he is unable to produce a full report of the situation inside East Timor because the Indonesian military prevented him from contacting or travelling to Fretilin-held areas.

May 15 Fretilin holds a two-week national conference in the central region, to co-ordinate the campaign of resistance to the invasion.

May 31 An East Timorese 'Popular Assembly' is convened by the Indonesian military. It approves a petition, addressed to President Suharto, calling for full integration into Indonesia.

Jul 12 First reports are received of resettlement camps being set up in East Timor.

Jul 17 President Suharto signs a bill integrating East Timor into Indonesia.

Sep 29 The Australian Government confiscates a transmitter used to receive messages from East Timor.

Nov 19 Indonesian relief workers visit East Timor and report that 100,000 people have been killed since the invasion.

Nov 19 The UN General Assembly rejects Indonesia's annexation of East Timor, and calls for an act of self-determination to be held in the territory. (The voting is recorded as 75 in favour, 20 against, with 52 abstentions.)

1977

Feb 2 First reports are received of American Bronco OV-10 jets being used in East Timor.

Mar 13 US congressional hearings on East Timor commence in Washington. Former Australian Consul to East Timor, James Dunn, provides details of Indonesian atrocities in East Timor in the months following the invasion, on the basis of interviews he conducted with East Timorese refugees in Lisbon.

Mar 17 Lt-General Howard Fisk of the US air force testifies to the congressional hearings that US military equipment was used in the invasion of East Timor.

May 7 Fretilin forces report that they control just over 80 per cent of the territory. Radio broadcasts from Fretilin areas describe food production and distribution, the use of traditional medicines and the conduct of anti-illiteracy campaigns.

Sep 5 Fretilin forces report heavy bombing raids on Bobonaro and a long military engagement with the Indonesian army in Quelicai. The bombing raids mark the beginning of the Indonesian encirclement and annihilation campaign of 1977-8.

Sep 7 The President of Fretilin, Xavier do Amaral, is arrested by the Central Committee of Fretilin, allegedly for opening negotiations with the Indonesian military. Nicolão Lobato subsequently is elected president in early November.

Sep 23 First reports are received of East Timorese being imprisoned without trial on the island of Atauro, north of Dili.

Nov 28 The UN General Assembly rejects integration and calls for an act of self-determination to be held in East Timor. (The voting record is 67 in favour, 26 against, with 47 abstentions.)

1978

Jan 20 The Australian Government gives *de facto* recognition to Indonesia's occupation of East Timor.

Apr 4 The British Aerospace Company signs a contract with the Indonesian Government to supply eight Hawk ground-attack aircraft to the Indonesian air force. These planes are ideally suited for use against ground forces in difficult terrain.

Apr 6 Lt-General Andi Mohammad Jusuf is appointed Commander in Chief of the Indonesian armed forces. He states that a resolution of the war in East Timor is one of his priorities.

May 12 Letters received by East Timorese refugees in Lisbon provide evidence of the first campaigns of enforced sterilization organized by the Indonesian military.

May A special co-ordinating group for East Timor is established by the Ministry of Defence. It is chaired by Brigadier-General Benny Murdani.

Jul 18 President Suharto pays a brief visit to the towns of Dili and Maliana.

Aug 4 The US Government sells 16 A4E Skyhawk counter-insurgency bombers to the Indonesian air force.

Aug 30 Former Fretilin president Xavier do Amaral is captured by Indonesian troops.

Sep 7 Ambassadors from several countries visit Dili, Baucau, Remexio, and Maliana, to assess food shortages and medical supplies. They are shocked by the extent of malnutrition.

Nov 20 The UN General Assembly calls for the withdrawal of Indonesian troops and for the right of self-determination to be exercised in East Timor (voting record: 59 in favour, 30 against, with 46 abstentions).

Dec 12 Fretilin's Radio Maubere ceases transmitting.

Dec 31 Fretilin's President, Nicolão Lobato, is shot and killed by Indonesian troops after a six-hour gun-battle on Mt. Maubisse.

1979

Apr 2 The ICRC concludes that 'tens of thousands of people displaced by military operations are facing starvation unless aid is brought to them rapidly' (cited in *East Timor News,* Sydney, **6** (12), November 1979).

Oct 19 The ICRC begins a relief programme in East Timor.

Nov 2 Peter Rodgers, Jakarta correspondent of the *Sydney Morning Herald* publishes photographs taken in East Timor. They reveal that malnutrition is widespread throughout the territory.

Nov 12 In London, Indonesian Foreign Minister Mochtar Kusumaatmadja admits that only half of the pre-1975 population of East Timor is under Indonesian control, and that 120,000 people have died since the 'civil war' began in East Timor in 1975.

Dec 13 The UN General Assembly passes a resolution condemning the Indonesian occupation and calling for an act of self-determination to be held in East Timor (voting record: 62 in favour, 31 against, with 45 abstentions).

Dec 25 A report in the *Times* of London claims that the Indonesian military are using napalm in East Timor.

1980

Jan 16 East Timor is designated an official resettlement area for Indonesian transmigrants from Java and Bali.

May 13 It is reported by Associated Press from Dili that there are 150 resettlement camps in East Timor.

Jun 10–11 A six-hour attack on Dili is mounted by Fretilin forces.

Nov 11 The UN General Assembly again calls for Indonesian withdrawal and self-determination for East Timor (voting record: 58 in favour, 35 against, with 46 abstentions).

Dec 4 A set of secret documents on Australian foreign policy on East Timor during the 1970s is published in the Melbourne *Age*. The documents show that the government had an extensive knowledge of, and acquiesced in, events prior to the invasion.

Dec 17 An American CIA official states that the US Government could have prevented the invasion of East Timor, without any adverse effects on its long-term policy aims towards Indonesia.

1981

Jun 3 A report written by the members of the Indonesian-appointed East Timor Regional People's Assembly (the parliament set up by the Indonesian military in 1976) is sent to President Suharto. It is highly critical of the Indonesian presence, citing cases of torture, maltreatment and disappearances. It complains bitterly of the actions of PT Denok Hernandes, a trading company controlled by the Indonesian military.

Jul Reports are sent from East Timorese students in Baucau, Laclo and Manatuto to Jakarta and thence to Australia, describing preparations for a new Indonesian offensive, referred to as *Operasi Keamanan*.

Aug 19 The forced recruitment of the East Timorese population into 'fence of legs' *(pagar betis)* operations begins, as part of *Operasi Keamanan*.

Oct 24 The UN General Assembly repeats its call for self-determination for East Timor (voting record: 54 in favour, 42 against, with 46 abstentions).

Dec 20 The ICRC is given permission by the Indonesian Government to re-enter East Timor.

1982

Jan 11 Mgr Costa Lopes, Catholic Apostolic Administrator of East Timor alleges that at least 500 East Timorese were massacred by Indonesian troops at the Shrine of St Antony, near Lacluta in September 1981.

Feb Catholic Church sources in East Timor report that approximately half the population is facing serious food shortages.

May 4 Elections are held in East Timor, in which the Indonesian military party, Golkar, obtains 98.8 per cent of the votes cast. The London *Economist* (8 May) describes the election results as 'hard to swallow'.

May 16 The Pope states that the Vatican will not accept East Timor as part of Indonesia.

May 18–28 A small group of journalists visits East Timor and produces reports highly critical of the actions of the Indonesian military. Their reports are published in the *Philadelphia Inquirer*, 28 May, and the *Asian Wall Street Journal*, 14 June.

Jun 10 The newly elected President of Portugal, António dos Santos Ramalho Eanes, initiates a new policy on East Timor, calling for a 'common front' of Portuguese-speaking nations to oppose the Indonesian occupation.

Aug 4 Figures for detention on the island of Atauro indicate that 6800 people are imprisoned there.

Oct 13–14 During President Suharto's visit to Washington, many of the major American newspapers are highly critical of Indonesia's occupation of East Timor.

Nov 3 The UN General Assembly again condemns the annexation of East Timor and calls for an act of self-determination. The motion, which is passed by 50 votes to 46 with 50 abstentions, also instructs the UN Secretary-General to initiate consultations with all concerned parties in order to 'achieve a comprehensive settlement of the East Timor issue' (*UN General Assembly Report*, 4 November).

Dec 30 Indonesian military manuals, captured by Fretilin troops, are released in

Lisbon. They deal with such issues as the destruction of Fretilin networks, the interrogation of prisoners and the control of resettlement villages.

1983

Feb 7–12 Portuguese television journalist Rui Araújo visits East Timor for two days with the permission of the Indonesian Government. His report, which is deeply critical, describes conditions on the island of Atauro, the daily oppression experienced by East Timorese and the use of the contraceptive drug Depo Provera.

Feb 16 The UN Human Rights Commission condemns human rights abuses in East Timor, and calls for self-determination (voting record: 16 in favour, 14 against, with 10 abstentions).

May 13 A document signed by a group of priests in Dili states, 'We foresee the implacable extermination of the people'.

May 16 Mgr Costa Lopes resigns as Apostolic Administrator of East Timor. He is replaced by a young East Timorese priest, Mgr Carlos Felipe Ximenes Belo, who has been out of East Timor for most of the time since the Indonesian invasion.

Jun 25 A ceasefire is reported to have been signed by the Indonesian Commander of East Timor, Colonel Purwanto, and Fretilin President Kay Rala Xanana Gusmão.

Jul 28–31 An Australian Parliamentary Delegation visits East Timor.

Jul (late) The ICRC halts its operations as Indonesia withdraws facilities in preparation for a new offensive.

Aug 8 The Indonesian military launches a new campaign against Fretilin forces, thereby breaking the ceasefire.

Aug 16 Fretilin forces attack the military section of Dili airport.

Aug 21–2 200-300 people are executed by Indonesian troops in the village of Kraras, near Viqueque.

Sep 9 A state of emergency is declared in East Timor by the Indonesian Government.

Sep 14 President Suharto orders a 'clean sweep' of East Timor.

Sep 23 The UN General Assembly discusses East Timor and votes to defer

consideration of the issue for a year, giving the secretary-general time to complete his report requested in 1982's resolution.

1984

Jan 6 Reports in both the Indonesian and international press describe how the offensive begun in September (code-named *Operasi Persatuan*) has severely disrupted food production.

Feb 24 First reports are received of trials of political prisoners in Dili.

Mar 16 The ICRC is allowed to visit prisoners in Dili, but is still prevented from resuming its food aid programme in mainland East Timor.

Mar 31 The Portuguese Government announces that talks are planned with the Indonesian Government on the East Timor issue.

Apr 1 22 US senators write to Secretary of State George Schultz, asking him to raise East Timor as an issue on his forthcoming trip to Jakarta.

May 2 A letter written by Mgr Belo, received in Lisbon, refers to disappearances, trials and 'popular judgements' carried out 'on the spot' by the military. He refers to settlement villages as 'corrals', and criticizes mass conscription for 'fence of legs' operations by the military. He claims that the Indonesian army is not winning the war despite the presence of ten battalions (10,000 troops).

Jul 12 When the new Indonesian Ambassador to the Vatican presents his credentials, the Pope hopes of East Timor that 'every consideration will be given in every circumstance to the ethnic, religious and cultural identity of the people' (*Washington Post, Le Monde, Vatican Daily*).

Jul 21 Portuguese President Eanes and Prime Minister Mario Soares make a joint statement on East Timor, calling upon the Portuguese Government to assist in 'bringing about the inalienable right of the people of East Timor to self-determination' (Melbourne *Age*).

Jul 25 The UN Secretary-General publishes his 'progress report' on negotiations between Indonesia and Portugal. He concludes that little progress has occurred. The General Assembly agrees subsequently to defer discussion of East Timor to its 1985-6 session.

Dec 17 General Murdani, Indonesian Armed Forces Commander in Chief. states that the East Timor conflict 'will take some time to resolve' *(Reuter,* Jakarta).

1985

Jan 1 A statement written by the Council of Catholic Priests in East Timor refers to the military organizing regular 'clearing up' operations, using children in 'fence of legs' operations, arresting people *en masse,* promoting resettlement and demanding that the inhabitants of resettlement villages undertake 'night watch' duties. It describes the 'Indonesianization' of the administration and the suppression of Christianity and animism.

Jan 5 The Indonesian Government publishes a Five-Year Plan for 1984-9. For East Timor it plans birth control for 95,000 women and the resettlement of 6800 transmigrants from Indonesia. The birth control campaign is to be supported by the World Bank.

Mar 15 The UN Human Rights Commission removes the charges against Indonesia on East Timor from its agenda.

May 8 131 members of the US Congress send a letter to President Reagan before his visit to Lisbon, expressing concern at the situation in East Timor.

Jul 3 A US government State Department report estimates that there are approximately 12,000 Indonesian troops in East Timor.

Jul 7, 10 Reporting from East Timor, a correspondent of *Agence France Presse* states that he was not allowed to visit Baucau because it was considered unsafe by the military.

Aug 8 Reporting on a trip to East Timor a journalist states that the Chinese population has been reduced from 20,000 in 1975 to a 'few thousand'. He reports fighting five miles from Dili and describes recent transmigration and political trials in Dili *(Far Eastern Economic Review,* Hong Kong).

Aug 16 In a speech marking the fortieth anniversary of Indonesia's independence, President Suharto justifies the invasion of East Timor as 'a positive response to the people's movement in East Timor to set themselves free from the shackles of foreign colonialism' *(Agence France Presse,* Hong Kong).

Aug 18 Australian Prime Minister Bob Hawke recognizes Indonesian sovereignty over East Timor on behalf of his Labour Government.

Aug 22 The UN General Assembly again votes to defer action on East Timor pending reports from the secretary-general on the talks initiated under UN auspices between the Portuguese and Indonesian governments in the 1983 General Assembly resolution.

Sep 14 Reports from East Timor describe intense bombardment by the Indonesian air force between August 1983 and June 1984.

Sep 24 The first formal diplomatic contacts are established between the Portuguese and Indonesian governments since the 1975 invasion.

Oct 27 The Indonesian and Australian governments begin discussions for a joint exploration programme in the disputed Timor Gap area, south of East Timor.

Nov 28 The Indonesian Government states that it intends to set up 400 strategic villages in East Timor.

Dec 9 The Indonesian and Australian governments announce that they will jointly develop the petroleum resources of the Timor Gap.

Dec 12 An upsurge in fighting in East Timor is reported, with ambushes of Indonesian troops by Fretilin forces across the territory.

Dec 20 A massacre by Indonesian soldiers of 60 inhabitants of a village is reported *(Guardian,* London).

1986

Mar 4 Bids from oil companies for drilling sites in the Timor Gap area have already produced $Aus 31.5 million for the Australian Government, according to the *Sydney Morning Herald* (4 March).

Mar 7 Reporting from Dili, a journalist is told by Govenor Carrascalão that 100,000 East Timorese have died since the 'civil war' of 1975.

Mar 31 In Lisbon, Fretilin's External Delegation and representatives of the Timorese Democratic Union (UDT) announce the formation of a coalition.

Apr 17 70 Japanese parliamentarians from both houses of the *Diet* call for self-determination in East Timor in a letter to UN Secretary-General Perez de Cuellar.

Apr 18 A set of maps, some captured from the Indonesian military and some drawn by Fretilin units in East Timor, is released in Lisbon. They indicate that most military activity is occurring east of a line from Baucau to Viqueque. The Indonesian army appears to have built a military gate across the island, with the aim of moving eastwards from the Baucau-Viqueque line to encircle Fretilin areas.

Jul 11 The European Parliament passes a motion criticizing the Indonesian annexation of East Timor, and calling for the exercise of self-determination.

Jul 11–15 Portuguese parliamentarian Miguel Anacoreta Correia, of the Christian Democratic Party, visits East Timor. His report concludes that although there have been some economic gains from integration, 'rejection and mistrust towards Indonesia are generalized feelings throughout East Timor' *(Christian Science Monitor)*.

Jul 17 Governor Carrascalão is reported to be critical of Indonesian control over East Timor's administration *(International Herald Tribune,* Paris).

Sep 16 The UN General Assembly agrees a motion, sponsored by Malaysia, that postpones further discussion of East Timor until the UN Secretary-General delivers his final report on negotiations between the Portuguese and Indonesian governments.

Sep 19 Letters received by refugees in Lisbon and Darwin, Australia, describe a wave of arrests in eastern areas, with those arrested being taken to Baucau.

Nov 16 Fretilin's external delegation describes a new offensive in East Timor, involving 50 Indonesian battalions, 12 of which are searching exclusively for Xanana Gusmão.

Dec 21 Fretilin military successes are reported during the previous month's fighting in the western, central and eastern sectors, notably in the Viqueque area.

1987

Jan 2 A new military commander of security operations, Brigadier-General Mantiri, is appointed in East Timor.

Jan 3 Governor Carrascalão calls on Fretilin members 'to come home and build the province' *(Jakarta Post)*.

Feb 10 The UN Human Rights Commission reinstates hearings on East Timor.

Mar 6 It is reported from Dili that 38,000 East Timorese children under the age of five are suffering from malnutrition *(Jakarta Post)*.

Mar 20 A new offensive is launched by the Indonesian military, deploying 30,000 troops.

Apr 13 The US Catholic Bishops' Conference officially criticizes the Indonesian occupation. Its statement focuses particularly on the enforced birth control campaign.

Apr 15 The Indonesian Ambassador to Australia states that there are 15,000 Indonesian troops in East Timor.

Apr 25 Elections are held in East Timor resulting in an overwhelming majority for the Indonesian military party, Golkar.

Jun 5 40 members of the US Senate criticize the Indonesian occupation of East Timor in a letter released to the press.

Jul 14 Another offensive is launched by the Indonesians, to coincide with the appointment of a new military commander, Colonel Soenarto.

Sep 2 The UN Sub-Commission on Prevention of Discrimination and Protection of Minorities (the committee preparing the agenda for the Human Rights Commission) adopts a resolution on East Timor, calling for a negotiated settlement and requesting the Indonesian Government to grant improved access to East Timor.

Sep 4 In Lisbon, a spokesman for the newly-elected Social Democratic Government states that it has dropped the demand for East Timor's self-determination from its programme because it is seeking greater flexibility in negotiations with Indonesia and a rapid diplomatic solution to the problem.

Sep 8 The UN Secretary-General's report on East Timor is published. It concludes that limited progress has been made to diminish the differences in the positions held by both sides. The General Assembly decides to adjourn debate on East Timor for a further year.

Oct 5 20 prisoners are released from Dili prison. According to Amnesty International, 136 prisoners were held in Dili prior to the release of the 20–63 in Becora prison, 73 in Comarca prison.

Nov 14 It is reported (in the *Jakarta Post*) that in the southern region of East Timor thousands of adults and children are short of food. Overall, 38,000 children in East Timor are in a state of malnutrition.

Dec 23 Accepting the credentials of the new Indonesian Ambassador to the Vatican, Pope John Paul states: 'The Church's universal mission of service leads her to hope that particular consideration will be given to the protection of the ethnic, religious and cultural character of East Timor' (*UCA News*, Hong Kong).

Dec 31 Governor Carrascalão concludes that 'although integration exists on paper ... it still has to be given content' *(Kompas,* Jakarta).

1988

Jan 4 East Timorese refugees in Australia who are in contact with relatives in East Timor claim that Javanese are increasingly taking over the best housing and land in the centre of towns, and moving East Timorese out to suburban areas *(Diario de Noticias,* Lisbon).

Feb 18 Indonesian Government representatives invite members of the Portuguese parliament to send a delegation to East Timor on an 'observer' mission.

Mar 9 Reports from East Timor describe an upsurge of fighting, with increases in Fretilin ambushes, an infiltration of Fretilin troops into Baucau and Fretilin attacks in areas near the border with West (Indonesian) Timor.

Mar 9 The Plenary Session of the European Parliament approves a draft

resolution condemning the Indonesian occupation of East Timor.

Mar 14 A former Portuguese civil servant, detained by the Indonesians after 1975 and then residing in the territory, manages to leave East Timor for Australia. Arriving in Lisbon, he claims that 200,000 East Timorese have been killed since the Indonesian invasion.

May 2–3 For the first time, the 12 EC governments adopt a common position on East Timor, agreeing to support the UN Secretary-General's efforts at achieving a fair and internationally acceptable settlement which 'will safeguard the rights of the people of East Timor and their cultural identity' (*O Seculo,* Lisbon, 4 May).

Jun 20 Governor Carrascalão asks President Suharto to declare East Timor an open province, in order to speed up the process of economic development.

Jul 29 It is reported that a new Indonesian military offensive has been underway in East Timor since May. It is entitled Operation Clean Up *(Diario de Noticias,* Lisbon).

Sep 15 By 164 to 12 votes, with 15 abstentions, the European Parliament calls for the withdrawal of Indonesian troops from East Timor, and affirms that the people of the territory should exercise their right to self-determination.

Oct 30 182 members of the US House of Representatives and 47 members of the Senate send letters to Secretary of State George Schultz, stating their continuing concern over events in East Timor. They focus particularly on torture, imprisonment and denial of access to international human rights organizations.

Nov 5 President Suharto announces that from January 1989 eight of East Timor's 13 districts will be opened up to entry by Indonesians and foreigners.

Nov 16 The Council of Europe's Committee of Ministers, meeting in Strasbourg, refers to East Timor for the first time in its final communiqué, expressing its members' hope for a 'fair, global and internationally acceptable solution, respecting the interests of the East Timorese people'.

Dec 12 It is reported that between 26

October and 21 November a total of 3000 people were arrested in connection with intelligence surveillance before, during and after a visit by President Suharto to the territory on 2-3 November.

Dec 29 The Indonesian Government grants East Timor 'equal status' with the provinces of the Indonesian Republic.

Dec 31 Fretilin units attack Dili's Lahane and Taibesse neighbourhoods. 84 Indonesian soldiers are killed and several East Timorese soldiers desert their Indonesian units.

1989

Feb 6 Mgr Belo writes to UN Secretary-General Perez de Cuellar, calling upon the UN to hold a referendum on the future of the territory.

Mar 16 The ICRC is allowed to visit one of Baucau's prisons for the first time in the town since the 1975 invasion.

Mar 17 A reporter travelling to Viqueque states that villagers have been ordered to build walls around their resettlement villages. He concludes that security is tight, with 40,000 troops stationed in the territory *(Daily Telegraph,* London).

Apr 26 In discussion with President Suharto, American Vice-President Dan Quayle raises the subject of East Timor, focusing on the issues of political prisoners and 'repressive practices' in the territory *(Diario Popular,* Lisbon).

Jun 9 118 members of the US Congress write to President Bush requesting him to discuss East Timor with President Suharto during the latter's forthcoming visit to Washington.

Jul 15 Documents received by East Timorese refugees in Lisbon claim that 1500 people have been arrested in East Timor since the beginning of the year. Almost all of these have been interrogated and many of them have 'disappeared'.

Jul 15 A short Indonesian military offensive is carried out in advance of the Pope's visit to East Timor. Its primary aim is to capture Fretilin President Xanana Gusmão.

Aug 5 In a speech to the Indonesian House of Representatives in Jakarta, Governor Carrascalão states that in East Timor malaria is endemic, 70 per cent of the population are infected with tuberculosis, of 61 districts only 40 have physicians and that the illiteracy rate is 92 per cent.

Aug 25 The UN Sub-Commission on Prevention of Discrimination and Protection of Minorities recommends to the UN Human Rights Commission that it continues to consider the human rights situation in East Timor.

Sep 5 Leaders of the East Timorese National Convergence are received officially by the Vatican State Office.

Sep 14 UN Secretary-General Perez de Cuellar releases a report on the current state of progress on the East Timor issue. It states that, despite difficulties, negotiations between the Portuguese and Indonesian governments are proceeding, concluding that a proposed visit by the Portuguese Parliamentary Mission to East Timor will help in creating an atmosphere conducive to the achievement of an internationally acceptable solution.

Oct 12 Pope John Paul II visits Dili. He consecrates the cathedral and celebrates Mass in the open air at Taci-Tolu, before a congregation of 100,000. At the end of the Mass, a demonstration takes place, supporting independence. The demonstrators are beaten by the police, and the scene is observed and photographed by foreign journalists.

Oct 13 40 young people are arrested after the Pope's visit, and interrogated. Some are tortured in order to extract confessions of involvement in the demonstration.

Nov 4 The Indonesian military organizes a demonstration outside Bishop Belo's residence, calling on him to release students who took refuge in his house after being chased by Indonesian troops following on from the demonstration during the Pope's visit. A counter demonstration develops, and is suppressed by Indonesian troops.

Nov 5 Children and young people from St Joseph's primary and secondary schools are arrested by Indonesian troops that forcibly enter the school.

Dec 11 The Australian and Indonesian governments sign a treaty to jointly explore the Timor Gap area.

Dec 17 100 members of the United States Congress call on the State Department to launch an official enquiry into claims of torture of East Timorese by the Indonesian military after the Pope's visit.

Dec 26 East Timorese students in Bali, Indonesia, stage a demonstration against suppression of students in Dili in November.

1990

Jan 17 During a visit to Dili, the US Ambassador to Indonesia meets with a group of demonstrators outside the Hotel Turismo. They are dispersed violently after his departure. At least two are reported killed. The violence is witnessed by US diplomats and Australian tourists.

Feb 3 General Murdani visits East Timor and addresses a meeting of all the senior military and non-military personnel in the territory. He threatens brutal reprisals if there is any recurrence of the demonstrations held during the recent visits of the Pope and the US ambassador.

Feb A joint statement on East Timor is made by 12 members of the EC to the UN Human Rights Commission. It notes the human rights violations in the territory and requests entry for human rights organizations.

Mar (mid–) A new offensive is launched by the Indonesian military, involving 40,000 troops, 6000 East Timorese conscripts and two helicopter squadrons.

Apr 19 A seminar to be held at Gadjah Mada University, Jogjakarta, to discuss a critical report on the situation in East Timor is cancelled by the military, following the publication of highlights of the report in the Indonesian paper, *Kompas*.

Apr 20 The International Committee of the Red Cross reports that it was allowed to visit 82 prisoners in six detention centres in East Timor between January and March, and that all the prisoners seen were detained for security reasons.

Jul 17 School girls and boys raise the Fretilin flag in Dili during Indonesian independence day celebrations. Many are subsequently arrested.

Sep 4 A pro-independence demonstration by East Timorese youth held at the end of a mass in Dili Cathedral to commemorate the fiftieth anniversary of the founding of the Dili diocese. Arrests follow on the 6th and 10th September.

Sep 27 Xanana Gusmão is interviewed by an Australian journalist, Robert Domm. Published worldwide, the article outlines his views on strategy, tactics, political perspectives, and the forthcoming visit of a Portuguese Parliamentary Delegation.

Nov 19 170 Democrat and 53 Republican members of the United States Congress write to Secretary of State, James Baker, expressing concern at the situation in East Timor.

1991

Jan (early) It is reported from East Timor that a new Indonesian military offensive has been underway since late November. It is directed not only against the armed resistance, but also against the youth and student networks in the towns. In the latter, it is marked by killings, disappearances and arrests.

Feb 27 Mgr Martinho da Costa Lopes, head of the Catholic Church in East Timor from 1977 to 1983, dies in Lisbon, aged 73. A key figure in the publicizing of events in East Timor during the early eighties, he was forced into retirement by Indonesian pressure on the Catholic hierarchy.

Mar 11–12 During a visit to Jakarta, Japan's Deputy Foreign Minister, Hisashi Owade, formally raises the Japanese Government's concern about human rights abuses in East Timor.

Jun 28 The Parliamentary Assembly of the Council of Europe calls for an arms embargo on Indonesia, due to its occupation of East Timor.

Sep 12 In a letter to the UK Human Rights Organisation, Tapol, Xanana Gusmão details Indonesian military preparations for the forthcoming visit of the Portuguese Parliamentary Delegation. These include the arrival of seven new battalions – one commanded by Suharto's son-in-law, and the continual rehearsal of pro-integration rallies. The delegation is scheduled to arrive on 4 November.

Nov 12 Indonesian troops open fire on groups of East Timorese as they walk from Motael Church to the Santa Cruz Cemetery in Dili to place flowers on the grave of Sebastião Gomes, shot dead by troops at the church two weeks earlier. The subsequent events – in which an estimated 180 people are killed and many injured – are filmed by cameramen and journalists in Dili to cover the visit of the Portuguese delegation, subsequently cancelled just before its departure from Lisbon. The events are shown on TV screens worldwide.

Nov 14 United States Senate and House Members adopt a declaration on East Timor for incorporation into the 1992/3 Foreign Relations Authorisation Act, calling for the suspension of military training programme funds for the Indonesian Government as a result of the Santa Cruz massacre.

Nov 18 In the aftermath of the massacre at Santa Cruz, it is reported from Dili that about 80 prisoners taken to Bé-Musi – near Comaro, on the western outskirts of Dili have been killed by firing squad.

Nov 19 Whilst taking a petition to the United Nations Office in Jakarta, East Timorese students are attacked by anti-riot police. Some are arrested.

1992

Mar 14 As a sign of his determination to maintain law and order in East Timor, the new Dili commander, General Theo Syafei, interviewed in the Indonesian press, states, 'So, as I have said, if something similar to the 12th November event were to happen under my leadership, the number of victims would probably be higher' (*Editor*, March 14th, 1992)

Mar 16 In Jakarta and Dili, the trials begin of 13 East Timorese arrested in the wake of the Santa Cruz massacre. They are charged with subversion and face the death penalty.

May–Jun (various dates) The 13 East Timorese receive sentences ranging from 30 months to 15 years and life

imprisonment for their participation in the Santa Cruz and Jakarta demonstrations.

Aug 11 Reports from Dili (by *Agence France-Presse* and *Reuters*) describe a new offensive, *Operasi Tuntas* (literally: 'Operation Wring Dry') whose main objective is to capture Xanana Gusmão.

Aug 27 The United Nations Sub-Commission for the Prevention of Discrimination and the Protection of Minorities, meeting in its 44th Session, deplores the Santa Cruz massacre, and calls upon the Indonesian government to set up an independent enquiry into the November events.

Nov 20 Xanana Gusmão is arrested by Indonesian soldiers in Lahane, Dili. After being held *incommunicado* and denied legal assistance, he is charged with rebellion, undermining national stability, and masterminding the November 12th demonstration.

1993

Feb 1 Xanana's trial commences in Dili.

Apr 3 Ma'Huno, the National Resistance's second-in-command, is captured by Indonesian troops near Ainaro in the centre of East Timor.

May 21 Xanana Gusmão is sentenced to twenty years imprisonment. The trial judge stops his reading of his defence plea as he reaches its third page.

Jun 22 The International Committee of the Red Cross issues a statement deploring the difficulties placed in its path by the Indonesian Government in its attempts to visit prisoners in East Timor.

Jun 23 Seven East Timorese, in hiding since the Santa Cruz massacre, are refused protection at the Finnish and Swedish Embassies in Jakarta.

Jul 20 The Indonesian Government gives the go-ahead for talks between pro- and anti-integration East Timorese. The 'pro' faction is headed by former UDT leader Lopes da Cruz, now Suharto's personal emissary on East Timor. The 'anti' faction features Abílio Araújo, head of Fretilin's external delegation. Criticized for not consulting other members of the delegation, Araújo is subsequently voted to be removed from his post.

Sep 5 Bishop Belo receives a group of

100 East Timorese during a visit to Dili by three United States Congressional staff members. On the following day, many of this group are taken to military headquarters, where they are beaten and tortured.

Dec 14–17 'Reconciliation talks' between pro- and anti-integration East Timorese, together with Indonesian Government representatives are held at a secret location in the UK.

Dec 30 The 7 East Timorese seeking asylum in embassies in Jakarta are allowed to leave for Lisbon.

1994

Jan (mid) Two senior United Nations officials visit Lisbon, Jakarta and East Timor, to formulate new initiatives in time for the next round of talks between Indonesian and Portuguese government representatives, under the auspices of the UN Secretary-General, in Geneva, in May. They visit Xanana, in prison.

Feb (late) Xanana Gusmão and Bishop Belo respond negatively to the 'reconciliation talks'; Belo in a letter to Abílio Araújo, and Xanana in a taped statement, published in the Portuguese Daily, *Diario de Noticias*.

Apr 15 The new Governor of East Timor (appointed September 1992), Abílio Osorio Soares, interviewed in the *Sydney Morning Herald*, states that the figure of 200,000 killed since the invasion is correct.

May 20 At the request of the Indonesian Government, Philippines President General Fidel Ramos bars foreigners from attending an Asia-Pacific Conference on East Timor, claiming that their presence would be inimical to the national interest.

Jun 28 In Remexio, two soldiers participating in a communion service desecrate the church by spitting out wafers and trampling them underfoot.

Jul 15 In an interview with film-maker and journalist, John Pilger, Bishop Belo claims that two attempts have been made on his life, in 1989 and 1991.

Jul 31 Bishop Belo calls for a series of dialogues to be held between the Indonesian government and representatives of the pre-1975 political parties, with the Church as mediator. Concomitantly, Konis Santana – replacing Xanana Gusmão as leader of the independence movement – offers a unilateral ceasefire in return for a commitment by the Indonesian military to enter into serious negotiations.

Sep 25–8 A second set of 'reconciliation talks' are held in the UK. The UDT, Fretilin and the East Timorese Council for National Resistance (CNRM) denounce the talks as unrepresentative and divisive.

Nov 12 Following the murder of an East Timorese by a Buginese trader in Becora market, Dili, there are riots and attacks by East Timorese on Indonesian shops and military barracks.

Nov 12 Twenty-nine East Timorese students enter the United States Embassy compound in Jakarta during the Asia-Pacific Economic (APEC) Forum meeting, attended by President Bill Clinton. They call for the release of Xanana, the entry of an impartial mission into East Timor to investigate human rights abuses, and for the participation of all East Timorese political groups in any future negotiating process. Their actions are given widespread international profile and support.

Nov 13 Three East Timorese are reported killed by the army in Dili.

Nov 14 During a post-APEC bilateral meeting with President Suharto, United States President Bill Clinton is reported to have been 'firm and forceful' on the issue of human rights in East Timor. Similar views had already been expressed by Secretary of State Warren Christopher, arriving in Jakarta for the summit on 11 November.

Nov 15 Six hundred students stage a demonstration at East Timor University, Dili, in favour of the release of Xanana Gusmão and political independence.

Nov 17 Hundreds of people assemble at Dili Cathedral for a mass celebrating Christian martyrs. They unfurl independence banners on the cathedral steps.

Nov 23 In Dili, the Indonesian military announce that thirty East Timorese will be prosecuted for their alleged involvement in the pro-independence protests since November 12.

1995

Jan 1 Three civilians are killed when Indonesian security forces open fire on East Timorese rioters following an ethnically-inspired clash with Bugis traders and migrants in Baucau. The main market is burnt.

Jan 10 Indonesian Foreign Minister Ali Alatas states that a settlement of the East Timorese issue remains a distant prospect, despite the inclusion of CNRM's external representative, José Ramos-Horta, in an expanded round of talks.

Jan 12 Indonesian troops execute six civilians near Liquiçá to the west of Dili, in reprisal for a Fretilin attack in which one Indonesian soldier was wounded. Following investigations and protests by several Western embassies in Jakarta and NGO groups, the Indonesian governement announces (11 Feb) that a military inquiry has discovered 'an action by military personnel...not based on proper procedure.' An Honorary Military Council is established to take disciplinary action.

Jan 13 Following the completion of an investigation into human rights abuses in East Timor, the United Nations Special Rapporteur on Extrajudicial, Summary or Arbitrary Executions, the Senegalese jurist Bacre Waly N'Diaye, publishes a report that is highly critical of the Indonesian military and government. It concludes that members of the army planned and perpetrated the killing of civilians participating in a peaceful demonstration on November 12th, 1991 at the Santa Cruz cemetery in Dili, and calls for the Indonesian Government to establish a new working group to undertake a thorough investigation into the massacre.

Jan/Feb The local security situation in East Timor declines dramatically as a result of attacks on civilian communities by black masked armed thugs – the so-called *Ninja* – linked to the military, who terrorize those suspected of harbouring anti-integrationist feelings.

Index